£15.95

REG
GL
1978

AN INTRODUCTION TO REGIONAL PLANNING

D0510567

J3

AN INTRODUCTION TO REGIONAL PLANNING

Concepts, Theory and Practice
Second edition

JOHN GLASSON

Head of Department of Town Planning,
Oxford Polytechnic

UCL
PRESS

First published in 1974
Second edition 1978
First published in 1992 by UCL Press as a sixth impression

UCL Press Limited
University College London
Gower Street
London WC1E 6BT

The name of University College London (UCL) is a registered
trade mark used by UCL Press with the consent of the owner.

ISBN: 1-85728-062-8

A CIP catalogue record for this book
is available from the British Library.

Typeset in Monotype Garamond
Printed in Great Britain by
St Edmundsbury Press Limited, Bury St Edmunds, Suffolk

To Carol, Rebecca and Claire

Contents

6

Preface to the first edition

Regional planning means many things to many men. For some, regional planning has an economic bias and is primarily concerned with the centrally directed allocation of resources between regions to achieve certain regional and national objectives. For others, regional planning involves the physical, economic and social planning of development within regions and sub-regions and has more of a land use content. Not surprisingly it tends to be something of an enigma and is often regarded as an intruder in the planning fraternity. Nevertheless it has given rise to a diverse literature in many countries although much of this tends to be rather specialised covering only narrow areas of the wider field.

This book is intended as a general and introductory text in regional planning, particularly oriented to the United Kingdom context. It seeks to provide an insight into the nebulous subject, attempting to integrate the various aspects into a systematic framework. As such, the aim is to avoid the narrow specialist approach yet provide sufficient depth into regional analysis and practice necessary for a meaningful understanding of the subject area.

It has been designed and written with the requirements of undergraduate education in mind but it may also prove useful to certain postgraduate courses. It is hoped that it will be of particular use to students in urban and regional planning, geography, economics, business and other related subjects such as surveying and architecture. It is also designed to form a survey of the subject for those involved professionally, either directly or peripherally, as well as for the interested layman.

The book is subdivided into three major parts—the Conceptual Basis of Regional Planning, the Analysis or Anatomy of Regions and Regional Planning in Practice. Of course the wide scope of the subject means that argument may be compressed in places. For example, the text does not attempt to provide a comprehensive guide to the regional planning process, nor indeed a detailed examination of specific regional plans and strategies. In such cases it is hoped that the references will help to fill the gaps.

In Part One a distinction is made between inter- and intra-regional planning. This simple taxonomic device provides the framework for the discussion of the regional analysis and the practice of regional planning in Parts Two and Three. It must be noted at the outset however that there is a considerable overlap and interrelationship between inter- and intra-regional analysis and likewise between inter- and intra-regional planning—both of which may be involved in the development of a region.

Of course, regional planning, involving an interference with the existing patterns of activity within a region, requires some knowledge of the 'laws' that underlie their structure and growth. Part Two examines the anatomy of regions, critically discussing the various regional theories. Chapters 3 to 5 adopt an inter-regional approach, seeking to explain the differences between regions, taking regions as a whole. The following Chapters, 6 to 8, examine the theories of the internal structure of regions. The former, concerned with growth and change, draw heavily on economic concepts, and the latter, concerned with locational analysis, derive much from the geographer's spatial theories. All the theories serve the basic descriptive function providing an aid to the understanding, comparison and further analysis of a variety of unique regions. Several also have useful predictive and prescriptive attributes and these are discussed.

Regional science is one of the popular names given to this study of the regional anatomy. It is not a pure discipline, drawing heavily on the theories of regional economics—perhaps the parent discipline—geography, mathematics, physics and more recently certain socio-political concepts. However, as yet, the body of theory is still rather indeterminate, as aptly illustrated by Hilhorst

'regional planners have set to work openly confessing that although they knew more about their profession than others, they still have not mastered their trade, if only because no adequate theory of regional development exists.'*

There have been several important developments in the practice of regional planning over the last few years. These are discussed in Part Three with particular reference to the United Kingdom but with a limited discussion of some European practice of relevance to the British situation. Of course, in such a rapidly evolving area this should be seen as part of an ongoing discussion and indeed new developments are imminent, notably in the field of regional administration and European regional policy. Thus before too long—hopefully—we should have the report of the Commission on the Constitution, set up to examine the administrative and other relationships between the various parts of the United Kingdom, and by 1974 there should be available the new European Economic Community regional policy called for by the 1972 EEC Summit Conference.

*J. G. M. Hilhorst, *Regional Planning*, Rotterdam University Press (1971).

Preface to the second edition

The aims and scope of this revised edition are unchanged from the first edition. But, as noted in the first preface, regional planning is evolving rapidly and any commentary on the subject must be seen as part of an ongoing discussion. The last few years, in particular, have witnessed some important changes in the theory, practice and 'climate' of regional planning. Reflecting such changes, this revised edition seeks to update the commentary by introducing and developing a number of issues which are seen as of growing importance for the student of regional planning.

The structure of the first edition has been retained, plus most of the original material, but variations and additions have been made to specific sections. Some limited developments have been made of the material in Parts One and Two, the Conceptual Basis and the Analysis of Regions. Some aspects not directly covered in the first edition, such as the rôle of multi-national firms, transport factors and socio-political factors in regional development, have been introduced; others, such as the rôle of regional planning in guiding regional development, have been expanded.

The most substantial changes however have been made in Part Three, The Practice of Regional Planning, with an updated and expanded discussion of changing regional planning practice in the UK, including a reappraisal of regional policy and an assessment of recent developments in regional strategic planning. In addition there is a much fuller discussion of the institutional environment of regional planning and the related devolution issue. Regional planning in its European context has been revised to include an updated discussion of the evolving rôle of EEC regional policy, plus an addition of Eire to the French and Dutch comparative case studies. The material in the appendices has also been developed.

John Glasson
Oxford 1978

Acknowledgements

My grateful thanks are due to the many people in practice, teaching and research who have introduced me to the field of regional planning. I am particularly grateful to my colleagues at Oxford Polytechnic who have helped me to develop my interest and to my students who have critically tested many of my ideas. But above all I owe a special debt of thanks to my wife. She has typed and retyped the manuscript and provided me with that most valuable of commodities, time. Without her help and encouragement the book would never have been produced.

PART ONE
The Conceptual Basis of Regional Planning

1   The context of regional planning

Regional planning has tended to be somewhat of an intruder in the planning fraternity for several reasons. Its rôle in the planning framework is not very clearly defined, nor are its aims fully worked out or generally agreed. Comprehension is further complicated by the very flexibility of the actual concept of the 'region'. Thus there is a need to set regional planning in its planning context, and this will be considered in the first chapter; the actual concept of the region will be left open until the second chapter. The placing of regional planning in its context involves asking certain very basic questions. Why in fact is there a need to plan at all? What is 'planning', and how does regional planning fit in? Why is there a need for regional planning and what form does it take?

1 Why plan?

Planning has been going on throughout history and it is tempting to explain it away by merely stating that man has a natural urge to plan, it is part of his organisational make-up. This could be the psychologist's approach, setting 'planning' up as one of the basic 'social drives' of society—a drive which is not biologically inborn, but which is learned in society, and upon the satisfaction of which rests the survival of society.

Although relevant, this does not explain the rapid increase in planning over the last 100 years. There has been a rapid evolution from a society dominated by *laissez-faire* principles to one where state intervention is accepted to varying degrees in many aspects of everyday life. But why this increase in planning? It has been demonstrated over time that the normal interplay of private action and market forces often results in situations which the nation is not willing to tolerate and which can only be improved by means of a control mechanism—planning. Such an explanation is applicable at most scales and in most contexts; thus the lack of family planning and the problems of oversize families, the lack of national economic planning and the problem of oversize dole queues.

Particular problems of the *laissez-faire* approach are the inequalities of income distribution between groups and regions, as evidenced, for example, by the income gaps between old-age pensioners and motor-workers and between South East England and Northern Ireland in the United Kingdom. Another problem is the divergence between the voluntary private costs and benefits and the involuntary social costs and benefits of private actions. The limited provision of 'public goods' such as open space and fresh air; the wastes of competition and the dangers of monopoly; and the problems of economic instability—in particular, the problem of unemployment, are also synonymous with the *laissez-faire* approach. More recently, the rapid rise in population (especially urban population), increasing affluence and rampant technology have all increased the need for planning; but what is this control mechanism called planning?

2 What is planning?

Individual definitions of planning are abundant, but a general theory of planning has not yet been written. Indeed, with a subject which is so obviously evolutionary and responsive to its own history of development and to the wider developments taking place in society as a whole, it is perhaps too much to expect a final statement on what constitutes 'planning', and this will certainly not be attempted here. However, certain features of planning in general, features common to all types of planning, can be identified. In addition, certain alternative types of planning of some relevance to the regional form can be identified within this general framework.

Major features of general planning include a sequence of actions which are designed to solve problems in the future. The planning problems vary but tend to be primarily economic and social; the planning period, the time horizon of 'the future', also varies according to the type and level of planning; but all planning involves a sequential process which can be conceptualised into a number of stages, such as:

the identification of the problem;

the formulation of general goals and more specific and
    measurable objectives relating to the problem;

the identification of possible constraints;

the projection of the future situation;

the generation and evaluation of alternative courses of action;

and the production of a preferred plan, which in its generic
    form may include any policy statement or strategy as well
    as a definitive plan.

This process is relevant to the whole spectrum of planning problems—how can I get from London to Manchester as quickly as possible? How can an extra 2 000 000 people be accommodated in South East England over the period 1971–91? How can the British economy achieve a growth rate of 4% per annum? Summing up in Friedman's words:

'planning is primarily a way of thinking about social and economic problems, planning is oriented predominantly toward the future, is deeply concerned with the relation of goals to collective decisions and strives for comprehensiveness in policy and program. Wherever these modes of thought are applied, there is a presumption that planning is being done.'[1]

Within this general planning framework, there are a wide variety of types of planning. Certain basic distinctions between the various types are particularly useful in our analysis of regional planning. The first and perhaps most fundamental distinction— and one which has been a constant source of confusion in regional planning—is that between *physical planning* and *economic planning*. Physical planning is the planning of an area's physical structure —land use, communications, utilities and so on, and has its origins in the regulation and control of town development, which outstripped the ability of the market mechanism to cope. Economic planning is concerned more with the economic structure of an area and its overall level of prosperity. It works more through the market mechanism than physical planning which relies heavily on direct controls. Unfortunately many see this physical/economic division as absolute, which is misconceived because physical planning is an important means in the implementation of plans and vice versa.[2]

A second distinction is between *allocative* and *innovative planning*.[3] These are the names given to two instrumental models of planning divided according to 'function' or 'area of concern'. Allocative planning is concerned with co-ordination, the resolution of conflicts ensuring that the existing system is ticking over efficiently through time in accordance with evolving policies. Hence it is sometimes known as regulatory planning. In the context of a small firm, it would involve the planning of the deliveries of inputs of raw materials and labour and the distribution of the final goods. In the context of the national economy, it would involve the month-to-month regulation of the economy using fiscal and monetary policy. Innovative planning, on the other hand, is not merely concerned with planning for the efficient functioning of existing systems, but is more concerned with improving/developing the system as a whole, introducing new aims and attempting to mould change on a large scale. For this reason, it is sometimes known as development planning. In our small-firm example, the marketing of a new product or the opening of a factory extension within a specific period of time, would involve innovative planning. Of course, as with physical and economic planning, there is a great deal of overlap between the two and any planning action may involve both allocative and innovative elements.

A third distinction is between *multi* or *single objective planning*. Whatever its type or form, planning has certain aims, or in the planner's jargon, goals and objectives. The distinction between the latter is clearly made by Young[4]: 'a goal is an ideal and should be expressed in abstract terms' (for example, 'to improve the standard of living in Scotland'); 'an objective is capable of both attainment and measurement, its inherent purpose is explicit rather than implicit' (for example, 'to improve all the houses in

Glasgow to Parker Morris standards'). Planning may have single or multiple goals and objectives. A local authority may plan to build a new road to improve internal accessibility, but also to attract new firms and to widen its shopping hinterland. Similarly an individual may plan to build an extension to his house to accommodate his growing family, gain more privacy from his neighbours and increase the market value of his property. Goals and objectives are usually social and/or economic in nature. This raises another distinction, that between 'manifest' and 'latent' aims. Manifest aims are obvious and explicit, latent aims are less obvious and quite often unconsciously pursued.

The final distinction between *indicative* and *imperative planning* relates to the method of implementation of planning. Indicative planning merely lays down general guidelines and is advisory in nature, imperative or command planning involves specific directives. The distinction can clearly be seen at a national level by comparing the indicative UK *National Plan* (1965)[5] with the imperative USSR seven year plans, or at an individual level by comparing the approaches to family planning in different countries.

This planning typology is particularly relevant at the regional level. Regional planning usually involves both physical and economic planning. Some regional plans may be purely allocative, but the majority include certain innovative elements—an extreme example being that of the Dutch Polders Scheme. In addition, regional planning is invariably multi-objective, but the method of implementation may vary greatly between the 'advisory' British regional plans and the 'command' Eastern European and Russian versions.

3   Levels of planning

Regional planning is thus similar to other types of planning in that it possesses the same basic features and may be a combination of the variety of alternative forms already outlined. But it is also distinct from other types of planning in that it is planning for a region. In general terms, a region is a flexible concept, referring to a continuous and localised area intermediate between national and urban levels. As such, regional planning can be seen as fitting

21

into a continuum of planning—'regional planning is the process of formulating and clarifying social objectives in the ordering of activities in supra-urban space.'[6] For some, this arbitrary division into levels would seem to contradict the essentially comprehensive and theoretically indivisible nature of planning, while others would argue that there is no natural continuum, and merely disparate existence. However, from a practical viewpoint, some sub-division is necessary to allow an understanding of such a comprehensive subject and as a basis for administration.

In the United Kingdom, planning is most clearly identified at the national and local levels. This obviously reflects in part the government and administrative systems, which in contrast to countries with strong federal systems, are clearly polarised at these levels.

Planning at the *national level of government* tends to be strongly economic in content. This certainly is the case in Britain although other countries do have a system of national physical planning. National economic planning can be subdivided into the short-run allocative form concerned with the stabilisation of the 'ups and downs' of the economy, and the long-run innovative form concerned primarily with the achievement of certain rates of economic growth. The UK *National Plan* (1965) and the various post-war French five-year plans, are examples of the long-run form. The plans are multi-objective, and differ in implementation according to the ideology of the country involved. The medium/long-run form of national planning is not well developed in this country. Both the 1965 Labour national plan and the earlier Conservative proposals[7] came to ignominious ends, owing to a combination of reasons. The plans were weak in methodology and hurriedly produced; they were over-ambitious in the light of the prevailing economic climates; and being of an indicative form, carried little weight and were difficult to implement. This lack of an effective national planning framework of course has important implications for the lower levels of planning. In contrast, in France, there is a long history of successful national planning, with the production and fulfilment of five plans since the War and the sixth currently in progress.

Planning in Britain is particularly well developed at the *local authority level*. Here, town and country planning has played a more

22

dominant rôle resulting in a more land-use orientated approach. The Town and Country Planning Act (1971) provides for two tiers of plans, with the preparation of structure plans—setting out the local authority's policy and general proposals in respect of the development and other use of land, including measures for the improvement of the physical environment and the management of traffic; and local plans—formulating in detail the ways in which the policy and general proposals are to be worked through.

However over the last few decades, the need to plan for an *intermediate level* has gained momentum in many countries, including Britain. The *regional level* of planning straddles the national-local gap. It is concerned with the planning for an area with distinctive economic and social characteristics, opportunities and problems—setting it apart from other regions. Economic factors are again of major importance when dealing with areas at this level, such as the North West and Northern Ireland; but there are of course also fundamental physical problems, as in the South East. Hence, as noted earlier, the introduction of a physical/economic split into the continuum must be kept in perspective, as physical and economic elements are generally present to varying degrees at all levels. Indeed, at the regional and sub-regional levels, economic and physical elements would appear to be inextricably woven together.[8] The *sub-regional level* is perhaps the most difficult to define. It is something of a 'hybrid', relating to a part of a larger region, and although it may not be too clearly definable, it has a certain logic in practical terms. In Britain, the sub-region may overlap local authority boundaries relating more to specific problems than administrative convenience. It is a more localised area with its own particular structure, problems and potential. There is more emphasis on physical elements at this level, and the sub-region can be regarded as the highest level at which physical elements are major components of the plan.

Of course, not all these levels may be present in any one country at any particular time. In some small countries, the national and regional levels may be collapsed into one, in others, there may be little distinction between regional and sub-regional. In Britain, the regional-sub-regional distinction can be misleading and the concepts and analysis of later chapters are certainly assumed to be relevant to both these levels. Perhaps at this point we should switch from this rather arbitrary continuum to a consideration of why in fact there is a need for regional planning. Indeed, for reasons already outlined, the levels approach should not be over-emphasised.

4 The need for regional planning

Pressure for governmental action for the regional level may come from a variety of sources. Regional planning can be seen as a response to certain problems with a regional dimension, that is, a response to pressing regional issues. In the United Kingdom and several other countries, two dominant regional issues have been the problems of urban regions arising from rapid population growth, increasing urbanisation and increasing standards of living and personal mobility; and the problems of depressed industrial and rural regions suffering from 'economic malaise'. Unfortunately, because of these two distinct origins, regional planning, certainly in the UK, has been dichotomised throughout its history. Other regional issues, however, have been, and are also important in generating regional action. Particular note should be made of the existence of separate regional cultures, political identities and their desire for autonomy and self fulfilment; and of the search for administrative efficiency at a supra-urban, sub-national level. These various pressures for regional action are now explored further with particular reference to the UK context.

The problem of congested urban regions has resulted in an aspect of regional planning that has been largely physical or environmental in nature. It grew up in Britain during the late nineteenth century and its original motivations were largely social, stressing the health hazards of living in congested, smoky, noisy, dirty cities as compared with the delights of garden suburbs or, later, new towns. In essence, it is a land-use planning approach evolved through the early Health Acts with the aim of improving living conditions and creating a better environment. It has been primarily physical based involving the location of land uses within the region, although recent strategies have adopted a wider approach. Although, originally concerned with the major

24

conurbations, it is equally of concern to other smaller 'urban regions' based on smaller towns and cities.

The problem of depressed industrial and rural regions has resulted in an aspect of regional planning that is primarily economic. It developed virtually independently of the physical aspect, germinating in the depression years of the 1920's/1930's but only really coming to the fore in the 1960's. It is derived from social welfare and seeks to find solutions to the economic inequalities between regions. In Britain, this inequality or regional imbalance can be clearly illustrated by drawing a line from the Humber to the Exe, and comparing the 'divided nation' with the prosperous regions to the east and south and problem industrial and rural regions to the west and north. Mackinder in his classic text *Britain and the British Seas*, called these two areas Metropolitan England and Industrial England. It is interesting to note that even before Mackinder in 1902 novelists such as Mrs Gaskell and Disraeli were drawing attention to the 'two nations'.

Originally, however, it may have been the existence of separate regional cultures and political identities that produced the necessary pressure for action, with regional planning being a response to regionalism. Although the United Kingdom is a national territory in political terms, it does include several countries with clearly defined ethnic and geographical variations. Over time, these countries acquired varying special arrangements—separate civil services in Scotland and Wales run by Cabinet-rank Secretaries of State, and an elected Parliament in Northern Ireland until the 1970's. Such arrangements provided opportunities for the development of regional planning. Events in the 1970's have fuelled this desire for autonomy in decision making, reflected in Scotland and Wales in the growing strength of nationalist political parties. Similar pressures for regional autonomy are also present and developing in other countries in Western Europe.

The movement towards a regional structure of administration and decision making is also a response to the problems of administering certain services by local or central agencies. In the search for administrative efficiency, many UK central government departments and agencies have devolved responsibilities to regional tiers, and certain formerly local authority functions are now being carried out at the regional level—recent examples being the Regional Health Authorities and Regional Water Authorities established in 1974.

In addition, regional planning can also be seen as a supportive device for national and local planning, with the actual stimulus to action coming not from within the regional level but from the adjacent national and local levels. There is now general agreement that overall national planning should take into account the problem of the inter-regional allocation of resources. Further, regional information is a major element in the formulation of national plans and policies, and regional policies are of some importance in their implementation. At the other end of the scale, it is recognised that a city or large urban centre cannot be planned in isolation from its hinterland. For physical, economic and social reasons, it must be seen and planned in its regional context.

Finally, however, it should be noted that the climate of need for regional planning is not constant. In the United Kingdom it has changed and warmed rapidly in the last few years and is likely to continue to do so. There have been significant changes in the institutional environment of regional planning with the re-organisation of local government and membership of the European Economic Community. The revival of nationalist pressures in Scotland and Wales has already been noted. Other important and sometimes related factors include the economic recession of the mid-1970's leading to cries of help even from the 'prosperous' South East and West Midlands regions; a collapse in birth rates resulting in a switch in metropolitan regions from a policy of finding overspill sites to one of helping the inner cities; and the discovery and exploitation of oil and gas resources along the East Coast from Sullom Voe in the Shetlands to Great Yarmouth in East Anglia, leading to some undermining of the established views of what are the peripheral regions. Such changes have important implications for regional planning.

5 'Inter' and 'intra' regional planning

The regional planning response to the various problems outlined can and does take many forms, and regional planning can perhaps best be seen as a planning response to the regional issues which appear most pressing in any particular country at a particular

26

point of time. However, although as a branch of public planning, regional planning does take many forms, its concern for area has two main strands reflected in the following quotation from the 1970 *Strategic Plan for the South East*.

'The rôle of regional planning . . . On the one hand it is an extension of local planning, dealing particularly with those matters—the movement and distribution of population and employment, the complex interaction or social and economic needs, the provision of major recreational facilities and the main communications network, for example—which can only be decided for areas much larger than the areas of existing local planning authorities.

'On the other hand it is concerned with inter-regional flows of population and employment, with the availability and use of resources, and with long term economic prospects which cannot properly be considered except in the context of the balance to be achieved between growth in one region and growth requirements in other parts of the country, on which only the Government can decide.'[9]

This quotation reflects the planning response to the specific problems previously outlined. Firstly, there is that type of regional planning which is directed towards resource allocation *within* regions. This type can be regarded as *intra-regional planning* and its concern is with the allocation of resources between the sub-regions of the region, and between various policy fields— economic development, social, environmental, transport, etc.— within the region and its sub-regions. Its aim is to achieve a satisfactory relationship between people, jobs and the environment within the region. More specifically, social objectives concerned with factors such as the provision of housing, social, cultural and recreational facilities; economic objectives relating to the control of the diseconomies of the congested cities and the distribution of new investment; and environmental objectives relating to issues such as the quality of urban form and the prevention of urban sprawl, can be identified. Obviously, with such multiple objectives, there may be conflict, for example, socially desirable housing distribution may conflict with the preservation

27

of areas of attractive landscape, and a ranking of priorities and trade-off between them may be necessary.

The content of intra-regional planning varies from region to region. For a congested metropolitan region, the emphasis may be on controlling the location of population and employment, that is, accommodating growth. For a depressed industrial region, measures may be more related to the stimulation of industrial development, that is, generating growth. Examples of intra-regional planning in Britain date back to the proposals around the turn of the century for 'garden cities' to deal with the problems of the overcrowded city. More recently, in the 1940's, Abercrombie prepared a series of regional plans for some of the major conurbations of the country. During the 1960's and early 1970's, this trickle of planning has turned into a flood with plans, studies and strategies being produced at both the regional and sub-regional levels.

Secondly, there is that kind of regional work which is directed towards the inter-regional relationship. This type can be regarded as *inter-regional planning* and its concern is with the allocation of resources *between* regions. It has developed largely as a response to the problems of economic imbalance between regions resulting from the changing locational preferences of industry. The prime aim is obviously more economic in nature, relating to the achievement of a satisfactory relationship between people and jobs.

As with its intra-regional counterpart, it is also multi-objective, drawing in particular on the national economic objectives of economic growth, full employment and social equity, and giving them a spatial dimension. Economic growth involves the efficient utilisation of resources to achieve a higher rate of output, yet some regions may have high levels of unemployment and under-utilised capital assets. The injection of investment into such regions, in the form of new infrastructure or industry, may provide the necessary catalyst for regional economic growth, thereby also aiding national economic growth. The former UK Department of Economic Affairs can be quoted as saying that for them 'regional planning is an integral part of the steps being taken to implement the National Plan and to raise industrial efficiency'.[10]

Most countries are also now committed to a national economic objective of full employment. But employment and unemployment have a spatial as well as a time dimension, and the eradication of major inequalities in regional unemployment has been the major factor behind inter-regional planning. Related to this full employment objective is that of social equity, which is often equated with the reduction in inter-regional differences in *per capita* incomes. Unfortunately there may also be conflict between these regional economic objectives. Time horizons are important here, especially in the allocation of investment between 'strong' and 'weak' regions. Allocation of preferential investment to the 'weak' regions on equity grounds may limit economic growth in the short run, by failing to take advantage of the economies of scale of the 'strong' regions. However, in the long run, the situation may be quite different, for with the removal of barriers to growth in the 'weak' regions and the prevention of possible diseconomies in the 'strong' regions, the various objectives may be consistent with one another.

The terms 'balanced growth' and 'regional balance' have often been explicitly linked with, or implicitly implied in, discussion of the above objectives. The achievement of a regional balance between people, jobs and the environment is fine rhetoric, but the term 'balance' is somewhat confusing and has been given a variety of meanings. For instance, what is really meant by the term 'balanced growth'? It could mean that poorer regions should grow faster than rich ones so that income levels tend to equalise; in this context, 'balance' means 'convergence'. Another interpretation could mean that the rate of growth in the poor regions should keep pace with that in the prosperous regions. In this case, the nation and the constituent regions would grow at the same rate, but a consequence of this would be a widening of the absolute income differentials between rich and poor regions.

But what of the second of these grandiose terms, 'regional balance'—a term that has been referred to as 'the most secret and unexamined of sacred cows'?[11] Is it the same as the first or something much wider? In the UK, the term was first widely used by the Barlow Commission in 1940, but since they failed to define it adequately at that time, it has since been, as Hall puts it, 'flung around as an all-purpose phrase in lieu of thought'.[12] It could be interpreted as equal population density in each part of the country, or zero net migration between regions with the distribution of activities and people remaining for ever the same as it is now. It is worth considering that if such rules had been followed in the eighteenth century there would have been no industrial revolution in Britain. A more acceptable interpretation might be that the government should use a combination of policies to ensure that the level of economic activity is the same in each region. But is this the meaning of 'balance'? 'Balance', in the regional context, does not imply equality, uniformity or conformity. It does however imply equality of opportunity for each region to redress demographic, economic, social and environmental weaknesses and to achieve its full potential, thus ensuring that the 'quality of life' is not a function of the area of the country in which people happen to live and work.

Inter-regional planning is a top-down process of resource allocation, and the inter-regional planning activity is concentrated within national (central) government agencies—government departments, public corporations and nationalised industries. The degree of concern for inter-regional disparities varies between these agencies. In the UK, the most explicit regional policies are the Department of Industry Assisted Area policies. Such policies have a long history in the United Kingdom dating back to the inter-war depression years. This period saw the introduction of the 'Special Areas' and the development of a variety of measures to deal with their problems, ranging from labour migration schemes to the building of trading estates. Following the 1940 Barlow Report,[13] the immediate post-war years saw a vigorous development of inter-regional planning with the advent of many policies—such as the designation of Development Areas and the use of controls on industrial location—which have persisted to the present day. But this was quickly followed by a decade of 'freewheeling' in the 1950's. Since 1960 however, there has been a considerable re-emphasis of policy with a widening and strengthening of the range of measures to help a wide variety of problem regions. Over time, the Assisted Areas policy has also provided a framework for other policies of inter-regional resource allocation (e.g. discriminatory house improvement grants).

The balance between these two strands of regional planning varies from country to country. In a Western European context, for example, inter-regional planning is most apparent in those countries with large regional imbalances, e.g. Italy and Norway. On the other hand, in West Germany, a country with a more limited economic imbalance, the focus is on intra-regional planning. Of course, there are some countries where both strands are significant. This is certainly the case in the UK where there are some fairly serious regional imbalances, which have given rise to over forty years of regional policy, as well as a good deal of 'supra-urban' planning within regions, reflected in sub-regional plans and regional strategies.

The two strands are of course interrelated in many ways. They may be complementary, and there have been some notable examples of harmony. The Barlow Report in the 1940's and the 'growth area' philosophy of the 1960's represent occasions when the two aspects did come together, even though their stated aims were often in contention. They may also conflict—in the UK, the South East policy of developing growth centres which are very attractive to industry can be seen as conflicting with inter-regional policy which seeks to disperse industry to the Assisted Areas. The two strands may also be seen as substitutes—the spatial discrimination of Assisted Areas (Intermediate Areas, Development Areas) within very close proximity in South Wales is an important influence on intra-regional resource allocation in that area. As such, a regional planning agency for a particular region must not only seek to influence resource allocation within its region but also seek to influence inter-regional resource allocation.

6 Regional planning and the management of regional development

Regional planning, in its various forms, can be seen as an attempt to guide the development of a region. The concept of *development* as applied to society is a complex one. Development is not the same as societal change. The latter includes changes in society which may be detrimental as well as beneficial, whereas development tends to be equated with the beneficial side only, with progress or improvement—for example, improvements in living standards, the adoption of new technologies, the establishment of new institutions. Development as such involves implicit and explicit value judgements about the direction and speed of change. However, it should be noted that the distributional impact of development may not be even and development for one person may not be development for another (for example, the opinions of a motorist commuter and a local house owner on a new motorway development). The generation of a consensus on the future development of a particular region may thus encounter many conflicting views. Further, even if a consensus on ends can be achieved, there may still be conflict on the means, the policy tools, to achieve those ends.

Although economic factors are of fundamental importance, development is much more than economic development or economic growth. It can be seen as a *multi-dimensional process*, including in addition to the economic development process, social development processes concerned with the distributional aspects of development; and political/administrative development processes concerned with the shifts in the influence and power of groups and individuals. All these processes are complexly interrelated and interdependent—the distributional impact of economic growth, the productivity effect of social factors and so on.

Building on this discussion, *regional development* can be seen as the process of development in a particular area, a region. Friedman[14] defines regional development as follows:

'regional development concerns the incidence of economic growth. It is ultimately the result of the location of economic activities in response to differential regional attractions. Shifts in the location pattern have direct repercussions on income, employment and welfare. Since spatial organisation is a function of activity and interaction patterns, regional development is simply an expression of these patterns.'

This definition includes several important aspects. But from the previous discussion it can be seen as perhaps somewhat limited in scope, for regional development involves a number of interrelated processes, including economic, social and political, taking place within a supra-urban/sub-national spatial–temporal framework.

Regional development is often used in a relative context, comparing problem regions with the prosperous regions, or with the national context, on the basis of a variety of socio-economic indicators. It can also be used in an absolute context—the development within a particular region. This approach is as relevant to the South East or West Midlands as it is the North East or Mid-Wales; but unfortunately, perhaps reflecting the economic development emphasis, regional development has been used mainly with reference to the 'problem' regions.

But who *manages* this process of regional development? Management, in the societal context, involves 'the powers of decision to influence social change'.[15] Thus, following on from the previous section, the management of regional development includes all the powers of decision through which the multiplicity of relevant agencies can influence the process of development in a beneficial way (towards higher positions on the value continua) for a region. The agency context of regional planning varies from situation to situation, but the management of the regional development process invariably lies in the hands of a large number of agencies—both public and private, operating at a variety of levels, with varying scopes of concern and perhaps, most important, with varying degrees of power. If regional planning is to be effective in guiding regional development, it must seek to influence the various agencies with the powers to act, encouraging them to adopt and use regional plans and policy guidelines.

7 Summary

The regional level can be viewed as an intermediate level between national and local. At this level, particular functional problems of growing urban regions and depressed industrial and rural regions have given rise to the need for an intermediate level of planning. Yet despite the urgency and convincing nature of the reasons for and aims of regional planning, its rôle has remained imprecise and capable of a variety of interpretations. For the purposes of this text, a simple taxonomic approach is adopted dividing regional planning into 'inter' and 'intra' forms.

To conclude with a more general definition of regional planning, Mr. Claudius Petit, one of the pioneers of regional planning and for many years French Minister for Reconstruction, commented that 'regional planning really means the planning of our society.[16] There could be no better way of summing up in a few words the vital importance of the problem facing many governments, and certainly most European governments, today.

References

1 Friedman, J., Regional Planning as a Field of Study, in Friedman, J. and Alonso, W., *Regional Development and Planning*, page 61, MIT Press, Cambridge, Mass. (1964).

2 For a discussion of the interrelationship of physical and economic planning, see: Robertson, D. J., The Relationship between Physical and Economic Planning, a Paper delivered to the *Town and Country Planning School, St. Andrews* (1965).

3 Friedman, J., A Conceptual Model for the Analysis of Planning, *Administrative Science Quarterly*, **12,** 12 (1967).

4 Young, R. C., Goals and Goal Setting, *Journal of the American Institute of Planners*, pages 76–85, **32** (1966).

5 *The National Plan*, Cmnd. 1764, HMSO (1965).

6 Friedman, J., Regional Planning as a Field of Study, *op cit*, page 64.

7 *Growth of the UK Economy to 1966*, NEDC, HMSO; *Conditions Favourable to Faster Growth*, NEDC, HMSO (1963).

8 Robertson, D. J., *op cit*.
Also Lichfield, N., Scope of the Regional Plan, *Regional Studies*, page 15, **1,** 1 (1967).

9 South East Joint Planning Team, *Strategic Plan for the South East*, HMSO, page 4 (1970).

10 Rodgers, W. T., The Future of Regional Planning, *Journal of the Town Planning Institute*, June 1966.

11 Ash, M., Realism and Regionalism, *Town and Country Planning*, **36,** 4 (1968).

12 Hall, P., Regional Balance, *Town and Country Planning*, June 1968.

13 *Report of the Royal Commission on the Distribution of Industrial Population*, Cmnd. 6153, HMSO (1940).

14 Friedman, J., and Alonso, W., *op. cit.*

15 Friend, J., Power, J., and Yewlett, C., *Public Planning: the Inter-Corporate Dimension*, Tavistock (1974).

16 Council of Europe, *Regional Planning: A European Problem* (1968).

2   The Region in Regional Planning

Planning has been identified as a future-oriented problem-solving process, which may be classified in a variety of ways. Regional planning fits into this general classification, but differs from other forms of planning in that it is specifically concerned with the regional level. This level lies somewhere between the national and local levels, and the region is a continuous and localised area at this level. But this is all very vague and provides little insight into the actual concept of the region. The idea of the region has been much used and abused over the years and there have been numerous controversies and disagreements over its meaning, perhaps reflecting the variety of disciplines involved in regional studies. To some, the region is a real entity that can be positively identified—a 'natural region'; to others, it is merely a product of the imagination, a method of classification. This chapter seeks to clarify the concept of the region, outlining alternative forms and discussing their relevance as planning regions.

1 The concept of the region

THE REGION: FACT OR FALLACY?

A first step in an outline of the concept of the region is to examine whether regions are natural phenomena or merely mental constructions. There are two divergent views—one objective, the other subjective. The subjective view sees a region as a means to an end, simply an idea, a model, to help in the study of the world. It is a method of classification, a device to segregate areal features, with the only 'natural' region being the surface of the earth on which man finds his home. The objective view adopts an opposite stance, seeing the region as an end in itself, a real entity, an organism, that can be identified and mapped.

The *subjective view* is now generally accepted. Hartshorne[1] wrote that attempts to see the region as a unitary concrete object 'have passed into history'. Regions are seen as descriptive tools, defined according to particular criteria, for a particular purpose—there being as many regions as there are criteria to define them. In this context they perform a particularly useful function, avoiding the extremes of description. Without the regional concept, for example, a description of Britain would either be so general as to be meaningless—'an industrial nation, with a cool climate, capital London'—or so complex as to be incomprehensible, cataloguing every single feature of the local landscape.

The *objective view* that regions actually exist was held by many academics in the early twentieth century, and was linked with the search for the elusive 'natural' region. The famous Oxford geographer, A. J. Herbertson,[2] adopting an analytical approach, divided the world into 'natural regions' on the basis of four criteria—land configuration, climate, vegetation and population density, but with climate as the dominant factor. Numerous followers applied his analytical approach at more local levels. Unstead;[3] on the other hand, approached the problem from the other end of the scale. He adopted a synthetic approach building up a series of British regions based on physical factors, extending outwards from the centre of a region until the periphery no longer shared the characteristics of the centre. Vidal de la Blache adopted a similar approach in France, although he used population as the basic criteria and starting point for his identification of *pays*. All these approaches have obvious geographical determinism undertones with the physical factors determining the human environment. In the words of de la Blache 'man and nature have become moulded to one another over the years rather like a snail and its shell'.[4]

However, most academics have now come round to the

subjective way of thinking, although there are important exceptions. There is an important East/West ideological split with many
Russian geographers repeatedly stating that economic regions
objectively exist.[5] In addition, in this country, the regionalism
movement with its demands for various forms of regions for
political, administrative and planning purposes could be seen as
taking a more objective view of regions. The topical idea of the
city region, linking a central town or city with its rural hinterland,
has been put forward as much for the purpose of creating regions
as for simply describing them. R. E. Dickinson,[6] a constant
advocate of the city region sees it as a 'natural social unit'.
Certain other recent studies could also be seen as lending limited
support to the concept of the region as a 'natural' entity. Carter,[7]
in an interesting analysis of *Referenda on the Sunday Opening of
Licensed Premises in Wales*, correlates 'wet' and 'dry' votes with
the ability to speak Welsh, and identifies a distinct 'cultural core'
zone in Wales—albeit a declining zone. Perhaps this cultural core
could be seen as the remainder of a natural region? In another
equally fascinating study, Gould and White[8] attempt to draw the
mental maps of British school leavers. These maps, based on the
ranking of alternative areas in Britain as residential locations,
contain a series of 'perception surfaces' with distinct 'peaks'
(e.g. the Lake District) and 'troughs' (e.g. Greater London)
which might also be interpreted as unique 'natural regions'.

THE REGION: FORMAL OR FUNCTIONAL

The concept of the region as a method of classification has evolved
through two distinct phases reflecting the economic advance
from a simple agrarian economy to a complex industrial system.
The first phase saw the 'formal region'—concerned with uniformity, and defined according to homogeneity. The second phase
saw the development of the 'functional region'—concerned with
interdependence, the interrelationship of the parts, and defined on
the basis of functional coherence.

A formal region is a geographical area which is uniform or homogeneous in terms of selected criteria. In early definitions of formal
regions, the criteria were predominantly physical (such as top-

37

ography, climate or vegetation), linked with the concept of geographical determinism. Later there was a shift to the use of economic criteria (such as industrial or agricultural types), and even social and political criteria (such as party political allegiance). The 'natural region' was a physical formal region. Interest in this form of region stemmed partly from the fact that physical factors are more stable than dynamic economic factors and hence much easier to study, but also from the influence of Darwin's Theory of Evolution. Following from Darwin's concept of natural selection, geographers believed that the survival of man depended on his adaptation to his environment. Hence, it was thought that the human environment could best be understood by isolating and studying the physical environment.

Economic formal regions are generally based on types of industry or agriculture (such as the South Yorkshire coal mining region or the Cotswolds sheep farming region), although there are obvious physical undertones. A traditional sub-division of Britain into economic formal regions is that by Stamp and Beaver,[9] who divided Britain into 19 agricultural regions upon which were superimposed 13 industrial regions. More recent attempts to delimit economic formal regions have been based on criteria such as income level, rate of unemployment and rate of economic growth. An interesting development of this approach is used by Smith[10] who divides the North West into several 'economic health' sub-regions using multiple socio-economic criteria.

A functional region is a geographical area which displays a certain functional coherence, an interdependence of parts, when defined on the basis of certain criteria. It is sometimes referred to as a nodal or polarised region and is composed of heterogeneous units, such as cities, towns and villages, which are functionally interrelated. The functional relationships are usually revealed in the form of flows, using socio-economic criteria such as journey-to-work trips or shopping trips linking the employment or shopping centre with subsidiary centres.

Ebeneezer Howard[11] was one of the early pioneers of the concept of the nodal region. He suggested that the solution to the problems of a large urban area such as London lay in developing a cluster of new towns linked to the central city in a functional relationship. Patrick Geddes[12] also stressed the interdependence and interrelationships of factors in a region, using his famous 'place–work–folk' diagram. It was Geddes also who coined the term 'city-region' which has come to be the most widely used form of nodal region. Rather more recently, Dickinson,[13] Smailes,[14] Green[15] and others have pioneered research into nodal regions, attempting to identify the region by deductive processes. Dickinson attempted to determine the nodal region of Leeds by analysing the distribution of the Leeds based *Yorkshire Evening Post*. Green used the frequency of bus services to determine the hinterland of urban centres. Foreign researchers, such as Christaller and Lösch have used a more inductive approach, concentrating on the hierarchical relationships between centres within the functional region.[16]

This brief analysis of the concept of the region suggests that regions are a means to an end, rather than ends in themselves. They may be formal or functional based on a single or multi-criteria. The development in Europe from vertically related primary producing economies to modern economies characterised by high levels of specialisation and horizontal relationships has tended to continue the trend towards a classification by functional regions, using mainly economic criteria. However, the formal region defined on the basis of socio-economic criteria is also useful, but the physical formal region, in particular the 'natural region' is of declining importance.

Formal or functional regions, or a combination of both, may provide a useful framework for a third type of regional classification into *planning regions*. There have been numerous definitions of planning regions. Boudeville[17] defines planning regions (or programming regions) as areas displaying some coherence or unity of economic decisions. Keeble[18] sees a planning region as an area which is large enough to enable substantial changes in distribution of population and employment to take place within its boundaries, yet which is small enough for its planning problems to be seen as a whole. Klaassen[19] believes that amongst other things, a planning region must be large enough to take investment decisions of an economic size, must be able to supply its own industry with the necessary labour, should have a homogeneous economic structure, contain at least one growth point and have a common approach to and awareness of its problems.

In the context of earlier discussion, such definitions suggest that planning regions are geographical regions suitable for the designing and implementing of development plans for dealing with the regional problems outlined earlier in Chapter 1. The problem of economic malaise displays a considerable degree of homogeneity in areas such as North East England and Central Scotland. On the basis of criteria such as unemployment levels, activity rates and migration trends, formal regions could be defined. The problem of congestion in South East England is more concerned with journey-to-work and service flows between major and subsidiary centres. Using these flows as criteria, functional regions could be defined. In practice, the formal and functional regions very rarely overlap neatly, and often vary markedly. The identification of satisfactory planning regions may therefore involve some compromise. This also assumes that the formal and functional regions can actually be delineated and that the resultant regions are administratively viable, which introduces the problems of regionalisation and regionalism.

2 Regionalisation and the delineation of regions

Regionalisation is the process of delineating regions. This process may take several forms depending on the purpose of regionalisation, the criterion/criteria to be used and data availability. Thus, as previously mentioned, a resolution of the problem of economic malaise may involve the delineation of formal regions using certain relevant criteria, and similarly the resolution of the congestion problem may involve the delineation of functional regions. In the absence of adequate data, qualitative intuitive approaches have been used, but this tends to lead to very 'misty' regional boundaries which, the more closely they are examined, the more vague they appear. Understandably, there has been a shift to a more quantitative approach to regional identification.

The delineation of formal regions involves the grouping together of local units which have similar characteristics according to certain clearly defined criteria, but which differ significantly from units outside the region on the basis of the chosen criteria. The resultant formal region will never be perfectly homogeneous, but must be homogeneous within certain clearly defined limits.*

If the criteria are simple and static, such as 'land over 500 feet', identification is relatively simple. But if there are a variety of criteria, such as unemployment rates, activity rates, and migration trends, and many of the criteria are dynamic and constantly changing, the task becomes more difficult. Several techniques have actually been used to delineate formal regions. Two of these, representing the extremes in sophistication, will now be briefly outlined.

a The weighted index number method has been outlined in its simplest form by Boudeville,[20] and has been developed by others into more sophisticated techniques such as cluster analysis and social area analysis. Figure 2.1 presents a very much simplified example of the method. The study area contains nine localities varying according to unemployment rates and per capita income levels. For policy reasons, there is a need to isolate the main problem region, the area of 'economic malaise'. Taking the criteria individually, it is difficult to isolate the problem region; but taken together and weighted, region *B* can be isolated. Problems implicit in this method are of course the choice of the original criteria, the choice of weights and the determination of acceptable homogeneity limits. Nevertheless, because of its simplicity, it is a well-used method.

b The factor analysis method is a more sophisticated approach to regionalisation which owes much to the pioneering work of

* Here, use can be made of simple statistical variation tests. For example, in the regionalisation of localities on the basis of unemployment rates, it may be decided that no unit within the region must diverge from the mean unemployment rate by > one standard deviation. Thus, if the mean $(\bar{x}) = 4\%$, and standard deviation (SD) = $\frac{1}{2}\%$, a locality with an enemployment rate of 3% would not be included in the formal unemployment region.

41

Berry[21] in the USA. The technical details of the method are more complex,[22] but the basic principles can be illustrated with reference to the economic health regionalisation of North West England by Smith.[23] Smith identified 14 industrial criteria on a

Fig. 2.1   *Delineation of formal regions (simple weighted-index number method)*

Applying a statistical variation test to the weights, Region *A* has a mean ($\bar{x}$) of 4·5 and standard deviation (SD) of 0·5, and Region *B* has ($\bar{x}$) = 8·5, (SD) = 0·5. Therefore, both regions are homogeneous within the limits ($\bar{x}$) ± 1 (SD).

local employment exchange area base and 14 socio-economic criteria on a local authority base. Many of these criteria were obviously interdependent, and determined by some underlying

42

factors. The factor analysis method can be used to isolate these basic factors, and to group areas on the basis of factor loadings. A contiguity constraint can be applied to give continuous regions. In his analysis, Smith identified 'industrial change' and 'industrial structure' as major industrial factors, and 'social structure' and 'population change' as major socio-economic factors. On the basis of these factors he was able to delineate economic health regions, highlighting East Lancashire and the 'cotton–coal belt' of Central Lancashire as distinctive problem areas.

The method is of course only as good as the choice and quality of data employed. But with the rapid development of associated computer 'software' and relevant statistical techniques, such as multivariate analysis, the method would seem to have considerable potential, not only for delineating regions, but in the wider field of planning.

THE DELINEATION OF FUNCTIONAL REGIONS

The delineation of functional regions involves the grouping together of local units which display a considerable degree of interdependence. The concern is thus more with flows linked to a central point rather than with the uniformity of the region as a whole. Two basic approaches to functional regionalisation will be outlined—'flow analysis' based on actual observations of what people do, and 'gravitational analysis' based on theoretical observations of what they might do.

a Flow analysis builds up functional regions on the basis of the direction and intensity of flows between the dominant centre and surrounding satellites. Each flow will show decreasing intensity as it becomes more distant from the main centre and increasing intensity as it approaches another centre. The boundary of the sphere of influence of the dominant centre will be where the flow intensity is at a minimum. The flows may be of several types. They are often economic, categorised according to type (such as cargo or passenger, road or rail) or purpose (such as shopping or commuting). They may also be social (such as the flow of students or hospital patients); political, especially the flow of government expenditure; or information, such as telegrams,

43

newspapers and telephone calls, which in fact may provide a good proxy indicator for the rest.

Green[24] and Carruthers[25] have attempted to delimit the sphere of influence of a centre, its functional region, using bus services as indicators of economic linkages. Green worked on the assumption that bus services were economic concerns, and would therefore choose the most economic routes which would similarly reflect the areas of greatest demand and functional linkages with the dominant centre. From bus timetables, he constructed flow diagrams of the frequency of service and from the latter he deduced the sphere of influence of centres, drawing up functional regions. The value of Green's approach is somewhat reduced by the impact of increasing competition from other forms of transport, especially the private car, and the fact that some public transport services are run on a social rather than on an economic basis.

An interesting variation of simple flow analysis is *graph theory*. This is again a very simple approach, but a more ordered and systematic way of identifying functional or nodal regions. The approach has been employed by Nystuen and Dacey,[26] and Boudeville,[27] and measures the relationships between selected groups of centres on the basis of flows between the centres. The number of telephone calls is the usual flow criteria, and provides a useful index of a wide range of economic and social relationships. The flows are plotted in matrix form, from which the primary and secondary flows into and out of each centre can be identified. The resulting hierarchy of nodes can be plotted as a simple network, providing an insight into the form and extent of functional relationships within an area. Figure 2.2 provides an example of simple graph theory, showing that D is the major centre, with B, E and G subsidiary centres. Figure 2.3 illustrates the use of both simple flow analysis and graph theory in the identification of sub-regions in South East England.

b Gravitational analysis is concerned with the theoretical forces of attraction between centres rather than the actual flows. As such, it could be regarded as a second-best approach, but if used with care it can provide a good guide to the actual flows and, perhaps more important, the potential flows between centres.

44

This rapidly developing field of 'social physics', as developed by Zipf, Reilly, Stewart, Stouffer and others, is based on a probability view of human interaction, and originates from the

Telephone calls ('000's per day) to centre;

	A	B	C	D	E	F	G	H	I
A		40		20					
B	10			60					
C				30					10
D		60			40				
E				30	10				
F					20	10			
G				50				20	
H				20		30			
I			10	40					

Telephone calls ('000's per day) from centre;

Flow matrix (primary and secondary flows only)

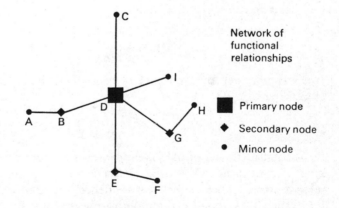

Network of functional relationships

■ Primary node

◆ Secondary node

● Minor node

Fig. 2.2 Graph theory: a simple illustration

application of analagous reasoning to Newtonian Physics.[28] Only the simple principles relevant to functional regionalisation will be discussed here, as interaction models are discussed in Chapter 8.

The simple gravity model assumes that the interaction between two centres is directly proportional to the 'mass' of the centres and inversely proportional to the 'distance' between the centres. The variables used to measure 'mass' and 'distance' depend on the problem and data availability. In recent planning developments of the model, 'mass' has been represented by such variables as population, employment, income, expenditure and retail turnover, and 'distance' in physical terms (miles), time, price and intervening opportunities. In mathematical notation:

$$T_{ij} = k \left[\frac{P_i P_j}{d^2_{ij}} \right]$$

where T_{ij} is the gravitational force between towns i and j, P_i and P_j are the masses of the two centres, d_{ij} is the distance between them, and k is a constant.

The concept of demographic or gravitational potential is a development of the original concept of particular relevance for regionalisation. The demographic potential at a centre i caused by a mass at centre j, $(_jV_i)$, is defined as:

$$_iV_j = k \left[\frac{P_j}{d_{ij}} \right]$$

If i is surrounded by a number of centres, n, the total potential at Centre i will be:

$$_iV = k \sum_{j=1}^{n} \left[\frac{P_j}{d_{ij}} \right]$$

By calculating the potential for the centres in a study area, contour lines of equal potential can be plotted on a map, illustrating the relative attractiveness, spheres of influence, of the various centres. From such lines, functional regions can be identified.

Thus, regions can be identified in practice. Indeed there are several quantitative approaches to the delineation of both formal

46

and functional regions. However, there are problems—the first one being the invariable lack of correlation between regions defined according to different criteria. Although there may sometimes be a general resemblance, it would be a great coincidence if different functional flows, such as journey-to-work, shopping or recreation flows were spatially matched. It is even more unlikely

Fig. 2.3(a) *Functional sub-regions in South East England*

that regional boundaries defined according to both functional and formal criteria would also be closely matched. The dynamic nature of regional activities presents a further problem. Firms are continuously expanding and contracting, with some regions becoming more prosperous, others becoming less so. The flows

47

of functional regions and the spheres of influence of centres are also constantly changing, particularly in response to transport developments. One only needs to note the impact of the Severn Bridge on the nodal relationships of Cardiff and Bristol, or to speculate on the possible impact of a Humber Bridge or a Dee Barrage to illustrate this point.

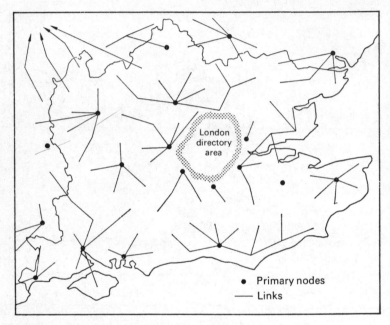

Fig. 2.3(b)   Telephone linkages, South East, 1967
Use of graph theory for identification of sub-regions

SOURCE   *Strategic Plan for the South East, Studies **4**; Strategies and Evaluation*

But, in spite of these difficulties, the regional types outlined may provide a useful basis for planning regions if delineated on the basis of 'problem' criteria. Although even if regions could be defined on the basis of such criteria, there are additional problems of whether they are administratively suitable and whether they

48

closely reflect the regional consciousness, the 'regional identity' of the areas concerned.

3 Regionalism and the administration of regions

Planning regions, however precisely defined on the criteria of formal or functional problems, may not correlate with administrative areas, and the latter are obviously important if the regional plan is to be implemented. Indeed, planning is not really planning unless it is related to implementation programmes and administration. To be administratively viable, Smith[29] believes regions must satisfy at least five criteria:

a they must be large enough to support a team of professional administrators;

b they must take in the main commuter hinterlands (this is especially important when considering traffic control);

c they must take in human catchment areas (of particular importance for the administration of services such as health);

d they must be able to provide the necessary talents for their services;

e they must consider topographical factors (especially important with regard to administration of services such as sewerage systems).

In addition to these administrative criteria, the factor of 'regional consciousness', which is particularly strong in areas such as Lancashire and Yorkshire and has developed 'nationalist' movements in Wales and Scotland, also merits consideration in the delineation of regions. Unfortunately, there is often little correlation between the problem defined regions, administrative regions and areas of regional identity, and this has been a major constraint on effective regional planning. However, there have been many suggestions and approaches to a resolution of this conflict which can be discussed under the umbrella of 'regionalism'.

REGIONALISM

'Regionalism' has been used by many people—geographers, political scientists, town planners and economists—to mean many different things. Hence, there is much confusion attached to the term. In the standard text on regionalism, Smith attempts to clarify the confusion and offers the following definition:

'Regionalism may thus be defined as an attempt to delimit areas usually larger than those of local government structure, with a view to making local and national government and planning more effective and efficient. Regionalism in this sense is essentially concerned with the problem of defining areas for a new, intermediate level of government and administration, rather than with the purely geographical function of delimiting areas of the earth's surface according to physical features.'[30]

The pressure behind regionalism comes from three major groups— those seeking administrative devolution from central government, those seeking local government re-organisation and those seeking a more efficient land-use planning system.

France was one of the first countries to consider regionalism. Many moves were made to replace *départements* as political units, but it was not until the 1950's, with the introduction of 22, and later 21, 'program regions', that the first steps were taken towards a nationwide system of administration and planning at the regional level. In the United Kingdom, the regionalism movement dates back to the beginning of this century, but it was only in the mid-1960s, with the arrival of the Regional Economic Planning Councils and Boards (1965), that there was any substantial progress.

THE EVOLUTION OF REGIONALISM IN THE UNITED KINGDOM

A review of some of the major stages in the evolution of regionalism in the United Kingdom will serve to illustrate some of the confusion associated with the term, and also clarify certain meanings relevant to regional planning. Since 1900 there have been numerous attempts to formulate an intermediate administrative level between the local and national levels and to reduce the fragmentation of administrative boundaries which initially date back to 1888 but which in shape and extent date back to 1066. Suggestions for reform have been mainly limited to England, with

50

Scotland, Wales and Northern Ireland already possessing some degree of regional autonomy within their 'cultural' regions. The majority of suggestions usually outlined a limited number of large regions or provinces. All tended to be rather limited being heavily weighted by the particular service(s) or policy they had in mind.

H. G. Wells in his *Anticipations* in 1902 predicted the development of urban regions or 'city regions', but it was the Fabian Society[31] in 1905 who were the first to advocate a series of large-scale regions as a basis for administrative reform. Their 'new heptarchy' was made up of seven great provinces, each incorporating several counties, and based on the major centres of Newcastle, Leeds, Liverpool, Manchester, Birmingham, Nottingham and London.

Somewhat later in 1919, the geographer, Fawcett,[32] in *The Provinces of England* divided England into 12 provinces on the basis of six principles:

1. The provincial boundaries should be so chosen as to interfere as little as possible with the ordinary activities and movements of the people.
2. There should be in each province a definite capital, which should be the real focus of its regional life. (This capital should be easily accessible from every part of the province.)
3. The least of the provinces should contain a population sufficiently numerous to justify self-government. (Fawcett suggested a figure of at least one million.)
4. No one province should be large enough to be able to dominate the others.
5. The provincial boundaries should be drawn near watersheds rather than across valleys, and very rarely along streams.
6. The grouping of areas must pay regard to local patriotism and to tradition.

Fawcett believed that this 'systematic application of geographical science to the existing conditions' provided the most practical and satisfactory delimitation of provinces. His twelve provinces are illustrated in Figure 2.4. This framework was later modified, and in 1942 he produced a revised version, the major difference being the elimination of the Peakdon province based on Sheffield.

Regionalism as a whole, however, never really came alive as a political issue in the inter-war years, and it was not until the war years of the 1940's that the movement gained a fresh impetus. To meet the war emergency, Regional Commissioners were appointed to control the affairs of nine groups of counties termed Civil Defence Regions. The various Ministries of Transport,

Fig. 2.4 Fawcett's original provinces

SOURCE C. B. Fawcett, *Provinces of England*, rev. edn. by W. G. East and S. W. Wooldridge. Hutchinson (1961).

Education, Labour, Agriculture and so on, had representatives and staff at the regional capitals. The validity of these regions as a basis for post-war regional administration was hotly disputed during this period. The geographer, Gilbert, made use of them in postulating his ideas for 13 provinces (the main difference from Fawcett being the subdivision of the Northern province and a different grouping in the South East). Others such as the geographer, Taylor,[33] preferred a more radical change.

The need for postwar reconstruction did in fact result in the government maintaining a regional framework. Nine Standard Treasury Regions were established in 1946 and other departments adopted the same boundaries to facilitate co-operation between regional officials. With minor modifications (in 1956) the Standard Regions formed the backbone of regionalism into the 1960's. Yet the subdivision did have its problems. The approach to dealing with the different areas of the South West and South East illustrated some of the problems of splitting up the UK on a regional basis, and displayed a certain inconsistency of approach. In the South West there was only one region stretching from Gloucester to Land's End, including areas with little community of interest; whereas in the South East there were three subdivisions—East Anglia, London and the South East, and the South.

At roughly the same time (1945–51), several statutory boards and corporations were established. These bodies related to major aspects of the life of the country, such as hospitals, railways, gas coal and electricity. Each had a regional framework, and although there was some general similarity of boundaries between them, there were also some major anomalies and often little correlation with the Standard Regions.

During the 1950's there was a wane in administrative regionalism and some dismantling of the post-war machinery. The reawakening came in the late 1950's and early 1960's linked to the growing recognition of regional problems, especially those of economic malaise in the depressed areas; the recognition of the need to plan vital infrastructure on a large scale as outlined in the Buchanan Report; and the resurgence of a regional consciousness possibly encouraged by the development of the new universities and regional TV, such as Granada and Tyne-Tees. New forms of regions were outlined, and the *Economist*,[34] for example,

53

produced an imaginative plan for dividing up Britain into 15 regions. The culmination of this movement was the establishment of the Regional Economic Planning Regions under the new Labour Administration in 1965. (See Figure 2.5.) These regions,

Fig. 2.5   United Kingdom: economic planning regions (1975)

eight English plus Northern Ireland, Scotland and Wales are very similar to the original Standard Regions, except for the creation of a larger South East and an integrated Yorkshire and Humberside. However they are far from standard in size and Table 2.1 gives a population breakdown illustrating the regional disparity, with the population of the new South East region larger than the sum of the population of the next three regions.

Table 2.1 *UK Economic Planning Regions: Population (1977)*

Region	Population (000's)
North	3116
North West	6519
Yorkshire and Humberside	4876
West Midlands	5154
East Midlands	3747
South West	4279
South East	16834
East Anglia	1827
Scotland	5196
Wales	2768
Northern Ireland	1537

SOURCE CSO, *Abstract of Regional Statistics,* 1979.

The establishment of the Economic Planning Regions each with its council and board (with special arrangements for Northern Ireland), represents the present state of affairs in UK regional administration. But this is not to suggest that a satisfactory system of administrative regions are now generally agreed and are operating effectively. The dissatisfaction with the economic planning councils and boards in their rôle of planning and co-ordination at the regional level, the electoral successes of the Scottish and Welsh Nationalists, and the creation of the Commission on the Constitution at the beginning of 1969, have all contributed to a resurgence of interest in regionalism in the late 1960's and early 1970's. (See Chapter 11.)

But in addition to this revival of interest in the need for a limited number of large regions, between 10 to 15, the 1960's have also witnessed growing support for a larger number, between 30 to 60, of smaller regions or sub-regions integrating town and country, based on the organic concept of the relationship between a town or a city and the surrounding area. The system of local government created in the nineteenth century with its division into administrative counties and county boroughs effected a cleavage in this organic relationship. Geographers such as Smailes[35] and Dickinson[36] sought to identify alternative 'city-regions', but it was not until 20–25 years afterwards that the concept was seriously considered as a viable administrative unit in the UK. In the mid 1960's, Senior,[37] a latter-day 'city-regionalist' revived interest in the concept. He was fortunate in that his interest coincided with the establishment of a Royal Commission on Local Government in 1966. Over the next few years, alternative frameworks were proposed for local government reform, ranging from Senior's advocacy of 30 to 35 city regions to the Maud Report[38] suggestions for approximately 60 unitary authorities.

The problem of the existing regional administrative framework and the proposals for reform at both the level of the large planning region and the smaller city region will be examined in more detail in a later chapter. Suffice it to say at this stage that these two types of regions have evolved out of the history of regionalism in the UK. In this context, it is relevant to note that for the Scottish and the Welsh, Scotland and Wales are of course nations. Indeed, Scotland itself has, since local government reorganisation (1975), been divided into regions. The region is a flexible concept and varies with purpose, perception and time.

The factor of *regional perception* or regional identity has been noted several times in the preceding discussion, but this factor has been somewhat ignored in regional research. Each resident of a country sees his/her country in a different way; that is everyone has a personal mental map broadly reflecting the rival forces of distance and knowledge. But how important is the concept of the region in that mental map? An attitudes survey[39] carried out in the researches of the *Royal Commission on the Constitution* provides some qualified support for the existence of a regional identity factor in the United Kingdom. The survey showed that 77% of 4892 informants were able to think of themselves as part of a region larger than a county. There was also some evidence that people had a mental image of the relative attributes of their particular region, for example, whether it was industrial, well-off financially or particularly proud of its own culture and traditions. The feeling of regional identity, although fairly strong throughout the country, did vary, being stronger in Scotland, Wales and the northern regions of England. In another study based on a survey of people in four towns in the North East of England only, Townsend and Taylor[40] also illustrated the presence of a regional identity. Their results reveal a reasonably uniform picture of people's identity of the North East, closely correlating with industrialisation and social deprivation and transcending local authority boundaries.

4 Summary: planning regions and regional planning

As outlined earlier, subjective and objective views can be taken of the concept of the region. The subjective view regards regions as descriptive tools, defined according to particular criteria for a particular purpose. On this basis, formal and functional regions can be identified. Such regions may provide the basis for ideal planning regions, with for example the identification of an economic planning region on the basis of homogeneity in a certain criteria such as unemployment, and the identification of city regions on the basis of functional flows. But this assumes that the regions can actually be delineated on the basis of available data. It also assumes that the regions thus identified reflect the underlying regional consciousness of the areas concerned and are administratively viable. In most cases there will undoubtedly be conflict between these criteria, and the need for compromise. As such, the region will generally be 'satisfactory' rather than 'ideal'. In practice, planning regions may be more determined by administrative expediency than by theoretical excellence.

In the United Kingdom context, there appears to be the emergence of two new intermediate levels of administration and planning region—with the large 'economic planning regions' representing a devolution from above, and the smaller 'city regions' representing scale enlargement from below. Inter-regional planning, concerned with the allocation of economic

57

resources between regions, demands the large region with some uniformity of problem. Intra-regional planning, with rather more emphasis on land-use planning, is of relevance equally to the large regions as it is to their constituent sub-regions.

References

1 Hartshorne, R., *Perspective on the Nature of Geography,* Chicago, page 31 (1959).
2 Herbertson, A. J., The Major Natural Regions, *Geographical Journal,* XXV (1905).
3 Unstead, J. F., A synthetic method of determining geographical regions, *Geographical Journal,* XLVIII (1916).
4 De la Blache, Vidal, in Wrigley, E. A., *Changes in the Philosophy of Geography* (in Chorley, R. J. and P. Haggett, *Frontiers in Geographical Teaching,* London (1965) page 8).
5 Alampiev, P. M., The objective basis of economic regionalisation and its long range prospects, *Soviet Geography* II, pages 64–74 (1961).
6 Dickinson, R. E., *City and Region: A Geographical Interpretation,* Routledge and Kegan Paul (1964).
7 Carter, H. and Thomas, J. G., Referendum on Sunday Opening of Licensed Premises in Wales, *Regional Studies,* pages 61–71, **3,** 1 (1969).
8 Gould, P. R., and White, R. R., The mental maps of British school leavers, *Regional Studies,* pages 161–82, **2,** 2 (1968).
9 Stamp, L. D., and Beaver, S. H., *The British Isles,* Longmans (1933).
10 Smith, D. M., Identifying Grey Areas—a multivariate approach, *Regional Studies,* **2,** 2 (1968).
11 Howard, E., *Garden Cities of Tomorrow,* Faber and Faber (1945).
12 Geddes, P., *Cities in Evolution* (1915).
13 Dickinson, R. E., *op cit.*
14 Smailes, A. E., The Urban Hierarchy in England and Wales, *Geography,* pages 41–51, **29** (1944).
15 Green, F. H. W., Urban Hinterlands in England and Wales, *Geographical Journal,* **116** (1950); also: Green, F. H. W., Urban Hinterlands: Fifteen Years On, *Geographical Journal,* **132** (1966).
16 Christaller, W., *Central Places in Southern Germany,* (Trans. C. W. Baskin), Englewood Cliffs, New Jersey (1966).
17 Boudeville, J. R., *Problems of Regional Economic Planning,* Edinburgh U.P. (1966).

18 Keeble, L., *Principles and Practice of Town and Country Planning,* 4thedition, Estates Gazette, page 47, London (1969).

19 Klaassen, L., *Area Social and Economic Redevelopment,* OECD (1965).

20 Boudeville, J. R., *op cit.*

21 Berry, B. J. L., A method for deriving multifactor uniform regions, *Przeglad Geograficzny,* pages 263–82, **33** (1961).

22 See: Bruton, M. J., An introduction to factor analysis and its application in planning, *Oxford Working Papers in Planning Education and Research,* W.P.8, Oxford Polytechnic, November 1971.

23 Smith, D. M., *op cit*; also Spence, N. A., A multifactor uniform regionalization of British counties on the basis of employment data for 1961, *Regional Studies,* **2,** September 1968.

24 Green, F. H. W., *op cit.*

25 Carruthers, I., A classification of service centres in England and Wales, *Geographical Journal,* pages 371–85, **123** (1957).

26 Nystuen, J. D. and Dacey, M. F., A graph theory interpretation of nodal regions, *Papers and Proceedings of the Regional Science Association,* pages 29–42, **7** (1961).

27 Boudeville, J. R., *op cit,* Chapter Two.

28 For a discussion of the principles, problems and application of gravitational analysis, see: Dept. of Town Planning, Lanchester Polytechnic, Coventry, *Gravity Models in Town Planning,* October 1969.

29 Smith, B. C., *Regionalism 3: the new regional machinery,* Acton Society Trust, page 36 (1965).

30 Smith, B. C., *Regionalism 2: its nature and purpose,* Acton Society Trust, pages 22–3 (1965).

31 Sanders, W., *Municipalisation by Provinces,* Fabian Society (1905) ('New Heptarchy' series).

32 Fawcett, C. B., *Provinces of England,* London (1919), revised edition, London (1961).

33 For Prof. Taylor's suggested regions, see *Geographical Journal,* page 62, **99** (1942), and those of Professor Gilbert on page 76 of the same volume.

34 *The Economist,* Federal Britain's New Frontiers, 18 May 1963.

35 Smailes, A. E., *op cit.*

36 Dickinson, R. E., *op cit.*

37 Senior, D., The City Region as an Administrative Unit, **36,** *Political Quarterly,* January–March 1965.

38 *Report of the Royal Commission on Local Government in England 1966–69* (Chairman: Lord Redcliffe-Maud), 3 Volumes, Cmnd. 4040 (1969).

39 *Royal Commission on the Constitution, Research Papers No. 7, Devolution and Other Aspects of Government: An Attitudes Survey,* HMSO (1973).

40 Townsend, A. R., and Taylor, C. C., Regional Culture and Identity in Industrialised Societies: the Case of North-East England, *Regional Studies,* **9,** 4 (1975).

PART TWO
The Analysis of Regions

A: Inter-regional Analysis

3 The regional framework

The quality of the regional data base is a major influence on regional planning. Adequate data is essential both for the initial definition of regions and for their subsequent analysis and planning. The formal and functional regional definitions of Chapter 2 and the 'inter' and 'intra' regional analysis of later chapters require a wide range of spatially aggregated and disaggregated data on people's activities (such as employment, education), land use, and flows (such as journey-to-work patterns). This chapter seeks to generally examine the British regional data base, outlining available sources, their adequacy or otherwise for regional planning and possible refinements. In particular, it is interesting to investigate whether Prof. Chester's view that the 'existence of large gaps in our statistical information about regional problems is by now well recognised as a major obstacle of realistic planning'[1] is still borne out by the facts. The possibility of establishing a framework of regional accounts including input-output tables is discussed rather more fully. Such accounts and tables are spatially aggregate, abstracting from the locational differences within the region, and looking at the region as a whole. They thus provide a valuable context for further inter-regional analysis in the following chapters.

1 The adequacy of the UK regional data base
Appendix A lists some of the major sources of regional statistics,

63

subdividing them into *general sources* and *supplementary sources* (including both activities and land use). But are such sources adequate? There are limitations and inadequacies in all statistics which can only be clearly identified when they are required for a specific purpose. At this level of discussion of statistics for general use for regional definition, analysis and planning, only general comments on their adequacy or otherwise would appear justified. As such, adequacy will be stressed against the general criteria of availability, frequency of publication, time lag in publication comparability and overall relevance.

The range of sources in the Appendix clearly suggests that a large body of regional statistics is readily available in published form. But it must be remembered that although two series may be equally available in the objective sense that they both appear in official publications, in the subjective sense they may differ widely if one is a regular publication and the other is more obscure.

Associated with the criteria of availability is that of frequency of publication. Some of the most useful data is that which is available on a frequent and regular time series. Employment data is available at monthly intervals, housing data at three-monthly intervals, and much other useful information is available annually. However, other very important sources, such as detailed Inland Revenue data and the Censuses of Population, Production and Distribution are more infrequent with five-year and ten-year intervals, and this of course reduces their value. The decennial Population Census is particularly infrequent, although the insertion of a 10% sample census in 1966 gave some hope of improvement.*

The non-comparability of the data from various sources presents another problem. This is largely due to the use of different regional boundaries. It may occur at one point in time where different statistical sources use different boundaries—for example, the non-comparability of data based on hospital, electricity board and economic planning regions. It may also occur over a period of time for one particular series of statistics. Thus the population statistics for the standard regions of the early 1960's are not directly comparable with the more recent population data based on the new economic planning regions.

* Later dashed by the abandonment of the 1976 sample census.

But even if data is immediately available, published regularly and comparable in time and space, it is still useless unless it is relevant to the broad uses outlined earlier. From the list of sources, one immediately apparent inadequacy would seem to be the lack of information on land use and flows as compared with the considerable amount of published information on activities. This data is in fact normally available from a different set of sources collected on a unified basis by local surveys and censuses conducted by planning bodies. Broad national land use surveys are provided in a limited form by the Ordnance Survey and by the *National Land Utilization Surveys* of Stamp and Coleman, but it is arguable that there is a need for a more comprehensive national land use survey to complement the national population census.

With regard to this question of general relevance, another inadequacy is the limited nature of information on the regional economic structure. A knowledge of the latter is essential in assessing the problems and potential of the region, yet available information is primarily related to employment characteristics, with very infrequent censuses on production and distribution. There is a need for a more comprehensive framework with data on the internal and external interrelationships of industrial sectors in the regional economy.

Therefore in spite of a reasonable coverage of many areas of relevance to regional planning, regional statistics do have their problems. But it would probably be unfair to say that these deficiencies constitute the main obstacle to regional planning at the present time. Administrative problems may be much more fundamental here. But what of the future for regional statistics, how can the various problems be overcome? One interesting possibility is the development of data collection on a more disaggregated basis. Another is the development of regional accounts.

To be of maximum use to planning, relevant data from all agencies needs to be disaggregated to a common level of small and spatially regular units. These can then be aggregated into whatever geographical units are necessary. Aided by the rapid advances in information processing technology, many countries are now, in fact, introducing data collection based on metric grid systems. In Sweden, an information system links a basic population register (with data on income, employment, education, migration, etc. for individuals or groupings) and an enterprise register (providing data on the economic life of individual concerns) to a property register which can provide the locational element based on grid references. In Britain the 1971 Population Census collected information on a 100-metre grid square basis in many areas. This represents a major advance in British data collection, and opens up many possibilities for the future including the production of computer based census maps. The implicit problems however of extending this system to give a comprehensive statistical framework for not only regional and sub-regional planning but also for more local levels of planning should not be underestimated. How should it be organised—by a national collecting agency with an expanded census or by local collecting agencies using standardised methods or by a combination of both? How can a wide variety of agencies, some producing handwritten statistics, others producing them on magnetic tape be physically integrated into a unified system? And finally and most important, what of the cost and confidentiality aspects of obtaining this information? Many agencies, firms and private individuals, as revealed in the 1971 census, may object to the increasing intrusions of 'Big Brother'.

2 Regional accounts

A comprehensive picture of the regional economic structure is vital for regional planning. One possible approach is through the development of regional accounts. These accounts are similar to national accounts, which in the UK provide an annual picture of monetary flow, traditionally using a 'treble entry' system with Income = Expenditure = Output. However, an interesting and more recent development is the presentation of the economic interrelationships of the major sectors of the economy—households, firms, government, financial sector and rest of the world—in a series of social accounts, presented in a matrix form.

McCrone[2] believes that the development of accounts at the regional level is an essential prerequisite before regional planning can be undertaken. They have already been developed in several other countries at this level. Italy, for example, has a comprehensive set of regional accounts for the Mezzogiorno; Belgium has estimates of regional product by industry at the provincial level and France has comprehensive income data by *départements*. But enthusiasm for their development in the UK must first be qualified by an examination of their potential role in regional planning and the data and conceptual problems involved in their construction.

Besides providing a detailed picture of the interrelationships of the major sectors of the regional economy, regional accounts can also provide a valuable basis for regional policy and decision making. With information on topics such as regional income, output, investment and productivity, regional policy need no longer rely solely on political and social arguments and the dubious economic criteria of unemployment. Estimates of regional product by industry would facilitate the isolation of strengths and weaknesses in the regional economy, while data on investment could indicate which industries in which regions would give the best returns for a given level of investment.

However these advantages are only achieved at a cost, for regional accounts have heavy data requirements which raise a number of problems. Conceptually, regions are not micronations and perhaps need a different form of accounts to those used at the national level. In addition, the economic structure also varies greatly from region to region, yet for comparison between regions, standard accounts must be used which may mask important aspects of a particular region's economy. As compared with nations, regions are also 'open' economies with numerous cross-boundary transactions but no trade barriers and hence little information on such movements. (It is particularly difficult to balance the income and expenditure approaches at the regional level as a person may work in one area and live in another.)

Specific data problems include most of those already outlined in the previous section on regional statistics—infrequency of some series, time delay in publication and non-comparability in time and space. But there are also additional problems. The disaggregation of national data raises the problem of confidentiality, with a regional industry composed of perhaps only a handful of firms. Disaggregation also raises the question of the statistical accuracy at sub-national levels of national sample based surveys. With the growth of multi-product, multi-plant firms it may also be difficult to identify and obtain the relevant data for the specific plants in the region under study.

In spite of these problems there have been several attempts to construct regional accounts. Estimates of gross domestic product (GDP) for Wales,[3] Scotland[4] and Northern Ireland[5] have all been prepared. Statistically these 'national' areas present fewer problems than the English regions, and until the recent publication of regional accounts by Woodward arising from research done at the National Institute of Economic and Social Research,[6] accounts for English regions were limited to tentative calculations by Deane[7] and Stone,[8] both for 1948. Woodward, using disaggregated national accounts and a wide variety of regional sources such as Inland Revenue Reports and Family Expenditure Surveys, draws up comprehensive tables for GDP (including industrial subdivisions), domestic expenditure and personal income. The accounts provide a fascinating insight into regional variations, suggesting many of the underlying factors responsible for the variations. For example, the wide divergence in GDP per head of population at factor cost between South East England and Northern Ireland in 1961—£503 (SE) as compared with £289 (NI)—is clearly shown to be influenced by several factors such as the economic composition of the regional population, variations in regional productivity and the different industrial structures.

Notwithstanding that regions are not micro-nations, most attempts to draw up regional accounts have opted for the traditional national accounts approach. This approach as has been shown, does have many problems, especially income spillovers, and although recent works have met with some success it is arguable whether such accounts do provide the most useful framework of the regional economy. There is the general question of divergence between economic welfare and general welfare with only the former reflected in the accounting framework. There is also the point that regional accounts tend to focus on 'the wood and not the trees'. However changes in individual 'trees' sometimes bring about substantial changes in the 'wood' as a whole. Concentrating on the production sector, an industrial breakdown of a region, showing inter-industry relationships in the form of an input-output matrix, may be more useful than income and expenditure components enabling us to see both the 'wood' and the 'trees'. This particular aspect of the wider regional accounts will now be examined in more depth.

3 Descriptive regional input-output tables

INPUT-OUTPUT TABLES

Since the pioneering work of W. W. Leontieff[9] in the 1930's, input-output has grown into one of the most widely accepted methods of not only describing the industrial structure of an economy but also, linked with other techniques, of predicting changes in that structure. This section will be limited to an examination of input-output as a descriptive framework. Discussion of input-output as a predictive technique and examples of its predictive use are discussed more fully in the next chapter.

The input-output table is a set of accounts, usually in monetary form, prepared for an economy. It pays explicit attention to inter-relationships between different sectors of the economy, concentrating in particular on inter-industry relationships. The format of the input-output table is outlined in Table 3.1. Usually the framework is a matrix of '$n \times n$' dimensions divided into four parts with each part describing a particular relationship. The overall system is a series of correlating rows (output) and columns (input).

Sector 1 is usually the largest sector and describes the inter-industry relationships as sales from one industry representing inputs to the production process of other linked industries. For example, in the hypothetical three-industry economy of Table 3.1, Industry 1 has sales of £50m to Industry 2 and £20m to Industry 3, and receives inputs of £20m from Industry 2 and £40m from Industry 3. Sector 1 is generally referred to as the intermediate or processing sector.

Sector 2 represents the sales from the industries to the external sectors of the economy. This sector, the final demand or household sector, consists of relationships more dependent on socio-political factors than economic criteria and includes commodities

69

for personal consumption, public expenditure, exports and the like. Thus Industry 1 has sales of £40m to final demand (including home consumption and exports), giving total sales or output of £110m.

The third part, Sector 3, refers to external inputs to industrial production, including factors such as wages for labour, taxes and subsidies, profits and imports. In our example, Industry 1 has household inputs (primarily wages for labour) of £40m and £10m of imports, giving total inputs of £110m.

Inputs From:	Output To:	Industry 1	Industry 2	Industry 3	Final Demand	Total Output
Industry	1	—	50	20	40	110
	2	20	--	80	110	210
	3	40	50	—	60	150
Household Inputs		40	100	50	—	190
Imports		10	10	—	20	40
Total Inputs		110	210	150	230	700

Sector 1 · Sector 2 · Sector 3 · Sector 4

Table 3.1. *Simple Input-Output Flow Table for One Area. (£ million).*

Sector 4 represents the relationships between the external sectors. In Table 3.1 half of the total imports go straight to final demand. In practice this sector is not too important, mainly serving as a balancing factor in the total accounts. Finally, by summing the rows, total outputs are obtained. Likewise by summing the columns, total inputs are obtained. Obviously total inputs must equal total outputs, and the inputs and output of each industry and the external sectors must also balance out.

This combination of the four sectors presents a sophisticated method of describing an economy by input and output relationships, and has been enlarged to include a large number of industrial and external sectors in several national studies. However, the format of Table 3.1 limits relationships with other economies to simple import and export rows and columns. But regional economies are much more open than this with numerous cross-boundary transactions and consequently present more problems.

REGIONAL INPUT-OUTPUT TABLES

The problem of constructing regional tables can be approached in three ways. The first, and simplest, is to use a single region table identical in form to the national tables with all trade with the rest of the world relegated to a single row and column (as in Table 3.1).

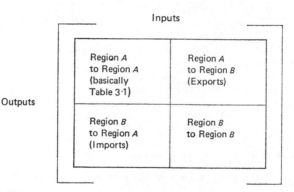

Inputs

Region *A* to Region *A* (basically Table 3·1)	Region *A* to Region *B* (Exports)
Region *B* to Region *A* (Imports)	Region *B* to Region *B*

Outputs

Table 3.2 *Outline framework for a two-region input-output table*

The second method is more sophisticated using two regions, with both the region of primary interest and a second region (often the rest of the nation) treated in detail. A further three matrices are added to the original model of Table 3.1. The first matrix relates to the intra-regional system; the second and third to relationships between the primary region and the other region (regional exports and imports); and the fourth to the other region as a whole. Table 3.2 illustrates this approach.

The third and undoubtedly most difficult approach is the construction of a multi-region input-output table. This extends the second approach by treating three or more regions on an equal

71

footing. Table 3.3 illustrates the approach, with each block representing an input-output system for a region, each consisting of the basic framework similar to that described in Table 3.1. Although the multi-region tables add greatly to the realism of

Inputs

A/A	A/B	A/C	A/D
B/A	B/B	B/C	B/D
C/A	C/B	C/C	C/D
D/A	D/B	D/C	D/D

Outputs

Table 3.3 *Outline framework for a multi-regional input-output table*

the approach, implicitly or explicitly introducing distance as a factor affecting inter-regional flows, they also impose extra data problems.

INPUT-OUTPUT DATA PROBLEMS

Regional input-output tables require two broad types of information: firstly, regional accounting data and secondly, inter-regional and inter-industry flow estimates. The problems of regional accounting data have already been outlined, but with the recent NIESR[10] study there are signs of improvement. Data on the second area however is much thinner. The problem of disaggregating inter-industry inputs presents a major problem. The most accurate method would probably be to survey the industries within the region to identify their input composition. This however, is usually ruled out on cost grounds and tends to be replaced by a disaggregation of national input-output data. Thus if 10% of the inputs for the engineering industry nationally come from the manufacturing industry, then it is also assumed that 10% of the inputs for the regional engineering industry also come from the same industry. This use of national input coefficients represents a considerable economy in data collection and is probably not too misleading provided that the regional industry does not differ too markedly in technology from the same industry in other regions.

In addition, regional input-output tables also need to identify the regional source of the inputs. Data on regional trade in the UK is of limited availability. Even the 1962 MOT Road Goods Transport Survey[11] data and British Rail Wagon Movements Survey data are of dubious reliability for inter-industry flows. Direct surveys would again appear to be the panacea, although even here the presence of middlemen may distort the picture. Faced with these problems most input-output tables assume that regions are self-supporting wherever possible. If an industry requires an input which is produced within its own region, it will use the internal source, only drawing on other regions when the internal supply is insufficient. Similarly only when an industry can more than meet internal demands will there be any export of its commodities to other regions. This approach, implying no cross-hauling of the same commodity between regions is of doubtful validity.

A more interesting approach to inter-regional trade flows is the use of synthetic trade coefficients based on a gravity formulation. From their recent work on patterns of flow for Severnside, Edwards and Gordon[12] suggest the possibility of developing a synthetic model relating inter-regional trade flows in a particular commodity directly to the supply and demand for the commodity (using either gross output or proxy employment data) and inversely to the distance between the regions involved, with constants for relative accessibility and competitive factors. Such an approach not only provides a rational basis for trade coefficients, but may also introduce a more spatial element into this basically non-spatial input-output approach.

REGIONAL INPUT-OUTPUT IN PRACTICE*

In spite of the basic problems, a large number of regional input-output tables have been constructed. Table 3.4 summarises

* This section draws partly on Fletcher, R. J., *Regional Input-Output Analysis,* unpublished thesis, Department of Town Planning, Oxford Polytechnic.

Input-Output Studies — Characteristics	1 New England	2 New York – Philadelphia	3 Interregional USA Model	4 Utah Model	5 Pacific NW. Study	6 St. Louis Study	7 California Study	8 Los Angeles Study	9 Philadelphia	10 Washington State	11 Rio Grande Valley	12 Stockholm	13 Welsh Study	14 Dundee Study	15 W. Midlands	16 S.E. Kent	17 Peterborough
1 Origin																	
Year of Completion (19)	53	53	55	57	59	59	63	64	66	68	69	59	67	67	67	70	71
Sponsorship : Research Project	X	X	X	X	X	X	X	X	X	X	X	X	X	X	X	X	X
Public Policy																	
2 Scale and Size																	
Regional	X	X	X	X	X		X	X	X	X	X		X		X	X	X
Urban																	
Single Region	X	X		X	X	X		X	X		X	X		X	X	X	X
Two Regions						X						X		X			
Multi-Regional			X				X			X			X				
3 Table Composition																	
Number of Processing Sectors	45	45	11	26	45	27	28	41	496	54	12	31	31	12	45	45	38
Number of Final Demand Sectors	4	–	–	7	–	–	7	–	86	6	–	15	–	6	–	–	5

Table 3.4 shown below (rows = study characteristics; columns = individual regional input–output studies, identified by the base year of their table). An "X" indicates the characteristic applies to that study.

4 Data																	
Coefficients:	National	X												X	X	X	X
	Modified National		X	X													
	Direct Survey				X	X	X	X	X	X	X	X	X				
Base Year of Table (19)		47	47	47	55	47	60	60	59	63	64	50	64	55	54	63	68
Units:	Monetary	X	X	X	X	X	X	X	X	X	X	X	X	X	X	X	X
	Labour						X										
5 Planning Functions																	
	Descriptive	X	X	X	X	X	X					X	X	X	X	X	X
	Predictive		X					X	X	X	X						
Specific Uses:	Structural Analysis	X	X			X	X					X	X				X
	Trade Flow Analysis		X			X						X	X				
	Production Output Forecast								X				X				
	Impact Analysis	X		X		X		X	X		X	X					
	Income Multipliers			X		X		X	X		X	X					
	Employment Multipliers	X		X		X											

Table 3.4 Examples of regional input-output studies and their characteristics

a sample of such tables. Although the sample is small and limited to a number of general criteria on primarily British and American studies, it does give some indication of the evolution of the approach over a period of 20 years or so.

The first section in the table contains information on the year of construction and form of sponsorship. It is interesting that all are research projects—although this is not true of every input-output study. The second section illustrates the predominance of regional scale studies, although the approach can also be used with effect at 'sub'-regional levels, and Artle's[13] famous Stockholm Study and recent British work on a table for Peterborough[14] provide interesting examples. The single region approach with all external trade relegated to a single row or column is the most common. However the Welsh Study by Nevin[15] provides an interesting example of a two-region approach, using Wales and the rest of the UK as the two regions.

The third section illustrates the range of size in processing and final demand sectors. The tables have tended to be limited to approximately 45 processing sectors and seven final demand sectors, partly due to the difficulties of dealing with large matrices on limited financial budgets. However, the recent study by Isard[16] for the Philadelphia Standard Metropolitan Statistical Area demonstrates the feasibility of a highly detailed (500–600 sector) regional input-output study, using the capacity of modern computers. In several of the studies some final demand sectors have been integrated into the processing sector to close the table for predictive purposes.

The fourth section shows that the majority of studies use national or modified national data. The time span between the base year for this data and the publication date of the study is seldom less than three years, those with the shorter periods being based on direct survey material. Most inputs are expressed in monetary terms which can be readily converted into approximate labour equivalents if required.

The final section shows that input-output has the valuable dual function of not merely describing the inter-industry relationships of a region but also predicting how they may change in the future. As a descriptive device, Isard sees input-output tables as extremely useful because:

'1 they record rather concisely, in an internally consistent manner, a large amount of information about a regional economy and the interrelations of its sectors

2 they impose a desirable statistical discipline on data collection agencies and empirical investigations

3 they reveal gaps in our data and may help in filling them

4 they present an economy in perspective and facilitate comparison of the magnitudes of its major sectors and bonds with other economies.'[17]

One particularly useful descriptive role is that of 'structural analysis'. This is concerned with the qualitative properties of an input-output table, especially the properties of the processing matrix. From this matrix, the extent of technical interdependence among sectors can be seen, and by comparing two tables covering different time periods, trends in inter-industry dependences become apparent. There are also a whole range of predictive roles, which will be outlined in the next chapter, and it is this wide practical flexibility of input-output which urges on development in face of all the constraining problems.

4 Summary

The quality of the regional data base is a major influence on the definition, analysis and planning of regions. With the increasing demand over the last ten to fifteen years, UK regional statistics are fairly comprehensive in some areas and are improving all the time. However, as has been shown, there are some major inadequacies, although these would not appear to constitute an unsurmountable obstacle to effective regional planning. This is not to suggest that there is not room for further improvement. One possible line of development could be through the construction of regional accounts, and in particular, regional input-output tables. Such tables provide a comprehensive and ordered picture of the regional economy, and it is interesting to speculate that if the resources were available, a nested hierarchy of such tables as in Figure 3.1, relating region and sub-region to their adjacent levels, would be of considerable value.

77

Fig. 3.1   A nested hierarchy of input-output tables

References

1 Chester, T. E., The Challenge of Regional Planning, *District Bank Review*, page 20, June 1964.

2 McCrone, G., The application of regional accounting in the UK, *Regional Studies*, pages 39–45, 1, 1 (1967).

3 Nevin, E. T., *et alia*, *The Structure of the Welsh Economy*, Univ. of Wales, Welsh Economic Studies 4 (1966).

4 McCrone, G., *Scotland's Economic Progress 1951–60*, Allen and Unwin, (1965).

5 Carter, C. F., Estimates of the Gross Domestic Product of Northern Ireland 1950–56, *Journal of the Social and Statistical Inquiry Society of Ireland*, (1958–59).

6 Woodward, V., *Regional Social Accounts for the United Kingdom*, National Institute of Economic and Social Research (NIESR) (1970).

7 Deane, P., Regional Variations in UK Incomes from Employment, *Journal of the Royal Statistical Society*, (Series A), pages 123–35, 116, 2 (1953).

8 Stone, R., Social Accounts at the Regional Level: A Survey, in *Regional Economic Planning*, O.E.E.C., pages 263–96 (1961).

9 Leontieff, W. W., *Input-Output Economics* (1966).

10 Woodward, V., NIESR, *op cit*.

11 Ministry of Transport, *Survey of Road Goods Transport 1962, Final Results*, Part IV (London, 1965).

12 Edwards, S. L., and Gordon, I. R., The application of input-output methods to regional forecasting: the British experience, *Proceedings of the Twenty-Second Symposium of the Colston Research Society*, Bristol, April (1970), 1971.

13 Artle, R., *Studies in the Structure of the Stockholm Economy*, Stockholm (1959).

14 See: Centre for Environmental Studies, *Seminar on the Construction and Use of Small Area Input–Output tables*, CES, CP1, June 1970.

15 Nevin, E. T., *et al*, *op cit*.

16 Isard, W., and Langford, T. W., *Regional Input-Output Study: Recollections, Reflections and Diverse Notes on the Philadelphia Experience*, MIT Press (1971).

17 Isard, W., *Methods of Regional Analysis*, p. 327, MIT Press (1960).

4 Regional change—short run

The fortunes of regions and sub-regions vary greatly. Some are relatively prosperous, others are not so fortunate. A basic factor in this variation is the economic structure of the region. The various sources of regional statistics and the development of regional accounts and input-output tables, outlined in the last chapter, can provide a descriptive framework of this structure. But this is essentially a static picture and of course regions are not static, with prosperity changing according to the ability of the region to produce goods and services that are in demand. The decline of a firm within a region, perhaps owing to the cancellation of a government contract or because of an unexpected loss of export trade, may result not only in a loss of jobs for workers in that firm but may also have a 'multiplier' impact on the wider regional economy. Auxiliary industries will be affected and service trades will also feel the pinch. On the other hand, if a firm expands, the process is reversed with a beneficial 'multiplier' effect.

There are a series of economic theories, known collectively as regional multiplier theories, which seek to explain these changes, stressing the interrelationships of sectors within the regional economy and the spread of impulses originating in any one sector to all other sectors either directly or indirectly. The economic base theory is the most simple and probably the most well known. More complex approaches include the development of inter-regional trade multipliers. Input-output analysis can also be utilised as a technique for analysing and predicting short-run change in the regional economy. Unfortunately these approaches tend to suffer from either over-simplicity or over-complexity, and more recent models suggest the emergence of a middle course between the economic base and other aggregate models and the input-output approach. All the approaches are similar however in that they are spatially aggregate, abstracting from space and looking at the region as a whole. They are also all basically attempts to explain short-run change rather than long-run trends of growth or decline which will be considered in the next chapter.

The various models are not only useful in explaining regional change and in predicting the implications of economic decisions, they are also useful in forward planning. It is obvious that many different industries, having different structures, will affect the regional economy in different ways. One may import most of its inputs, another may obtain them within the region. One may employ a large quantity of labour, another may be capital-intensive. Thus, although most regions, especially depressed regions, would welcome almost any type of industry, some industries may be better than others and, given the ability to plan and choose, it would be advantageous to know the relative contribution of each industry to an overall strategy and to concentrate encouragement on those which make the greatest contribution.

1 Economic base theory

ECONOMIC BASE CONCEPT[1]

Academically, the regional economy can be subdivided into two sectors: basic activities and non-basic activities. Basic activities are those which export goods and services to points outside the economic confines of the community, or which market their goods and services to persons who come from outside the community's economic boundaries. Non-basic activities are those which provide for the needs of persons resident within the community's economic limits. They do not export any finished goods or services, but are primarily local in their productive scope and market areas.

Implicit in this division of activities is the cause and effect relationship which constitutes the economic base theory. An increase in the amount of basic activity within a region will increase the flow of income into the region, increasing the demand for goods and services within it and effecting a corresponding increase in the volume of non-basic activity. Alternatively a decrease in basic activity would lead to a fall in income coming into the region, and a decline in demand for the products of the non-basic sector. Hence, basic activity as its name suggests has the prime mover rôle with any changes having a multiplier effect on the regional economy.

The economic base multiplier is usually calculated in terms of employment and can be expressed as:

$$\frac{\text{total employment in basic and non-basic activities}}{\text{total employment in basic activities}}$$

For example, a region with 500 000 persons in employment, 250 000 in basic activities and 250 000 in non-basic activities, that is a 1 : 1 basic : non-basic ratio, will have a multiplier of:

$$\frac{250\ 000\ +\ 250\ 000}{250\ 000} = 2$$

Extensive use has been made of the employment multiplier for projection purposes. By evaluating the future prospects of the basic activities in the regional economy, and then applying the employment multiplier derived from the total : basic ratios relating to existing industrial composition, future employment totals have been forecast. This predictive rôle can be illustrated by considering the impact of an increase in employment of 20 000 in a basic industry in the above region. With an employment multiplier of 2, an extra 20 000 non-basic jobs will be created, and total employment will increase from 500 000 to 540 000. That is:

$$\triangle T = \triangle B\,(k)$$
$$40\ 000 = 20\ 000\,(2)$$

where $\triangle T$ = change in total employment
$\triangle B$ = change in basic employment
k = employment multiplier

82

There will also generally be a similar relationship between total employment and the regional population. If, in our study region, total employment of 500 000 supports a population of 1 500 000, there is a 1 : 3 ratio, and the extra 40 000 jobs would increase the population to 1 620 000.

Unfortunately, the attractive simplicity of the economic base theory can be deceptive and misleading, and there are several technical and conceptual problems which, although they do not disprove the theory, cast some doubt on the use of economic base studies in forecasting changes in the regional economy.

LIMITATIONS

The major technical problems involve the unit of measurement, the identification of basic and non-basic activities and the choice of study area. Taking the first problem, until now almost all economic base studies have used employment (number of jobs) as the unit of measurement. This partly reflects the fact that employment figures are relatively easy to obtain compared with other economic data. It may also reflect the political significance of employment totals. But employment as a unit of measurement has serious drawbacks. It does not consider the fact that equal changes in employment in two basic industries paying widely differing wage levels, such as farming and computer technology, may have significantly different multiplier effects, Not does it consider changes in productivity whereby a firm may increase output dramatically leading to higher wages and more spending without increasing its labour force. The use of total payroll data as a unit of measurement may overcome these difficulties, although the associated problems of allowance for inflation and non-consideration of numbers of jobs should not be discounted.

The identification of basic and non-basic activities is a particularly thorny problem. In most economic base studies the general practice with respect to industrial and commercial firms has been first to divide them into those that are wholly basic, then those that are wholly non-basic, and finally those that are 'mixed'. In one study by Mattila and Thompson,[2] aircraft firms were considered wholly basic, construction firms wholly non-basic, and wholesale and retail trading firms, mixed. It is in dealing with the

83

'mixed' class of firms that the serious allocation problems arise.

The basic/non-basic allocation of the 'mixed' firms can be done by either direct survey of the individual firms or by some indirect approach making use of information already available such as the levels and kinds of employment in individual industries. The direct empirical 'firm-by-firm' approach seeks information regarding each firm's proportion of export and local sales, usually by personal interview or questionnaire. These proportions are then applied to the firm's total employment or payroll to determine the basic and non-basic components. There are a number of limitations to this method. In addition to being tedious, time-consuming and expensive to carry out at the regional scale, it is also heavily dependent on the estimates of the firms which may be misleading with respect to the final destination of a firm's sales. An associated problem is that of intermediate sales—for example, the sale of coal mined locally as fuel for a local steel producer exporting finished steel—which may result in seemingly basic industries being classified as non-basic.

The indirect approach to the basic/non-basic split may use one or a combination of three methods, none of which is completely satisfactory.

1. The assumptions or arbitrary method simply assumes that all primary and manufacturing industry (SIC 1–20) is basic, and all service industry (SIC 21–27) is non-basic. No recognition is given to the fact that any one order can contain industries which are either export or local or both in some proportions.

2. The second method, that of location quotients (LQ) has greater academic respectability but very little if any more reliability than the first method. The location quotient for each industry in a region can be derived from the following ratio:

$$LQ = \frac{\text{percentage of regional employment in industry } A}{\text{percentage of national employment in industry } A}$$

Ratios greater than unity are taken to indicate an export or basic activity, and the number of workers surplus to those necessary to give an LQ of 1 (that is surplus to regional self-sufficiency) are assumed to serve the export market. Ratios of less than unity indicate a local or non-basic activity. This method has some advantages. It does take care of intermediate sales (thus the local

84

coal industry selling to the local steel industry will appear as basic if the LQ is greater than unity) and it is inexpensive and easy to apply. However some of the underlying assumptions, such as the uniformity of regional and national demand patterns and the uniformity of regional productivity by industrial sector, do weaken its reliability.

3. The third method, minimum requirements,[3] is a modification of the LQ method, using the minimum distribution of employment necessary to support a regional industry rather than the average distribution. For each region, a computation is made of the percentage share which each industry claims of the region's labour force. The percentages are then compared and discounting atypical situations, the lowest percentage is taken as the minimum requirement for that particular industry. This minimum represents the benchmark and all employment in other regions above this percentage share is considered as basic employment. This process can be repeated for each industry in the region to give the total basic employment. This method would seem to be even more arbitrary than the LQ method, being highly dependent on the selection of the minimum percentage and the level of industrial disaggregation—a very fine disaggregation would in fact turn most sectors into basic, export activities.

The fact that all three methods can produce very different estimates of basic and non-basic activities for any one particular region underlines the difficulty of identifying the split. Table 4.1 illustrates the divergence of results when the three methods were applied to the South East of England.

The choice of study area constitutes the third technical problem. This obviously depends on a whole range of factors discussed in earlier chapters, such as the purpose of the study, administrative factors, regional consciousness and data availability. But whatever the choice of area, it must be remembered that the basic/non-basic split changes as the analyst proceeds from the one extreme of a small hamlet to the other of the entire nation. In the small hamlet, the country inn and petrol station are primarily export activities. At the urban level, these functions become service and non-basic; and at the national level, the majority of activities are non-basic with a relatively limited export sector.

85

Additional to these technical problems are a number of more conceptual problems. The theory assumes that basic industry is the prime mover behind regional change and that for any region there is a given basic/non-basic employment ratio which remains constant as changes in the economic structure of the region take place. Although basic industry probably is a major factor behind

Employment Method	Basic Employment		Non-Basic Employment	
	Numbers	% Total	Numbers	% Total
Assumption Method	2 561 180	32	5 445 250	68
Location Quotient Method	1 040 800	13	6 965 630	87
Min. Requirements Method	3 266 623	41	4 739 807	59

Table 4.1. *Basic/Non-Basic Employment in South East England (1966)*.

SOURCE: *Strategic Plan for the South East, 1 Population and Employment* (Appendix 2D), HMSO, London (1970).

many changes in the regional economy, there can be little doubt that in certain situations well developed non-basic activities will themselves attract basic industries to a region and may therefore be amongst the determinants of that area's level of economic activity. It also appears more than likely that the basic/non-basic ratio will actually change with the very growth or decline it is supposed to estimate—with the non-basic element becoming relatively more important over time.

By concentrating on basic or export activity, the theory also unfortunately turns a blind eye to the importance of imports. An increase in basic employment and income may have a very limited multiplier effect on non-basic activity if much of the extra income

86

flows out of the region in the form of expenditure on imports. Although it must be noted that the influence of the trade factor may not always be negative, for as the regional economy grows, there may come a point when it can produce a service or good for itself rather than importing it.[4] The resultant increase in non-basic activity may attract new basic industry, which again generates yet more non-basic activity. The fundamental point here of course is that an economy may grow not only by increasing exports from basic industries but also by replacing imports.

RELEVANCE OF THE THEORY

The outline of only some of the limitations of economic base theory would seem to suggest that it is of little practical relevance in regional analysis and planning. This is not the case. It has the undoubted advantages of simplicity and easy application and can shed useful light on a region's economic structure and the general impact of short-run changes. In certain situations, for example when dealing with small regions with a high level of dependence on specialised export activities, the limitations are least severe and it can provide a very useful basis for short-run forecasting. It can also serve as an important point of departure for more elaborate models. These include more sophisticated methods of analysing aggregate regional change and also the more recently developed spatially disaggregated land-use models, such as the Garin-Lowry Model.[5]

2 Inter-regional trade multipliers

Many of the criticisms levelled at economic base theory can be avoided by the use of a more sophisticated inter-regional trade multiplier. This is a rather more realistic but also rather more complicated approach, accepting that regions receive imports from other regions and are affected by national economic factors such as levels of direct and indirect taxation.

This multiplier, calculated in money terms as compared with employment in the base theory, is much more akin to the short-run Keynesian income type multiplier of macro-economics. It is based on the fact that an injection of a certain amount of money into the regional economy will increase regional income effecting an increase in consumer spending (although by an amount less than the original injection). The proportion of income spent becomes someone else's income, some of which they spend, and so the procedure is continued through several rounds. The question is what will be the impact of this injection of say £x million in Region A? Will it generate three times its own value through the multiplier effect or perhaps only one and a half times its own value? The difference is obviously of some importance to the planner.

DETERMINANTS OF THE MULTIPLIER

If the initial injection of money is passed on intact at each round, the multiplier effect would be infinite. The £x million initial injection would provide £x million extra income to workers in Region A which would all be spent on locally produced goods, which in turn would generate an extra income of £x million for local producers, who would then spend it and so on *ad infinitum*.

But the multiplier is not infinite because there are a number of fairly obvious leakages out of the stages of the multiplier process, which quickly bring about convergence. Three major leakages are savings, taxation and imports.

a Savings. People do not spend all of their extra income, generally preferring to save some proportion of the increase. The proportion of extra savings to extra income is known as the marginal propensity so save (s). The marginal propensity to consume (c) is of course ($1-s$).

b Taxation. Extra income is also reduced by taxation. This may be directly in the form of income tax or indirectly in the form of purchase tax.

c Imports. A substantial proportion of regional income is usually spent in goods produced outside the region, which represents an important leakage to other regions and countries.

Allowing for these leakages, the regional multiplier (k) can be expressed as:

$$k = \frac{\text{Initial Injection}}{\Sigma \text{ (Leakages)}}$$

For example, if a major regional industry injects an extra £1 000 000 into a regional economy through its expansion programme, it will generate an extra £1 000 000 of regional income. However, if £100 000 of this extra income is lost to the government via taxes, £200 000 is saved and £200 000 is spent on goods and services imported into the region, the resultant multiplier will be:

$$k = \frac{£1\ 000\ 000}{\Sigma\ (£100\ 000\ +\ £200\ 000\ +\ £200\ 000)}$$

$$= \frac{£1\ 000\ 000}{£\ 500\ 000}$$

$$= 2$$

Thus, because of the various leakages, the initial injection will only have limited multiplier effects. The basic problem is how to calculate the regional multiplier in a real-life situation with limited data resources.[6]

BRITISH REGIONAL MULTIPLIERS

Given a planned injection into a regional economy, it is of course impossible to observe and measure directly the round-by-round leakages. As such, the multiplier must be estimated by some indirect method. This involves the estimation of the regional marginal propensities to consume, save, import and the marginal rates of taxation, which can then be incorporated into a Keynesian type formula from which a general regional multiplier can be derived. Even this unfortunately presents problems, for several of the factors, especially the import relationship, are difficult to estimate. Nevertheless, there have recently been some interesting attempts to estimate British regional multipliers.

A very general and intuitive approach has been used by Archibald.[7] His multiplier is:

$$k = \frac{1}{1 - (c - m)\,(1 - t)}$$

where c = marginal propensity to consume,
m = marginal propensity to import,
and t = marginal rate of taxation.

89

Using approximate estimates of the factors involved, he placed UK regional multipliers within the range 1·2 to 1·7.

To be more precise than this requires more accurate and empirically based estimation of the various marginal propensities. Amongst British regional multiplier studies, some of the most empirically based estimates are those compiled by Steele.[8] He uses a modified Archibald multiplier, including both direct and indirect taxation. Estimates of the various factors are made primarily from regional Family Expenditure Survey consumption and income data, although estimates of the difficult regional import factors are derived largely from statistics for freight flows. Table 4.2 illustrates the multiplier estimates for

Table 4.2. *British Regional Multipliers*

Region	Multiplier	with Feedback
North	1·37	1·42
Yorkshire and Humberside	1·19	1·26
East Midlands	1·37	1·45
West Midlands	1·20	1·33
East Anglia	1·22	1·33
South East	1·41	1·57
South West	1·37	1·42
Wales	1·33	1·38
North West	1·27	1·39
Scotland [a]	1·70	1·77

SOURCE: Steele, D. B., *Oxford Economic Papers,* July 1969, by permission of The Clarendon Press, Oxford.

[a] Steele did derive two possible estimates for Scotland based on differing import factors. This is the lower multiplier estimate.

each of the British regions. It also includes Steele's estimates of the regional 'feedback effect'. This is the effect of the import leakage from a particular region stimulating, via increased income in other regions, an increased demand for the exports of the original region.

Although too much should not be read into Steele's results,

they do illustrate several important features of regional multipliers which are of some relevance to an understanding of short run regional change and the guidance of that change. Firstly, the multiplier is low. This of course makes the resolution of regional problems more difficult, for pouring aid into a region may be like pouring water into a bath with the plug out. This can also be embarrassing for the rest of the country, for if Scotland, by way of example, has a regional multiplier of 1·7, then approximately 60% of any extra investment into the region will inevitably leak into other regions, much of it into pressured areas such as the South East. The results also suggest a considerable regional variation in multipliers ranging from 1·7 in Scotland to 1·19 in Yorkshire. The high Scottish figure is not explained by a high marginal propensity to save (contrary to expectations!), but is more influenced by a much lower import ratio than any other region. This no doubt reflects the relative geographical isolation of the region. The low multipliers for Yorkshire, the West Midlands and East Anglia are mainly explained by high savings and high import ratios. These variations indicate that in some regions investment in the short run may be more effective than in others. Steele's detailed results also emphasise the relative importance of the import factor. Whereas the combined marginal savings and direct tax ratios are low and vary only from 0·14 to 0·22, the ratio of imports to final demand is much higher and varies more widely from 0·41 to ·074.*

However, the regional multiplier is not without problems. It suffers from severe data problems, with the most vital factor, that of imports, the most difficult to estimate. In addition, the problem of integrating the 'feedback effect' is only partially solved. Like the economic base theory, it is also an excessively aggregated approach, abstracting from specific industries and inter-industry linkages. This is an important consideration for although a region may overall have a low multiplier, specific industries within that region may have much higher multipliers with their individual actions exerting a substantial influence on the wider regional economy.

* More recent estimates by Steele indicate a range of 0·44 to 0·82. See Steele, D. B., A Numbers Game (or The Return of Regional Multipliers), *Regional Studies*, pages 115–130, 6(1972).

3 Regional input-output analysis

The input-output matrix previously presented as a descriptive framework can also be used in the analysis and prediction of short-run changes in the regional economy. To some, this is indeed its most valuable use and it has several advantages over the approaches already outlined, providing an industry-by-industry breakdown of the regional economy and placing particular emphasis on inter-industry relationships. This use of input-output for predictive purposes involves a number of additional procedures and basic assumptions extra to its descriptive rôle. The procedure will first be outlined and then the vital assumptions will be examined.

PROCEDURE

The procedure for using input-output for analysing and predicting short-run changes can be illustrated by using the hypothetical situation outlined in Table 4.3. This table is a simple two-region

Inputs From:	Output To:	Region A Industry			Region B Industry			Final Demand		Total Output
		1	2	3	1	2	3	A	B	
Region A Industry	1		10		50	10		30		100
	2									
	3	20						30		50
Region B Industry	1									
	2	20	20				60	20	80	200
	3	20			50				30	100
Households	A	40	20		20					80
Households	B				80	30				110
Total Inputs		100	50		200	100		80	110	640

Table 4.3 *Input-output inter-regional flow table for two regions, A and B* (£ million).

input-output matrix, based on a subdivision of Table 3.1, but with foreign trade (imports and exports) omitted for simplicity in exposition. Region A is dependent on Industries 1 and 3 with a combined output of £150m. Region B on the other hand is dependent on Industries 2 and 3, which have a combined output of £300m. twice that of Region A. This difference is to some extent reflected in the differences in household output, with the payments for labour being £110m in Region B as compared with only £80m in Region A (although relative population figures would be necessary for an estimate of relative prosperity between the two regions). Although the regions do specialise, they are also very much interdependent. For example, Industry 1 in Region A sells over half its output to Industries 2 and 3 in Region B, the rest going to its own Industry 3 and internal final demand. Similarly, it also derives much of its inputs from Region B, although it is, as would be expected, dependent on labour inputs from its own household sector.

But this is a simple descriptive picture of inter-regional relationships. Prediction requires the calculation of Table 4.4.

Inputs From: \ Output To:	Region A Industry 1	2	3	Region B Industry 1	2	3	Final Demand A	B
Region A Industry 1			0·20		0·25	0·10	0·37	
Region A Industry 2								
Region A Industry 3	0·20						0·38	
Region B Industry 1								
Region B Industry 2	0·20		0·40			0·60	0·25	0·73
Region B Industry 3	0·20				0·25			0·27
Households A	0·40		0·40		0·10			
Households B					0·40	0·30		
TOTAL	1·00		1·00		1·00	1·00	1·00	1·00

Table 4.4 *Input and supply coefficients for Table 4.3 (direct inputs per £ of output)* *(Rounded to the nearest penny)*

This table shows the direct inputs per £ of output for the various industries in both regions. Thus, to produce £1 of output, Industry 1 in Region A requires 20p of inputs from its own Industry 3, 20p of inputs from both Industries 2 and 3 in Region B, and 40p of inputs from the household sector in Region A. Hence, this table of coefficients shows not only the input coefficients but also the regional origins of the inputs in percentage terms, the supply coefficients.

The table of coefficients is the key to the predictive rôle, for by assuming constant coefficients (an assumption that will be examined later) the impact of any change in either of the regional economies on the rest of the inter-regional economic structure can be traced. Suppose that population projections indicate a rapid increase in the population of Region B over the next five years, leading to a doubling of its final demand for the output of its own Industries 2 and 3. At the same time there will be no change in final demand in Region A. What will be the impact on the inter-regional economies?

The projected change, the doubling in final demand in Region B, will mean an increase in output of £80m for Industry 2 and £30m for Industry 3 in Region B. But both industries rely on inputs from elsewhere. The size and incidence of these inputs can be found by multiplying down the column for Industry 2 (Region B) in the coefficient table (Table 4.4) by the £80m, and likewise down the column for Industry 3 by £30m.* The results of this first multiplication are an increase in demand for Industry 1 of £23m (£20m and £3m), for Industry 2 of £18m, and for Industry 3 (Region B) of £20m. These are the first round of input requirements. But of course they must be produced too, and they will also need extra inputs. For example, the £23m increase in Industry 1 will necessitate extra inputs of approximately £5m from each of three other industries. This is the second round of the process, which will generate a demand for further inputs, and so the iterations continue.

After about seven iterations, however, the extra input require-

* The household sector (both column and row) however, is eliminated from this procedure, because projected household expenditure (final demand) has already been stated. It was the starting point and its inclusion would lead to double counting.

ments are minimal and the process converges. The use of an 'inverse matrix' and a computer facilitates this process for more complex situations.[9] The original increase plus the summed round-by-round input requirements can then be added to the original table, providing a full picture of the predicted inter-regional economies in five years' time. In our example, the net result of the doubling of final demand in Region B is a two-thirds increase in the total industrial output of Region B from £300m to approximately £500m, but also an increase, although more limited, in the industrial output of Region A from £150m to £200m, thus reflecting the economic interrelationships of the two regions.

THE COEFFICIENT PROBLEM

Unfortunately, the benefits of the regional input-output approach have their price. There are the numerous data problems outlined in Chapter 3, especially the problems of disaggregating inter-industry inputs and identifying their regional source; but for prediction, there is also the problem of the validity of the assumption of constant coefficients. The assumption that an industry will constantly use the same composition of inputs is undoubtedly dubious for many industrial sectors over anything but a very short time period. Changing technology, relative movements in price level, the development of economies of scale and a wide variety of social, psychological and political factors can all radically alter an industry's input pattern. Trends in technology are particularly difficult to forecast although change does appear to be occurring at an increasing rate. (Servan Shreiber[10] has pointed out that the time lag between invention and manufacture was 112 years for photography (1727–1839), twelve for television (1922–34) and only three years for the integrated circuit (1958–61).) When, as in regional input-output analysis, the assumption of constant supply coefficients is also added, the whole approach looks rather problematic.

But this is too pessimistic a view. All projections guess at some factors, and less factors are overlooked in the disaggregated input-output approach than in the more aggregated methods already discussed. Further, it may also be possible to build rather more flexibility into the determination of the input-output coefficients, by anticipating future changes. If it is argued that under a given technology there is only one best input combination for a specific industry, and that once adopted it will be retained for some time, then the incorporation of this combination into the analysis may ensure some consistency in the short run. This depends on 'the assumption . . . that the average input pattern of the most efficient establishments at time t will approximate the average input patterns of all establishments at $t + k$, where k is a time period to be determined'.[11] In time, it is also hoped that the more frequent production of input-output tables based on more up to date survey data will, besides producing a more accurate static picture, also allow the measurement of trend changes in average regional input coefficients. Since these trends would include both technological input and supply pattern influences, they could also be used for forecasting.

THE USE OF PREDICTIVE INPUT-OUTPUT ANALYSIS

There have been several regional applications of input-output models in predictive rôles, mainly in the USA but also more recently in Britain. Some of these were outlined in Table 3.4, where the various predictive rôles were noted. Of particular importance is the rôle of impact analysis assessing, for example, the impact of a sudden population influx into a region, the impact of the abandonment of the Concorde project on the Bristol sub-region, or the impact of changes in the US space programme or American involvement in the Vietnam War on certain areas of the USA[12]. An early and well known impact study is that by Isard and Kuenne[13] on the impact of the establishing of three-million-ton-capacity iron and steel mills at Trenton, New Jersey, in the Greater New York–Philadelphia industrial region. After estimating the size of new steel fabricating and other activities linked directly to the basic iron and steel activity, the impact of the investment was forecast using an incremental input-output model—providing a round-by-round insight into the impact on 45 sectors of the regional economy.

Input-output can also be used for estimating income and employment multipliers for each industrial sector within the region. Thus, given some target such as the maximisation of regional income or, more usually, regional employment, the analysis can be used to isolate the industrial sectors in which expansion induced by an investment injection would have the greatest effect. Recent work at the University of North Wales provides interesting examples of such applications. In a study, *Regional Income Multipliers*,[14] developed from an attempt to assess the impact of a new aluminium smelter on the economy of the county of Anglesey, an input-output matrix was constructed for thirty-three sectors of the economy, and a series of multipliers were derived. Interestingly some of the highest multipliers were found in the agriculture sector. Of course this is not to say that Anglesey's future should necessarily be tied to agriculture, for local authorities may wish to encourage balanced employment opportunities. Nevertheless the varying multipliers should not be ignored in policy decisions. Other interesting results cast doubt on the usual assumption that no matter how small a region any extra expenditure which takes place has positive multiplier effects, for they show that the increase in income of some consumers can change consumption patterns in such a way that the net multiplier effect is negative. A second study, *The Impact of Domestic Tourism*,[15] showed that an increase of £10 000 in tourist spending would on average generate an additional £3000 of income in the Anglesey study area. It also showed, however, that the multiplier effect varied between different categories of tourist, with the £10 000 increase in the 'hotel' and 'tent' categories generating the average figure of £3000; 'farmhouse and bed and breakfast' accommodation (with a lower income leakage)—an extra £7 600; and 'caravans' (with a higher income leakage)—only a little more than £2 000.

Future developments suggest even more potentially useful rôles in regional planning. In addition to the development of dynamic coefficients, the whole input-output process could be made more dynamic.[16] The approach to date has been primarily of a comparative static form, with the emphasis on the new equilibrium level of output following a change, rather than on the processes in production and especially the time required in reaching that new equilibrium. The time factor is crucial. Some inputs to supply increasing output demand may meet capacity constraints and demand may divert elsewhere. There has been some interesting research into ways and means of incorporating these wider dynamic aspects into the approach. Other interesting general developments are the widening of the input-output approach to include spatial land use implications[17] and, as at the national level, a growing interest in the inclusion of the wider environmental impacts of growth and change, 'the effluence of affluence', into the accounting framework.[18]

It would therefore seem that this wide range of rôles would make input-output a very valuable approach for understanding and predicting short-run regional change—that is change in the regional economy over a period of possibly five to ten years when the assumption of constant coefficients is less dubious. The situation is neatly summed up by Stone: 'we buy the possibility of answering complicated questions at the price of building in certain rigidities.'[19]

4 A compromise approach

Although the various approaches outlined so far have many advantages, they also have many problems; and more recent models do suggest the emergence of a middle course, a compromise approach, between the oversimplicity of the highly aggregated economic base and inter-regional trade multipliers and the complexities and heavy data requirements of input-output.

Moving from one end of the spectrum, Weiss and Gooding[20] have outlined a method of disaggregating the export base of a region into a small number of significant sectors and calculating multipliers for each sector. In a case study of the small regional economy centred around Portsmouth, New Hampshire, USA, they have calculated employment multipliers for three major export employment categories. Private export employment is shown to have the highest multiplier of 1·8, civilian employment at the local naval shipyard has a multiplier of 1·6, and employment at a local air force base has the lowest multiplier of 1·4. The low nature of all the multipliers reflects the 'open' nature of the small regional economy, with numerous import leakages out of the area. They also suggest however that in a small region such as the study area the loss of private export jobs will have a greater impact on the regional economy than a loss of the same number of jobs from a government defence installation.

Moving from the other end of the spectrum, the Regional Economic Development Institute of Pittsburgh have developed Technique for Area Planning (TAP).[21] This is a technique which simplifies input-output relations and restricts the expensive data collection process. It is a cross between economic base and input-output and divides the economy into a limited number of major sectors and minor sectors. The major sectors would be made up of large, predominrntly basic firms, experiencing considerable change and hence exerting considerable influence on the regional economy. A full inter-industry analysis is computed only for these major sectors, with the minor sectors being consolidated within the household sector. Examples of the application of the approach in impact analysis show it to give results deviating by at the most ± 5% from those produced for full input-output analysis. As with the other compromise approaches, TAP is most effective in small specialised regions.

5 Summary

Over the years there has developed a considerable armoury of economic models concerned with analysing short-run changes in the regional economy as a whole. Such models are of considerable value to the regional planner, providing an understanding of regional change, predicting the implications of economic decisions and thus aiding forward planning. However, as with all models, they have their limitations.

The attractiveness of the simple economic base theory relating changes in total regional employment to changes in basic employment, must be balanced against the numerous conceptual and technical problems, especially the thorny and perpetual problem of identifying the basic/non-basic split. The highly aggrcgated inter-regional trade multiplier introduces relevant import, savings and taxation factors and throws interesting light on to large-scale regional multiplier variations, but it is severely limited by the assessment of the regional import leakages. Data problems, plus the assumptions of constant coefficients, also constrain the more technical input-output approach, which is nevertheless potentially a most valuable method of regional analysis. The recent developments also have their problems, but they do suggest that the modification and integration of some of the other approaches may offer useful rule-of-thumb methods of analysing short-run regional change which will be of considerable practical value in regional planning.

References

1 Useful source references on the economic base concept include:
   Pfouts, R. W., *The Techniques of Urban Economic Analysis,*
   Chandler-Davis (1960);
   Andrews, R. B., series of articles in *Land Economics,* 29–31
   (1953–6);
   Blumenfeld, H., The Economic Base of the Metropolis, *Journal of the American Institute of Planners,* 21 (1955);
   Thomas, M. D., The Economic Base and a Region's Economy, *Journal of the American Institute of Planners,* 23 (1957).
2 Mattila, J. M., and Thompson, W. R., Measurement of the Economic Base of the Metropolitan Area, *Land Economics,* 31 (1955).
3 See: Ullman, E., and Dacey, M. F., The Minimum Requirements Approach to the Urban Economic Base, *Papers and Proceedings of the Regional Science Association,* 6 (1960);
   Ullman, E., Minimum Requirements after a decade, *Economic Geography,* 44 (1968).
4 See for example: Jacobs, J., *The Economy of Cities,* Jonathan Cape (1969).
5 For a recent survey of land-use modelling in Britain, see:
   Batty, M., Recent Developments in Land-Use Modelling: A Review of British Research, *Urban Studies,* 9, 2 (1972).
6 See for example: Allen, K. J., *The Regional Multiplier: Some Problems in Estimation,* Chapter 4 in Cullingworth, J. B., and Orr, S. C., *Regional and Urban Studies,* Allen and Unwin (1969).
7 Archibald, G. C., Regional multiplier effects in the UK, *Oxford Economic Papers,* 19 (1967).
8 Steele, D. B., Regional Multipliers in Great Britain, *Oxford Economic Papers,* 21 (1969).
9 See: Isard, W., *Methods of Regional Analysis,* pages 363–71, MIT Press (1960);
   also: Yan, C. S., *Introduction to Input-Output Economics,* Holt, Rinehart and Winston, New York (1969).
10 Servan-Schreiber, J. J., *The American Challenge,* page 59, Penguin (1969).

11 Miernyk, W. H., Long-Range Forecasting with a Regional Input-Output Model, *Western Economic Journal*, pages 165–76, **VI** (1968).
12 See: Isard, W., and Langford, T. W., *Regional Input-Output Study: Recollections, Reflections and Diverse Notes on the Philadelphia Experience*, MIT Press (1971).
13 Isard, W., *Methods of Regional Analysis, op cit*, pages 349–62.
14 Sadler, P. G., Archer, B. H., and Owen, C. B., *Regional Income Multipliers*, Bangor Occasional Papers in Economics: 1, University of Wales Press (1973).
15 Archer, B. H., *The Impact of Domestic Tourism*, Bangor Occasional Papers in Economics: 2, University of Wales Press (1973).
16 See: Yan, C. S., *op cit*.
17 Hirsch, W. Z., Input-Output Techniques for Urban Government Decisions, *American Economic Review: Papers and Proceedings*, **58** (1968).
18 Isard, W., and Langford, T. W., *op cit*.
19 Stone, J. R., Social Accounts at the Regional Level: A Survey, in *Regional Economic Planning*, page 289, OEEC, Paris (1961).
20 Weiss, S. J., and Gooding, E. C., Estimation of Differential Employment Multipliers in a small Regional Economy, *Land Economics*, **44** (1968).
21 Regional Economic Development Institute of Pittsburgh, *Technique for Area Planning: A Manual for the Construction and Application of a Simplified Input-Output Table* (1967).

5 Regional growth—long run

All regions and sub-regions experience the short-run ups and downs outlined in the previous chapter. But the long-run rate of growth of regions, usually measured in terms of otuput and/or income varies widely, and some regions may actually experience long-run decline. At the regional level in the United Kingdom the South East has been more prosperous than the North East over a long period of time. Similarly, within regions, certain sub-regions are considerably more prosperous than others. But what factors account for these variations?

Theories of long-run regional growth must obviously consider those factors held constant in short-run analysis—that is factors such as population, wages, prices, resources, technology and the distribution of income. The mobility of factors, especially labour and capital is a particularly important consideration. However, as yet, there is no one generally accepted theory of regional growth (or development). Indeed it is doubtful whether a single comprehensive theory is possible, although recent attempts at synthesis by Hilhorst[1] and Siebert[2] are interesting. There are, however, a number of partial theories and concepts which between them focus on the major determinants of regional growth.

It is generally accepted that regional growth may result from either endogenous or exogenous determinants, that is from factors inside the region or outside the region, or more usually from some combination of both. Major internal determinants include the distribution of factors of production such as land, labour, capital, while a major external determinant is the level of demand for the region's commodities from other areas. This endogenous/exogenous split is similarly reflected in the theories; some such as the sector theory suggest that regional development is essentially an internal evolutionary process, others such as the export base theory emphasise demand for the region's exports.

As with short-run analysis, the theories can be subdivided into those which are highly aggregated and those that are more disaggregated. The aggregate models include those already mentioned plus several more sophisticated but spatially abstract models derived from national economic growth theory. An example of the disaggregated approach is industrial structure analysis which, although perhaps more a technique than a theory, provides a useful insight into both the internal and external elements of regional growth.

In addition to gaining an understanding of the process and determinants of regional growth which explain regional variations it is also useful to know whether the various regional imbalances are self-righting. The question of whether regional growth is convergent or divergent is debatable, and an outline and discussion of certain relevant concepts, such as 'cumulative causation' and the centre-periphery concept conclude the chapter.

1 Aggregate growth models

GROWTH FROM INSIDE

One of the simplest theories of regional growth is the so-called *sector theory*. The theory arises from empirical observations by Clark and Fisher[3] that a rise in per capita income in different areas at different times is generally accompanied by a resource reallocation, with a decline in the proportion of labour force employed in primary (agriculture) activities, and a rise first in secondary (manufacturing) and then in tertiary (service) activities. The rate of occurrence of such sector shifts, and the resultant internal evolution of specialisation and division of labour, is seen as providing the main dynamic of regional growth.

The rate of shift in the relative importance of different sectors is explained by the income elasticity of demand for their products and by the different rates of change in labour productivity. As incomes rise, the demand for commodities supplied by the secondary and tertiary sectors rises faster than the demand for primary products, and thus these sectors grow faster. But it is also argued that the secondary and tertiary sectors benefit more from productivity advances and are therefore able to offer higher earnings to factors of production, thus causing a shift from sectors in which rewards are low to those in which they are high.

An extension of the basic theory is the *stages theory*[4] which suggests that regional development is primarily an internal evolutionary process with the following stages:

a The first stage is that of the self-sufficient subsistence economy, with little investment or trade. The basic agricultural population stratum is distributed according to the localisation of natural resources.

b With the improvements in transport, the region develops trade and specialisation. A second stratum develops carrying on simple villages industries for the farmers. Since the materials, market and labour are all furnished originally by the agricultural population, this new stratum is located in relation to the basic stratum.

c With increasing inter-regional trade, the region progresses through a succession of agricultural crops from extensive grazing to cereals to intensive dairying and fruit growing.

d With increasing population and diminishing agricultural returns, the region is forced to industrialise. Secondary industry develops, at first processing primary products but then becoming more specialised. (A failure to industrialise would lead to population pressure, a fall in living standards and general stagnation and decay.)

e The final stage is the development of tertiary industry producing for export. Such a developed region exports capital, skills and specialised services to less advanced regions.

Implicit in this process of growth to maturity are fundamental changes in the organisational structure of industry. The major change is the decrease in the number of establishments within a particular industry, with the closure of small establishments and the concentration into a limited number of bigger and stronger firms. This organisational rationalisation plus the original internal

104

reallocation between sectors also causes major changes in the locational and settlement patterns within regions, favouring migratory movements from small to bigger centres, from rural to urban areas. (Such locational changes are discussed in more detail in later chapters.)

But does the sector theory and its extension into the stages theory constitute a useful and adequate explanation of regional growth? There are several objections to the approach. In particular, the rigid 'primary–secondary–tertiary sequence', or the five stages with their heavy emphasis on the necessity of industrialisation, invariably bear little resemblance to the actual development of regions. This is especially true of regions which were developed primarily to serve external markets. This of course introduces a second criticism—the lack of insight provided into the external relationships of a region. Although the theory does not rule out external shifts in demand, it is much more useful the greater the degree of self-sufficiency in the regional economy. However, regional economies are open economies and the one-sided nature of the approach is a fundamental weakness. A third criticism which can be applied to all the aggregate theories, is the grossness of the factors. Primary, secondary and tertiary categories can hide a multitude of industrial variations. A final criticism questions whether the approach does in fact constitute a 'theory' of regional growth. Such a theory would clearly focus on the critical factors that aid or impede growth. The sector approach merely outlines a process of growth, on the assumption of a rise in per capita income, failing to provide any insight into the causes of growth and change. However, the approach is not without merits. It does provide a general picture of the stages of regional development and throws light on the conditions for moving from one stage to another. It focusses on the major factors of industrial and occupational structure, and changes in the pattern of demand and sector productivity, and as such provides a useful starting point for the disaggregated analysis of regional growth which will be outlined in a later section.

A more recent approach to an explanation of the internal determinants of regional growth is via the use of *macro-economic models*[5] used in national economic growth theory. These models are supply oriented and seek to explain regional output in terms of certain regional factors, each of which can be analysed individually. Thus:

$$O_n = f_n\,(K, L, Q, Tr, T, So\,)$$

where O = Potential Output of Region n
$\quad\quad K$ = Capital
$\quad\quad L$ = Labour
$\quad\quad Q$ = Land (Natural Resources)
$\quad\quad Tr$ = Transport Resources
$\quad\quad T$ = Technology
$\quad\quad So$ = Socio-Political System.

Taking the more important, and more easily quantifiable factors, a growth equation can be produced, for example:

$$o_n = a_n k_n + (1 - a_n)l_n + t_n$$

where o, k, l and t = growth rates of output, capital, labour
$\quad\quad\quad\quad\quad\quad$ and technology
$\quad\quad\quad\quad a$ = capital's share of income (the marginal
$\quad\quad\quad\quad\quad\quad$ product of capital).

This simple neoclassical growth model can be adjusted to provide a model of steady regional growth, and tests with US data show a high degree of correlation between the results of such a model and reality.[6]

Although this macro-economic approach does isolate some of the major determinants of regional growth and can be adapted to describe growth in a system of regions, it still possesses certain basic weaknesses—in particular its highly aggregate nature and its concentration on the supply side.

GROWTH FROM OUTSIDE

The emphasis of the last section was on the internal productive capacity of a region and on the supply of factors such as capital, labour, natural resources and technical progress which determine that capacity. These internal supply factors are undoubtedly major determinants of regional growth, but their narrow emphasis on 'closed' regions can be misleading. In the highly interdependent economies of today, regions are not vacuum sealed against all external impulses, but are 'open' to the flows of trade and information from the outside world. The degree of 'openness' does vary according to factors such as topography, the stage of economic development and the size of the region, but external factors must be considered in any explanation of regional growth.

The *export base theory* provides one possible explanation of the external demand factor in regional growth. The theory is simply an application of the short-run comparative static economic base model to long-run dynamic growth situations. It states that a region's growth is determined by the exploitation of natural advantages and the growth of the regional export base which are in turn largely influenced by the level of external demand from other regions and countries. The income from export sales will lead to the development of residentiary activities, capital and labour movements, the development of external economies, and further regional growth. Thus, the level of external demand for the products of a region's export industries is set up as a critical determinant of regional growth. (One of the main exponents of the theory, North,[7] uses some 'colonial' examples—the decline in demand for beaver hats and the growth in demand for wheat from England in the late nineteenth century, with the resultant impacts on certain US export industries and regions—to illustrate the relationship.)

Unfortunately, this attractively simple concept is not without problems. In addition to the various technical and conceptual limitations outlined in the previous discussion of the economic base concept in short-run analysis, there are several other problems when the theory is adapted for long-run dynamic analysis, many of which are outlined in the published discussion between North and Tiebout.[8] The highly aggregate nature of the theory can be particularly misleading. The simple split into the region and the rest of the world hides the interrelationships between regions which are of considerable importance in regional growth. Aggregation also masks the fact that an increase in some export base industries may have much greater regional growth effects than others in particular regions.

But there are also other fundamental questions. Will export growth always lead to regional growth? Is export growth solely determined by external demand? What of the other internal and external influences that are relegated into insignificance in the theory? Taking the first question, the successful translation of the export sector growth into residentiary growth and large-scale regional growth depends on several variables—variables such as the income and expenditure patterns of the export sector, the initiative of local business and the rôle of the government. If export income goes mainly on imported luxury goods, or local businessmen fail to invest in the region, or the government fails to provide the necessary infrastructure, the region may remain in a state of colonial dependence on external areas, and will experience only limited growth.

Secondly, even if the export base is a major determinant of regional growth, its fortunes may not be solely determined by the level of external demand. Internal factors may be of considerable importance. Such factors were in fact recognised by supporters of the theory although the emphasis of the theory was still on the level of external demand as the major determinant. North, for example, recognised that the reasons for the decline of an existing exportable commodity might include the exhaustion of natural resources (e.g. coal seams), the increasing cost of land and labour within the region relative to those of competing regions (e.g. the decline of the Lancashire cotton textile industry), and technical progress changing the relative composition of inputs. Further, the growth of new exports may be influenced by factors such as major transport developments (canals and railways) allowing a region to compete in commodities from which it was previously barred by high transfer costs.

Thirdly, there are other influences on regional growth besides the fortunes of the export base. The internal growth influences may be vital factors in their own right. The growth of local (residentiary) activities by replacing imports may stimulate regional development. Other exogenous influences, such as the level of government spending, shifts in investment and consumption patterns, may also have a greater impact on regional growth than changes in the export base.

But the theory does stress the important fact that the growth of any sub-national unit is directly tied to developments within the national economy and international trade as well, suggesting that regional growth cannot be studied in isolation from changing patterns of national demand and investment. It clearly introduces the Keynesian concept of aggregate demand as a growth determinant, although highlighting exports as the primary component in that demand.

A more comprehensive and equally familiar method of incorporating the external factors in regional growth is through the application of the theory of international trade to regions. The *inter-regional resource allocation models*, first developed by Ohlin,[9] assume that factors of production, especially labour and capital will flow from regions in which the rewards are low to those in which the rewards are high. For example, if the wages for labour were lower in one region than all the others, there would either be an outflow to other regions or an inflow of capital to take advantage of the low labour costs, or some combination of both. This inter-regional resource allocation provides the major growth factor.

As might be expected, *national economic growth models* have also been adopted in an explanation of the external determinants of regional growth. Richardson[10] provides an example of the use of the Harrod-Domar group of models in regional analysis. This formulation is a demand-dominated theory which explains rates of growth in terms of exogenous demand factors such as investment and exports. It is wider in scope than the export base theory, but is similarly limited by its one-sided approach and high level of aggregation.

2 A disaggregated approach

INDUSTRIAL STRUCTURE ANALYSIS—ORIGINS

Although the general growth theories recognise the importance of industrial structure in the process of regional growth, their aggregate nature often hides important industrial variations. Industry is not homogeneous and some industries grow much faster than others. Similarly, some regions grow faster than others. As industrial structure varies from region to region, it is tempting to draw the obvious conclusion that there is a causal relationship between industrial structure and regional growth. Industrial structure analysis examines this relationship.

The approach was pioneered by Jones[11] and Leser[12] in the UK and was later rediscovered and further developed by Dunn and Perloff[13] in the USA. An early UK application was by Hemming,[14] and more recently under the new title of 'shift-share analysis', the approach has enjoyed great popularity. Recent applications to British regional problems include studies by Brown,[15] Stilwell,[16] the Hunt Report on Intermediate Areas[17] and the South East Economic Planning Council.[18]

INDUSTRIAL STRUCTURE ANALYSIS—SHIFT-SHARE COMPONENTS

The approach requires an isolation of the effects of a region's industrial structure on its growth over a particular period of time. This involves the breaking down of a region's growth performance, as indicated by some representative variable (such as employment, population or income) into a number of components. The usual variable is employment, and total regional employment growth (G) can be separated out into 'shift' and 'share' components.

The 'national share' component (N) represents the amount by which regional employment would have grown if it had grown at the national rate over the study period. This is the norm for the region from which deviations can be measured.

The 'shift' component represents any deviations in regional employment growth from the national share. It is positive in prosperous growth areas and negative in relatively depressed areas. Net shift for any region can be subdivided into two components:
    the 'proportionality shift component' (P), sometimes known as the 'structural' or 'industrial mix' component, measures the amount of net regional shift attributable to the composition of industrial sectors in the region. This component would be positive in areas specialising in nationally fast-growing sectors and negative in areas specialising in nationally slow-growing or even declining sectors.
    the 'differential shift component' (D), sometimes known as the 'locational' or 'regional' component, is the remainder. It measures the amount of net regional shift resulting from specific industrial sectors growing faster or slower in the region than

nationally owing to internal locational factors. Thus, a region with locational advantages, such as good resources, would have a positive differential shift component, whereas a region with locational disadvantages would have a negative component.

These two shift components separate out the external and internal elements of regional growth, with the proportionality shift resulting from the influence of 'outside' influences operating nationally and the differential shift resulting from the influence of factors operating 'inside' the region.

In algebraic notation, the various components can be expressed as follows:

$$G_j = E_{j_t} - E_{j_o} \dots\dots\dots\dots\dots\dots\dots\dots\dots\dots\dots 1$$
$$= (N_j + P_j + D_j)$$
$$N_j = E_{jo}(E_t/E_o) - E_{j_o} \dots\dots\dots\dots\dots\dots 2$$
$$(P+D)_j = E_{j_t} - (E_t/E_o)E_{j_o} \dots\dots\dots\dots\dots\dots 3$$
$$= (G_j - N_j)$$
$$P_j = \Sigma_i[(E_{i_t}/E_{io}) - (E_t/E_o)]E_{ij_o} \dots\dots\dots\dots 4$$
$$D_j = \Sigma_i[E_{ij_t} - (E_{i_t}/E_{i_s})E_{ij_o}] \dots\dots\dots\dots\dots 5$$
$$= (P + D)_j - (P_j)$$

where G_j, N_j, $(P + D)_j$, P_j, D_j are the total regional employment growth, national share component, net shift component and proportionality and differential shift components respectively for region 'j'

and E_j = total employment in region 'j'
        E = total national employment
        o, t = initial and terminal time periods
        i = industry subscript.

BRITISH REGIONAL GROWTH—SHIFT-SHARE COMPONENTS

Stilwell[19] has isolated the shift and share components of regional employment growth in Britain between 1959 and 1967, using Department of Employment and Productivity statistics, and the results are presented in Table 5.1. The results show four areas of substantial absolute and percentage employment growth, with the remaining regions lagging far behind. An insight into these

Table 5.1. *Analysis of the regional pattern of employment growth (1959–67)*

Region [a]	Absolute increase in employment (in thousands and as percentage of employment in region) G	National Share N	Total Shift P + D	Proportionality Shift P	Differential Shift D
South East	+ 691 (8·9)	+ 460 (5·9)	+ 230 (+2·9)	+ 251 (+3·2)	− 21 (−0·3)
South West	+ 114 (9·5)	+ 71 (5·9)	+ 44 (+3·6)	+ 3 (+0·2)	+ 41 (+3·4)
West Midlands	+ 175 (8·2)	+ 126 (5·9)	+ 49 (+2·3)	+ 29 (+1·4)	+ 20 (+0·9)
East Midlands	+ 133 (10·3)	+ 76 (5·9)	+ 57 (+4·4)	− 60 (−4·7)	+ 117 (+9·1)
Yorkshire and Humberside	+ 64 (3·2)	+ 116 (5·9)	− 52 (−2·6)	− 64 (−3·2)	+ 11 (+0·6)
North West	+ 25 (0·9)	+ 171 (5·9)	− 146 (−5·0)	− 24 (−0·8)	− 122 (−4·2)
North	+ 15 (1·2)	+ 75 (5·9)	− 60 (−4·7)	− 64 (−5·0)	+ 4 (+0·3)
Scotland	+ 28 (1·3)	+ 122 (5·9)	− 95 (−4·6)	− 40 (−1·9)	− 55 (−2·7)
Wales	+ 28 (3·0)	+ 55 (5·9)	− 27 (−2·9)	− 32 (−3·5)	+ 5 (+0·6)
Great Britain	+1272 (5·9)	+1272 (5·9)	—	—	—

a The regions used are the current Economic Planning Regions with the exception that East Anglia is included in the South-East Region for statistical comparability over the study period.

SOURCE: Stilwell, F. J. B, Regional Growth and Structural Adaptation, *Urban Studies*, June 1969.

growth variations is provided by the identification of the shift and share components using the approach outlined in the previous section.

For example, in the prosperous South East, only two-thirds of the regional employment growth (G) is explained by the national share component (N). The remaining positive deviation of 230 000 must be explained by the shift components ($P + D$). Indeed it is more than explained by the proportionality shift component (P) only, which suggests that the main reason for the growth in the South East is its industrial mix with the specialisation in nationally growing industries,* such as services and electronics. The negative differential shift component (230 000–251 000) suggests in fact that certain locational factors in the South East, perhaps congestion, are actually inhibiting the growth potential reflected in the industrial mix.

Another region with a negative differential shift component is the North West, but unlike the South East it is not offset by a favourable industrial structure, and this is reflected in the poor growth performance of the region between 1959–67. The only other region experiencing a negative differential shift component is Scotland—no doubt influenced by its relative isolation. In contrast, six of the nine regions have negative proportionality shift components, reflecting the overwhelming dominance of the South East with regard to possession of growth industries.

AN APPRAISAL OF THE APPROACH

There has recently been much discussion on the relative merits of the approach (see: Stilwell, Buck[20]). It is now generally accepted that industrial structure analysis is not in itself a theory of regional growth. This would require a fuller explanation of the underlying factors influencing the two shifts—why do some

* By way of example, if the South-East economy was dependent on two industries only: A, employing 5 million people at the beginning of the period, and B, employing 3 million, and both were growing faster than the national rate of approximately 6%, A at 8% and B at 11%, then from Equation (4), the proportionality shift component would be:

$$= \Sigma\,[\,(8\% - 6\%)5\text{m} + (11\% - 6\%)3\text{m}\,]$$
$$= (100\,000 + 150\,000)$$
$$= 250\,000$$

industries grow faster than others nationally and what are the location factors encouraging an industry to grow faster in one region than another? It is indeed doubtful whether such a disaggregated approach, considering a wide variety of regions and industrial sectors, could in fact be easily handled in the form of a theory.

There is also some scepticism about its value in other rôles, such as the description, analysis and prediction of regional growth and its general use as a guide to regional policy. This results from fundamental criticisms of some of the basic concepts of the approach. Mackay[21] and Buck[22] question whether the proportionality and differential shifts truly reflect the relative influences of industrial-mix and locational factors in a region. Because of industry interdependence in the regional economy, the proportionality shift may be underestimated. For example, a depressed region with a below average representation of national growth industries will also have less of the auxiliary industries supplying the growth industries, and consequently part of the negative differential shift may be traced back to industrial structure. The proportionality shift may also be underestimated owing to the non-homogeneity of industry groups. Thus, demand for particular models of cars made on Merseyside may be growing faster than the demand for cars nationally, and hence the application of national car industry growth rates to the Merseyside sub-region may underestimate the proportionality shift. In addition, differential shift may also be distorted by the impact of factors such as the positive inducements and the negative controls of regional policy.

Industrial structure analysis is also highly sensitive to the level of aggregation of data input. Analysis of employment growth by the finer Minimum List Headings (MLH) will usually reveal a larger proportionality shift than analysis at the SIC order level, and Buck presents empirical evidence to illustrate this in the North West Region.[23] The analysis is also sensitive to the base year of the data input. The proportionality shift reflects the relative industrial specialisation of the region at the beginning of the study period. It takes no account of the change in the industry mix of the region over the study period.

A final criticism concerns the policy implications to be drawn from the analysis. It has sometimes been assumed that a region with poor differential effects would benefit from improved locational advantages, such as better infrastructure, and that a region with poor proportionality effects requires an injection of new growth industry. But this mechanical relationship to policy is an over-simplification, for a region with poor differential effects could also benefit from new industry, as could the region with poor proportionality effects benefit from improved infrastructure.

Despite this barrage of problems, the approach still has much to commend it. Although not a growth theory, it does complement the other more formal theories emphasising the relationship between industrial structure and regional growth, and separating out the internal and external elements of that growth. Its industrial emphasis suggests a particular affinity to the sector theory and export base theory approaches. Certain modifications and assumptions can also maintain the approach as a useful method of analysis. The assumption that the proportionality shift represents only a minimum estimate of the influence of industrial structure; the recognition that the level of data aggregation is to some extent dependent on the scale of region to be investigated; and the inclusion of a 'proportionality modification shift'[24] to accommodate the impact of time on the industrial structure counter some of the major problems.

3 Regional Growth—convergence or divergence?

A question of some importance to the regional planner is whether regional growth is convergent or divergent. Will the gaps between the prosperous and the depressed regions widen or narrow over time? Some of the regional growth theories outlined suggest that regional imbalance may be self-righting, thus reducing the need for intervention. The sector theory suggests that the scope for internal resource reallocation is greater in the poorer agrarian regions than in the more developed regions, eventually leading to a convergence of regional prosperity. Similarly, the factor flows of the inter-regional trade models also suggest convergence of regional per capita income. The development of diseconomies of scale may also limit the growth of the prosperous areas. In practice however, convergence trends may be limited by the

115

immobility of factor movements between sectors and regions, and the failure of diseconomies to have impact on the growth of the prosperous regions. Thus, if regional balance is an objective, policies to improve factor mobility would be necessary.

One final hybrid group of regional growth theories which clearly recognise that regional growth may be divergent rather than convergent are the *centre–periphery* theories of Hirschman,[25] Friedman[26] and Myrdal.[27] The general argument of such theories can be simply illustrated by comparing the relative fortune of two regions, A and B. Region A initially develops faster than Region B because it possesses a variety of natural and/or man-made advantages. However, contrary to many growth theories, this divergence may not be self-righting and indeed the process may be cumulative with the 'rich getting richer and the poor getting poorer', or using Myrdal's biblical quotation:

'for unto everyone that hath shall be given, and he shall have abundance, but from him that hath not shall be taken away even, that which he hath.' (St. Matthew xxv. v 29).

Myrdal explains this process of *cumulative causation* in terms of the relative strength of *spread* and *backwash* effects. The spread effects are those forces favouring convergence between the rich and poor regions. As the rich region grows it may demand more products from the poor region thus stimulating its growth. Similarly, outmigration of factors from the poor region may induce a more efficient use of resources, with the internal reallocation from low wage to high wage/high productivity sectors generating growth. Diseconomies of scale may also set in in the prosperous region. However, Myrdal believed that such spread effects will invariably be more than offset by backwash effects. The increased demand for peripheral goods resulting from an increase in the prosperity of the centre may not materialise if the peripheral goods are primarily agricultural goods with a low income elasticity of demand. In addition, the selective outmigration of capital and skilled labour from the poor region to the rich may do more harm than good, reducing the ability of the poor region to compete, Finally, as already mentioned, the diseconomies of the rich region have also little impact being offset by other

116

economic and socio-psychological benefits ('better the devil we know . . .'!).

The centre–periphery theories with their emphasis on cumulative causation and divergent regional growth provide a valuable insight into the growth process, bringing together many of the elements of the other theories. They also have important policy implications for if the economic growth process is not self-equilibrating there may be need for government intervention to help the poorer regions. The initiative may come from within the problem region. In Britain, the strength of the Northern Region lobby has had some impact on government intervention in the region. Similarly, at the sub-regional level, the political opposition of North East Lancashire to Central Lancashire New Town, has brought Intermediate Area status and large-scale public investment in the infrastructure of the area in an attempt to break out of the 'vicious circle' of stagnation. However, a history of economic backwardness may so debilitate the poor region that there is a failure to perceive economic opportunities and the whole socio-political structure becomes incompatible with rapid regional growth. In such a situation, the initiative may have to come directly from the central government.

The concept of divergent regional growth is also supported by a growing number of theorists who believe that the control, as well as the structure, of industry is central to the explanation of regional growth variations. Holland,[28] for example, argues that the fundamental cause of regional imbalance is capitalism itself, and especially the rising power of the *multi-nationals*. He sees the multi-national, multi-product, multi-company enterprises occupying a 'meso-economic' sector midway between micro- and macro-economics, and argues that the distribution of such enterprises in a country is fundamental in perpetuating and developing regional imbalance. The enterprises are seen as concentrating in the most prosperous regions of a country, and there remaining, impervious to policy measures to relocate them to problem regions, and threatening to leave the country altogether if they do not get their own way.

Multi-nationals are without doubt of growing importance, and a limited number of large firms now dominate manufacturing industry in both the USA and Western Europe. Prais[29] has estimated that in Britain the top 100 companies controlled 20% of net output in the manufacturing sector in 1950, 50% in 1970, with a projected 70% in 1985. Multi-nationals are also important in regional development. In some cases, Holland's diagnosis of the multi-national impact on regional development may be accurate, but there is much contradictory information in this area and Yannopoulos and Dunning,[30] for example, suggest that in the UK context many multi-nationals have been influenced by regional policy measures. They also note that multi-nationals come in many varieties, and their locational activities are very much a function of the characteristics of the firm (product and enterprise related variables) and the characteristics of the regions concerned. Overall, they reasonably conclude that 'it is not possible to take any dogmatic position regarding the influence of the locational strategies of multi-national enterprises on regional disequilibria within countries'.

Table 5.2. *Location of ultimate ownership of Scottish manufacturing plants and employment (1973)*

Location of ultimate ownership	Plants		Employees		Average size of plant (employees)
	number	(%)	number	(%)	
Scotland	2176	71·6	243 440	41·2	111·9
England	640	21·0	234 990	39·8	367·2
Rest of United Kingdom	4	0·1	160	—	40·0
EEC	29	1·0	8 760	1·5	302·1
Europe non-EEC	15	0·5	3 800	0·6	253·3
North America	148	4·9	87 730	14·9	592·8
Other	5	0·2	370	0·1	74·0
Joint-owned	24	0·8	11 450	1·9	476·7
Total	3041	100·0	590 700	100·0	194·2

SOURCE Firn, J. R., External Control and Regional Development: the Case of Scotland, *Environment and Planning* (1975).

In one of the few regional level studies on the control of industry, Firn shows that one problem region, Scotland, already had by 1973 a high degree of dependence on externally controlled enterprises (Table 5.2). Only 41% of Scottish manufacturing employment was controlled within Scotland, and usually the larger the enterprise, and the faster the growth of the industrial sector, the greater the likelihood of external control.* The implications of such external dependence are complex. On the one hand, externally controlled enterprises are often dynamic multinationals bringing many jobs and advanced technology to hard pressed regions. On the other hand, the region may become more vulnerable to sudden change in employment and also prone to a more long run negative multiplier process, with very limited linkages from the new firms into the regional economy, high leakages out of the region and a lack of 'white collar' headquarter jobs, all of which might sap the region's economic prosperity and viability. A problem region's acquisition of externally controlled multi-nationals may be a mixed blessing.

4 Social and political factors in regional growth

Our theorising thus far has largely focused on the economic dimension of regional development, and indeed this is the area in which most theoretical advances have been made. Yet, as noted in the last section, social and political factors are also of considerable significance in regional growth, but to date they have figured little in regional growth theory. However, such inputs are developing and certain possible lines of investigation are now briefly noted.

The class structure, socio-economic structure, life styles or expectations of social groups may have a significant effect on the growth capacity of a region.[31] Within the United Kingdom there are considerable regional differences in socio-economic structure. For example, a comparison of the percentage economically active men by SEGs (Socio-Economic Groups) for the Northern Region and the South East (1971) reveals greater proportions of low SEGs (skilled manual and semi-skilled) and lower proportions of high SEGs (managerial and professional) than the national

* The whole field of external control is a semantic minefield—e.g. what is 'external', what is 'control'. See: Dicken, P., The multiplant business enterprise and geographical space: some issues in the study of external control and regional development, *Regional Studies*, **10**, 4 (1976).

average in the Northern Region, with the reverse situation in the South East.[32] In the North this situation may reflect the industrial base and the corporate structure of enterprises, which are often subsidiaries of companies located elsewhere, plus limitations in the educational and cultural environment and in opportunities for social and economic advancement in the region. With regard to the latter, Klaassen[33] has drawn attention to the importance of social amenities in economic growth, although largely from the perspective of attracting industrial development. Pahl,[34] on a slightly different tack, contends that an individual's location in a spatial sense fundamentally influences his life chances because of constraints it may impose on his access to social facilities, such as education. But whatever the merits of these ideas, the existence of an 'imbalanced' social structure has implications for the future development of a region. Thus in the Northern Region, the imbalance may limit the proclivity for entrepreneurship and reinforce social and occupational immobility, which may themselves limit indigenous self help and hinder the adoption of new concepts and technologies.

A wider perspective to include social factors also raises questions on the measurement of regional growth. Conventional measures of the levels and rates of growth, such as regional output and regional personal income *per capita*, may be too narrow as indices of regional welfare. Indeed, when regional economic objectives are broadened to include equity objectives, it may be that investment in regional welfare facilities (e.g. hospitals) may bring more benefits than investment in increased industrial output. In addition, broad economic criteria may be too aggregate. Indicators reflecting an improvement in the position of a poor region may not necessarily reflect an improvement in the position of the poor people within that region.[35]

Political factors are of course central in regional policy making, and regional policy decisions are political decisions about the spatial allocation of resources. Political awareness that regional problems existed in the first place was instrumental in drawing the professional economist's attention to regional problems, but there have been only limited advances in building political factors into regional growth theory.

In addition to Holland's arguments discussed in the previous section, one possible line of investigation is the relationship between political concern for the problems of a region and the distance of that region from the political centre. Kohr, in an adaptation of Prebisch's[36] 'Law of Peripheral Neglect', argues that 'the concern of the capital for its surrounding political space decreases with the square of the distance from it'.[37] Such a formulation may overdramatise and oversimplify the relationship—population mass and political marginality may be as significant as distance in the equation—but it does provide an interesting complement to the centre–periphery/cumulative causation arguments previously outlined. The implications of such a formulation for regional growth, might be the need to manipulate political space as well as economic space to generate regional growth, giving peripheral regions greater political representation, either at the centre or the periphery, to overcome the 'distance' factor.

Finally, in similar vein, Hechter[38] suggests that within a unitary nation there may be internal colonies, areas which have an ethnic or cultural identity different from that of the state, which have been treated in effect as colonies. A recent socio-economic strategy for the South Wales valleys,[39] for example, suggests that nineteenth-century Wales was treated very much as a colonial territory, with the coalfield producing wealth for the controllers of capital and enterprise in Bristol and London.

Thus, regional policy decisions often reflect a trade-off between economic efficiency, equity, and political expediency, and this should be recognised in a discussion of regional growth. The nature, extent and distributional impacts of such trade-offs vary greatly from country to country and region to region, depending on factors such as social and political structure and the 'normal' degree of government intervention in regional issues.

5 Summary

Regional growth is a product of many factors, some internal to the region, others external. The complexity of this variety of economic and socio-political factors, makes the formulation of a single, generally accepted and comprehensive regional growth theory very difficult. The simple aggregate models, such as the sector theory and export base theory are only partial attempts.

The new generation of macro-economic models offer an interesting development but as yet have limitations as explanatory tools of the process of regional growth. In this situation, there does seem to be a case for considering approaches, which although of limited theoretical pedigree, do attempt to identify some of the underlying internal and external determinants of inter-regional differences in regional growth in a simple but comprehensive framework. Industrial structure analysis is such an approach which, in spite of its weaknesses, is of considerable practical value in examining variations in regional growth. Finally, the concept of cumulative causation suggests that the inter-regional differences may not be self-righting, at least in the short run. Even if they do eventually converge over a longer period, the hardship in the poorer regions in the intervening period may necessitate some form of intervention.

References

1 Hilhorst, J., *Regional Development Theory: An Attempt to Synthesize,* Institute of Social Studies, The Hague (1967).
2 Siebert, H., *Regional Economic Growth: Theory and Policy,* International Textbook Co., Pennsylvania (1969).
3 Clark, C., *The Conditions of Economic Progress,* London Macmillan (1940); Fisher, G. B., Production, Primary, Secondary and Tertiary, *Economic Record,* **15,** June 1939.
4 Hoover, E. M., and Fisher, J., Research in Regional Economic Growth, Universities—National Bureau Committee for Economic Research, *Problems in the Study of Economic Growth,* N.Y., Chapter V (1949).
5 See: Richardson, H. W., *Regional Economics,* Chapter 13, Weidenfeld and Nicolson (1969).
6 Romans, J. T., *Capital Exports and Growth among U.S. Regions,* Wesleyan University Press (1969).
7 North, D. C., Location theory and regional economic growth, *Journal of Political Economy,* **63,** pages 243–58 (1955).
8 Tiebout, C. M., Exports and Regional Economic Growth, *Journal of Political Economy,* **64** (1956). Reply by North, D.C. and Rejoinder by Tiebout, C. M., **64.**
9 Ohlin, B., *Inter-regional and International Trade,* Cambridge, Mass. (1933).
10 Richardson, H. W., *op cit.*

11 *Report of the Royal Commission on the Distribution of the Industrial Population* (Cmnd. 6153), Appendix II, London (1940).
12 Leser, C. E. V., *Some Aspects of the Industrial Structure of Scotland*, Univ. of Glasgow, Dept. of Social and Econ. Research, Occ. Paper V (University of Glasgow) (1951).
13 Perloff, H. S., Dunn, E. S., Lampard, F. F., and Muth, R. F., *Regions, Resources and Economic Growth*, Resources for the Future Inc., Johns Hopkins Press, Baltimore (1960).
14 Hemming, F. W., The Regional Problem, *Nat. Inst. Econ. Review*, August 1963.
15 Brown, A. J., Regional problems and regional policy, *Nat. Inst. Econ. Review*, November 1968.
16 Stilwell, F. J. B., Regional Growth and Structural Adaptation, *Urban Studies*, June 1969.
17 *Report of the Committee on the Intermediate Areas* (The Hunt Report), Cmnd. 3998, London, HMSO (1969).
18 South-East Economic Planning Council, *South-East Kent Study*, Economic Planning Council, London (1969).
19 Stilwell, F. J. B., *op cit.*
20 See: Buck, T. W., Shift and Share Analysis—A Guide to Regional Policy?, *Regional Studies*, **4**, 4, pages 445–8 (1970); also Stilwell, F. J. B., Further Thoughts on the Shift and Share Approach, *Regional Studies*, **4**, 4, pages 451–8.
21 Mackay, D. I., Industrial Structure and Regional Growth: A Methodological Problem, *Scottish Journal of Political Economy*, **XV,** June 1968.
22 Buck, T. W., *op cit.*
23 Buck, T. W., *op cit.*
24 Stilwell, F. J. B., Regional Growth and Structural Adaptation, *op cit.*
25 Hirschman, A. O., *The Strategy of Economic Development*, Yale (1958).
26 Friedmann, J., *Regional Development Policy: A Case Study of Venezuela*, MIT Press (1967).
27 Myrdal, G., *Economic Theory and Underdeveloped Regions*, Duckworths (1957).
28 Holland, S., *The Regional Problem*, Macmillan (1976), and *Capital versus The Regions*, Macmillan (1976).
29 Prais, S. J., A New Look at Industrial Concentration, *Oxford Economic Papers* (July 1974).
30 Yannopoulos, G., and Dunning J., Multinational enterprises and regional development: an exploratory paper, *Regional Studies*, **10,** 4 (1976).

31 Kuklinski, A. R. (ed.), *Social Issues in Regional Policy and Regional Planning*, Mouton, The Hague (1977).
32 Northern Region Strategy Team, *First Interim Report*, NRST (1975).
33 Klaassen, L. H., *Social Amenities in Area Economic Growth*, OECD (1968).
34 Pahl, R. E., *Whose City?*, Longman (1970); and *Patterns of Urban Life*, Longman (1970).
35 Richardson, H. W., *Regional Growth Theory*, Macmillan (1973).
36 Prebisch, R., *The Economic Development of Latin America*, United Nations (1950).
37 Kohr, L., *Is Wales Viable?*, Christopher Davies (1971).
38 Hechter, M., *Internal Colonialism*, London (1975).
39 Ty Toronto, *A Socio-Economic Strategy for the Valleys of South Wales*, Ty Toronto, Aberfan (1977).

B. Intra-regional Analysis

6 The location of industry

A knowledge of the 'laws' underlying regional structure is essential if the regional planner is to predict the reaction of particular areas to particular pressures and policies. Interference in the existing patterns of activity within a region is of fundamental importance in structuring economic opportunities, and regional development strategies are invariably expressed in terms of patterns of relative locations. The location of industry is of particular importance and provides a useful starting point for an explanation of the internal structure of regions.

1 Location of industry: theory and practice

Production involves the use of inputs—factors of production—to produce output—goods and services—as efficiently as possible. The location of the unit of production, the firm, will obviously be determined in relation to the source of the inputs and the market for the output. The various factors of production—land, labour, capital and enterprise—plus the market factor, thus constitute primary determinants of location. These factors can of course be refined into more specific determinants such as the quality and quantity of labour, the geographical location of a site and the availability of the necessary infrastructure. Other determinants, such as central and local govenment policy and behavioural factors can also be added. There have been two main approaches to the study of these factors of industrial location—one theoretical and the other empirical. This divergence reflects the difference of approach between the economist with his love of abstract theories and the geographer with his concern for empirical study and generalisation from real world situations.

The theoretical approach attempts to abstract from reality, constructing an all-embracing system of 'pure' rules. The search is for a general theory of industrial location, which can explain the existing structure of industrial location and changes in that structure.

The empirical approach involves the listing of factors which might be important, together with examples of situations where they have in fact been important, in the location of particular industries. There is usually little or no attempt to formulate such factors into a general theory, and hence this approach is generally limited to the provision of a descriptive picture. Unfortunately the two approaches have developed independently with little attempt at reconciliation. This chapter will first consider the theoretical approach, and then attempt to marry it into the general complexities of the real world.

2 Industrial location theory

The major work on industrial location theory has been carried out by economists attempting to integrate location into the main body of economic theory—in particular, into the 'theory of the firm'. However, location is concerned with spatial relationships, and this has over time also attracted the attention of numerous geographers. The resulting contributions have aimed at providing an all-embracing system of 'pure rules' of location, attempting to derive the 'optimum location' for the individual firm. But such a goal is very difficult to achieve when one considers:

a the wide range of industry—including the primary sector, such as mining and quarrying; the secondary sector with a multitude of manufacturing industries, the tertiary sector with rapidly growing service trades, and the so-called 'quaternary sector'— composed of high expertise information based industries;

b the wide variety of firms, each with its own input combination and market characteristics, within each industry.

Forerunners of the theoretical approach include Adam Smith, Ricardo, Von Thünen and Mill, but here the outline will be limited to post-1900 developments. Even within this context, space restricts analysis to a very limited number of the numerous contributions on the subject. The analysis is structured around three approaches to industrial location theory:

a the *least cost approach*, which attempts to explain location in terms of the minimisation of factor costs;

b *market area analysis*, where there is more emphasis on the demand, or market factors;

c *the profit maximisation approach*—the logical outcome of the other two.

These three 'umbrella' approaches provide a useful framework for the analysis of the theoretical approach to industrial location, although they are by no means mutually exclusive.

The differences in approaches can be clearly illustrated by using the recent work of Smith,[1] who seeks to synthesise the various theoretical statements to produce an approach of more practical relevance. Smith's diagrams (Figure 6.1) present cost-price situations in a simplified and very useful way. Assuming a profit maximisation objective, the most profitable location for a firm will be where total revenue exceeds total cost by the greatest amount. Figure 6.1 shows three examples of how cost and revenue curves for the individual firm might vary according to location. Profitable locations lie between points *A* and *B*, and *O* is the optimum point. The historical evolution of the three approaches will now be considered in a little more detail.

THE LEAST COST APPROACH

Alfred Weber[2] (1909) was the first person to work up a comprehensive theory of industrial location—although many of his ideas had been partially formulated by another German, Launhardt, some 20 years earlier. Weber's basic principle was that a businessman would choose a location where his costs were least. For the purposes of his model, he made the following simplifying assumptions:

Fig. 6.1   Optimum locations (re profitability to firm) in different cost-price situations—assuming constant output

SOURCE   D. M. Smith, 'A theoretical framework for geographical studies of industrial location', *Economic Geography*, **42** (2), (1966).

a the unit of study is a single isolated country, homogeneous in climate, with consumers concentrated at certain given centres; conditions of perfect competition are implied with all firms having access to unlimited markets;

b some natural resources, such as water, sand, and clays are 'ubiquitous', that is, widely available;

c other materials, such as mineral fuels and ores, are 'sporadic' with availability limited to a number of sites;

d labour is not ubiquitous, with several fixed labour locations and fixed labour mobility.

Within these assumptions, Weber believed three factors influenced industrial location. These are transport costs and labour costs—general regional factors which determine the fundamental location pattern and the geographic framework; and agglomerative or deglomerative forces—local factors which determine the degree of dispersion within the general framework. The locational objective for the businessman involves an optimum in substitution between these factors, selecting a site which minimises total costs.

Weber first considered the impact of transport costs, the primary location determinant and then showed how the other two factors might modify the location. He assumed transport costs to be directly proportional to distance moved and weight carried. Thus the point of least transport costs is that at which the total weight movement of assembling inputs and distributing output is at a minimum. He illustrated the concept using his famous *locational triangle*, (see Figure 6.2*a*), where the optimum location (T) is a balance between the forces exerted by the material sources (M_1 and M_2) and the consumption point (C). To indicate whether the optimum location was closer to the source of materials or to the market, Weber devised a *material index*, which is:

$$\frac{\text{(Weight of Local Material Inputs)}}{\text{(Weight of Final Products)}}$$

If the index was greater than one, the firm was material oriented; if the index was less than one, it was market oriented.

Labour costs, the second location factor, can attract a firm to a location other than the least transport cost if the savings in labour costs per unit of output are greater than the extra transport

T = optimum location
M1, M2 = material sources
Mk = market
y,x,z = weights of inputs
and outputs
a,b,c = distances between
location,inputs
and market

(a) Locational triangle

Isodapanes

£3
£2
£1

T = 'least-cost
transport
location

L = 'cheap
labour'
locatior

(b) Impact of labour costs on
least cost transport location

Fig. 6.2   The Weber 'least-cost' approach

costs per unit involved. This is illustrated in Figure 6.2*b*, where *T* is the point of least transport costs and the contour lines, *isodapanes*, show the increase in unit transport costs away from this point. *L* is a labour market where labour costs are £2 per unit less than that at *T*. As *L* is within the critical £2 isodapane, the firm would, other things being equal, substitute between transport costs and non-transport costs and divert its location to a new location at this point of reduced labour cost. Similarly, a firm may be diverted away from both the least transport and labour cost locations if cost economies can be achieved through the third location factor of agglomeration. The advantages of agglomeration might include the development of a pool of skilled labour and the establishment of specialist services, although of course there may also be diseconomies such as rising land prices and congestion which may eventually encourage deglomeration.

Since its publication, the Weberian model has been subjected to a great deal of criticism and has been regarded as very 'noisy' in terms of its abstraction from reality.[3] It has been criticised for some of its assumptions, such as constant transport costs and production costs, and for its disregard of institutional factors, such as government policy. But in particular, the model is very one-sided, assuming perfect competition with all firms having access to unlimited demand. The least cost approach can be clearly illustrated using Smith's diagrams (Figure 6.1a). Average cost (AC) varies according to location, but average revenue (AR) is assumed to be constant. The optimum location is O where average costs are at a minimum and unit profits are at a maximum. However, market demand obviously also varies, with firms locating so as to gain some control over that demand. Nevertheless, Weber's contribution to industrial location theory should not be underestimated. He did identify many of the key factors involved and his work provides a very valuable base for the further development of the theory.

Hoover[4] (1948) elaborates on the Weberian model, making far more realistic cost assumptions than Weber, and attempting to modify some of the inherent weaknesses. Compared with Weber, Hoover divides costs into transport (procurement and distribution) and production, each of which is analysed in a more detailed and realistic way. For example, transport costs are not directly proportional to distance and weight as Weber assumed, but may vary according to the length and direction of haul and the composition of the goods involved. Hoover also gives more emphasis to institutional factors, such as local taxes, which may have a considerable impact on locational decisions. He also mentions market areas, but only from an assumed location, and his

131

concern is much more with cost than with demand. Thus, although Hoover's approach is more one of location within a capitalist economy compared with Weber's general theory, it still remains firmly within the least cost approach.

MARKET AREA ANALYSIS

One of the fundamental weaknesses of the least cost approach is the overemphasis of the input side (cost minimisation), and the underemphasis of the output or demand side, simply assuming that the firm can sell all it produces wherever it locates. But the market is a variable. Buyers are scattered over a wide area and the intensity of demand varies from place to place. Firms will seek to gain access to the market and serve the greatest demand. The market may therefore be a major location determinant, perhaps overriding the least-cost location, and its rôle in industrial location has been analysed by serveral scholars.

Lösch[5] realised that the optimum location is the place of maximum profits, where revenue exceeds costs by the largest amount. However, a theoretical formulation of this optimum is very complex. As such Lösch to some extent compromises, and in *The Economics of Location* (1954) attempts to incorporate demand into the theory by considering the optimum size of the market. On the basis of the following assumptions:

a no spatial variations in the distribution of factor inputs—raw materials, labour and capital—over a homogeneous plain;
b uniform population densities and constant tastes;
c no locational interdependence between firms;
he considered a fixed individual producer, a farmer, producing beer, and attempted to determine his market area and market revenue.

For the analysis, Lösch uses and adapts a simple demand curve. (Figure 6.3). At the centre of the market area near to the farm (*P*), the unit price of beer is *OP*, with demand *PQ*. Further from the centre (*R*), extra distribution costs result in a higher price, *OR*, and demand falls to *RS*. At the far extremities of the market area, extra distribution costs are prohibitive, pushing up the price to *OF*, and demand is nil. If the shaded quadrant, *FPQ*, is now rotated around the axis, *PQ*—*P* being the farm at the centre of the market, a 'demand cone' is produced (Figure 6.3). The base of the cone represents the market area, the height represents the quantity sold at any one point, and the volume represents the total revenue from the market demand. In time, if beer production is profitable, other farmers will develop their own circular market areas, which, according to Lösch, will finally adjust into a series of hexagonal market areas covering the entire plain.

Figure 6.3. Löschian Demand Curve and Cone

But this is the other side of the coin to the Weberian approach and equally one-sided. For by assuming no spatial variations in the distribution of factor inputs, Lösch eliminates spatial cost variations. Thus, where Weber neglects demand in his attempt to find the least cost location, Lösch neglects input supply, and the optimum location is primarily a function of market demand. The overall approach can be seen in Figure 6.1*b* where average revenue (AR) varies according to location, but average cost (AC) is assumed to be constant. Optimum location is at O, where average revenue is at a maximum.

There have been several attempts to modify some of Lösch's assumptions in an attempt to create a more realistic model. Richardson[6] is particularly concerned with the limiting assumption of a uniform population density. Densities do of course vary, being high in urban areas and low in rural areas. Demand and potential sales revenue will therefore vary markedly from place to place. Harris[7] shows the variation in market demand between different locations in the USA, using a simple index of gravitational potential, as outlined in Chapter 2.

THE PROFIT MAXIMISING APPROACH

The *least cost* and *market area* approaches are both one-sided, although in different ways—holding either the input supply or market demand constant. In practice, both costs and revenue vary with location and the optimum location is the one which yields the greatest profit. Figure 6.1c conceptualises the approach, showing both cost and revenue varying with location. In such a situation, the optimum, profit-maximising location may be neither the least cost nor the maximum revenue location. Recent theorists, Isard[8] and Greenhut[9] in particular, have attempted to remould the Löschian approach into a more profit-maximising approach. (However, the idea is not at all new. Loria, an Italian, suggested that industrialists seek locations that will give them maximum profits, considering both markets and costs, in 1884. But, owing to Weber's influence, the least cost approach dominated early twentieth-century thinking.) However, as Lösch concluded, there are problems in deriving the profit-maximising location.

There is firstly the question of *locational interdependence*. In the typical modern oligopoly structure, a major location determinant for an individual firm is the location and markets of like firms. Firms manoeuvre to control or share competitors' markets ('follow the crowd'). This is very difficult to incorporate into a theory as it involves a consideration of not only what rivals have done, but what they might do in the future. Nevertheless, several theorists, such as Hotelling[10] and Greenhut[11] have suggested certain general rules. Perhaps a possible approach in this area of uncertainty lies in the use of game theory[12].

A second problem is the difficulty of evaluating the relevant variables. In practice, the determination of the profit-maximising location is difficult and involved. Major areas of difficulty are the evaluation of differing costs in differing locations, differing market conditions and the policy of rival firms. Hence most locations may be sub-optimal, and the Weber least cost location

134

may be more common in reality than it should rationally be if profit maximisation was the locational criterion.

The impact of large modern corporations[13] constitutes a third problem. It is difficult to incorporate large concerns such as ICI and Unilever into location theory as they contain a wide variety of plants which may originally have located for reasons independent of the present concern. They may also produce a wide variety of products, not all of which can be produced at one optimum location.

The fourth problem raises the evergreen question of whether firms actually do 'maximise' profits. For a state concern, an 'adequate' return on public money with some consideration of social costs and benefits may be more important than maximum returns. Alternative aims have also been suggested for non-state concerns. Firms may have philanthropic motives (but with profit maximising undertones?). They may only maximise in the long run or concentrate more on maximising turnover (equating revenue with the ego of the management?). Simon[14] suggests that firms are 'satisficers' seeking locations giving a satisfactory level or profits and growth, and that the difference between optimising and 'satisficing' is similar to 'the difference between searching a haystack to find the sharpest needle in it and searching the haystack to find a needle sharp enough to sew with'.

The fifth and final problem introduces the long neglected subject of behavioural factors. To consider only the simple mechanical factors so far discussed is to deny that man is human. Behavioural factors, such as the businessman's attitude to the troubled labour conditions of certain areas, or his attitude to the 'social life' of 'the North' compared with that of 'the South', may play an important rôle in industrial location. Certainly if, as Figure 6.1c shows, profit may vary little over quite a large area (A to B), then a firm may locate within fairly wide limits without too much concern. Within these limits, other factors, especially behavioural factors, may become relatively more important. There is certainly a growing awareness of the importance of these factors and Pred has attempted to structure them presenting 'a verbal formalisation of the fairly obvious'.[15]

In summary, there have been several theoretical approaches to the complex problem of industrial location. Each has something to contribute to the general body of theory, providing a valuable insight into the relevant locational factors. But there are also several problems. In particular, there are the problems of formulating a general theory for a wide variety of industries and firms, the problem of searching for an 'optimum' rather than a 'satisfactory' location, and the various problems of the profit-maximising approach outlined above.

3 Industrial location in practice

To accept that a businessman will fall in with a plan based solely on the concepts of location theory may be very misleading. More subjective criteria may be important. Hence, if bad location decisions are to be avoided, it is necessary to examine location determinants in practice. Clark[16] illustrates the importance of location decisions quoting an American researcher in Chicago who found that 20 location decisions by major retailers would control the location of 20 000 other retailers for the next twenty-five years.

THE CONTEXT OF LOCATION/THE LOCATION PROBLEM

The location problem must be faced not only by new firms seeking their first site, but also by established firms relocating. That new firms face a location decision is self-evident. That established firms must also face locations decisions is perhaps less obvious. The relocation of an established firm can result from pressures both internal and external to the firm. Several studies[17] have shown that the main *internal* pressure comes from growth in output, which itself imposes pressure on the existing location, in particular on the limited floorspace. However a decline in output with a subsequent rise in unit fixed costs may also sometimes encourage a reduction in floorspace and a move to smaller premises. *External* pressures may come from a variety of sources: from other firms bidding up the price of labour, or perhaps from the government with its local planning controls and national taxation policies.

Faced with these pressures, most firms would first investigate whether or not their existing site could be used more efficiently,

136

perhaps by an increase in shift working. If the pressures are too great, there are several options open to the firm. It may do nothing, forgoing the increase in output, or it may possibly increase the amount of sub-contract work put out. It may also choose to relocate. If the decision is taken to move, involving either the entire firm, or as is more common, merely a branch of the parent concern, a new site must be chosen, and this choice involves a consideration of several general location factors.

THE CHOICE OF A NEW LOCATION/GENERAL FACTORS
AFFECTING INDUSTRIAL LOCATION

Location factors are difficult to quantify, varying from firm to firm, and are difficult to rank in any order of importance. For many large-scale capital intensive projects, such as steelworks or oil refineries, physical location factors may be of overriding importance. For many others—particularly those involving factory processes—physical considerations are less important, and the analysis here is mainly concerned with these. There have been several surveys[18] of mobile firms seeking to identify the major location factors, and they seem to suggest the following as major categories:

a Labour—quality and quantity;
b Transport and communications;
c Site and premises;
d Government aid;
e Environmental factors—in the widest sense.

The first two factors influence variable costs, whereas the third factor is concerned with capital costs. Government policy may affect both cost categories. The final factor may also affect costs, but is more concerned with attitudes.

Labour—quality and quantity. Most research indicates that labour availability is the most important single factor. This does not necessarily equate with high levels of unemployment. Indeed long dole queues, with their degrading effect on labour morale, may be more of a deterrent than an attraction. Firms however, are particularly concerned with local competition for the labour supply and the quality of that supply. Many firms show a preference for small localities where there is sufficient labour for their immediate requirements and anticipated build-up, but not enough to attract other firms into the area. Such firms, by becoming the principal employer in a locality, hope to keep labour turnover to a minimum. Other firms on the contrary, for advantages of linkage, prefer to be close to other establishments. The quality of labour is particularly important. This does not necessarily mean a large supply of trained labour, for inbred skills may often be more of a hindrance than a help. However, a large supply of adaptable, trainable labour is particularly attractive, especially if complemented by the existence of local training facilities. With the rapid growth in light industry, a large supply of female labour is at a special premium.

Contrary to expectations wage rates tend to be of only marginal importance as a location factor in Britain. This is partly because collective national union agreements tend to standardise rates and make any wage advantage only short term, and also because lower wage rates often equate with lower productivity. The history of labour relations on the other hand, is a factor of increasing importance. Once an area has established a bad reputation for labour relations it is very difficult to shake off, and this can have a deterrent effect on new industry.

Transport and Communications. Transport factors are usually regarded as major locational determinants. Yet certain studies tend to query this. The Toothill Report on the Scottish Economy,[19] from a survey of firms operating on industrial estates in Scotland, showed that more than half of the firms had total transport costs not above 2% of turnover. But despite this evidence (and it may be somewhat biassed relating to firms that have actually moved to distant locations and which could therefore be assumed to have low transport costs) it remains true that many firms are still strongly influenced by communications. One only needs to witness the pressure on industrial sites close to the motorway network to illustrate the point, at a local level.

A location giving good access to the main markets is still important. A remote location may involve two drivers and an overnight stop for a distribution journey—hence increasing costs. In addition, and perhaps more important, rush orders may be more difficult to meet on time, which may encourage consumers to buy elsewhere, hence revenue also suffers. A location giving good access to linked producers is also important. If the firm is a branch concern, this would allow the minimisation of transport costs between the parent factory and the branch and easier executive control by main plant management. Good access by road, rail and air also reduces the feeling of geographical isolation of a relocated plant.

Site and premises. Although land cost may be a major cost item in the initial setting up of a firm, it becomes much less important when costed over a long period and may be relatively insignificant in determining choice between comparable sites, although of course it may rule out certain very expensive locations. The provision of a wide variety of ready-built factories on fully serviced sites, facilitating immediate production and minimum 'teething' problems, can be a more important factor. Factory rents for similar properties in similar locations do not vary too markedly; although certain areas with a supply of old, but sound, industrial accommodation (such as Lancashire with its legacy of cotton mills 'built to last') may be able to offer 'cut price' rentals. However even such premises may constitute a 'mixed blessing' in that they hinder the efficiency and constrain the innovative spirit of the occupant firms.

Government aid. Many countries now seek to actively divert industry to particular problem regions using a wide variety of measures. These measures emanating from a variety of sources at national, regional and local levels can have a major impact on a firm's location and will be briefly outlined here prior to a more detailed discussion in Chapter 9. The UK has a long history of 'carrot and stick' incentives administered by central government. The positive incentives, including capital cost grants, subsidies to variable costs via measures such as the Regional Employment Premium, and numerous tax and depreciation allowances, appear quite generous bait. But a recent costing by Professor Wilson[20] suggests that they may represent no more than 5% of a firm's total costs. In Eire, the Shannon Free Airport Scheme provides a rather different example of government aid.

139

Under this scheme, firms operating for export markets can import and export without customs restrictions, and also benefit from investment grants and tax exemptions on export profits. Such measures have obviously played a major rôle in the rapid development of this area of South West Eire in recent years.

Aid at the local level is more organisational than financial. Local help, with regard to matters such as housing requirements and planning permission, can be a real factor in the choice between alternative locations. In addition many local authorities band together to sponsor regional scale industrial development associations, each seeking to lure the limited supply of mobile industry to its own constituent authorities through a combination of publicity campaigns, industrial promotion and political pressure. Some development associations, such as those for North East and North West England have had considerable success, despite the inherent difficulties of selling their regions. An official of the North West Industrial Development Association summed up the problem and the rôle of the association as follows:

'To sell a region is a very difficult task. The main functions of an association like the North West Industrial Development Association in the field of industrial development are to smooth the path of expanding firms by having the right information available, and the right contracts, to advise on locations where the firms have not already made up their minds and to emphasise the advantages of the region to those people from outside whose impressions of Lancashire are still dominated by Coronation Street and the paintings of L. S. Lowry.'[21]

Environmental factors. If economic criteria suggest a limited number of satisfactory locations, environmental factors may come into play in deciding the final choice. The factors considered may be simply the climate and landscape or perhaps the wider concept of the total environment. Climate and landscape appear to be of growing importance as location determinants. This is particularly true for the new lighter industries—such as computers, electronics and research establishments—which are less constrained by raw materials and transport factors. Such industries are prospering in the Californian sun; in Britain, locations in the South West, South Hampshire and perhaps the periphery of the Lake District may be equally attractive.

But climate and landscape are only part of the total environment which help to determine the 'quality of life'. Other major determinants include the quality of the social infrastructure—housing, schools, roads and town centres—and also various social and psychological factors. The latter have been entertainingly discussed by Eversley,[22] who suggests that businessmen prefer the 'good life' of the South, with its good schools, clubs, shops, theatres and common accent, fearing that many of these social attributes may not exist in other areas. As the divorce between business ownership and management grows, and the maximisation of profits perhaps diminishes in importance in management priorities it would appear likely that these environmental factors will become of increasing importance.

Finally, it should be noted that many of the locational determinants discussed here depend on 'agglomeration economies' derived not from a specific geographical position but from the stimulus given by a concentration of firms. Advantages of such a concentration might include the provision of a skilled labour pool, the greater availability of local ancillary industry and improved social infrastructure—such as educational and entertainment facilities.

EMPIRICAL STUDIES

The location factors outlined are those commonly listed in surveys of mobile firms. For example, in a survey by Cameron and Reid,[23] 18 firms, which considered a Scottish location but then decided to locate elsewhere, were given a list of location factors and asked to rank them in order of importance and to compare them with the facilities of their chosen site. The results in Table 6.1 clearly emphasise the factors already discussed.

Of course, the relative importance of location factors varies from industry to industry and firm to firm and there have been numerous specific studies. Cameron and Clark[24] have attempted a classification of industry and location factors into a limited number of categories. From a sample survey of mobile firms, they identified several location types varying from small market

Table 6.1. *Location Factors: An Empirical Study*—factors effecting the rejection of Scotland as a production location by 18 firms. The factors are ranked in order of importance to the industrialists and are compared with the facilities at the chosen site.

Main location category	Location factor	Ranking	Compared with selected site			$\dfrac{(A+B)}{(B+C)}$
			Better A	Same B	Worse C	
Labour	1 Supply of trained labour	8	3	6	2	9/8
	2 Supply of trainable labour	1	2	9	2	11/11
	3 Low labour rates	—	1	6	4	7/10
	4 High productivity of local labour	16	2	5	4	7/9
	5 Good local management relations	5	1	3	7	4/11
Geographical location	6 Access to main markets	2	2	—	14	2/14
	7 Access to main suppliers	12	—	2	15	2/17
	8 Access to linked producers	8	—	3	11	3/14
Factory/Site	9 Ready built factories	5	—	2	6	2/8
	10 Factory rents	8	2	5	1	7/6
	11 Fully serviced site	5	1	4	2	5/6
Local	12 Transport facilities for goods	4	—	5	8	5/13
Services	13 Transport facilities for personnel	12	1	7	4	8/11
	14 Local technical education facilities	12	2	6	1	8/7
Environment	15 Attractiveness of local environment for transferred key workers and executives	8	2	2	5	4/7
Agency	16 Local authority co-operation	2	1	9	—	10/9
co-operation	17 Local agency co-operation	12	1	9	—	10/9

NB: Government inducements ignored as they are generally in a standard form in each development area.

SOURCE: Adapted from Cameron, G. C., and Reid, G. L. *Scottish Economic Planning and the Attraction of Industry*, University of Glasgow Social and Economic Studies, Occ. Paper number 6, Oliver and Boyd, Edinburgh (1966), pages 15–17.

oriented firms, often retail or wholesale concerns, which were mainly attracted by ready-built factories and access to the parent concern, to companies establishing divisions or large branches, which were more concerned with labour, transport and government aid factors.

LOCATION FACTORS IN THE FUTURE

As with most things, location factors change over time. The growth of light industry may result in a decline in the importance of proximity to markets and supplies. Similarly, improvements in transport and communications are also likely to make movement over larger distances more acceptable, with the emphasis changing from 'how far' to 'how long'. The capital intensive nature of new industry may also diminish the power of attraction of the labour factor. On the other hand, with increased automation and rationalisation and more space intensive processes, sites and premises are likely to become of increasing importance. Further, for the new quaternary industry and office employment freed by new developments in telecommunications and data transmission, the environmental advantages of new locations may outweigh the environmental consequences of congested conurbations. Finally, as noted in Chapter 5, the changing control of industry and the growing presence of large multi-nationals adds a further dimension to the analysis.

4 Summary

This analysis of industrial location factors in theory and practice illustrates the divergence between the two approaches but also isolates certain factors of fundamental importance. The key elements in location theory—transport, labour, agglomeration and market factors—are all seen to be of importance in practice, setting the basic parameters to any location decision. But practice suggests that there are also behavioural and institutional factors, difficult to quantify in a simple model, which may also influence location decisions within the framework provided by the other factors. Hamilton combines these various influences in diagrammatic form, as illustrated in Figure 6.4

All this is of considerable importance to the regional planner. It provides him with a valuable insight into the economic structure of regions. It also provides him with basic information for future planning, and a starting point for the identification of suitable industrial locations and the formulation of inducements to attract firms to them. Thus, the industrial revitalisation of an area may require a restructuring of certain factors—an improvement of communications, labour retraining, improved sites and financial aid to new industry—but also some interference in more

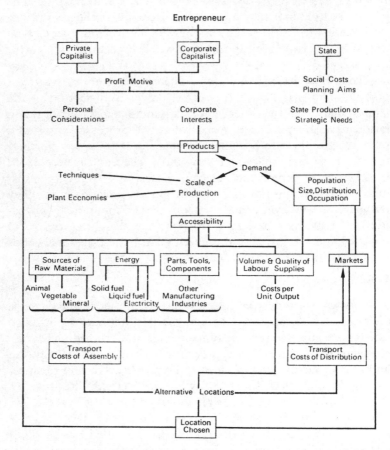

Fig. 6.4   A basic model of the factors influencing industrial location decisions

SOURCE   F. E. I. Hamilton, 'Models of industrial location' in R. J. Chorley and P. Haggett (eds.), *Models in Geography*. Methuen (1968).

behavioural type factors. As such, attempts to improve the 'image' of an area through improvement to both the physical and social environment, via campaigns like the North West's 'Operation Springclean', may be of considerable importance.

Overall however, the study of industrial location is an inexact science and it would not be surprising if most firms did not consider, specifically, all relevant factors. The Hunt Committee came to a similar conclusion:

'We have also, in the course of our enquiries, talked with a large number of industrialists in large, medium and small firms throughout the country and we are concerned that the quality of many firms' investment decisions is not as sophisticated and thorough as would be desirable. This reflects a number of factors—notably the fact that major investment decisions are taken relatively rarely by a large number of firms, so that they lack experience and expertise; and the speed with which decisions sometimes have to be taken.'[25]

It may also reflect that the costs and benefits of choosing one site rather than another may be minimal in terms of percentage profit.

But industrial location theory, even when modified by empirical evidence, is still essentially a theory of the location of the firm. It cannot properly explain the spatial structure of regions, even though it does isolate the major industrial factor. We now need to turn to more general spatial theories.

References

1 Smith, D. M., A Theoretical Framework for Geographical Studies of Industrial Location, *Economic Geography*, **42,** 2 (1966); see also: Smith, D. M., *Industrial Location,* Wiley (1971).
2 Weber, A., *Alfred Weber's Theory of the Location of Industries,* translated by Friedrich, C. J., from *Über den Standort der Industrien* (1909), Chicago (1929).
3 Hamilton, F. E. I., *Models of Industrial Location,* in Chorley, R. J., and Haggett, P., *Socio-Economic Models in Geography,* page 373, Methuen (1968).

4 Hoover, E. M., *The Location of Economic Activity,* McGraw-Hill, New York (1948).
5 Lösch, A., *The Economics of Location;* translated by Woglom, W. H., from *Die räumliche Ordnung der Wirtschaft* (1940), Yale (1954).
6 Richardson, H. W., *Regional Economics,* Weidenfeld and Nicolson, Part A (1969).
7 Harris, C. D., The Market as a Factor in the localisation of Industry in the U.S., *Annals of Association of American Geographers,* **44** (1954).
8 Isard, W., *Location and Space Economy,* Wiley (1956).
9 Greenhut, M. L., *Plant Location in Theory and Practice,* University of North Carolina Press (1956).
10 Hotelling, H., Stability in Competition, *Economic Journal,* **39**, pages 41–57 (1929).
11 Greenhut, M. L., *op cit.*
12 Isard, W., Game Theory, Location Theory and Industrial Agglomeration, *Papers and Proceedings of the Regional Science Association,* pages 1–11, **18** (1967).
13 See: Galbraith, J. K., *The New Industrial State,* London, Pelican (1969).
14 March, J. G., and Simon, M. A., *Organisations,* pages 140–1, NY, (1958).
15 Pred, A., *Behaviour and Location: Foundations for a Geographic and Dynamic Location Theory,* Part 1, Lund Series in Geography, Series B, **27** (1967).
16 Clark, C., *Population Growth and Land Use,* pages 281–2, Macmillan (1967).
17 See: Cameron, G. C., and Clark, B. D., *Industrial Movement and the Regional Problem,* Univ. of Glasgow Social and Economic Studies, Occ. Paper 5, Oliver and Boyd, Edinburgh (1966);
Luttrell, W. F., *Factory Location and Industrial Movement,* 2 vols., NIESR, London (1962);
McGovern, P. D., Industrial dispersal, *Planning* **31**, No. 485 (1965);
Townroe, P. M., Locational Choice and the Individual Firm, *Regional Studies,* pages 15–24, **3**, 1 (1969);
Townroe, P. M., *Industrial Location Decisions: A Study in Management Behaviour,* Centre for Urban and Regional Studies (University of Birmingham), Occ. Paper 15 (1971).
18 *Ibid.*

146

19 Scottish Council, *Report on the Scottish Economy,* pages 72–5, (1962);
   See also: Luttrell, *op cit*
20 Wilson, T., Finance for Regional Industrial Development, *Three Banks Review,* September 1967.
21 Nuttall, T., The Work of an Industrial Development Association, *Regional Planning Seminar: Paper 5,* Dept. of Town Planning, Lanchester Polytechnic (1971).
22 Eversley, D. E. C., Social and Psychological Factors in the Determination of Industrial Location, *Papers on Regional Development* (supplement to the *Journal of Industrial Economics*), page 105 (1965).
23 Cameron, G. C., and Reid, G. L., *Scottish Economic Planning and the Attraction of Industry,* University of Glasgow Social and Economic Studies, Occ. Paper 6, Oliver and Boyd, Edinburgh (1966).
24 Cameron, G. C., and Clark, B. D., *op cit.*
25 *Report of the Committee on the Intermediate Areas* (The Hunt Report), Cmnd. 3998, paragraph 358, London, HMSO (1969).

7 The spatial structure of regions

The spatial structure of most regions can theoretically be sub-divided into three basic elements:

a a backcloth of service or tertiary industry locations, including administration, finance, retail and wholesale trades and other similar services, which tend to group into systems of central places uniformly distributed over the landscape giving access to the largest market population;

b a scattering of locations with specialised industry such as manu-facturing, mining and recreation, which tend to group into clusters or agglomerations according to the localisation of physical resources such as coal, and physical features such as river valleys and beaches;

c a pattern of transport links, for example roads and railways, which may give rise to a linear pattern of settlement.

These basic elements, *a* and *b* in particular, have been investi-gated within a number of conceptual frameworks, but as yet no one framework has satisfactorily taken into account all three elements. However, the various frameworks or models have one thing in common in that they all assume a measurable degree of order in spatial behaviour—although in certain cases possible chance factors seem to have played some part in deciding specific locations within the regional framework (for example, William Morris (Lord Nuffield) and the development of the motor industry at Cowley, Oxford). Garner[1] believes the assumption of order rests on the following six premises, which form the basis of most models of regional spatial structure:

a the spatial distribution of human activity rests on ordered adjustment to the factor of distance, which may be measured using linear or non-linear criteria

b location decisions are taken in general so as to minimise the frictional effects of distance, this concept is generally known as 'the principle of least effort'

c all locations are endowed with a degree of accessibility but some locations are more accessible than others

d there is a tendency for human activities to agglomerate to take advantage of scale economies, that is—advantages of specialisation made possible by concentration at common locations

e the organisation of human activity is essentially hierarchical in character, the hierarchy resulting from the interrelationship between agglomeration and accessibility

f human occupance is focal in character.

Of all the models of spatial structure, *central place theory* is probably the most researched and well known. The theory seeks to relate central places to their hinterlands and defines a central place as a settlement providing services for the population of its hinterland. However, although of considerable importance in an explanation of the size and spacing of settlements within a region, it should be noted at the outset that the theory is only concerned with the intensity and location of service industry—only one of the basic elements—and as such can only provide a *partial* explanation of regional structure.

1 Central place theory

The notion of central place theory is linked with the name of Walter Christaller and his pioneering work on *The Central Places of Southern Germany*.[2] However, several of the concepts of the theory were anticipated by others such as Dickinson,[3] and there have been numerous developments since, in particular by Lösch,[4] Berry and Garrison.[5] From the voluminous literature on the subject, certain basic concepts can be abstracted.

Service activities can be classified in a variety of different ways. A recent EFTA study[6] classifies them into four homogeneous trade groups on the basis of functional qualities:

a repair work and other services carried out directly on physical objects

b distribution and transport of goods

c processing and distribution of information including organisation, administration and education

d attendance to various personal and collective needs, such as security and health.

Within these groups activities may vary greatly in scale. Thus postal services may vary from a rural post box to a General Post Office, retail trades may vary from a small corner shop to a large departmental store. In other words, there is a *hierarchy* of service activities, ranging from 'low order' services found in every centre—city, town or village—to 'high order' services found only in the major centres. Thus major towns and cities are likely to have most services, with smaller towns and villages having a more limited number. Each service activity has a threshold population and market range.

The *threshold population* is the minimum population necessary to support the service activity. It may be as low as 250 for a corner shop or as high as 150 000 for a theatre. If the population falls below the threshold level, the activity will run at a loss and will face closure in the long run. If the population increases above the minimum, the activity will increase its profits, which may also lead to increased competition through increased provision of service activities. The frequency of use of the service is of course a vital influence on the threshold population. A theatre needing 500 visitors per night will need a threshold population of approximately 150 000 if the average number of visits per head of population is only one per year. But if the average number of visits is three per year the theatre could exist on a threshold population of only 50 000.

The *market range* of a service activity is that distance which people are willing to travel to reach the service. It is the outer limit of the market area for the service activity beyond which people will look to another centre. For example, people may be willing to travel to the nearest large town for jewellery and good clothing but only to the local corner shop for sweets and tobacco. The market range may be a simple function of linear distance but will more likely be influenced by time and cost factors. Nor is it a constant factor for a particular service activity, for range may vary between centres according to such factors as the size and importance of the centre and the income level of the hinterland. Figure 7.1 summarises the relationship between threshold and range for three levels of centre.

The Lösch analysis of Chapter 6 is also relevant to the demand

Fig. 7.1   Service activities: hierarchy, threshold and range

SOURCE Adapted from B. J. L. Berry, *Geography of Market Centres and Retail Distribution*, page 28. Prentice-Hall Inc. (1967). (Reproduced by permission of Prentice-Hall, Inc., Englewood Cliffs.)

situation for any service activity. Lösch's demand cone, in his example for a farmer selling beer, produces a circular market area for a good or service with market demand greatest at the centre and tailing off to the periphery—the market range.

SPATIAL COMPETITION BETWEEN PROVIDERS OF AN INDIVIDUAL SERVICE

The various service activities are distributed over the landscape and to explain this distribution, central place theory makes the usual simplifying assumptions. The landscape is assumed to be an even plain with an even distribution of natural resources and an even spread of population—invariably assumed to be farmers! In this landscape, the individual farmer retailing beer or his wife taking in laundry or running a small store may service a circular market area as illustrated in Figure 7.2*a*. Other farmers are willing to travel up to a distance *a* to purchase from the farmer. But beyond *a*, the benefits of purchase are out-weighed by the travel costs involved. In time, if retailing is profitable, other enterprising farmers may develop their own circular market areas, as in Figure 7.2*b* and spatial competition will develop between providers of the service activity. But at this stage not all the market area is being served.

If it is assumed that with improved transport and communications, consumers are willing to travel further, and that with improved production methods, producers can lower their prices, market areas will expand, with radius *b* as in Figure 7.2*c*, to cover most of the landscape. But although the market areas are now touching, certain consumers are still left out. Figure 7.2*d* illustrates the next stage where the market areas with radius *c* overlap. The white area is that in which consumers make exclusive use of one centre, but in the shaded areas consumers may actually use more than one centre. However, if those in the shaded areas are assumed to be rational beings seeking to minimise transport costs they will choose the nearest centre. This results in a division of the shaded area and the development of hexagonal market areas (Figure 7.2*e*) around a system of central places. This hexagonal packing of trade areas, each tangential to the other, is mathematically the most efficient system.

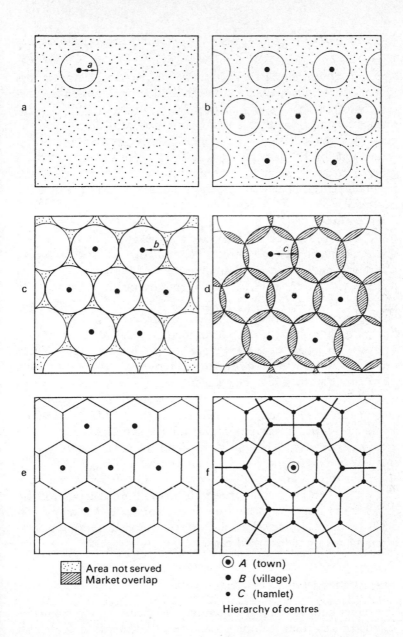

Area not served	⊙	A	(town)
Market overlap	•	B	(village)
	•	C	(hamlet)
	Hierarchy of centres		

Fig. 7.2 *Evolution of hierarchy of central places*

With the consideration of more than one service activity the situation can develop in several ways. The original central places may attract additional services such as doctors and banks, with threshold populations and market areas similar to the original service activity. Smaller central places may also develop at the points where the hexagonal service areas meet, perhaps providing more 'low order' service activities. As these service activities require smaller threshold populations and market areas, the resultant central places will be more numerous than the original centres.

In addition, certain of the original central places may attract more 'high order' service activities such as a cinema or a supermarket, requiring a larger threshold population and market range. There will only be a limited number of these higher order central places. Already three levels in a hierarchy of central places are apparent, with a 'nesting' pattern of lower order trade areas within the trade areas of higher order centres. Figure 7.2f illustrates this hierarchy. A centres might possess service activities 1 to n, with 1 being the local store and n a large supermarket. B centres would possess a more limited range of activities, perhaps from 1 to $(n - 10)$, while the smaller C centres would only possess a small number of service activities, perhaps from 1 to $(n-20)$.

In his study of Southern Germany, Christaller identified seven levels of central place ranging from the small hamlet to the metropolitan city. The initial distance of 7 km between the smallest centres is based on the assumption that half that distance, approximately 4 km, roughly represents the distance one man can walk in an hour and appears to be the normal range for the smallest centre. Table 7.1 outlines the Christaller hierarchy and offers a comparative classification of English central places, based mainly on the work of Smailes.

ALTERNATIVE FORMS OF HIERARCHY

Christaller believed that the hierarchy of central places could be organised according to one or other of the following principles (see Figure 7.3).

154

a The marketing or supply principle gives maximum choice of central places to individual sub-centres. In this hierarchy, the central place has the allegiance of one third of each of six sub-centres plus the original centre, giving a total equivalent of three dominated centres. Christaller termed this three the *k*-value, which is the total number of settlements of a certain order served by a central place of the next higher order.

General Hierarchy	Christaller Hierarchy					English Equivalent
	Central Place	Towns		Hinterland		
		Distance Apart (km)	Popn. (000's)	Size (km²)	Popn. (000's)	
1st (lowest)						Roadside hamlet
2nd	Marktort	7	0·8	45	2·7	Village
	Amtsort	12	1·5	135	8·1	
3rd	Kreisstadt	21	3·5	400	24·0	Sub-town
	Bezirkstadt	36	9·0	1200	75·0	
4th	Gaustadt	62	27·0	3600	225·0	Town
5th	Provinz-haupstadt	108	90·0	10 800	675·0	Major Town City
6th	Landstadt	186	300·0	32 400	2 025·0	Major City
7th	Reichstadt					World City

Table 7.1. *Christaller's hierarchy*

b The transporting principle leads to a hierarchy which minimises the distance between the sub-centres and the main centre, with as many important places as possible lying on one traffic route between main centres. As the sub-centres lie along the routes between main centres they have only dual loyalty. Thus, under the transporting principle the *k*-value is four.

(a) 'marketing' principle
(k = 3 hierarchy)

(b) 'transporting' principle
(k = 4 hierarchy)

(c) 'administrative principle
(k = 7 hierarchy)

● Village

• Hamlet

0 2 4 6 8 Miles

Fig. 7.3   Alternative hierarchies

c The administrative principle requires that each centre has complete control of the six surrounding sub-centres with no divided allegiances. In this case the *k*-value is seven.

Obviously, when $k = 3$ or 4, there are the problems of divided allegiance of sub-centres. Christaller recognised this and suggested that in practice 'nesting' of centres would occur with, for example when $k = 3$, one centre gaining complete allegiance of two sub-centres, but losing all allegiance to the remainder. According to Christaller, once the *k*-value has been determined it remains fixed throughout the hierarchy. Under the marketing principle, the progression of central places runs 1, 2, 6, 18, 54 . . . , and the progression of market areas at each level is 1, 3, 9, 27, 81 . . .

MODIFICATION TO THE CHRISTALLER HIERARCHY

Lösch attempted to incorporate more realism and flexibility into Christaller's rigid hierarchy. He did not accept that there was a *discontinuous* hierarchy of settlements with a rigid *k* system determining the number of settlements at each level. Instead he believed that settlements were of a *continuous* distribution, with for example populations ranging from 100 in the smallest hamlet to over 10 000 000 in the largest metropolitan complex. This dichotomy between the Lösch continuum and Christaller's rigid hierarchy of urban centres has led to much debate. Lösch believed that Christaller's hierarchial principles were merely special cases of a whole series of possible central place systems. He illustrated his theory by combining the various Christaller hierarchies producing an 'economic landscape' characterised by six densely developed 'city rich' sectors and six sparsely developed 'city poor' sectors radiating from a central metropolis. Thus, although both Lösch and Christaller agree on many basic principles of spatial structure, Christaller's approach is purely an explanation of the service element in spatial structure, whereas that of Lösch could be said to be more an explanation of the spatial distribution of market-oriented manufacturing industry.

But how valid and useful are these theoretical frameworks? We must now turn to an examination of empirical evidence for central place theory and an assessment of its relevance in regional planning.

2 The validity of central place theory

There has been a considerable amount of work in various countries in the search for empirical regularities to support the theoretical systems. The various studies can be classified into inter-urban and intra-urban. *Inter-urban studies* which will be briefly outlined, involve the classification of towns into a hierarchical framework. This may be on a national basis, such as the early pioneering work by Smailes[7] and its recent updating by Smith,[8] or on a regional basis, such as the studies of Brush and Bracey,[9] Carter,[10] and Berry and Garrison.[11] *Intra-urban studies* involve the classification of centres within an urban area into a hierarchical framework. The works of Carruthers,[12] Smailes and Hartley,[13] and Thorpe and Rhodes[14] provide examples of this scale of study. Admittedly, the distinction between the two approaches may not be all that clear when the urban areas considered are conurbations such as Greater London, Tyneside and Manchester.

To Smailes[15] goes the credit for the first hierarchical classification of central places on a national scale. His hierarchy for England and Wales was formulated on the basis of certain selected activities, which he considered to be the retail and service attributes of a 'fully-fledged' town. These activities were:

a banks
b branches of major chain stores (Woolworths)
c secondary schools
d hospitals
e cinemas
f weekly newspapers.

In order to qualify as a 'fully-fledged' town a centre had to possess all these functions, with the exception of hospitals and secondary schools which Smailes treated with some flexibility. Above this 'town' level, Smailes identified three higher levels of central place. At the top came 16 'major cities', with London as the world city and provincial centres such as Manchester and Glasgow. Next came 21 'cities' such as Carlisle and Exeter, and almost 100 'major towns' such as Barrow and Burnley. Below the 'town' level, itself with approximately 300 centres, were two further levels of 'sub-towns', lacking from two to four of the basic activities, and 'urban villages' possessing at the most two of the activities. The Smailes approach has been criticised on many counts, in particular for its interpretation of what constitutes a central function, and has been recently updated by Smith. Nevertheless, it does provide a hierarchical ordering of centres based on service activities—although it should be noted that the clustering of some of the major centres, such as Liverpool and Manchester or Leeds and Bradford, suggests evidence of some distortion of the regular hierarchy.

At the regional scale, Dickinson[16] in his early work in East Anglia, established a definite hierarchy of towns. Using bus route data and information obtained from auctioneers, he established a regular pattern of small market towns, such as Stowmarket and Debenham, approximately eight miles apart. On top of this basic tier, were two further levels—a top level of large centres such as Norwich, Cambridge and Ipswich and a lower level of smaller centres such as King's Lynn and Bury St Edmunds. In another regional example, Brush and Bracey[17] compared the central places of South West Wisconsin and South West England —two areas differing markedly in economy, history and population density. Different methods of identifying centrality were used. Brush in Wisconsin used the Smailes method of identifying centres on the basis of the possession of certain service activities, whereas Bracey ranked centres by assessing their hinterlands for four representative services (chemist, ordinary shopping facilities, local bank and cinema). Yet despite these differences in setting and method, both studies showed two distinct tiers of central places, with high order centres, such as Oxford, Reading, Banbury and Swindon, at approximately 21 miles apart, and lower order centres, such as Witney, Woodstock and Chipping Norton at 8–10 mile distances.

Such empirical evidence, plus other studies such as Carter's[18] study of the towns of Wales, lends support to the existence of central place hierarchies. They may vary from the rigid theoretical system, but they appear to exist nonetheless.

SPATIAL HIERARCHIES AND THE RANK SIZE RULE

Central Place Theory of course considers not only the spacing of settlements but also their size. It has already been shown that there are many small centres with small market areas but only a limited number of large centres with large market areas. The vertical relationship between the number and population size of these settlements has been formalised as the *rank size rule*. This rule, which originated from the work of Auerbach and Singer,[19] but which has been most popularised by Zipf,[20] says that if urban settlements in an area are ranked in descending order of population size (from 1 to *n*), the population of the '*n*th' settlement will be 1/*n* the size of the largest settlement. That is:

$$P_n = \frac{P_1}{n^q}$$

where P_n = population of the *n*th settlement,
  P_1 = population of the largest settlement,
  n = settlement rank,
  q = an exponent which usually approximates to unity.

Although several theorists are sceptical of the rule, there has been a considerable body of empirical support.[21] However, there has been much disagreement as to whether the ranking of settlements forms a continuum or a tiered hierarchy, conforming more to the Christaller theory. The problem appears to be mainly one of scale. When all the centres of a country are considered, industrial centres are inevitably included and the rank-size relationship approximates to a continuum. However, with a more limited area, at the regional or sub-regional level, the ranking tends to be more tiered and discontinuous providing empirical support for the central place hierarchy. As an example, Batty[22] tested the distribution of zonal populations in three sub-regions (Central Lancashire, Notts–Derby and Bedfordshire) for rank-size regularity. Although the results are probably somewhat biassed by the arbitrary definition of population zones, they do provide strong evidence of rank-size regularity at the sub-regional scale and indicate a definite hierarchy of centres.

PROBLEMS OF CENTRAL PLACE THEORY

Yet in spite of the empirical evidence, central place theory, as a model of regional spatial structure, has been subject to numerous criticisms. In particular, many areas seem to contradict the basic hierarchial rules. This is partly because the theory relates only to the service element. But of course settlements may develop due to the localisation of natural resources—for example a tourist centre may develop in an area with a good coastline and fine climate, while a coalfield may give rise to a manufacturing centre. The Christaller model holds such factors constant assuming an even plain and a uniform distribution of natural resources. In rural areas where the conditions are comparable with this ideal Christaller landscape, as in many of the empirical studies, the theory may provide a good explanation of reality; but in other areas, such as industrial Northern England, resource localisation distorts the regular hierarchy. As such, central place theory cannot provide an all inclusive general theory and there is a need to introduce other theories to explain the agglomerations of many areas—although even in these areas the service hierarchy invariably provides the backcloth.

The theory also assumes a uniform distribution of population. But this is unlikely to occur in practice since the factors upon which population density depends, such as soil fertility and climate, vary markedly from place to place and thus distort the picture. Another implicit assumption is that consumers will act rationally and patronise the nearest centre for the relevant service activity, giving rise to mutually exclusive hexagonal hinterlands. Several factors, especially the impact of multi-purpose trips to a centre, may undermine this assumption leading to overlapping market areas.

Central place theory has also been criticised from time to time for its apparently static and descriptive approach. It identifies the relationship between centres and their hinterlands at one point in time but fails to take into account the evolutionary process of spatial structure. A central place system indeed is not fixed and is in a constant state of change. Thus an increase in the service activity of one centre, perhaps with the development of a new multiple store, will have an impact on the service activity of other competing centres. The theory does not provide a thorough dynamic explanation of these changes, although some authors believe it is possible to place a limited dynamic interpretation on the theory in the explanation of changes in relative location.

Other more detailed criticisms include the possible distortion of the hierarchy by the domination of large centres which may create a 'shadow effect' discouraging the growth of appropriately sized smaller settlements. An alternative distortion could be caused by the development of a dispersed city—a group of cities which although physically separated function together as one unit. Interdependence between them is reflected in patterns of retailing and functional specialisation. Burton[23] believes the Derby–Chesterfield–Nottingham area of the East Midlands may develop into, or already be, an example of such a city. With the development of private transport the area would develop into a cohesive unit, truncating the hierarchical system.

One final technical criticism of the theory is the problem of actually ranking central places. This involves the dual problem of the actual identification of central places (which may be confused by the problem of sprawl) and the choice of criteria to rank the centres. Christaller realised that population alone was an insufficient measure of centrality—a mining or manufacturing centre may have a large population but exercise few central functions. Therefore, in addition, he used an index based on the number of telephone installations. This, in brief, involved the subtracting from the actual number of telephones in a centre, the number that it should have in proportion to its population, according to the average of the area. More recent approaches to the measurement problem have used mainly retailing information including simple numerical counts of the number of retail shops in a centre; the identification of key facilities and the ranking of centres according to the number they possessed (such as the Haydock method);[24] and more sophisticated quantitative approaches (such as Davies's[25] 'functional index' based on location coefficients). Unfortunately, as a recent study by McEvoy[26] demonstrates, different ranking methods may result in different rankings of central places within a particular area.

3 Central place theory and regional planning

In the face of encouraging empirical studies and discouraging criticisms, does the theory have any relevance for regional

162

planning? It would seem to have two potential rôles—firstly as a framework for understanding the regional spatial structure and secondly as a model for future planning. There is little doubt that central place theory does provide a very valuable partial framework for the understanding of regional structure, but what of its rôle for future planning?

A basic argument supporting the use of central places in regional planning is that a hierarchical system of centres avoids duplication and waste. It is a relatively efficient way of administering and allocating resources within a region, facilitating the realisation of social benefits accruing from economies of scale. In addition, the network of interrelated centres means that the planning of any centre within an area must take into account the implications for other centres within the area (the lack of recognition of this principle has led to much wasteful duplication of shopping facilities in certain areas of the country). Hilhorst,[27] in an interesting approach at a synthesis of regional theory, also suggests that a region's economic shock resistance is much greater where the region's spatial structure is 'closely knit'. An area with such a structure is one in which the distribution of settlements approximates to the rank size rule. It is an area which has reached a stage in its development in which certain sub-systems focussing on subsidiary centres are clearly discernible and there is no undue reliance on one primate city.

Yet, although the basic principles have been used in various shopping studies (such as those for the North West and West Midlands) and may be implicit in several regional strategies, there has been only a limited number of comprehensive practical applications of the theory in regional planning. Of these, recent schemes in Holland, Ghana and Israel are of particular interest providing examples of application in both developed and developing countries. The Dutch Physical Plan,[28] to be discussed in more detail in Chapter 12, recognises a four-tier hierarchy of settlements ranging from the smallest unit of 5000 people to major cities with populations in excess of 250 000. Within this framework, probably the most renowned applications of central place theory was that carried out when the North East Polder was reclaimed from the Ijsselmeer and a two-level hierarchy of market centres was established around the centre of Lelystad.

The application of the theory in the regional planning of a developing country, Ghana, has been examined by Grove and Huszar.[29] Like many developing countries, Ghana has initiated comprehensive economic planning in an attempt to achieve 'take-off' economically. Such planning involves the location of vast investments; but some locations may involve a better use of resources than others. In an attempt to identify such locations, Grove and Huszar drew up a hierarchy of central places. The ranking or centrality of towns was defined as a function of the quality (variety and level) of the services offered, rather than of the quantity of services (such as the number of shops). Services were weighted, with for example a specialised hospital ranking three times more important than a health centre, and a total service weight was established for each centre. When these weights were plotted in the form of a frequency distribution a definite five-tier hierarchy of centres was evident. When the centres were plotted on a map according to grade, the first tier centres were approximately 50 miles apart with service areas of 25 miles' radius. However, the hierarchy revealed certain first-tier 'gaps' with minor settlements in their place. These settlements represented potential first-tier centres, and twelve of them were identified for future population increase and economic development. The development of such centres would fit into the hierarchy, avoiding the waste of developing competing first-tier centres.

The development of a three-tier hierarchy of central places around the centre of Qiryat-Gat in the Lakhish Plains of Israel,[30] represents another application of the theory in a developing country. Here the development of a settlement structure is basically starting from scratch, for this previously barren area, 40 miles South of Jerusalem, was only opened up in 1955 with the advent of irrigation.

4 Information flows and spatial structure

A more recent area of investigation into regional and national spatial structure, and one associated with the concept of central places, is that of information flows and the diffusion of innovations in space. Much of the work on information flows was pioneered by Hägerstrand,[31] whose work and that of other researchers indicates the spread of information in a hierarchical form following a limited number of channels downwards from high-ranking central places to low-ranking central places. This reflects the hierarchy of economic activities and organisations, with the head offices and centres of decision making located in the metropolitan centres with their decision trees spreading out spatially down the urban hierarchy.[32]

It is in the large urban centres, with their concentrations of the highest levels of decision making, that entrepreneurs can make essential face to face contacts and exchange information. Tornqvist[33] sought to quantify the opportunity for such contacts for major urban regions in Sweden, using the concept of contact potential. Through a study of largely tertiary employment job types, such as senior management, clerical, etc., he identified those occupations which required considerable personal contact outside the job base (office, factory). For each urban region, he calculated the contact potential by weighting the number of persons employed in contact intensive job functions within the region, by national daily average hours of contact for each job function, and by the length of time in a single working day it was possible to remain in the region after a return journey to another region. Fig. 7.4 shows that Stockholm has the highest contact potential, with a decline in potential with distance from the capital; but there are some other notable high values in the urban regions of Gothenburg and Malmo. There are thus considerable variations between urban regions in the possibility for access to specialised information.

Access to information is being increasingly seen by researchers as one of the principal determinants of regional economic growth and adaptation to change. Thus, a small firm in an isolated location may not pick up as many new ideas from the 'business grapevine' as a firm in a major metropolitan centre. The national trend towards the concentration of headquarter offices and high level administrative, research and development and support functions in and around capital cities, such as London, together with the steadily rising importance of 'knowledge and information' activities in all spheres of the economies of many countries, puts problem regions, such as the North of England, in a

Fig. 7.4   Contact potentials for major urban regions in Sweden, 1970.
(*Stockholm*= *100*)
SOURCE   Tornqvist (1973).

disadvantaged position as locations for advanced industries and for the exercise of high level and decision making activities in commerce and industry. To plug into the national communications network for innovations and information flow, a backward region may need a city high in the national urban hierarchy.[34]

So far this discussion has focused on the diffusion of entrepreneurial innovations down the urban hierarchy, but Pedersen[35] suggests a distinction between such entrepreneurial innovations (E) and household innovations (H). Whilst the flow of information between entrepreneurs may be particularly significant for the economic development of a region, the flow of information down to individual households may be of considerable significance in generating an awareness of a region's problems and opportunities. A newspaper may be particularly important here, as evidenced by the impact of the *West Highland Free Press*, and its crusading reporting of oil developments, in the isolated and previously information-poor environment of the Western Highlands and Islands of Scotland.

4 Summary

Central place theory is probably the most researched and well known model of regional spatial structure, it is also the most criticised. It is a purely deductive theory of a highly simplified and abstract nature developed on the basis of very idealised assumptions. It relates only to the service element of regional structure, failing to explain distortions in that hierarchy caused by the location of primary and manufacturing industry which tends to group into clusters or agglomerations due to resource localisation. The theory is also essentially static, explaining the existence of regional spatial structure but failing to explain how that structure has evolved and how it might change in the future.

Yet to admit that the model has problems is not to discount it out of hand. Its value as an explanatory model of regional spatial structure is borne out by empirical studies, and even where other locational elements are dominant, the service hierarchy of central places invariably provides the backcloth—the theoretical norm from which deviations can be measured. Similarly, although its direct application in regional planning practice may be less

readily apparent, especially in developed areas with complex
settlement structures, it still serves a very useful rôle identifying
concepts of vital importance to the regional planner such as the
interdependence of city and region, a hierarchy of functions and
centres, and market range and threshold populations.

References

1 Garner, B. J., *Models of Urban Geography and Settlement Location,* in
   Chorley, R. J., and Haggett, P., *Socio-Economic Models in
   Geography,* pages 304–5 Methuen (1967).
2 Christaller, W., *Central Places in Southern Germany* (Trans. C. W.
   Baskin), Englewood Cliffs, New Jersey (1966).
3 Dickinson, R. E., The Metropolitan Cities of the United States,
   Geographical Reviews, 24 (1934).
4 Lösch, A., *The Economics of Location,* translated by Woglom,
   Yale (1954).
5 Berry, B. J. L., and Garrison, W., Recent developments of
   central place theory, *Papers and Proceedings of the Regional
   Science Association,* pages 107–20, 4 (1958);
   Berry, B. J. L., and Pred, A., Central place studies: a bibliography
   of theory and applications; *Regional Science Research Institute,
   Bibliography Series,* 1 (1961);
   Berry, B. J. L., *Geography of Market Centres and Retail
   Distribution,* Prentice-Hall (1967).
6 Allen, K. J., and Hermansen, T., *Regional Policy in EFTA,*
   page 147, EFTA Secretariat, Geneva (1968).
7 Smailes, A. E., The urban hierarchy in England and Wales,
   Geography, pages 41–51, 29 (1944).
8 Smith, R. D. P., The changing urban hierarchy, *Regional Studies,*
   pages 1–19, 2, 1 (1968).
9 Brush, J. E. and H. E. Bracey, Rural Service Centres in South
   Western Wisconsin and Southern England, *Geographical Review,*
   pages 550–69, 45 (1955).
10 Carter, H., *The Towns of Wales: A Study in Urban Geography,*
   Cardiff (1965).
11 Berry, B. J. L., and Garrison, W. L., The Functional Bases of
   the Central Place Hierarchy, *Economic Geography,* pages
   145–54, 34 (1958).
12 Carruthers, W. I., Service centres in Greater London, *Town
   Planning Review,* pages 5–31, 33 (1962).
13 Smailes, A. E., and Hartley, G., Shopping centres in the Greater

London area, *Institute of British Geographers, Transactions and Papers,* pages 201–13, **29** (1961).

14 Thorpe, D., and Rhodes, T. C., The shopping centres of the Tyneside urban region and large-scale grocery retailing, *Economic Geography,* pages 52–73, **42** (1966).

15 Smailes, A. E. (1944), *op cit.*

16 Dickinson, R. E., The distribution and functions of the smaller urban settlements of East Anglia, *Geography,* pages 19–31, **17** (1932).

17 Brush, J. E., and Bracey, H. E. *op cit*

18 Carter, H., *op cit*

19 Singer, H. W., The Courbe des Populations: À Parallel to Pareto's Law, *Economic Journal,* **46** (1936).

20 Zipf, G. K., *Human Behaviour and the Principle of Least Effort,* Addison-Wesley, Cambridge, Mass. (1949).

21 See: Haggett, P., *Locational analysis in human geography,* Arnold (1965).

22 Batty, M., *Spatial Theory and Information Systems,* W.P. 3/0, Urban Systems Research Unit, University of Reading, pages 31–3 (1970).

23 Burton, I., A restatement of the dispersed city hypothesis, *Annals of the Association of American Geographers,* **53,** 3 (1963).

24 Univ. of Manchester, *Regional Shopping Centres: A Planning Report on North West England, Parts 1 and 2,* Department of Planning, (1965).

25 Davies, W. K. D., Centrality and the Central Place Hierarchy, *Urban Studies,* **4,** 1 (1967).

26 McEvoy, D., Alternative methods of ranking shopping centres, *Tijdschrift voor Economische en Sociale Geografie* (1968).

27 Hilhorst, J. G. M., *Spatial Structure and Decision Making,* in Hilhorst, J. G. M. and D. M. Dunham, *Issues in Regional Planning,* Institute of Social Studies (The Hague), page 71, Mouton (1971).

28 *Second Report on Physical Planning in the Netherlands,* Government Printing Office of the Netherlands, The Hague (1966).

29 Grove, D., and Huszar, L., The Application of Central Place Theory in the Regional Planning of a Developing Country, *Town and Country Planning School,* Exeter (1964).

30 *Operation Lakhish: Stage 2,* a publication of the United Israel Appeal;
Jackson, G., Regional Policy and Planning in Israel, *Oxford Polytechnic O.P.* (1970).

31 Hägerstrand, T., *Innovation Diffusion as a Spatial Process*, Chicago U.P. (1967).
32 EFTA, *National Settlement Strategies: A Framework for Regional Development*, EFTA Secretariat (1973).
33 Tornqvist, G., *Contact Requirements and Travel Facilities: Contact Models of Sweden and Regional Development Alternatives*, Lund Studies in Geography, Series B, **38** (1973).
34 See NRST, *Strategic Plan for the Northern Region*, HMSO (1977).
35 Pederson, P. O., Innovation Diffusion within and between National Urban Systems, *Geographical Analysis*, **2**, pp. 203–54 (1970).

8 Growth pole theory

Many of the criticisms levelled at central place theory as a model of regional spatial structure can be answered by the theory of growth poles. Although the concept can be traced back to the agglomeration factors of early location theories, outlined in Chapter 6, its modern development owes much to French economists, especially Perroux, who believed that the basic fact of spatial, as well as industrial development is that 'growth does not appear everywhere and all at once; it appears in points or development poles, with variable intensities; it spreads along diverse channels and with varying terminal effects to the whole of the economy'.[1] More specifically, Boudeville defines a regional growth pole as a 'set of expanding industries located in an urban area and inducing further development of economic activity throughout its zone of influence'.[2] Owing to its versatility, the theory has been adapted not only for understanding regional structure, but also as a method for predicting changes in that structure and prescribing solutions to certain regional problems. It has enjoyed great popularity in recent years becoming 'an idea in good currency', and if only for this reason merits further investigation.

Unfortunately though, application tends to have progressed further than the theoretical underpinnings. Because of some minor inconsistencies in Perroux's original works, there has been much confusion in subsequent literature. This can be clearly seen in the vast confusion of terminology with not only growth poles and growth points, but also growth centres, development poles, development axes, growth zones and growth areas. Indeed there seems to be as many definitions as authors writing about them. Darwent, who has written the most recent review of the growth pole concept states that 'it has become associated with an enormous variety of indistinct and ill-defined concepts and notions.'[3] Hansen believes that the whole of 'growth pole' literature is badly in need of a thorough semantic reworking. It is thus necessary to identify the basic concepts of this much used theory, first in outline and then in more detail.

1 Basic concepts of growth pole theory

The basic concepts and subsequent refinements and developments are to be found in the 'core' literature[4] of Perroux, Boudeville, Hansen, Hermansen, Hirschman and Myrdal. There is a definite French domination of this field of regional theory providing an interesting complement to the earlier German work on central place theory. In contrast to the deductive nature of the latter, the theory of growth poles is inductively derived from observations of the process of economic development.

Perroux's original work focusses on the development of growth poles in *economic space*. This was a deliberate attempt to break away from the limiting geographical dimensions adopted by Christaller and Lösch. He developed a typology of economic spaces, the most important being that of economic space as a field of forces, from which he derived the notion of a pole as a vector of economic forces ' . . . as a field of forces, economic space consists of centres (or poles or foci) from which centrifugal forces emanate and to which centripetal forces are attracted'. Perroux did acknowledge that growth poles would also exist in geographical space, but it was Boudeville who extended the original theory to include more comprehensively the geographical dimension. To keep the distinctions clear and in perspective, the term *growth pole* can be taken to refer to the original concept of Perroux without any specific geographical dimension, while the term *growth centre* or *growth point* refers to a spatial location.*

* Some writers see a scale distinction between growth poles and growth centres, with growth poles relating to the national scale and growth centres to the regional scale. See: Kucklinski, A. R., Regional Development, Regional Policies and Regional Planning, *Regional studies*, 4, 3 (1970).

From the various writings on growth poles (*pôle de crois-sance*) and growth centres, the following basic economic con-cepts and their geographical developments can be identified:

a The concept of leading industries (*industrie motrice*) and propul-sive firms, states that at the centre of growth poles are large propulsive firms belonging to leading industries which dominate other economic units. There may be just one single dominant propulsive firm or a core of them forming an industrial complex.

The original geographical location of such industries in certain focal points in a region may be due to several factors—the localisation of natural resources (water/shelter/fuel), the localisa-tion of more man-made advantages (communications or existing service-based central places with advantages of infrastructure and labour supply), or possibly just chance. In reality, the growth points are often grafted on to the existing framework of central places.

b The concept of polarisation states that the rapid growth of the leading industries ('propulsive growth') induces the polarisation of other economic units into the pole of growth. Implicit in this process of polarisation are the various agglomeration economies (internal and external economies of scale.)

This economic polarisation will inevitably lead to geographical polarisation with the flow of resources to and the concentration of economic activity at a limited number of centres within a region. Even when the original *raison d'être* of such locations disappears, they will often continue to prosper due to the presence of the agglomeration economies.

c The concept of spread effects states that in time the dynamic pro-pulsive qualities of the growth pole radiate outwards into the surrounding space. These 'trickling down' or 'spread' effects are particularly attractive to the regional planner and have con-tributed much to the recent popularity of the theory as a policy tool.

However, although these basic concepts might intuitively pro-vide a reasonable and· dynamic explanation of the industrial clusters or agglomerations in regional spatial structure, some regional theorists have cast doubt on their validity. Do growth poles grow indefinitely? What about the diseconomies of scale? Do the spread effects ever materialise? Before any attempt is made to draw out the relevance of growth pole theory for regional planning, it is first necessary to examine each of the basic concepts of the theory in rather more detail.

LEADING INDUSTRIES AND PROPULSIVE FIRMS

These concepts can be clarified by outlining their major characteristics. A leading industry has the following characteristics:

a it is a relatively new and 'dynamic' industry with an advanced level of technology injecting an atmosphere of 'growthmindedness' into a region;

b it has a high income elasticity of demand for its products which are usually sold to national markets;

c it has strong inter-industry linkages with other sectors, (these linkages may be 'forward' linkages where an industry has a high ratio of intermediary industry sales to total sales, or 'backward' linkages, where an industry has a high ratio of intermediary inputs from other industries to total inputs).

Similarly, a propulsive firm has the following characteristics:

a it is relatively large;

b it generates significant growth impulses into its environment;

c it has a high ability to innovate;

d it belongs to a fast growing industry.

By analysing some of these characteristics it is possible to identify leading industries and propulsive firms in the UK context. For example, a very approximate guide to leading industries can be found by identifying the income elasticity of demand and the inter-industry linkages of the main Standard Industrial Classification categories. The use of such broad categories does of course mask variations within subdivisions of the broad classification, but nevertheless provides a rough guideline. Income elasticity of demand measures the change in demand for a good resulting from a change in income. In general, industries with elasticities less than unity will be expanding less rapidly than the norm, whereas industries with elasticities greater than unity will be expanding faster than the norm. By comparing increases in total sales for the industrial groups with the increases in national income, elasticities can be deduced. Similarly, by analysing inter-industry input-output tables, the forward and backward linkages of each industrial group can be deduced. On the basis of such analysis, and applying the subjective criteria of 'newness', the following can be identified as leading manufacturing industries in Britain: chemicals (SIC V), electrical engineering (SIC IX), metal goods (SIC XII), furniture (SIC XVII) and other manufacturing industries (SIC XIX).

However, although most growth poles involve leading industries, not all leading industries necessarily generate growth poles. A much quoted example is the case of Lacq in South West France where it was anticipated that the discovery of large natural gas deposits would provide the growth pole focus for an industrial revitalisation of the whole of the South West Region. In reality, because of the presence of vastly greater external economies elsewhere, the Lacq complex has been essentially a local phenomenon, doing little to help the wider region and having little effect on the existing spatial structure. A further problem of leading industries is the inherent danger in relying on one particular industry. Many of the problem areas of today are the over-specialised growth points of yesterday. The development of an industrial complex with a variety of smaller firms is one solution to this problem.

POLARISATION EFFECTS AND AGGLOMERATION ECONOMIES

Once localised, the propulsive firm or complex of propulsive firms within the leading industry tend to grow rapidly reaping the advantages of agglomeration economies and effecting the polarisation of other economic activities around the original location. Three types of agglomeration economies can be identified.

a Economies internal to the firm. These are the lower average production costs resulting from an increased rate of output. Such large-scale production allows technical economies, such as job specialisation and the use of 'flow-line' processes instead of 'batch' processes, and various management, marketing and financial economies.

b Economies external to the firm but internal to the industry. These are the reductions in cost per unit of output to the firm as the industry expands at a particular location. Such 'localisation economies'[5] arise from the close locational proximity of linked firms, and include the development of a large and skilled labour pool, the easy interchange of materials and products ('the road is the conveyor belt'), the possibility of firms existing to process waste materials, and the development of specialised services available to all firms, such as access to R and D facilities and repair services.

c Economies external to the industry but internal to the urban area. These are the downward shifts in the average costs of each firm as many industries grow in one place. Known as 'urbanisation economies',[6] they include the development of urban labour markets, access to a larger market and the provision of a wide range of services by both the private and public sector for both people and industry. Such services might for instance include the availability of improved transport, commercial and financial facilities, and the development of a wide range of social, cultural and leisure facilities—hospitals, schools, museums, theatres and cinemas. In effecting polarisation, a highly developed infrastructure providing facilities at the centre for the wider region may be as important as the presence of a complex of leading industries.

History provides us with numerous examples of polarisation due to agglomeration economies—for example, the localisation of the textile industry in North East Lancashire and the development of the associated textile machinery industry. It is also possible to identify relatively recent examples of the localisation of economic units about propulsive firms. After the First World War, large firms of two leading industries (vehicles and aerospace) located in the town of Coventry. Associated metal and engineering firms have developed about these propulsive firms resulting in the development of a strong growth pole where approximately 90% of manufacturing employment is in the engineering and metal manufacturing industries. The growth pole has become localised in geographical space so that Coventry can be identified as a growth centre. The development of this growth centre has resulted in considerable increases in Coventry's population. Two more recent examples of polarisation are the development of an incipient electronics industry complex around 80 or so firms in the central valley of Scotland, and the growth of a scientific R and D complex West of London.[7]

176

However, there may be limitations on polarisation. As already indicated, the leading industry itself may decline, as in North East Lancashire. In addition, at some stage in the development of the growth point, diseconomies of scale may begin to outweigh the agglomeration benefits. Some diseconomies such as the rising costs of public services, rising factor prices such as wages and site rents, and congestion costs, may directly affect industrial growth. Other more general social costs—noise and air pollution and longer journeys to work—may initially have a more limited effect, but in the long run may also limit polarisation.

An interesting and much discussed offshoot of this question of diseconomies is that of optimum town size. This involves an analysis of how the agglomeration economies (the benefits), and the diseconomies (the costs), vary with population size. The benefits to industry and people, such as the advantages of good communication, theatres and a technical college, are very difficult to measure but would probably follow a form similar to Figure 8.1a. Here small centres have few advantages, but these generally increase with size, although they will probably level off as diminishing returns set in. However, whether they will actually fall or not is debatable. The other side of the equation, the cost side, is a little more manageable although still rather vague. Considering the costs involved, that is the specific costs such as infrastructure—costs of sewerage, roads and hospitals, plus the general social costs, it would seem that the cost curve is of a flat-bottomed U-shape (see Figure 8.1b). Average costs are very high for small centres, but then fall quite rapidly levelling off over a wide range of population, before rising again. Figure 8.1c shows the net (benefit-cost) to population and industry as a whole over the population range. Such crude figures are of course largely conceptual and in practice would differ widely between countries and regions within countries. However, they do suggest that 'optimum' town size may vary over a wide range.

Finally, another possible limitation on polarisation has been raised by Lasuen.[8] He questions whether the polarisation concept is as strong today as it used to be. Comparing the modern Litton Corporation of the USA with the Krupp Company of Germany, he argues that firms are becoming more multi-product, multi-plant and spread-oriented with the external economies of con-

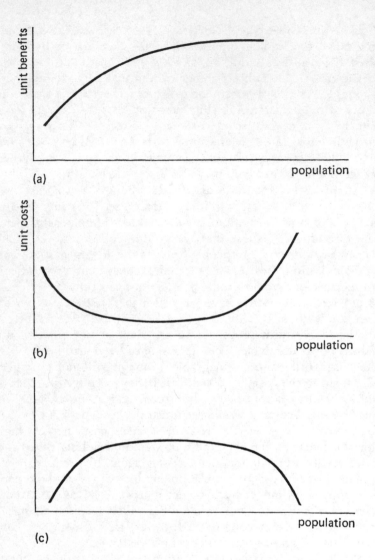

Fig. 8.1 The general relationships between agglomeration costs, benefits and population size

a *Gross benefits of agglomeration*
b *Gross costs of agglomeration*
c *Net (benefits—costs)*

centration becoming of decreasing importance. Such an argument, if valid, does not reduce the value of growth pole theory as an explanation of existing regional structure, but it may have some relevance to future structures.

SPREAD EFFECTS

This is the most difficult aspect of the theory to examine, and although there has been some general discussion of the question of whether growth will diffuse outwards from a growth pole there is little empirical evidence that this does in fact take place. Myrdal and Hirschman[9] have talked of the 'spread' or 'trickling down' effects of growth poles in contrast with the 'backwash' or 'polarisation' effects. However, as noted in the discussion of macro 'cumulative-causation' growth theory in Chapter 5, there is scope for considerable doubt over the relative strength of spread in comparison with backwash.

One of the few empirical studies which actually tries to assess the spread effects is that by Vida Nichols[10] who seeks to measure the spread effects from the growth pole of Atlanta into the rest of the relatively depressed state of Georgia, USA. She observed that the change in median income distribution over a 10-year period (1950–60) included a region-wide increase associated with a general shift in employment, but also a residual element which was highest in the suburban ring around Atlanta and in other large towns in the area. She concluded that the residual element to some extent reflected the influence of the Atlanta growth pole. The locations of the spread effects, with the propulsive influence of growth pole felt first in other major towns in the region and in the rural area immediately surrounding the growth pole, and then spreading to other interstitial rural areas are interesting in themselves. They tend to concur with the results of other diffusion studies by Hägerstrand[11] and suggest, from a policy viewpoint, the advantage of injecting growth into intermediate areas as well as into the focal pole.*

*For a study which tends to cast doubts on the efficacy of the 'trickling down' development processes from growth centres, see: Moseley, M. J.; The impact of growth centres in rural regions—I Brittany; II East Anglia, *Regional Studies,* 7, 1 (1973).

Drawing this more detailed outline of the concepts together, it can be seen that although the various concepts of growth poles can be identified and clarified and may appear intuitively attractive, their theoretical basis and empirical validity are still rather thin, relying heavily on support from associated concepts of location and agglomeration. In addition, there are numerous problems—the dangers of over-reliance on large leading industries, the limitations on polarisation from diseconomies of scale and 'footloose' firms, and the problem of imbalance between spread and back-wash effects. Yet, as a framework for understanding the regional anatomy it provides a valuable dynamic complement to central place theory and, despite its limitations, is of considerable value for regional planning. It introduces numerous planning-oriented concepts, stressing the advantages of industrial complexes, leading industries, polarised growth and agglomeration economies and the resultant spread effects, all of which are certainly robust if not rigorous.

2 Growth pole theory and regional planning[12]

The value of the growth pole theory as a policy tool in regional planning has been realised for some time. In Britain, it was first adopted in 1963 in plans for North East England and Central Scotland. The idea was later taken up in Northern Ireland and Mid-Wales. However, its relevance was not confined to declining areas, for as early as 1964 a policy of concentrating all industrial growth in a few large centres was proposed for the prosperous South East. 'Growth centre' policies have subsequently been proposed for the North West, South Wales, the Scottish Highlands and Eire, and modifications have been undertaken to the earlier applications.

Abroad, 'growth point' policies have been favoured in both advanced and under-developed countries. Well known examples are the Bari–Taranto–Brindisi industrial complex for the Mezzogiorno Region of Southern Italy, the national policy of growth points or *mêtropoles d'équilibrium* in France, and the development of new centres at Brasilia and Cuidad Guyana as attempts to generate growth into the backward areas of Brazil and Venezuela. The idea has also been recently accepted in the

USA to aid its depressed regions, and in the Soviet Union and India.

The theory is particularly attractive as a policy tool for several reasons:

a owing to the various agglomeration economies it tends to be a very efficient way of generating development

b the concentration of investment in specific growth points costs less in terms of public expenditure than wholesale grants to large areas

c the spread effects out of the growth point will help to solve the problems of depressed regions.

But the various and more and more frequent uses suggest some confusion over the rôle of the theory in regional policy, and there is a need for some clarification. Hermansen[13] originally introduced the idea of formulating distinctions in order to clarify this rôle, and building on his original ideas, a typology can be identified. This typology seeks to provide a comprehensive guide to the practical use of the theory, and consists of four categories, each with its own variations.

1. *Function*	Policy of Development	
	Policy of Relief	
	Policy of Development and Relief	
2. *Level*	Primary	
	Secondary	
	Tertiary	
3. *Strategy*	Active	
	Passive	
4. *Form*	Growth Pole Policy	
	Growth Centre Policy	

The first distinction is between the functions of the policy. This will be influenced by the particular problems of the region. The choice may be a pole of development which aims at generating growth in an area with no real industrial characteristics or where the economy is in a state of depression. In contrast, a pole of relief could be chosen which attempts to reduce the problems of a large industrial complex by establishing itself as a counter magnet. It is also possible for the pole to embody both functions. A second distinction is between poles belonging to different levels of the hierarchial system of settlements. The level of pole may vary from primary to tertiary depending on its function and the scale of the problem.

Another distinction is between an *active* and *initiating* growth policy or a *passive* and *reinforcing* approach. The former is more ambitious, involving a rejection of the existing settlement structure and the creation of new centres in an attempt to create development. The passive approach accepts the rationality of the existing system of centres and seeks to aid development by concentrating on the most promising of these centres.

The final distinction, but a most important one in the use of the theory, is between the use of a *growth pole policy* or a *growth centre policy*. The major difference between the two is that the pole policy necessitates the development of a selected industrial focus composed of propulsive firms from leading industries, the intention being to foster localisation economies. In contrast, the centre policy does not involve the selection of related industries, but rather entails the concentration of investment in the provision in a chosen location of those facilities which will create urbanisation economies that are attractive to industry. As industry must be localised, a growth pole policy will inevitably result in a growth centre and the resultant urbanisation economies. However this is not necessarily true in reverse for a growth centre policy may not lead to the development of a growth pole of linked industries.

Implicit in the growth pole explanation of regional structure and growth centre policy is intra-regional imbalance, at least in the short run. This imbalance however may be socially and politically unacceptable to certain areas of the region, and social and political factors can be of considerable importance in determining spatial structure. Such factors have been recognised by several theorists[14] although they are even more difficult to analyse than the predominantly economic concepts discussed so far.

3   The transport factor in regional development

Implicit in the discussions of central place theory and growth pole theory is a recognition of transport links and flows of goods and people. But the transport factor is important in its own right in

182

the development and spatial structure of regions and is now considered more explicitly, although unfortunately very briefly, here. Transport is a wide ranging term including road, rail, air and sea elements. In the context of regional development and planning, however, our concern is largely with the impact of transport developments on spatial accessibility. But accessibility is an elusive concept, with many interpretations. Here, the definition by Ingram[15] that 'accessibility may loosely be defined as the inherent characteristic (or advantage) of a place with respect to overcoming some form of spatially operating source of friction (for example, time and/or distance)' is offered as a reasonable starting point. But what are the impacts of improved spatial accessibility on regional development? The impacts can be most clearly seen by subdividing them into two categories, inter-regional and intra-regional.[16]

Inter-regionally, a region's economic growth depends on the efficiency with which it can manufacture and distribute its goods and services compared with other regions. A region's production advantage may be offset by high transport costs to other regions. Thus a transport development, improving the accessibility of a region and reducing transport costs, places greater emphasis on the production factor. But such a transport development, for example linking a region into a national motorway system, can be a two-edged sword. Some firms in the region may benefit and serve a wider market, but others may become much more vulnerable to extra-regional competition. The extent to which the region, as a whole, suffers or benefits, obviously depends on its mix of such firms. If it has a majority of firms with production cost advantages it may prosper from the change; although other factors—such as the price elasticity of demand for the region's products, the elasticity of supply of inputs into the region's firms (labour supply may be a constraint on growth) and the proportionate importance of transport costs in the original total costs of the region's products (the higher the proportion, the greater the scope for cost reductions)—may also influence the outcome.

Thus inter-regional transport improvements may be either positive or negative in terms of regional growth. Intra-regional improvements on the other hand will always be positive. An intra-regional road link will not only improve accessibility for the

183

local car owning public but will also reduce transport costs for local firms, thereby improving their efficiency and their cost position. The direct spatial impact of a transport improvement within a region depends on the nature of that improvement. Improvements with a limited access, such as motorways, railways or airports, may encourage activity concentration; others with easier access may have a more dispersed effect.

In practice it is often difficult to differentiate out the effects of transport improvements on a region. Nor is evidence which is available very conclusive. The most comprehensive British study, analysing the effects of the M62 Lancashire–Yorkshire motorway,[17] suggests that the impact of the road on industrial growth and economic performance in the study area was negligible. However, reflecting the earlier arguments, effects do depend very much on the economic conditions of the regions involved. In a study of the impact of the Severn Bridge, Cleary and Thomas[18] noted the most significant impacts on employment in wholesale distributive trades, where transport costs are particularly important. Impact also varies according to the nature of the improvement. The construction of an estuarial road bridge which dramatically reduces transport costs may have significant impacts. The construction of the Forth Road Bridge for example, is thought to have had a major impact on the fortunes of Fife in Scotland, providing a welcome impetus to the development of Glenrothes new town.[19]

Finally it should be noted that the impacts of transport improvements can be transitory. As a transport system fills out, a region having an initial advantage of good transport links may find its relative advantage being eroded. In Britain, the filling out of the motorway system is bringing more inter-regional time–space convergence. Similar convergence trends are also noticeable with improved motorway accessibility within regions like the North West and the West Midlands.[20] On the other hand, the pruning of the railway system may be having an opposite effect, only partially offset by the improved service on the remaining inter-city routes.

4 Models of spatial interaction

Taken together, growth pole theory and central place theory provide a partial explanation of the spatial structure of regions. However neither theory satisfactorily explains the elements of spatial interaction—the movement between activities in space—although such elements are implicit in both models. In recent years there has been much research into this important area of spatial interaction, with major developments in mathematical land-use modelling arising out of the systems approach to urban and regional planning. Therefore to conclude the section on intra-regional analysis we now turn to examine some of the more important models of spatial interaction. Unfortunately the survey must be brief, only scratching the surface of the rapidly growing and highly technical literature on the subject. There are however several useful reviews of modelling by Harris,[21] Lowry,[22] Wilson,[23] and most recently by Batty[24] which fill most of the gaps.

The starting point for many of the models is the gravity model of human interaction outlined in Chapter 2 . . . 'the force of interaction between two centres is directly proportional to the mass of the centre and inversely proportional to the distance between them'. There have been many developments and variations of this model (potential models, models of intervening opportunities); there have also been many criticisms particularly of the lack of theoretical underpinnings. This concern has recently led to a completely new approach—a general theoretical derivation of the gravity model based on the concept of entropy as used in statistical mechanics. Advocated by Wilson,[25] this approach is 'quickly becoming the basis of a general framework for spatial interaction modelling'.[26]

Spatial interaction models can serve basically two rôles. Firstly they can be seen as an integral part of the development of the theory of spatial structure of towns and regions; secondly, they can be used in predictive rôles—forecasting into the future. Although recent developments have been primarily oriented towards the second rôle, they also provide a valuable insight into spatial structure. Two main types of models can be identified on the criteria of comprehensiveness—partial models relating to only one aspect of the urban or regional system and general models relating to two or more aspects.

Partial models have been extensively developed in the study of retail behaviour. In the retail context the models seek to explain the interaction between the consumer and the retail sources (shopping centres) in terms of the attraction of the source and its distance from the consumer. The attraction factor could be total retail sales at the source and the distance could be in terms of driving time. One of the most well known and popular of shopping models is that derived by Lakshmanan and Hansen.[27] This model, which can take the form of an economic model or a traffic model, can be used in forecasting—for example predicting the effect of a new shopping centre. As an economic model it can be used to predict the values of the transfers of money from origin zones (residential areas) to destination zones (shopping centres); as a traffic model the aim is to predict the numbers of shopping journeys from the origin zones to the destination zones. The economic model uses the formula:

$$T_{ij} = \frac{A_i C_i F_j{}^b}{d_{ij}{}^a}$$

where T_{ij} = money transfer from zone i to zone j
C_i = total expenditure by consumers from zone i
F_j = mass of the shopping centre j
d_{ij} = distance from zone i to zone j
A_i = scaling factor
a and b are parameters.

A well known application of this model is in the Manchester University study of shopping centres in the North West.[28] In addition to shopping, partial models are also well developed in transport and are slowly being introduced into other areas.

Yet despite advances in partial modelling, *general* or *holistic* models are likely to prove the long-term goal of location land-use modelling, allowing the planner to take account of the effects of change in a single activity pattern on other activities in the urban/ regional system. Batty subdivides general models into optimising and non-optimising classes. As the specification and measurement of optimality in systems involving human values is very difficult, the majority of general models are of a non-optimising nature. Of these, the Garin Lowry Model is the most popular.

Lowry's original model of a metropolis involved, in his own

words, the following sequence of operations:

'We start with the given distribution of 'basic' workplaces by mile square tract, and with certain specifications as to the land available for residential settlement in each tract. The computer distributes around each cluster of workplaces a residential population which can supply an appropriate labour force . . . This spatially distributed residential population is then available as a base for the location of population serving activities, from department stores to elementary schools. The market potential of each location (in terms of accessible customers) is evaluated; and retail employment is spatially distributed in proportion to these potentials.

In a new round of calculations, the residences of retail and service employees are located. This event changes the distribution of residential population so that market potentials must be recalculated.'[29]

Iterations proceed until constrained by available land, efficiency scales of operation for enterprises and density ceilings for residential population. In short, the model is constructed around two structures: firstly population and service employment are derived from basic employment (this assumes a basic/non-basic split of economic activity) and secondly, service employment and population are allocated to zones of the system using sub-models based on potential models.

The original model has since been much modified. Of particular note are the improvements by Garin[30] who amended the model principally by simplifying the allocation process. Versions of the Garin-Lowry Model have been applied in Britain at both sub-regional and town scales. The sub-regional applications illustrate some of the uses. In Central Lancashire[31] and Bedfordshire[32] the model was used mainly for impact analysis—the impact of Central Lancashire New Town and Milton Keynes; in the Nottingham-shire–Derbyshire Study,[33] the model was used more to forecast the implications of alternative sub-regional strategies, and in Mersey-side[34] a model was developed primarily for educational purposes.

The Garin-Lowry Model typifies many of the attractions and problems of contemporary spatial interaction models. It pro-

187

vides a relatively comprehensive coverage of urban and regional
systems in that it is concerned with population and employment
and the interactions between them; its sub-models can be
developed and refined in themselves; it is simple to understand
and capable of practical application. However such sophistication
has its price. In addition to the problems of application, the
inevitable data problems, problems of measurement and estimation of variables and parameters, there are fundamental conceptual problems. It is a comparative static model describing the
system in equilibrium at specific points in time and giving no
explicit account of the dynamics of urban and regional systems.
It also assumes that population and service employment are
dependent on basic employment, and that basic employment
is not dependent on other activities, which, as discussed in
Chapter 4, is clearly unrealistic.

5 Summary

In many regions the regular central place spatial structure tends
to be rather distorted by agglomerations. Growth pole theory has
been adapted not only to explain such distortions but also as a
policy tool in regional planning. Unfortunately its value in both
explanatory and planning rôles suffers from much semantic confusion over the theory and its underlying concepts. This chapter
has sought to clear some of the haze—making a distinction
between growth poles and growth centres, outlining and examining the underlying concepts and suggesting a typology of applications. The basic concepts of leading industries, polarisation and
spread effects appear intuitively attractive, yet their theoretical
basis and empirical validity are rather thin. Nevertheless, when
taken together they provide a valuable complement to central
place theory in an explanation of the regional anatomy and provide several concepts of immediate value and relevance to the
regional planner. However if we wish to examine the movement
between activities within the region, a different form of model, a
model of spatial interaction, is required. The last few years have
witnessed considerable developments in mathematical land use
modelling, and a range of partial and general models now provide an increasingly comprehensive picture of both regional and
urban systems.[35]

References

1 Perroux, F., *La notion de pôle de croissance, l'économie de xxème siècle,* 2nd edition page 143, Paris, (1964).
2 Boudeville, J., *Problems of Regional Economic Planning,* Edinburgh U.P. (1966).
3 Darwent, D. F., Growth Poles and Growth Centres in Regional Planning, *Environment and Planning,* 1, 1 (1969).
4 Perroux, F., and Boudeville, J., *op cit;*
Hansen, N. M., Development Pole Theory in a Regional Context, *Kyklos,* XX, pages 709-25 (1967);
Allen, K., and Hermansen, T., *Regional Policy in EFTA: An Examination of the Growth Centre Idea,* EFTA Secretariat, Geneva (1968);
Hirschman, A. O., *The Strategy of Economic Development,* Yale (1958);
Myrdal, G., *Economic Theory and Underdeveloped Regions,* Duckworth (1957);
UNRISD, *Concept and Theories of Growth Poles and Growth Centres,* Geneva (1970).
5 See: Hoover, E. M., *The Location of Economic Activity,* McGraw Hill (1948); and Isard, W., *Location and Space Economy,* MIT Press (1956).
6 Hoover, E. M., and Isard, W., *ibid.*
7 Buswell, D., and Lewis, E., Geographical Distribution of Industrial Research Activity in the United Kingdom, *Regiona Studies,* 4, 3 (1970).
8 Lasuen, J. R., On growth poles, *Urban Studies,* pages 137-61, 6 (1969).
9 Myrdal, G., and Hirschmann, A. O., *op cit.*
10 Nichols, V., Growth Poles: an evaluation of their propulsive effect, *Environment and Planning,* 1, 2 (1969).
11 Hägerstrand, T., *Innovation Diffusion as a Spatial Process,* Chicago (1967).
12 UNRISD, *Growth Poles and Growth Centres in Regional Policies and Planning,* Geneva (1971);
Allen, K., and Hermansen, T. *op cit.*
13 Hermansen, T., Development poles and development centres in national and regional development—elements of a theoretical framework, in UNRISD, *Concepts and Theories of Growth Poles and Growth Centres, op cit.*
14 See for example; Friedman, J., *Regional Development Policy: A Case Study of Venezuela,* MIT Press (1967);

Hilhorst, J. G. M., Spatial Structure and Decision Making, in Dunham, D. M., and Hilhorst J. G. M. (eds), *Issues in Regional Planning*, Mouton, The Hague (1971).

15 Ingram, D., The concept of accessibility, *Regional Studies*, **5**, 2 (1971).

16 Gwilliam, K. M., The indirect effects of highway investment, *Regional Studies*, **4**, 2 (1970).

17 Dodgson, J. S., Motorway investment, industrial transport costs and sub-regional growth. Case study of the M62, *Regional Studies*, **8**, 1 (1974).

18 Cleary, E. J., and Thomas, R. E., *Economic Consequences of the Severn Bridge*, Bath University (1973).

19 McGregor, D., The Social and Economic Effects of the Forth Road Bridge, *Scottish Geographical Magazine* (September 1966).

20 Williams, A. F., Crossroads: the new accessibility of the West Midlands, in Joyce, F. (ed.), *Metropolitan Development and Change*, Saxon House (1977).

21 See: Urban Development Models—New Tools for Planning, *Journal of the American Institute of Planners*, May 1965.

22 Lowry, I. S., *Seven Models of Urban Development: A Structural Comparison*, P—3673, Santa Monica, California, RAND Corporation (1967).

23 Wilson, A. G., Models in Urban Planning: A Synoptic View of the Literature, *Urban Studies*, **5**, 3 (1968).

24 Batty, M., Recent Developments in Land Use Modelling: A Review of British Research, *Urban Studies*, **9**, 2 (1972).

25 Wilson, A. G., *Entropy in Urban and Regional Modelling*, Pion Ltd (1970).

26 Batty, M., *op cit.*

27 Lakshmanan, T. R., and Hansen, W. G., A Retail Market Potential Model, *Journal of American Institute of Planners*, **31** (1965).

28 Univ. of Manchester, *Regional Shopping Centres: A Planning Report on North West England, Part 2: A Retail Shopping Model*, Department of Planning (1965).

29 Lowry, I. S., *A Model of Metropolis*, RM—4035—RC, Santa Monica, California, RAND Corporation (1964).

30 Garin, R. A., A Matrix Formulation of the Lowry Model for Intra-Metropolitan Activity Location, *Journal of American Institute of Planners*, **32** (1966).

31 Batty, M., The Impact of a New Town, *Journal of Town Planning Institute*, pages 428–35, **55** (1969).

32 Cripps, E. L., and Foot, D. H. S., A Land Use Model for Sub-Regional Planning, *Regional Studies*, **3** (1969).

33 Steeley, G., Analysis by the Garin-Lowry Model, in *CES—IP— 11 Papers from the Seminar on the Notts–Derbys. Sub-regional Study,* London: CES (1970).

34 Masser, I., Notes on the Application of the Lowry Model to Merseyside, *Department of Civic Design, University of Liverpool* (1970).

35 See: Wilson, A. G., *Urban and Regional Models in Geography and Planning,* Wiley (1974).

PART THREE

The Practice of Regional Planning

9 Inter-regional planning in the United Kingdom

Inter-regional planning is primarily concerned with the centrally directed allocation of resources between aggregate regions to achieve certain regional and national objectives. This form of planning, often under the title of regional industrial development planning or regional policy, has been pursued in several countries for some years although its relative importance varies according to the stage of development of the country. Friedman[1] suggests that there are four stages of development: pre-industrial, transitional, industrial and post-industrial. In pre-industrial societies, such as Bolivia and Afghanistan, the policy emphasis is on the creation of preconditions for economic 'take-off' and regional policy is inappropriate. In transitional societies, such as Venezuela and Brazil, there is a need to create a spatial framework suitable for sustaining economic growth, and here regional policy becomes critical. The third stage, the industrial society, typical of much of Western Europe, including the UK, often reaps the costs of industrialisation, especially in the form of depressed regions resulting from overspecialisation. In the final stage, the post-industrial society, typified by the USA, there is a shift to a new focus with the emphasis on urban and metropolitan problems. Here the emphasis will be on the regional problems of industrial societies, concentrating on the UK situation. In the UK, the origins of inter-regional planning stem back to the depression years of the 1920's and 1930's, when there was government intervention to aid a few particularly depressed areas. Since that time the scope and content has widened and there are now a whole range of financial, infrastructural and control policies directed at a variety of problem regions.

An examination of the practice of inter-regional planning in the UK requires a consideration of several aspects. Firstly the broad problem regions must be identified. Conventionally, the problem regions in a country are those that as a whole are materially worse off, reflected by indicators such as unemployment, low activity rates, low growth rates and a high level of outmigration. There are however also those regions which because they are growing so fast are also suffering from certain problems such as congestion and rising factor prices.

But the identification of problem regions does not in itself constitute a case for intervention. Indeed, regional variations are universal and there is, therefore, secondly a need to investigate the case for intervention, outlining goals and specific objectives against which the effectiveness of any policy can be appraised. The ends of inter-regional planning, the goals and objectives, usually have a strong economic flavour such as the achievement of high growth rates and the efficient utilisation of resources. But what of the means to these ends?

Inter-regional planning can adopt a variety of broad strategies, but the two main approaches have usually been a Labour Migration Policy (workers to the work) or an Industrial Location Policy (work to the workers) or some combination of both. In Britain, a policy of encouraging the migration of labour out of the depressed industrial areas was adopted for some time in the depression years, but the emphasis quickly switched to a policy of industrial location which has been dominant ever since.

The actual tactics of inter-regional planning, the instruments for carrying out the broad strategies, provide a fourth area for investigation, and raise a multitude of questions. Should industry be encouraged to move to parts of problem regions rather than regions as a whole, concentrating aid on growth points with potential rather than spreading it thinly over a wider area? What type of industry should be encouraged to move—service or manufacturing, public or private? How should industry be encouraged to move, by controls over location, financial incentives or infrastructural investment?

A final and important factor in an examination of the practice of inter-regional planning, especially in the UK where there is a history of some 50 years of intervention, is a general appraisal of its effectiveness with regard to its intended goals and objectives. This general appraisal plus specific assessments of particular strategies and tactics may suggest possible new directions for future inter-regional planning in the UK.

1 The identification of UK problem regions—how many nations?

Every country has its regional variations, but it is probably true to say that Britain is more varied than most. The recent book by Rawstron and Coates[2] provides an interesting picture of some of these differences. These variations can be a source of strength, stability and progress to a country, but they can also indicate the presence of certain regions with deep-seated problems. These problems place the regions at a relative disadvantage to the rest of the country. The problem regions are usually identified by certain standard indicators or symptoms, such as income levels, activity rates, growth rates, unemployment levels and migration flows. Although such indicators are no more than the tip of the iceberg of the fundamental underlying economic problems, their variations do provide a useful picture of relative regional prosperity. The indicators tend to be largely interdependent and self-reinforcing. For example, low income levels, low activity rates and high levels of unemployment in themselves reflect slow economic growth and usually lead to a high level of outmigration.

Table 9.1 illustrates the application of these indicators to the UK Economic Planning Regions. At a first glance at the table it might seem that the UK subdivides simply into a prosperous South and East ('the centre') with generally higher than average income levels, activity rates and rates of employment growth, and lower than average unemployment levels plus net migration gains; and a relatively less prosperous North and West ('the periphery') with lower income levels, activity rates rates and of employment growth but higher levels of unemployment and outmigration. Such a broad division, however, hides many variations, for

197

Table 9.1. *Standard indicators of UK problem regions*

Region	Average total weekly household income (67–68) as % of UK	Activity rates (male and female) (June 1968)	Percentage change in employment (61–66) Total	Male	Unemployment average annual percentage (65–71)	Net migration average annual flow (000's) (61–66)
Northern Ireland	85	48·9			7·0	− 6·9
Scotland	96	56·4	+ 1	− 2	3·9	−38·8
Wales	90	47·1	+ 3	− 1	3·8	+ 1·9
North	91	51·8	+ 2	− 1	4·1	− 7·1
Yorkshire and Humberside	88	56·1	+ 3	+ 2	2·3	− 1·0
North West	96	58·1	+ 1	0	2·6	− 5·7
South West	96	47·0	+ 6	+ 4	2·5	+24·8
United Kingdom	100 (£29·1)	56·2	+ 4	+ 2	2·3	+15·7
West Midlands	105	60·2	+ 6	+ 5	2·0	+ 7·1
East Midlands	97	56·3	+ 6	+ 4	1·9	+ 8·7
East Anglia	97	48·5	+13	+11	2·0	+11·9
South East	112	59·7	+ 5	+ 4	1·5	+20·8

SOURCES: *Family Expenditure Survey; Abstract of Regional Statistics; The Intermediate Areas,* Cmnd. 3998 (Appendix C.)

regional problems take many forms and no two regions are alike. Because of this variety, it of course follows that any finer classification is bound to be somewhat arbitrary, with any one region overlapping more than one category. Nevertheless it does seem possible to identify three broad categories of problem regions: the underdeveloped region, the depressed industrial region and the pressured region, each with its own distinctive set of problems.

1 *Underdeveloped/Sparsely populated regions*. Although such areas are more prominent in several other European countries, for example the Mezzogiorno of Italy, large areas of northern Scandinavia and the Massif Central of France, they are also found in the UK, where the Highlands of Scotland, the Scottish Borders and Mid-Wales would come under this classification. Such regions often cover a large proportion of the area of the countries concerned, although their populations may be quite small and scattered. The Scottish Highlands cover about 23% of the total land area of the UK, yet have less than 2% of the total population.

They are heavily dependent on primary occupations, especially agriculture, forestry, fishing, mining and quarrying, which may be suffering from a variety of factors such as a low income elasticity of demand for their main products, low levels of productivity, exhaustion of natural resources, outdated technology and so on. This situation is reflected in unemployment problems, low levels of income and rates of growth and, consequently, high levels of outmigration. This migration may be first to the larger centres within the region, but this is often only a stepping stone to movement completely out of the region. The migration tends to be selective taking the young and skilled, and this factor plus the poor service provision and geographical isolation of the regions makes the areas less attractive to modern industrial development, creating a typical Myrdal 'cumulative-causation' process.

2 *Depressed industrial regions*. In contrast to the first category, the UK probably provides the most widespread examples of depressed industrial regions. These are areas which went through the process of industrialisation in the nineteenth century and are now

suffering from an over-reliance on declining and stagnating industries. The decline may be caused by a general contraction in the demand for the products of such industries or because productivity is increasing rapidly through technological progress. As a result, the regional economic base is unable to utilise the regional resources to the full, and the regions display all the usual symptoms of high rates of unemployment and outmigration, and low activity rates, growth rates and levels of *per capita* income.

UK examples of depressed industrial areas are, with the exception of South Wales, found in the northern part of the country. The intensity of the problem tends to vary according to the narrowness of the industrial base. Central Scotland and North East England have suffered from an overdependence on coal and shipbuilding; the decline of the textile industry has been a major determinant in Northern Ireland, Lancashire and Yorkshire; and the problems of the iron and steel industry, and again coal mining, have been the major factors in the declining prosperity of West Cumberland and South Wales.

It should be added that, although the poor industrial structure with a lack of national growth industries may be the fundamental problem of these regions, they may also have locational disadvantages, as illustrated in the analysis of Chapter 5. Thus, if an area is peripheral to national markets and has problems of industrial dereliction, pollution, an ageing infrastructure and an ageing workforce, it may be less attractive to new growth industries. This suggests that a resolution of the problems may not only require industrial restructuring to widen the industrial base but also some investment in new infrastructure.

3 *Pressured regions*. These regions are found in most countries, and in the UK, large areas of the South East would fall into this category. The problems of the pressured regions are to some extent the reverse of the other problem regions. Because of an imbalance in their industrial structure in favour of growth industries and services, and the attraction of new industries to the agglomeration economies, these regions are developing at a rapid rate. Such growth brings undoubted benefits—full employment, high activity rates and high levels of income—but

there are also costs. There is too much development chasing too few resources and this is reflected in rising factor costs, congestion costs and the need for heavy investment in public infrastructure, (e.g. London's ringway system). In the long run, a wide range of social costs—noise, pollution and long journeys to work may effectively reduce the value of that ephemeral factor, the quality of life. The Barlow Commission recognised the existence of these problems in the South East as early as 1940, but it is only more recently that it has been recognised that the UK regional problems are not the monopoly of the depressed northern regions. It should also be recognised that the regional problems are interdependent. The growth of regions such as the South East is usually at the expense of the depressed industrial and underdeveloped regions. Conversely, any diversion of growth away from the pressured regions may have beneficial effects on the other problem regions.

There are of course alternative approaches to the 'underdeveloped/depressed/pressured' method of classification. Klaassen seeks to identify problem regions dynamically by means of a matrix approach as in Table 9.2. The criteria used here is regional income only, although multivariate analysis combining a range of socio-economic criteria can be used in a more comprehensive application. The advantage of the Klaassen approach is its emphasis on the dynamic characteristics of regional problems, identifying not only the prosperous regions and the 'hardcore' problem regions, but also regions that are developing out of problem situations and others that are facing potential decline. Policy characteristics would obviously vary according to the type of problem region, with for example an emphasis on the improvement of regional infrastructure to stimulate the continued growth of the industrial base of developing distressed areas; and a holding operation on the declining industrial base of potential distressed areas, while generally developing the growth of new light industries. Another classification by Friedman[3] similarly isolates the 'upward' and 'downward' moving regions, also stressing the relationship between 'core' regions and 'peripheral' problem areas.

The identification of problem regions is of major importance in inter-regional planning; but this identification, whatever the method adopted, does not in itself constitute a case to intervene to help the *whole* of any particular problem region. There may be a need for a more selective identification of particular areas of need and potential within the wider region. Nor of course, does the initial identification constitute a case for intervention at all.

Regional Income Level	High (≥ 1)	Low (< 1)
National Income Level Growth rate of Regional Income / Growth rate of National Income		
High (≥ 1)	Prosperity Area	Developing Distressed Area
Low (< 1)	Potential Distressed Area	Distressed Area

Table 9.2. *Klaassen's Typology of Problem Areas.*

SOURCE: Klaassen, L., Area Social and Economic Redevelopment, OECD (1965).

2 The case for intervention—goals and objectives

If the various regional problems were self-righting over a short period of time, there would be little case for intervention. However, Chapter 5 shows that regional growth may not be convergent. The diseconomies of prosperous regions may be offset by other economic and socio-psychological benefits; occupational immobility may hinder resource reallocation to more efficient growth sectors within the other problem regions; and interregional migration of firms and labour may be limited by economic and non-economic factors, such as uniform national wage rates for particular jobs and the strength of family ties. It must also be added that even if a *laissez-faire* approach was eventually self-righting, the inevitable distress of the intervening period would probably necessitate some form of intervention.[4] This suggests that there may be a case for intervention, but intervention is costly and there is a need for further evidence that such action is justified on economic and/or non-economic grounds. In particular, does intervention contribute to an achievement of the national economic goals of economic growth, full employment, price stability, a balance of payments and social equity?

Economic arguments figure prominently in the case for intervention. The indicators of the previous section reveal the imbalance between the depressed industrial and underdeveloped regions and the pressured regions. The former suffer from an 'under-utilisation' of scarce resources, reflected in high unemployment rates, low activity rates and a high level of outmigration; while the latter have an 'over-utilisation' of resources, reflected in immigration and high factor costs, congestion costs and levels of public expenditure. A reduction in this imbalance can have important implications for the regional and national economies.

The economic growth of the country could be substantially increased by utilising more fully the wasted resources of the depressed and underdeveloped regions. In the first British attempt at long-run national planning, the NEDC[5] estimated that a reduction in the differences between the problem region unemployment and activity rates and the corresponding national rates by half would add an extra 300 000 to the labour force. This represented a gain of 1·3% corresponding to an increase of £500m in GNP. Another constraint on economic growth is the rate of inflation. The regional imbalance tends to make the control of inflation difficult. Excess demand pulls up factor prices in the pressured regions, and these inflationary increases are passed on to the rest of the country via national agreements. In addition, the imbalance also limits government flexibility in the use of deflationary controls, as the latter have an exaggerated impact on the depressed and underdeveloped regions causing large rises in their unemployment levels. Thus, any reduction in regional imbalance will also facilitate a greater control over inflation, and likewise over the balance of payments situation.

Social arguments are also important in assessing the case for intervention. The cumulative process of regional growth increases the gap between the rich and the poor regions. The latter are trapped in a 'vicious circle', a downward stagnation spiral. The lack of economic opportunities and poor environmental conditions encourage selective outmigration, leaving a top-heavy population distribution, poorer services and an overall reduction in the growth potential of the area. By intervening in these problems and reducing differences in per capita regional income levels, regional policy can make a substantial contribution to the national goal of social equality.

Finally, *political arguments*, although often not explicit, are nonetheless of considerable importance. Their importance stems from the fact that they are felt directly in the areas in question. People feel very strongly about problems such as unemployment. It follows that in democratic countries it is a sound policy to appease depressed areas because such areas if neglected for some time will invariably vote against the government. If the neglect extends over a long period, nationalist tendencies may develop. It is arguable that the poverty of Ireland coupled with the unwillingness of Britain to help, precipitated Irish independence in 1916. The revival of Scottish and Welsh nationalism provides a more recent illustration. Similarly, although the roots of the more recent Northern Ireland crisis are complex and much deeper, recent economic problems of the province do not help the situation.

Thus, there would seem to be a case that intervention to reduce regional imbalance makes useful contributions not only to the 'manifest' national socio-economic goals, but also to more 'latent' political goals. These general goals and such comprehensive aims as 'regional balance', as has been noted earlier, are necessarily vague and generalised. Inter-regional planning requires their translation into more specific, quantitative regional objectives against which the effectiveness of policy can be appraised. These objectives will vary according to the problems of each region, but since these problems stem largely from structural and locational conditions, objectives should preferably be related to such factors. In practice, however, the achievement of certain standards in the various socio-economic indicators outlined earlier—per capita regional income, activity rates, growth rates, levels of unemployment and net migration rates—are the most usual regional objectives.

Conflicts are inevitable between the mass of goals and objectives. The national goal of social equity may be in conflict with the achievement of a high growth rate. Regional objectives, such as the maximisation of the regional growth rate, may conflict with the national goal of maximising growth. Similarly, the objectives of one region may conflict with those of another. Short-run objectives may conflict with long-run objectives and so on. The effective integration of these various goals and objectives is a particularly difficult problem, but it is hoped that the development of techniques such as Planning-Programming-Budgeting Systems will facilitate the task.[6]

3 A choice of strategy—labour migration or industrial location?

A policy of intervention to alleviate the regional problems, particularly the imbalance in the supply and demand for labour, requires firstly a choice of broad strategy. This choice has tended to be between two alternatives, a policy of labour migration or a policy of industrial location. Migration is basically the *laissez-faire* approach, while the encouragement of investment in the problem areas involves more public intervention, although this is not to say that there cannot be a policy for labour migration also. There has been much written on the advantages and disadvantages of the alternatives (see: West, Needleman and Nevin[7]), but the policy of industrial location has been dominant in UK inter-regional planning and in most other countries and its relative merits require some investigation.

Political and social considerations are again of considerable importance. Fear of election reversals and the development of separatist movements not only means intervention, but intervention not unfavourable to the problem regions. One could imagine the uproar from the Welsh Nationalists if the policy for Wales was one of outmigration, rural depopulation, making the area into 'a playground for the English'! Similarly, a policy of moving workers out of the depressed and underdeveloped regions would be contrary to the equity arguments of equal opportunity in all areas of the country. It would also erode the variety of regional identities reflected in the range of customs, backgrounds, languages and dialects, and many would regard this as a major social loss.

The whole case for moving the work rather than the workers is on a much more secure foundation however, if it can be shown that the policy of industrial location has undoubted economic advantages. In this respect, three economic arguments which justify some examination are: that there are economic disadvantages in labour migration; that not all under-utilised labour will in fact migrate resulting in a perpetual unemployment wastage; and that the guidance of industrial location may not be harmful and may indeed be beneficial to the individual firms involved as well as to the regions and the nation.

It can be argued that outmigration has disadvantages for the three parties involved—for the individual migrant, and for the regions of 'departure' and 'reception'. Migration undoubtedly involves a high private cost to the individual, involving quantifiable factors such as house removal and non-quantifiable factors such as the costs of leaving friends and relations. Even if a person does migrate, he may be quickly disillusioned by his new location and return to his 'native hearth'. (Although this is not to suggest that migration is not without benefits to the individual, for in our increasingly mobile society it can at times lead to the introduction of new personal opportunities and the breakdown of social barriers.)

Migration may also impose wider social costs on the region of departure. The loss of the migrant's income and expenditure will have a negative multiplier effect on local services, and low activity rates will be reduced even more making the area less attractive to incoming industry. In the extreme cases of heavy outmigration, there may also be some waste of valuable social capital—houses, schools, hospitals and so on—although much of this often needs scrapping anyway.

The costs imposed by migration on the receiving region have been the subject of much debate. Needleman[8] has argued that migration to the pressured regions of the South East and the West Midlands increases the inflationary pressures. An additional worker will not only create a positive multiplier effect through his own expenditure, but through his need for social capital (housing) and economic capital (plant/machinery) will generate a derived

206

demand for more labour, thus encouraging rising factor prices, congestion costs and demand for expensive public infrastructure. Needleman in fact suggests that the movement of one worker may create an extra two jobs. The argument obviously depends on whether the migrant demands more than he supplies, and Richardson,[9] introducing a time element, takes a rather different view. He argues that the immediate effect is to increase labour supply with extra demand being soaked up by the more intensive use of existing services. By the time the effects of the migrants on investment is felt, the supply position will have readjusted.

Whatever the inducements to migrate out of the problem regions, there will always be a 'hard core' of unemployed who for some reason will not leave the region. They may be unskilled workers who are not as mobile as the skilled; young school leavers and others tied to relations; and those who just cannot afford the cost of moving, especially if they are moving from an area such as Scotland with its history of artificially low house rents. In addition, there are in many problem regions a large number of people, especially married women, who are available for work but do not register as unemployed. Nor will they wish to migrate as long as their husbands have jobs. This is part of the pool of 'hidden unemployment' reflected in the low activity rates in many regions. Only by bringing work to the workers can these unemployed resources be fully utilised, and although it has been claimed that such labour resources are often 'rusty' and less productive than those in the prosperous areas,[10] the argument has tended to carry some weight.

Against these reasons for an industrial location policy, it has been argued that interference in the locational freedom of industry is harmful leading to a fall in efficiency and a decline in national economic growth. If a firm is prevented from expanding in the South East or the West Midlands, it may not expand at all or may even move abroad. Further, subsidisation to aid industrial mobility may also lead to stagnation by keeping inefficient firms in business. The analysis of Chapter 6, however, suggests that such arguments can be effectively countered. It was shown that profits may vary only slightly over a fairly large area, allowing a firm to locate within fairly wide limits without too much concern. Within this range, the final location is usually a 'satisfactory' rather than an 'optimal' location. Thus any guidance of a firm's location may impose little or no private costs to the firms. Indeed it may actually create benefits, breaking down socio-psychological barriers to certain regions and introducing more preferable locations not previously considered. The relocation of firms out of the pressured regions may also reduce social costs, provided that the new location avoids the equally congested urban areas in the other problem regions.

There would therefore appear to be some justification for the adoption of an industrial location policy in preference to one of labour migration. But the alternatives are not mutually exclusive and to completely rule out the migration of labour would be to oversimplify the situation. For some regions or parts of regions faced with a rapid decline in employment, the cost of moving in industry may be just too high, and a policy of encouraging inter-regional migration may be the only quick way of utilising otherwise wasted resources. As such, many countries include incentives to labour mobility as well as to industrial mobility in their tactics of inter-regional planning, although for political reasons the fact is not much emphasised.

4 The tactics of UK inter-regional planning

Britain was the first Western country to really come to grips with the problem of regional imbalance, and its history of intervention provides a good illustration of the various tactics of inter-regional planning and the associated problems.[11] Hence, this section seeks to outline the development of British policy, identifying the range of tactics used, prior to a discussion of their effectiveness and possible lines of improvement.

Any subdivision of policy over time is bound to be very arbitrary. However, there would seem to be four main periods with the first three providing the foundation for the rapid development of policy in the post-1960 period. These can be identified as:

a The Inter-war Period of the 1930's. This was the birth of the UK policy of intervention, and was mainly a response to the distressingly high levels of unemployment in the depression years. This was the only period when the strategy emphasis was more on moving the workers than the work.

b The Intermediate Post-war Years (1945–51). This post-war reconstruction period witnessed development of policy under a new Labour Government and the introduction of many measures, such as Development Areas and Industrial Development Certificates, which have been important ever since.

c The 1950's Lull. With the advent of a Conservative Government in 1951 and coinciding with a booming national economy, many regional measures fell into abeyance in the 1950's.

d The period from 1960 onwards. During this period a policy of intervention has been vigorously pursued under both Conservative and Labour governments, and a wide range of new measures have been introduced.

The measures can be subdivided into the various positive and negative tactics designed to facilitate industrial mobility; a series of measures to encourage labour mobility; and a more general but equally important range of measures designed primarily to improve the environment of the problem areas. Over time, these various measures have been largely administered by the central government through the Board of Trade, although the present responsibility now lies with the Department of Trade and Industry.* Within this UK framework Northern Ireland has enjoyed a certain degree of autonomy with regard to policy measures.

THE EARLY FOUNDATIONS OF UK POLICY

The inter-war period

Although there had been problems of rural decline before, the incidence of depression in the old traditional industrial areas of Britain in the late 1920's and 1930's created a new dimension in regional problems. Unemployment rates varied between 20 and 30% and even in the prosperous South East were as high as 10–15%. Such problems created untold misery and hardship, as revealed by H. Powys Greenwood in a study of West Cumberland in the 1930's.

'... West Cumberland, a district as favoured by nature as any in Great Britain for scenery, climate and natural wealth, has been in the grip of intense depression ever since the War. Only

* Department of Industry (DI) since 1974.

seven miles from Seascale, at Egremont, the long line of derelict mining villages begins, where over 10 000 good men are eating their hearts out in idleness and, what is far worse, losing little by little the capacity for work if it should come. If we drive along the endless straggling streets of Cleator, Cleator Moor, Frizingdon and Arlecdon, we shall hardly see a smiling face, only little groups of men, and women too, hanging about at every street corner with soured, hopeless, expressions.'[12]

The first response to these problems was a policy to encourage labour migration out of the worst areas. Under the Industrial Transfer Act of 1928, centres were established to retrain men in new skills and removal costs were subsidised. Approximately 250 000 people moved under the scheme between 1929 and 1938, but many returned somewhat discrediting the 'workers to the work' strategy in Britain, and indelibly stamping on many people's minds the impression that the geographical transfer of labour was a 'bad thing'.

As an alternative approach, the government introduced the Special Areas (Development and Improvement) Act, 1934, which was the first legislative measure affecting the distribution of industry. Four particular problem areas were designated as Special Areas—Clydeside, West Cumberland, the North East coast of England and South Wales—and two Commissioners were charged with the duty of facilitating their 'economic development and social improvement'. Their particular aim was to attract expanding industries to the areas. Unfortunately they had little financial power, although the introduction of the Special Areas Reconstruction Association (SARA) and Special Areas Loans Advisory Committee (SALAC) to provide loan capital for small and large firms in the areas, somewhat improved the position. However, probably the most positive achievement of this period was the formation of trading estates in the problem areas, and towards the end of the 1930's, 12 000 people were employed in factories, mainly on the three large estates at Hillingdon, Team Valley and Treforest.

The symptoms of the regional problems disappeared during the war, with the demand for armaments and shipping reviving the traditional heavy industries. But the deep-seated problems were still there, and this had prompted the government to set up the Royal Commission on the Distribution of the Industrial Population in 1937. The Commission subsequently reported in 1940 (the Barlow Report),[13] although the war prevented any immediate consideration of its recommendations. The terms of reference of the Barlow Report fell into three sections: to examine the causes of the present distribution of industry, population and future trends; to investigate the social, economic and strategic disadvantages of this distribution; and to suggest remedial measures to be taken to improve the situation.

The Report showed the trend to the South East to be a result of many factors, including the decline in the traditional basic industries, the destruction of the locational monopoly of coal, the growth of high-value, market-oriented light industries and the improvement in communications. The concentration of the industrial population in the South East was seen to have many disadvantages. Social costs, especially the dangers to health from overcrowding, were particularly stressed. The various economies of scale were shown to be offset by a wide range of diseconomies, and at the time the report was prepared, the concentration of the industrial population in the South East was also regarded as a strategic risk.

As such, the Commission recommended that a national agency should be established with the objectives of redeveloping congested urban areas, encouraging the decentralisation and dispersal of both industry and industrial population from such areas, encouraging a reasonable balance of industrial development throughout the regions of Britain and checking the continued drift to the South East. The Majority Report believed that this agency should be a small body under the Board of Trade with mainly advisory and research functions but with some control over industrial location in the South East. The Minority Report was more positive in its recommendations advocating the setting up of a Ministry to deal with the problems, and the extension of controls of industrial location to the entire country with the simultaneous application of positive inducements to promote balanced industrial development.

The Barlow Report has rightly been hailed as the foundation

of post-war British planning. It is a document of tremendous importance and such foresight that only now are some of its ideas being developed. The report showed that the regional problem was an economic as well as a social problem. It emphasised the relationship of physical planning and regional economic planning, and showed the connections between the problems of congested conurbations and the depressed regions (although it should be noted that depressed regions also have their congested areas).

The immediate post-war years

The Beveridge White Paper on Employment Policy in 1944,[14] followed many of the recommendations of the Barlow Report. It pledged itself to full employment and believed that regional unemployment could be combated by a combination of influencing the location of new industries, revitalising existing industries, retraining the labour force in new skills and encouraging labour mobility. The legislation for this policy introduced the 'carrot' and 'stick' tactics.

Under the Distribution of Industry Act, 1945, supplemented by the Distribution of Industry Act, 1950, the four Special Areas were extended, increasing in population from 4 to 6½ million, and were renamed Development Areas. Smaller problem areas were added in 1946 and 1949. In the Development Areas the Treasury could make loans and grants to prospective and established firms on the advice of an independent advisory committee (Development Areas Treasury Advisory Committee), provided that the firms had no alternative source of finance and had good prospects of success. Other inducements included tax allowances on new investments and limited grants for environmental improvements. But by far the greatest inducement was the accelerated development of industrial estates and advanced factories in the Development Areas. The Board of Trade had powers to acquire land and build factories for lease, or sale, and to make loans to trading or industrial estate companies. £40 million were spent on this policy during this short period.

The negative aspect of the policy was first effected through the extension of wartime building licence controls. Between 1945 and 1947, licences were freely given for the Development Areas but were strictly controlled in other areas. However, in 1947, the Town and Country Planning Act introduced a new method of control, the Industrial Development Certificate (IDC), which, in amended form, has been effective ever since. Any application for industrial development in excess of 5000 square feet required a certificate. By granting or refusing the certificate, the Board of Trade could channel development to problem areas.

The 1950's lull

The post-war boom in the early and mid-1950's temporarily masked the regional problem. Pent-up war demand for the products of the traditional industries (coal, iron and steel, ships) at times resulted in the problem regions' growth rates being higher than the national average. In the face of this prosperity, many regional measures fell into temporary disuse. Very little was spent on positive inducements (£4–5 million p.a. compared with the £10–12 million average in the earlier period), and IDC's were freely given for development in the Midlands and the South East.

But by 1957–58 the situation began to deteriorate rapidly. The post-war boom was seen to be the last fling of many traditional industries facing secular decline, and this decline was further exacerbated by national deflationary measures to combat inflation and balance of payments problems. The regional problem symptoms reappeared with a vengeance, and the government was spurred into action, tightening IDC controls and introducing the Distribution of Industry (Industrial Finance) Act, 1958—the only regional legislation of any importance during the period. This Act extended the power of the Treasury to give financial assistance, and designated several new development areas. These were certain belts of specialised unemployment, such as Cornwall and North East Suffolk, which had suffered rates of unemployment over 4% for twelve months prior to designation. But this Act was typical of an approach which appeared to be more concerned with containing the symptoms of the problem rather than eliminating the root cause. It also added to the confusion caused by the varying availability of inducements in different areas.

213

Several factors, such as the ineffectiveness of the then existing policy, the increasing severity of the regional problems and the realisation that their alleviation might be in the interests of national economic growth as well as social equality, prompted some fundamental rethinking at the beginning of the 1960's. During the following decade both Conservative and Labour governments ploughed through a welter of legislation seeking to introduce more effective tactics, all of which was at times rather confusing to the industrialist. Policy was pursued particularly vigorously under the 1964–70 Labour Administration. At first, the return of a Conservative Government in 1970 suggested a more 'conservative' attitude, but further legislation, the 1972 Industry Bill, marked a rather more positive approach. From the mass of legislation arising from this period, several important trends in the precise delineation of assisted areas and in the use of measures to aid these areas can be observed.

The delineation of assisted areas

In 1960, the Development Areas, evolved from the inter-war Special Areas and delineated almost exclusively by the criterion of unemployment, covered slightly less than 20% of the country with a population of approximately seven millions. By 1972, this 'blanket' approach had been replaced by a more sophisticated hierarchy of Special Development Areas, Development Areas and Intermediate Areas, based on multiple criteria including unemployment, and covering more than 50% of the country and including a population of approximately 25 millions (Figure 9.1).

However, the first stage in this replacement of the 'blanket' approach was rather a backward one. Under the 1960 Local Employment Act, the Development Areas were replaced by Development Districts. The criterion for delineation was basically the possession of an unemployment rate greater than $4\frac{1}{2}$% This unfortunately led to frequent re-scheduling as the unemployment in the areas improved or deteriorated. (Odber[15] provides an illustration of this situation in the North East). The policy also tended to aid those areas which had the least potential and were least attractive to industrialists.

214

Orkney Islands

Shetland Islands

Inverness

Glenrothes

Glasgow

Livingston

Newcastle upon Tyne

Belfast

Cockermouth

Skelmersdale

Leeds

Colwyn Bay

Manchester

Nottingham

Birmingham

Cardiff

Bristol

London

Plymouth

	Development areas		Overspill town where development area benefits are available
	Special development areas	▲	New towns where special development area benefits are available
	Intermediate areas	●	Departments of Industry Offices
	Northern Ireland	□	Ministry of Commerce Office Northern Ireland

Fig. 9.1   United Kingdom: the Assisted Areas (1978)

In 1963, Government White Papers on regional development programmes for Central Scotland and North East England marked an important turn in policy.[16] The designation of eight growth areas for Central Scotland and the growth zone for the North East (an area bounded by Tyneside, Teesside, the coast and the A1), allowed firms to choose the locations with maximum growth potential rather than those with hardcore unemployment problems and often limited prospects. But it was not until the Industrial Development Act (1966) that the narrowly defined Development Districts were finally abandoned and replaced by the Development Areas of today. Under this Act, *Development Areas* were selected on a wider range of criteria, including the actual and expected state of employment and unemployment, population changes, migration, and the objectives of regional policy, although the Board of Trade made it clear at the time that unemployment would still remain the main criterion. Five broad areas were identified covering most of Scotland and Wales, all the Northern Region and Furness, Merseyside and most of Cornwall and North Devon, allowing industrialists a wide choice of possible locations. These areas have since been supplemented by a system of Special Development Areas and Intermediate Areas.

Special Development Areas are those parts of the Development Areas likely to suffer from exceptionally high and persistent unemployment as a result of colliery closures. When initially designated in 1967, they were localised areas of West Central Scotland, West Cumberland, the North East and South Wales. But the addition of 71 Employment Exchange Areas in 1971 has greatly increased their scope and they now bear a remarkable resemblance to the original Special Areas of the 1930's. Firms choosing to locate in the Special Development Areas receive inducements extra to those locating in the Development Areas.

The latest stage in this delineation of problem regions is the introduction of an additional category of *Intermediate Areas*. In 1967, the Government established a committee (the Hunt Committee):

'to examine in relation to the economic welfare of the country as a whole and the needs of the development areas, the situation in other areas where the rate of economic growth gives cause (or may give cause) for concern, and to suggest whether revised policies to influence economic growth in such areas are desirable and, if so, what measures should be adopted.'[17]

On the basis of the following criteria:

a sluggish or falling employment
b slow growth in personal incomes
c slow rate of addition to industrial and commercial premises
d significant unemployment
e low/declining proportion of women at work
f low earnings
g heavy reliance on industry whose labour demand was growing slowly or falling
h poor communications
i decayed/inadequate environment
j serious net outward migration

the Committee concluded that quite large areas of the country, including the whole of the North West and the Yorkshire and Humberside regions, should be designated as Intermediate Areas and receive inducements proportional to those in the Development Areas. In the light of the Committee's Report, the Government decided to provide some additional assistance for industrial development to some areas, although they were much smaller than those recommended. These areas were Leith, North East Lancashire, the Yorkshire Coalfield, South East Wales and Plymouth. However, the 1972 extension of the 'Grey Areas' to include the whole of the North West and Yorkshire and Humberside represents an eventual triumph for the Hunt recommendations.

Measures directed at the individual firm

The *negative controls* over industrial mobility have been a constant feature of policy. The IDC policy has continued to the present day, although the severity of its application has varied from government to government. In 1965, the Labour Government lowered the limit above which it was mandatory to apply for an IDC to 1000 square feet. This low limit proved to be unduly restrictive and in 1966 was raised to 3000 square feet in the West Midlands and South East and 5000 square feet elsewhere. The advent of a Conservative Government has subsequently raised the limit again. In 1972 it was raised to 15 000 square feet in all areas except the South East where it was raised to 10 000 square feet (12 500 square feet in 1976). The need for IDC's in the Development and Special Development Areas has been dispensed with.

But IDC controls apply only to manufacturing industry. Yet since 1960, while national employment in manufacturing has actually been falling, employment in the service sector has increased at a rapid rate. This service growth was concentrated in the prosperous areas of the country, especially the South East. But it was not until 1965, with the Control of Office and Industrial Development Act, that negative controls were applied to the service sector. Under this act, Office Development Permits (ODP's) are required for office developments of more than 3000 square feet in Greater London and 10 000 square feet in the rest of the South East and the urban parts of the East and West Midlands. Criteria considered in the granting of ODP's in these restricted areas include whether the firm can work elsewhere, whether satisfactory alternative accommodation is available, and the public interest.

The *positive financial incentives* to attract industrialists to the scheduled areas have, in contrast with the negative controls, become increasingly important over the period. The expenditure on such incentives increased from under £10 million in 1959–60 to £691 million in 1975–6. Although these absolute figures of gross exchequer costs can be rather misleading in that loans are repaid, guarantees are not called upon and factory rents may increase from their low 'introductory offers', the trend is nevertheless highly significant. Three main categories of direct financial incentives to industrial mobility have been used over the period.

a Subsidies to a firm's capital costs. At first, loans and grants towards the costs of a new firm setting up in a scheduled area were at the discretion of the Board of Trade and assistance was provided to industrialists dependent upon the level of estimated employment likely to be created. The discretionary nature

218

of such loans and grants was their very weakness for firms never knew exactly what they would receive.

There was a need for a standard form of grant available to any firm moving to a scheduled area. The 'cost/value' building grant of the 1960 Local Employment Act, whereby a firm moving to a scheduled area received 85% of the difference between the estimated cost and the estimated value of the proposed premises in the open market, was an early attempt at such a grant. It was rather complicated though, and was replaced in 1963 by standard grants designed to make assistance both more generous and more predictable. The standard grants were payable at the rate of 25% of the cost of building, and 10% of the cost of acquiring and installing plant and machinery. This direct subsidy to capital investment has continued ever since although at times it has applied to buildings only, and the rates have varied considerably.

The 1963 Local Employment Act also introduced 'accelerated depreciation'. This allowed new investment in plant and machinery in the assisted areas to be written off against profits for tax purposes at whatever rate the company chose. This had the effect of providing firms with capital in the early periods when they most needed it and providing an incentive to efficiency and growth by rewarding profitability. As such, the measure was popular with firms. Nevertheless it was still shelved between 1966 and 1970 in favour of increased standard grants on the grounds that the latter were more practicable and, being independent of current profitability, would be particularly helpful to new firms initially making little profit. Second thoughts and a change of government have since resulted in a reintroduction of accelerated depreciation, but unfortunately its extension to the entire country (1972) has reduced its value as a regional incentive.

A particularly interesting innovation is the recent establishment (1972) of an entirely new Industrial Development Executive within the DTI to be largely concerned with the promotion of industrial growth in the assisted areas. It is anticipated that the existing standard grants, the regional development grants, will be administered through the regional offices of this executive, which will also have considerable powers of selective financial assistance to industry in the assisted areas.

b Subsidies to variable costs. The first attempt at subsidising labour costs rather than capital costs was more an afterthought of a national policy measure rather than a direct regional measure. The Selective Employment Tax (SET) introduced in 1966 was a *per capita* tax of £1·25 per week payable by all employers for each of their full-time employees. A weekly sum of £1·62½ per capita was paid back to manufacturing industry, but service industry received nothing. This transfer between sectors was designed to aid the export manufacturing industries. In 1967, the repayment to manufacturing industries was lowered to £1·25, with the exception of Development Areas which still received the full £1·62½, and thus received a preferential subsidy.

A more specific attempt at subsidising regional labour costs was the Regional Employment Premium (REP) introduced in 1967. This involved a payment toward the labour costs of all manufacturing industry in the Development and Special Development Areas at the rate of £1·50 per week for males, with lower rates for women and juveniles. In 1968–9 REP and the SET regional premium involved an expenditure of £125 million.

c Industrial estates and advance factories. The provision of fully serviced industrial estates and advance or custom-built factories has been one of the constant measures in regional policy. Firms can usually buy or rent such factories on very reasonable terms and in certain circumstances rent-free periods may be available.

Until 1960, the estates were run by five trading estate companies—the North East Trading Estates Ltd. (formed in 1936); the Wales/Monmouthshire Industrial Estates Ltd. (1936); the Scottish Industrial Estates Ltd. (1937); and the North Western Industrial Estates Ltd. (1946). Under the Local Employment Act (1960) these were reduced to three Industrial Estate Corporations for England, Scotland and Wales, under the overall control of the responsible Ministry.

Measures directed at the re-employment and mobility of labour

Chapter 6 showed that the presence of a large pool of unemployed labour in an area isn't necessarily attractive to industrialists. The labour is often immobile between occupations. It may be unskilled or skilled in the wrong trades and its utilisation requires considerable expense on retraining. *Government retraining grants* have been available since the Industrial Transference Act in the inter-war period, but have been developed considerably over the last ten years. The various schemes are co-ordinated by the responsible labour ministry—now the Department of Employment. They include national schemes operated by the Industrial Training Boards, established in 1964; and special training schemes for the scheduled areas. The various schemes provide a range of subsidies including a weekly *per capita* grant (averaging £25 in 1977) for 'on-the-job' training or 'off-the-job' training in one of the 65 Government Training Centres in the scheduled areas; financial assistance with training older workers, and grants to firms towards the cost of new machinery and equipment needed for training purposes.

The Government has also provided a *range of grants to encourage labour mobility between areas*. Grants to facilitate the movement of key workers into the problem areas have been available for some time. There has also been a Resettlement Transfer Scheme to give help to workers who are willing to move their homes to have a better chance of a satisfactory job. This remnant of a 'workers to the work' policy has recently been strengthened, and in 1972 the grant to a trainee to meet miscellaneous expenses, especially rehousing costs, involved in a move was increased from £100 to £600.

General measures

In addition to the various central government measures directed specifically at firms and labour, UK regional policy has also included a number of important more general measures. The importance of the preferential provision of infrastructure in the scheduled areas has slowly been recognised. The location of government establishments and the selective placing of government contracts has also been utilised as a policy tool. Finally, the whole gamut of central government measures are now being complemented by promotional bodies at the regional level.

Infrastructure and public investment. Many of the scheduled areas suffer from poorer than average social capital, for example education, housing and welfare facilities, reflected in criteria such as overcrowding, high pupil-teacher ratios, below average ratios of GP's to population and very much above average death rates. The severity of some of these social disparities contributes much to the cumulative process of regional imbalance. At last special urban programmes are being introduced to tackle the wider anomalies, and these will no doubt aid development in the areas.

Attempts are also being made to improve the inferior economic capital of many of the scheduled areas. In the 1960's, the 'growth policies' in the North East and Central Scotland involved considerable investment in 'promotional infrastructure'. The 1963 'growth zone' policy for the North East involved an increase in government public service investment in the area from £55 million (1962–3) to £90 million (1964–5), with 5½% of the nation's population receiving 7% of the public expenditure. This expenditure was earmarked for projects such as the building of the Darlington and Durham motorways, the expansion of new towns at Cramlington, Washington and Newton Aycliffe, and a new industrial estate on Teesside.[18]

Preferential investment has focussed heavily on the provision of communications (the 1972 White Paper on *Industrial and Regional Development* saw fit to provide for extra communications expenditure in the scheduled areas[19]). In contrast, there seems to have been less preference in the new town and expanded towns programme. Indeed there has probably been some bias towards the prosperous regions with the main aim being to accommodate the growing South East population.[20] Here, most of the new developments have taken place within or just over the borders of the region and overspill to the distant problem regions has been limited to small and isolated schemes (the GLC has overspill agreements with Bodmin and Plymouth in the South West and Burnley in the North West). The development of areas such as Severnside, Humberside and Tayside, identified as possible future major national growth poles, would provide more genuine counter magnets to the South East and aids to the scheduled areas. (Of course, all this investment in regional infrastructure is very much related to the field of *intra-regional planning* and this will be discussed more fully in the following chapter.)

222

The location of government establishments and the placing of government contracts. Government expenditure has also been used to aid the assisted areas by utilising the government's rôle as a major producer and purchaser of goods and services. The large nationalised sector and the numerous government offices mean that the government itself has effective control over many industrial location decisions. This control can be used in the interests of the assisted areas, although as yet there has been only limited interference in the locational decisions of public concerns perhaps reflecting the declining fortunes of many of them. Nevertheless, some investment programmes and 'run-down' programmes have been swayed. In addition, there is evidence of the increasing use of government offices in regional development, as witnessed by the establishment of the Royal Mint in Wales, the National Giro on Merseyside and the Post Office in the North East.

The public sector's position as a purchaser is a potentially most powerful policy tool. At present, the Department of Trade and Industry operates two relevant schemes. Under the general preference scheme, a firm in a scheduled area will receive preference over a firm from a non-scheduled area in tendering for a government contract where the tenders are equal. Under the contracts preference scheme, the firm from the scheduled area can still receive up to 25% of a government contract even if its original tender is not the lowest, provided that it can meet the price of the accepted tender.

Regional industrial development bodies. As the scheduled areas have increased in size, so a businessman influenced by the various central government measures to locate within them, faces, even subject to the locational considerations of his own particular industry, a wider and wider choice of final location. In an attempt to attract firms to their own particular location, many local authorities in the same region have sought to increase the expertise and financial resources available for the task by grouping together to form Industrial Development Associations. The rôle and development of such agencies is discussed further in Chapter 11.

(A brief summary of the major regional measures at present applicable (1978) in the Special Development Areas, Development Areas and Intermediate Areas can be found in Appendix B.)

5 The effectiveness of UK policy

A measure of policy effectiveness is an essential check on whether policies are achieving their intended objectives and on whether they are responsive to changing situations. It may also provide a guide for any necessary adjustments to future policies. Unfortunately there has in the past been little attempt rigorously to quantify the effectiveness of British regional policy, as exemplified by the following extract from the Second Report of the House of Commons Expenditure Committee on *Regional Development Incentives* (1973):

'We are far from satisfied that the continuing search for a viable regional policy has been backed by a critical economic apparatus capable of analysing results and proposing alternative courses. . . . Regional policy has been empiricism run mad, a game of hit and miss, played with more enthusiasm than success. . . . We regret that . . . efforts have not been better sustained by the proper evaluation of the costs and benefits of the policies pursued.'

The comprehensive aim of UK regional policy has been to right the 'regional imbalance', reflected in the under-utilisation of scarce resources in the depressed industrial and underdeveloped regions and their over-utilisation in the pressured regions, to achieve certain economic, social and political goals. Such goals include a halting of the 'vicious circle' of social decline in some areas and a containment of the 'costs of growth' in others. More specific objectives have been to achieve certain standards in socio-economic indicators, such as the achievement of the national norm in unemployment rates and per capita income in the problem regions (although for certain indicators such as growth in output and/or income, a poor region must grow faster than the national norm if it is to achieve parity).

As regional policy generally has no specific end date, effectiveness must be assessed on the basis of trends in the various indicators. For example, is the gap between per capita income in the poor regions and national per capita income narrowing? This form of assessment is not without problems. There are, firstly, statistical problems. The numerous changes in the boundaries of the scheduled areas makes the observation of trends over a reasonable period difficult. A compromise approach is to observe the trends in the larger problem regions, such as the Northern Region, Scotland and Northern Ireland, although it must be remembered that trends for such broad regions may hide numerous sub-regional variations. In addition, trends in particular indicators may often be misleading, masking more subtle variations in other factors. Thus a falling unemployment rate may be a function of rising outmigration, a rise in hidden unemployment or a fall in activity rates; while the achievement of a balance on net migration may hide the fact that a region is losing skilled young people and gaining old people. The most difficult problem however is to distinguish the effects due to regional policy from those that would have happened anyway. The improvement in a region's position may be due more to social and economic policies at the national level and nascent growth trends within the region rather than to specific regional measures. Finally, even if indicators such as unemployment levels are used, their short run trends may not accurately reflect changes in the underlying industrial structure of the region which are so fundamental to long-run regional recovery.

However in spite of these problems it is still a useful exercise to observe the trends in a number of indicators to gain at least a general picture of the effectiveness or otherwise of UK regional policy. Tables 9.3–9.6 illustrate some of these trends.

INDICATOR TRENDS

Unemployment trends are still the most popular indicator. Table 9.3 illustrates the persistent nature of the regional imbalance in the utilisation of labour over a 20-year period. Unemployment rates in the Northern Region, Scotland and Wales have been between 50–100% higher than the national norm, and in Northern Ireland the rates have been even higher. However recent figures do suggest some slight convergence in the disparity, and the 'hard

Table 9.3.   *Regional Unemployment Rates as ratios of national average (UK = 100).*

Region	1956	1961	1966	1971	1976
North	115	157	163	160	134
Yorkshire and Humberside	62	63	75	108	95
East Midlands	46	63	69	84	81
West Midlands	85	88	81	108	98
North West	100	100	94	111	121
East Anglia	} 69	} 63	{ 88	84	84
South East			{ 63	54	74
South West	100	88	113	92	114
Wales	153	163	181	127	131
Scotland	184	193	181	163	126
Northern Ireland	492	468	381	216	183
United Kingdom	100	100	100	100	100
	(1·3)	(1·6)	(1·6)	(3·7)	(5·8)

SOURCES: Hammond, E., *An Analysis of Regional Economic and Social Statistics.* University of Durham Rowntree Research Unit (1968).

Abstract of Regional Statistics
Ministry of Labour Gazette
Northern Ireland Digest of Statistics.

core' problem regions appear to have withstood the national economic troubles of the late 1960's and early 1970's 'relatively' better than other regions, such as the West Midlands. A cynic might conclude from this some fulfilment of Churchill's view of regional measures as a means of 'equalising misery'. The unemployment figures also of course serve to illustrate the importance of a buoyant national economy in the pursuance of regional balance.

·But as mentioned earlier a consideration of the unemployment indicator in isolation can be misleading, and other indicators must be considered. Many people in a region available for work but with no job may not show up in the unemployment statistics. These people, including a high proportion of married women who find it uneconomical to 'sign on', constitute the pool of *hidden unemployed*. Recent work by Taylor,[23] identifying 'cyclical' and 'structural' components of hidden unemployment, suggests

226

Table 9.4. *Regional Activity Rates as ratios of national average (UK = 100).*

Region	1956	1961	1966	1969
North	95	94	93	93
Yorkshire and Humberside[a]	104	103	102	100
East Midlands[a]	99	99	99	100
West Midlands[a]	110	108	109	107
North West	107	105	103	103
East Anglia ⎫	102	104	⎧ 87	89
South East ⎭			⎩ 104	104
South West	83	84	84	83
Wales	85	85	84	84
Scotland	100	99	99	101
Northern Ireland	84	84	85	88
United Kingdom	100	100	100	100
	(56·3)	(56·8)	(57·5)	(55·9)

[a] The figures for 1956 and 1961 refer to the previous regions—East and West Ridings, North Midlands and Midlands

SOURCE: *Abstract of Regional Statistics*

Table 9.5. *Regional Migration Trends (000's).*

Region	Ave. an. net migration			
	1951– 61	1961– 66	1966– 69	1971– 73
North	− 8·0	− 7·1	− 5·8	− 6·0
Yorkshire and Humberside	− 9·6	− 1·0	− 13·5	− 5·0
East Midlands	+ 3·9	+ 8·7	+ 4·5	+ 0·2
West Midlands	+ 4·7	+ 7·1	+ 6·7	− 4·1
North-West	− 12·4	− 5·7	− 15·1	− 16·1
East Anglia	+ 2·7	+ 11·9	+ 16·1	+ 21·6
South East	+ 43·8	+ 20·8	− 8·8	− 35·2
South West	+ 9·9	+ 24·8	+ 16·6	+ 38·0
Wales	− 4·9	+ 1·9	− 3·0	+ 8·4
Scotland	− 28·2	− 38·8	− 34·3	− 19·2
Northern Ireland	− 8·9	− 6·9	− 6·3	− 10·0
United Kingdom	− 7·9	+ 15·7	− 42·9	− 27·4

SOURCE: *Abstract of Regional Statistics.*

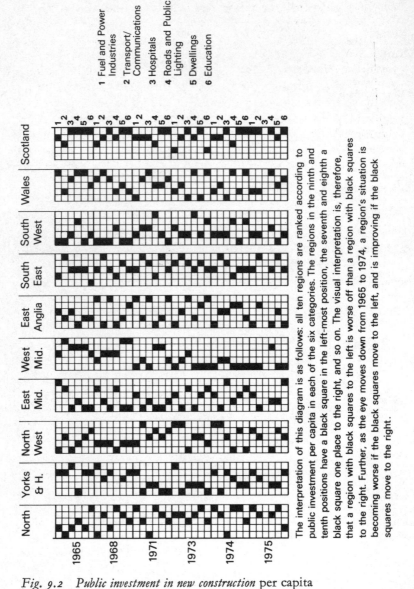

Category legend:
1 Fuel and Power Industries
2 Transport/Communications
3 Hospitals
4 Roads and Public Lighting
5 Dwellings
6 Education

The interpretation of this diagram is as follows: all ten regions are ranked according to public investment per capita in each of the six categories. The regions in the ninth and tenth positions have a black square in the left-most position, the seventh and eighth a black square one place to the right, and so on. The visual interpretation is, therefore, that a region with black squares to the left is worse off than a region with black squares to the right. Further, as the eye moves down from 1965 to 1974, a region's situation is becoming worse if the black squares move to the left, and is improving if the black squares move to the right.

Fig. 9.2 Public investment in new construction per capita

SOURCE West Midlands C.C., *An Economic Profile of the West Midlands Region/County*, WMCC (1977), adapted from *Abstract of Regional Statistics*.

that the recorded unemployment rate is on the whole, a poor guide to the unemployment situation in a region.

Table 9.4 summarises trends in *regional activity rates*. Over the period 1956 to 1966, national activity rates gradually rose but have recently fallen off sharply. This mainly reflects a fall in the male activity rate, although the impact of this fall has been partially cushioned by a rise in the female rate. The regional rates have tended to follow the national trend, although the decline has been more marked in the North West and Yorkshire and Humberside which are slowly losing their relative advantage. The other problem regions with much lower activity rates have generally failed to improve their relative positions.

Regional migration trends (Table 9.5) at first glance suggest a measure of success for regional policy.[24] The various policy controls appear to have halted the so-called 'drift' to the South East and the decline in the net annual loss from the Northern region is an encouraging sign. However, the South East reversal may be partly explained by trends in international migration. A closer examination of Table 9.5 also reveals increasing gains by neighbouring East Anglia and the South West but a changing picture in the West Midlands. Scotland continues to lose annually almost the equivalent of its natural increase, including a high proportion of young males, and the constant net migration losses from the North West and Yorkshire and Humberside suggests that their recent designation as Intermediate Areas was not before time.

Trends in public and private investment are more encouraging. The increase in public spending in the period 1965–70 was 44% in the UK as a whole, 33% in the South East, 100% in the Northern Region and 150% in Scotland. Fig. 9.2 similarly reveals some shifts in *per capita* public investment in new construction, especially in the North and West Midlands.

Figure 9.3 reveals the trends in industrial building (approved) over the period 1954–70. With the exception of the mid 1950's, the problem regions have fared rather better than their population size would justify in terms of gaining industrial floorspace. This represents a major policy achievement. Much of this extra

229

floorspace is attributable to new firms moving into the regions. In a valuable Board of Trade study[25] of the movement of manufacturing industry in the UK between 1945 and 1965, factory movements are subdivided into those destined for the 'peripheral areas' and those going to the 'remaining areas'. The peripheral areas are Northern Ireland, Scotland, Wales, the Northern Region, Merseyside and South West Lancashire and Devon and Cornwall. Figure 9.3 illustrates the large volume of factory movements to the peripheral areas in the post-war Labour period and in the post-1960 period when policy measures

Fig. 9.3   Trends in industrial building (approved)
'Problem' regions: North, Yorkshire and Humberside (East and West Ridings prior to 1960), North West, Scotland and Wales
'Other' regions: remaining British regions (northern Ireland excluded)

SOURCE   Abstract of Regional Statistics (1965, 1971).

were rigorously applied. In contrast, in the intervening period, the total volume of movements fell off markedly with the majority going to the Home Counties and the Midlands.

The number of factory moves however is not in itself a sufficient indicator of policy effectiveness. What types of moves are involved? Which industries are attracted to the problem regions?

Are the firms large or small and what of the employment created? The BOT study reveals that factories moving to the peripheral areas are mainly branch concerns. Of the 1101 complete transfers of factories recorded during the study period only 200 went to peripheral areas. Unfortunately branch concerns are usually more vulnerable in times of economic crisis, and this can have serious implications for the future economic stability of the problem regions. The factories moving to the peripheral areas include a wide range of industries, although the percentage of the total belonging to faster growing manufacturing sectors is only 60%

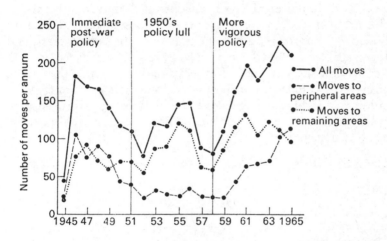

Fig. 9.4   The movement of manufacturing industry in the United Kingdom 1945–65

SOURCE   D. E. Keeble. 'Industrial movement and regional development in the United Kingdom', *Town Planning Review* (January 1972), page 6 (from Board of Trade 1968).

compared with 75% for migrant establishments in the South East and East Anglia. But this is still quite substantial, and an application by Stilwell[26] of the proportionality modification shift variation of the shift-share analysis outlined in Chapter 5, indicates some improvement in the industrial structure of the North West, Scotland, Wales, the Northern region and the South West between 1959 and 1967.

Yet despite this large-scale public and private investment in the problem regions, the growth in employment has generally been less than the national average (see Table 9.1). The usual explanation is that much of the new development has been capital intensive.[27] There is undoubtedly some truth in this argument, although if a more long-run view is adopted, industrial relocation should be evaluated more in terms of future income growth and the creation of a sound industrial structure rather than simply in terms of jobs. Two other factors are perhaps of equal if not more importance in explaining this slow employment growth. Firstly, the South East has had a monopoly of the rapidly growing service sector, which remained largely uncontrolled until 1965. Secondly, the problem regions have faced an unprecedented decline in employment in their basic industries over the last 20 years, and this had to be offset by new jobs. Thus if one considers that Scotland, Wales and the Northern Region together lost more than 300 000 jobs in the traditional industries of mining, agriculture and shipbuilding alone in the decade 1956–66, the maintenance of the employment *status quo* is in itself something of an achievement.

Table 9.6. *Average Total Weekly Household Income: Regional Trends (Index of UK Average).*

Region	1964–66	1969–70	1974–5
South East	113	113	113
West Midlands	110	102	101
East Midlands	99	95	97
South West	93	95	96
Yorkshire and Humberside	96	93	90
North West	96	98	93
East Anglia	94	93	96
Scotland	96	96	97
Wales	91	90	92
North	84	94	92
Northern Ireland	84	85	81
United Kingdom	100 (£25·2)	100 (£33·9)	100 (£65·9)

SOURCE *Family Expenditure Survey, Abstract of Regional Statistics.*

The *change in regional income levels* is a final indicator of the effectiveness of policy tools. This is generally regarded as the acid test of regional policy—does it make people better off, reducing the regional imbalance? The evidence in Table 9.6 is not too encouraging. There might be very limited convergence but the South East still remains well above the norm and problem regions, especially Northern Ireland, remain well below. There is also further evidence of a relative decline in the fortunes of the West Midlands; but no indicator is foolproof, regional cost of living variations may moderate the income differences. Nor do the latter necessarily reflect variations in the quality of life between the regions.

EMPLOYMENT CREATION
Another approach to policy effectiveness is directly to assess the number of jobs created by regional policy. Such an approach has been pioneered in the UK by Rhodes and Moore[28] who have attempted to measure the employment impact of regional policy post 1963, when policy measures were greatly strengthened. An initial investigation into the differences in employment growth between Assisted Areas and Non-Assisted Areas for four composite industrial categories revealed a marked improvement in the Assisted Areas performance—largely due to the differential performance of manufacturing industries. To assess whether this was due to regional policy, Rhodes and Moore calculated a 'non-policy' or 'passive' alternative position. This measure of 'expected' performance in the manufacturing sector in the Assisted Areas was calculated by applying cumulatively to each Assisted Area's employment figures for 1963, the UK growth rate for each industry annually from 1950–71. A comparison of the 'actual' and 'expected' manufacturing employment figures revealed a positive differential of 12% (1963–71). Prior to 1963, in the 1950's dormant policy period, there had been no such differential, and the actual and expected series had moved closely together. By way of supporting evidence, the researchers showed that the differential was even greater in N. Ireland where there were regional measures preferential even to those in the British Assisted Areas; that the differential was in reverse in the South East in the 1960's where

233

there were regional policy controls; and that the divergence was not observed in the service sector where there was little preferential regional treatment. In total, Rhodes and Moore estimated that the impact of regional policy during the 1960–72 period was the creation of 250–300 000 new jobs (i.e. approx. 185 000 direct × 1·4 service impact multiplier). The scale of these results relates broadly with a similar analysis carried out by Brown.[29]*

This approach has been developed in several directions, with area disaggregations for Scotland,[30] Wales[31] and the Northern Region,[32] and a policy tool disaggregation. With regard to the latter, Rhodes and Moore[33] sought to explain the number of firms moving to Assisted Areas in terms of policy tools, using a multiple regression approach. With the annual number of moves as the dependent variable and the 'strength' of various policy tools over time as the independent variables, various equations were tested until a good fit was derived, i.e.

$$MDA_t = a_1 + a_2 MU_t + a_3 II_{t-1} + a_4 IDC_{t-1} + a_5 REP_{t-1}$$

where MDA = annual number of moves to Development Areas.

MU = pressure of demand (male unemployment rate in GB).

II = amount of capital grant (aid per £100 expenditure on capital equipment.)

IDC = strength of IDC policy (as indicated by number of refusals).

REP = regional employment premium (value over time).

$a_{1,2,3,4,5}$ = constants.

t, t_{-1} = time periods.

---

* However, more recent analysis by Moore, Rhodes and Tyler in *The Impact of Regional Policy in the 1970's* (Centre for Environmental Studies, London, 1977) suggests that the regional policy employment effect may be levelling off. Over the period 1960–1976, the estimated direct effect of creating 282 000 jobs includes a rise to a peak of over 26 000 jobs per annum in the late 1960's, falling off by over a third to just over 17 000 jobs per annum in the mid 1970's. This may be explained by several factors, including a weakening of some policy measures, the political troubles in Northern Ireland, and the levelling out of effects after the initial impact following the marked lowering of factor costs in the Assisted Areas in the 1960's.

The general results of the analysis were that IDC policy was perhaps the major policy tool, closely supported by investment grants.

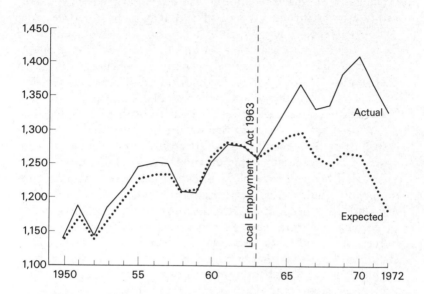

Fig. 9.5   Actual and expected employment in manufacturing industries (excluding shipbuilding and metals) in the assisted areas,* 1950–72

SOURCE   Moore, B., and Rhodes, J., 'The Effects of Regional Economic Policy in the UK,' in Sant, M. (ed.), *Regional Policy and Planning for Europe*, Saxon House (1974).

To conclude, this examination of a limited number of indicators offers little evidence to suggest that the regional imbalance will soon be a thing of the past. Policy to date has been basically a holding operation, running hard just to stand still. This in itself is a creditable achievement but there is still a long way to go and a relaxation of measures at this stage could be very damaging.

* Defined as Scotland, Wales, Northern England and Northern Ireland.

235

6 A reappraisal

The questioning of the form of regional policy has been accentuated in the mid to late 1970's by the major changes which have occurred in the macro-economic and demographic environment. For Western Europe in general and Britain in particular, the decades of economic growth which provided the context for regional policy gave way to a period of nil or very slow growth. High unemployment became a national phenomenon with problem pockets developing in the formerly prosperous regions. In a context of increased and widening demands on government aid and even scarcer resources, the redistributive effect of regional policy becomes increasingly painful for those not benefiting, for distribution then tends to be out of a fixed rather than a growing cake. Many academic commentators have called for a major reappraisal of regional policy, and politicians representing predominantly inner city locations in the South East and West Midlands have been, in essence, arguing for the total dismantling of regional policy. Such arguments have been countered by the Government, with for example the Secretary of State (DOE) stating in April 1977 that 'it would be great folly if we were now at this stage to start abandoning regional policy.* Yet there have been some significant changes in the 1970's with the ending of REP in late 1976 and the easing of IDC control.

A changing context, in particular a changing national economic context, may necessitate a reappraisal of regional policy measures. In addition, if certain policy measures are more effective than others, it may be beneficial to increase their use, reducing the rôle of more dubious measures. There may also be policy tools as yet unused which have an important rôle to play. However, the purpose here is not to suggest the optimal regional policy package, for what is optimal obviously varies according to region, industry and over time. The aim is more one of indicating certain possible adjustments in future regional policy.

THE CHOICE OF AREAS

A problem region is a relative concept, and its definition can vary with time and viewpoint (i.e. who is doing the comparing, and

* *Hansard*, 6 April 1977.

with what other area is the region being compared?). Although there is now a hierarchy of UK Assisted Areas, the system may still be too rigid.

Throughout the 40 years of UK policy there has been an undue emphasis on the level of unemployment as the major index, dividing the country into large development areas and the remainder. However, as Chapter 2 illustrates, homogeneous regions can be identified in a variety of ways and the use of a wider range of socio-economic criteria might provide a better indication of distress. In addition, regional problems are dynamic, some regions may be improving, others may be declining. In the UK, the West Midlands region has for some years been showing signs of potential distress. A major reappraisal of designated areas in favour of a region like the West Midlands is probably not justified, but some selective recognition of such an area's problems may usefully serve to nip a potential problem in the bud.

Inter-regional comparisons can also hide a multitude of intra-regional variations. Some of the traditional prosperous areas may have major pockets of depression; for example the London docklands area in the South East. Further, some of the traditional Assisted Areas may have major pockets of prosperity, such as locations in NE Scotland which have benefited from North Sea oil related developments—although it should be added that the traditional Assisted Areas also still tend to have the worst relative problem pockets.

The problem of pockets of distress poses a major dilemma in regional development policy. Should aid be focused on economically efficient locations, growth centres, within a region, in the hope that benefits will percolate into the wider region, or should aid be focused on the problem pockets, inner city problems and isolated industrial locations, in the interests of equity? The extent of the trade off between equity and efficiency is a difficult one. In the UK, the emphasis has tended to be on the growth centre approach but this approach, sometimes seen as discriminating against problem pockets, has been coming under increasing pressure.[34] Although it should be added that a condemnation of growth centre/pole policy *per se*, on the basis of net backwash effects can be premature, for net spillovers may take some time to materialise.[35] Overall however, the discussion would seem to suggest a case for more sub-regional and perhaps local flexibility in the identification of Assisted Areas. Increasing flexibility was reflected in policy terms with, for example, in 1977 the rescheduling of the Aberdeen area down from Development Area to Intermediate Area status, and the relaxation of IDC controls on inner city locations in London and Birmingham. In 1977 also, the Northern Region Strategy Team advocated a more flexible use of Special Development Areas, suggesting the designation of small and very localised areas where substantial regional aid would be available for a long period.[36]

THE COST OF NEGATIVE CONTROLS

The UK system of control over the location of new projects or major expansion of existing firms via the use of IDC's is the most comprehensive in Western Europe. Of all the policy measures used by the Government to influence the location of industry it is probably also the most criticised. Much of this criticism centres around the administration of IDC control. The application for an IDC is judged in complete secrecy by the civil servants of the responsible government department (now the DI), who themselves have been criticised for their lack of industrial experience and knowledge of the issues. The applicant is denied access to, and has little knowledge of the representation of his case and is thus incapable of correcting any misunderstandings that may arise. This situation makes it difficult for a firm to judge the reactions of the DI and leads to the non-presentation of some potentially successful applications and to accusations of unfairness between cases.

Another major criticism is that the full cost of the measure is not explicit. It is argued that a firm faced with IDC controls may not expand at all, or may expand abroad or even if it does move to an assisted area may do so with a marked rise in costs and loss of efficiency. Evidence on these issues is difficult to collect and rarely conclusive. Luttrell,[37] in a study of 98 firms that moved to Development Areas in the late 1950's compared the production costs at the new branch location with the actual costs at the mother plant to determine whether there were (i) initial costs, and (ii) continuing extra costs, in the development area location. Results showed that although the cost of the move may be

238

initially expensive, unit costs fall over time relative to the parent factory, with lower direct wage costs offsetting the higher overheads. (Further, such a comparison is probably somewhat biassed by the scale economies at the mother plant.)

The issues were also examined by the Hunt Committee,[38] which concluded that the volume of expansion which might have been lost through IDC control could not be quantified, although it doubted on the evidence available whether it was large. It showed for example that between 1964 and 1967, only 17% of the floorspace applied for in the South East and West Midlands was refused,* and of those firms refused 80% subsequently undertook expansion mainly in Development Areas.

Other criticisms relate to the operational difficulties of IDC control. There are loopholes. Firms may expand just beneath the IDC limit or may expand by building warehouses which have been exempt from control. Of course, some would regard these loopholes more as safety valves, allowing industry to expand in the West Midlands and the South East thereby maintaining economic growth and alleviating any development distress in the prosperous areas.[39] Finally, it has also been argued that IDC control may hinder self-help in the problem regions, developing a 'let's sit back and wait for the industry to come' attitude.

Balanced against these criticisms are several important advantages. The controls are in the narrow sense highly cost-effective, involving only the administrative costs of the DI. They may also encourage a more rational locational choice by firms, forcing them to consider a wider range of locations and perhaps making them realise that there are a wide range of external diseconomies in the prosperous areas. The controls may also help to take some of the pressure off the labour situation in such areas, thereby reducing the wastage imposed by labour 'poaching' between competing firms.

There have been several suggestions to modify the existing system, including the introduction of a sliding scale whereby the smaller the firm the greater would be the area for which a certificate was not required, and the allocation of IDC's by a system of

---

* Further, in the 1970's, the strength of IDC policy declined by 50% compared with the average prevailing in the 1960's.

auction.[40] Politically, it would be very difficult to tighten the controls any further in face of increasing representation from the controlled areas, although one minor extension, used in Norway and Sweden, might be acceptable. That is, that *any* firm intending to set up or expand whatever the size of the proposed development should automatically consult the Government on possible locations.

THE EVALUATION OF FINANCIAL INDUCEMENTS

The use of financial inducements on an ever increasing scale has raised a number of important issues. What should be the scale of such inducements and what is their value to the individual firm? Should the emphasis be on subsidies to capital or labour, and should there be more flexibility in the allocation of such inducements?

The relative scale of financial inducements has increased at a rapid rate over the last 20 years. However the absolute value of such inducements to the individual firm is difficult to assess varying according to factors such as the ratio of a firm's variable to capital costs, and the period of lapse between the start of production and the start of profits. A recent EFTA study[41] estimated that in 1971 the cash values of investment incentive benefits during the first three years of a project in a Development Area could be as high as 57·1% of capital costs in industrial buildings and 42·5% of machinery and plant costs. Such a subsidy is obviously substantial although it appears less dramatic when considered relative to a firm's total costs. Wilson[42] estimated that in 1967 the value of subsidies to both capital and labour costs might typically account for little more than 5% of a firm's annual total costs. This is less impressive. If inducements are to be effective they must be large and available over a long period, at least ten years, to give the businessman confidence in them. But this is not to belittle the scale of recent UK financial subsidies. At the margin even a 5% subsidy may still be highly significant, perhaps offsetting the extra costs of moving to the assisted areas.

Capital cost subsidies have been the predominant form of financial inducement in the UK although the introduction of the Regional Employment Premium in 1967 marked a certain shift

240

of emphasis. Capital subsidies have the advantages of usually being simple and explicit, of being a 'once and for all' subsidy rather than continuing subsidisation, and of encouraging new investment in buildings, plant and machinery and thereby improving the capital stock of the region. But they also have disadvantages. They have been validly criticised for encouraging capital intensive development. The new capital stock is often supplied from outside the assisted areas generating only a limited intra-regional spin-off. Similarly, although a capital intensive firm may sometimes 'trigger off' linked development in the depressed region, it often has a rather low multiplier effect with many of its complex components coming from outside the region.

Many of these problems can be overcome by the use of a labour subsidy such as the Regional Employment Premium (REP). Such a subsidy encourages labour intensive development, has less spillover effects to other regions, and may still have the same effect as capital subsidies in making the assisted areas more competitive. However the impact on employment of such a measure is difficult to forecast. It was estimated that the annual injection of £100 million into the assisted areas via REP would reduce labour costs by $7\frac{1}{2}\%$.[43] This would lead to a reduction in the price of goods produced in these areas, leading to an increased demand, increased industrial expansion and a rise in employment by 100 000 over a seven-year period. Such an estimation assumes that the demand for the goods of the assisted areas is price elastic, that firms can substitute between labour and capital and that firms, many of them branches of larger firms, can actually reduce prices. Many of these assumptions are undoubtedly dubious. It is probable that much of the subsidy will leak into profits and/or wage and salary increases. This in itself may generate more employment via the income multiplier and, in the profits case by attracting more firms to the area. But the total increase in employment may be considerably less than 100 000, reducing the cost effectiveness of the measure. A labour subsidy may also encourage labour hoarding, and its interference with a firms variable costs may lead to permanent subsidisation and the shoring up of inefficient concerns.

Financial inducements have also been largely directed at manufacturing industry, perhaps reflecting an economic base philo-

241

sophy that services would follow manufacturing, and/or that major services are perhaps less mobile. But the sectoral trends in most Western economies have been towards service employment. Between 1959 and 1973, service employment in Britain increased by 27% (or around 2 000 000 jobs) whereas manufacturing employment actually fell by 2%. Yet incentives to attract service industry to the problem areas have been minimal. Under the Local Employment Acts (1960–70), offices moving into Development Areas and creating more than 50 new jobs could apply for discretionary assistance in the form of removal and training grants and a 25% building grant if the move involved the firm building its own premises. But such aid was poorly publicised and very low in comparison with that available to manufacturing industry. Rhodes and Kan[44] estimated that a capital intensive manufacturing industry moving to a Development Area between 1967 and 1970 might well have received around £4900 per new job provided. The figure falls to £1900 per job for a labour intensive manufacturing industry, but is as low as £625 for office development. This constitutes a major failure in UK regional policy, and although the mid-1970's saw some improvement in the situation with a widening of service industry aid, the emphasis still remains strongly in favour of manufacturing industry.

There has also been an emphasis on aid to immigrant or mobile industry rather than indigenous industry. Admittedly, an industrial development policy for a region needs to consider both aspects, but the benefits of aid to indigenous industry, especially in periods of economic recession when there may be little mobile industry around, should be recognised. Indigenous industry is that industry controlled by, created by and having decisions made by management and personnel within the region concerned. Such control may create a more stable industrial base, less vulnerable to external management policies. It may also help to generate more management jobs, entrepreneurial talent and a self-help mentality, tackling the regional problem at root cause. Financial aid (especially initial risk capital) is important here, but sound business advice is also a necessary catalyst in fostering regional entrepreneurial skills.

In addition to incentives and disincentives to development in the private sector, use can also be made of the public sector in inter-regional planning. This has slowly been realised and as outlined earlier, public investment in infrastructure, the location of government establishments and contract preference schemes are now being used as policy tools.

Public investment in infrastructure has been used in several countries—in Languedoc in France, in the Mezzogiorno in Italy for example—as an instrument of regional policy. Investment in economic overhead capital such as roads, ports and public utilities can make an area economically more attractive; while investment in social overhead capital such as housing and recreational facilities can break down many social and psychological barriers. However the extent to which infrastructural investment can be the central instrument of inter-regional planning is not too clear. Very little is known of the ability of superior infrastructure to attract new industry. Improved inter-regional roads, for example, may open up a problem region to dangerous competition rather than encouraging new development.[45] The Hunt Report suggests that infrastructural investment may not be as cost effective as direct measures.[46] Therefore perhaps infrastructural investment should be regarded, as the French say, more as *accompagnement* rather than *entrainement*—that is accompanying growth rather than inducing it.

It contrast it has been suggested that more use could be made of public companies and the location of government establishments in the initiation of growth points in the problem regions. This could be in the form of government support for the development of industrial complexes, as in Bari–Taranto in Southern Italy;[47] or through the specific location of public sector industry. In Italy, the State has operated through a holding company, IRI (Istituto per la Ricostruzione Industriale), to further regional industrial development. Similarly, a regional dimension has been envisaged in the work of the National Enterprise Board in the UK. In the service sector, the Hardman Report, *The Dispersal of Government Work from London* (1973),[48] recommended the dispersal of 31 000 London-based civil service posts, in addition to the 7000 already in the pipeline. But the report proposed that more than one third of the 31 000 posts should remain in the South East, with little more than one half going to the Assisted Areas. With a change in government in 1974, the new Labour administration regarded the proposals as unacceptable and re-formulated the distribution with nearly 90% of the posts going to the Assisted Areas (e.g. about 7000 posts from the Ministries of Defence and Overseas Development to Glasgow).

The Labour Party[49] also note that much of the large demand for goods and services created by the public sector is at present privately supplied—electrical equipment for the GPO, surgical supplies for the National Health Service, school supplies, breath-alysers etc. More public control of these supplies could provide a source of mobile industry for the problem regions. An alternative approach is to extend the use of the distribution of public con-tracts as an instrument of regional policy. In 1976, total public sector purchasing was approximately £27000 million (at current prices), representing 25% of GNP (UK). The public sector's position as a purchaser is a most powerful government weapon; used as an instrument of regional policy it could be revolutionary.

FLEXIBILITY OF POLICY
Being centrally determined, regional policy operates through broad policies which tend to apply to all areas in a rather blanket fashion, irrespective of their particular problems. But problems vary greatly between and within regions and from situation to situation, and there is a need for selective government action. In the UK, the 1972 Industry Act (sections 7 and 8) makes some provision for selective aid, and such aid is on the increase. How-ever, another approach to a flexible and selective policy is to introduce a more devolved input into policy formulation. Again in the UK, there are some promising trends in this direction. The Department of Industry regional offices have an increasing amount of autonomy in the distribution of financial aid, and the establishment of new regional agencies such as the Scottish and Welsh Development Agencies (see Chapter 11) again reduces the distance between policy makers and problems.

But to conclude with one note of warning. Flexibility has its price, and it may be that many industrialists would react with mixed feelings to major policy changes. For them, stability and certainty of policy measures may be of major significance. (See Appendix D for recent developments.)

7 Summary

Despite the fluctuating fortunes during its 40-year history, inter-regional planning now appears to be well established in the UK. The case for intervention to help the problem regions, particularly the depressed industrial areas is now firmly based on economic, as well as social and political reasoning.

With the exception of the early inter-war period, the broad strategy has been predominantly one of 'work to the workers', but the range of tactics for implementing this strategy has shown some interesting trends. The delineated areas have evolved from the original Special Areas based almost exclusively on unemployment criteria and covering less than 20% of the country, to a hierarchy of Special Development Areas, Development Areas and Intermediate Areas, based on multiple criteria and covering more than 50% of the UK. To attract employment to these areas, the financial 'carrot' has become progressively larger, and more attractive, primarily through increased aid to a firm's capital costs. But the 'stick' in the form of IDC control has also constantly loomed menacingly in the background. Policies directed at the re-employment and mobility of labour have progressed quietly, and the rôle of direct public involvement via infrastructural investment and the use of the public sector's position as a producer and consumer of goods and services is slowly being recognised.

Yet in spite of this impressive array of measures, UK inter-regional planning has failed as yet to achieve anything more than a holding operation. Of course, this in itself can rightly be considered to represent some degree of success but there is still a long way to go. The process is long-drawn-out and premature relaxation could undo much good work.

'the economy of a less prosperous area is not static and while new employment is being introduced, job opportunities in other sectors may be lost. Indeed in areas suffering from deep-seated problems, the need for industrial renewal may extend even to a "second generation" of industrial mobility, with enter-

245

prises introduced some years before primarily to offset the decline in the traditional industries themselves having to adapt to changing circumstances, thus increasing local need for new employment.'[50]

Hence, the efficiency and effectiveness of existing measures must be kept constantly under review, and the possibility of new directions such as the greater use of the public sector and service industry must be fully investigated.

References

1 Friedman, J. F., *Regional Development Policy: A Case Study of Venezuela,* MIT Press, Camb. Mass. (1966).
2 Coates, B. E., and Rawstron, E. M., *Regional Variations in Britain,* Batsford (1971).
3 Friedman, J. F., *op cit,* page 41 ff.
4 Allen, K., and Hermansen, T., in *Regional Policy in EFTA; An examination of the Growth Centre Idea,* page 32, EFTA Secretariat, Geneva (1968), note 'that it was Joan Robinson who once made the pun that the trouble with the lazy fairies is that they are too lazy!'
5 National Economic Development Council (NEDC), *Conditions Favourable to Faster Growth,* page 16, HMSO (1963).
6 EFTA Economic Development Committee, *Regional Policy in EFTA; Industrial Mobility,* pages 68–74, EFTA Secretariat, Geneva (1971).
7 West, E. G., Regional Planning—Fact or Fallacy, *Lloyds Bank Review,* pages 33–49, April 1966;
Needleman, L., What are we to do about the regional problem? *Lloyds Bank Review,* January 1965;
Nevin, E. T., The Case for Regional Policy, *Three Banks Review,* December 1966.
8 Needleman, L., *op cit,* pages 46–7.
9 Richardson, H. W., *Regional Economics,* pages 393–7, Weidenfeld and Nicolson (1969).
10 Davies, G., Regional Unemployment, Labour Availability and Redeployment, *Oxford Economic Papers,* May 1967.
11 See: Odber, A. J., Regional Policy in Britain, Part 6 in *Area Redevelopment Policies in Britain and the Countries of the Common Market,* US Dept. of Commerce (1965);
McCrone, G., *Regional Policy in Britain,* Allen and Unwin (1969). The text by McCrone provides the most comprehensive study of

policy up to 1967, Odber's paper provides an excellent summary up to 1963.

12 Greenwood, H. P., *Employment and the Depressed Areas,* page 88, Routledge (1936).
13 *Report of the Royal Commission on the Distribution of Industrial Population,* Cmnd. 6153, HMSO (1940).
14 *Employment Policy,* Cmnd. 6527, HMSO (1944).
15 Odber, *op cit.*
16 *Central Scotland: A Programme for Development and Growth,* Cmnd. 2188, HMSO; Edinburgh (1963); *The North East: A Programme for Development and Growth,* Cmnd. 2206, HMSO, London (1963).
17 *Report of the Committee on the Intermediate Areas* (The Hunt Report), Cmnd. 3998, HMSO (1969).
18 Cmnd. 2206, *op cit.*
19 Secretary of State for Trade and Industry, *Industrial and regional development,* Cmnd. 4942 HMSO, (1972).
20 South-East Joint Planning Team, *Strategic Plan for the South-East,* HMSO (1970).
21 NEDC, *Tenth Annual Report, 1970–71.*
22 Cmnd. 4942, *op cit.*
23 Taylor, J., A Regional Analysis of Hidden Unemployment in Great Britain, 1951–66, *Applied Economics,* pages 291–303, 3 (1971).
24 For a fuller discussion, see: Eversley, D. E. C., Population Changes and Regional Policies since the War, *Regional Studies,* pages 211–28, 5, (1971).
25 Board of Trade, *The Movement of Manufacturing Industry in the UK (1945–1965),* HMSO (1968).
26 Stilwell, F. J. B., Regional growth and structural adaptation, *Urban Studies,* June 1969.
27 Bray, J., *Decision in Government,* Garden City Press (1970).
28 Rhodes, J., and Moore, B., Evaluating the effects of British regional economic policy, *Economic Journal,* 83, pp. 87–110 (1973).
29 Brown, A. J., *The Framework of Regional Economics in the UK,* NIESR (1972).
30 Rhodes, J., and Moore, B., *Regional Policy and the Economy of Wales,* Welsh Office (1975).
31 Rhodes, J., and Moore, B., Regional Policy and the Scottish Economy, *Scottish Journal of Political Economy* (November 1974).
32 NRST, *Technical Report No. 2: Evaluation of the Impact of Regional Policy on Manufacturing Industry in the Northern Region,* NRST (1975).

33 Rhodes, J., and Moore, B., Regional Economic Policy and the Movement of Manufacturing Firms to Development Areas, *RSA Conference on 'Reappraisal of Regional Economic Policy'*, Regional Studies Association (1975).

34 National Community Development Project, *The Costs of Industrial Change*, Home Office (1977).

35 Richardson, H. W., Growth Pole,Spillovers: the Dynamics of Backwash and Spread, *Regional Studies*, **10**, 1 (1976).

36 Northern Region Strategy Team, *Strategic Plan for the Northern Region*, HMSO (1977).

37 Luttrell, W. F., *Factory Location and Industrial Movement* (2 Vols), NIESR (1962).

38 Cmnd. 3998, *op cit*, paragraph 346.

39 Smith, B. M. D., Industrial development certificate control: an institutional influence on industrial mobility, *Journal of the Town Planning Institute*, February 1971.

40 Townroe, P. M., Industrial Development: What Alternatives?, *New Society*, 18/2/71.

41 EFTA, *Industrial Mobility, op cit*, pages 111–12.

42 Wilson, T., Finance for Regional Industrial Development, *Three Banks Review*, September 1967.

43 Brown, A. J., The 'Green Paper' on the Development Areas, *National Institute Economic Review*, May 1967.

44 Rhodes, J., and Kan, A., *Office dispersal and regional policy*, Occ. Papers 30, University of Cambridge, Dept. of Applied Economics (1971).

45 Gwillam, K. M., The Indirect Effects of Highway Investment, *Regional Studies*, pages 167–76, **4** (1970).

46 Cmnd. 3998, *op cit*, pages 155–65.

47 Newcombe, V., Creating an Industrial Development Pole in Southern Italy, *Journal of the Town Planning Institute*, April 1969.

48 *The Dispersal of Government Work from London*, Cmnd. 5322, HMSO (1973).

49 Labour Party, *op cit*.

50 EFTA, *Industrial Mobility, op cit*, page 108.

10 Intra-regional planning in the United Kingdom

1 The aims of intra-regional planning

Intra-regional planning is concerned with the planning of individual regions such as metropolitan South East England and the industrial North West and their constituent sub-regions. It has evolved out of the local land-use planning tradition and its objectives are social, economic and environmental.

The starting point of intra-regional planning in many countries is to be found in the problems resulting from urbanisation and population growth. This process has resulted in the growth of major metropolitan conurbations such as London, Paris, Randstad Holland and the Ruhr. But it is also a process which is affecting more than capital and major cities and can be observed in smaller towns and cities throughout the country. Such urban growth is invariably accompanied by a wide range of general social costs and increasing economic inefficiency within the urban/metropolitan regions themselves because of factors such as congestion costs and strains on public services. To cope with these problems there is a need to look beyond the existing urban area to the wider regional or sub-regional context. This need for a wider view is also reinforced by the increasing mobility of the population.

Intra-regional planning can also be seen as a necessary complement to the primarily economic based inter-regional planning geared largely to promoting economic development in the

249

depressed industrial and under-developed regions. It is here that the relationship between regional economic planning and regional physical planning is most clearly seen, for economic regeneration depends not only on labour supply and financial incentives to industry but also on the adequacy of the physical infrastructure such as roads, public utilities, housing and schools. A modernisation of industrial activity needs to be accompanied by a modernisation of the general physical and social environment and this requires careful planning.

Intra-regional planning usually involves the preparation of a plan for a region. The primary aim of this plan is to provide a framework for the region showing what it can do to improve the economic and social conditions and the quality of the environment . . . to achieve a satisfactory relationship between people, jobs and the environment within the region. In addition it can also be seen as providing an input into national planning and a basis for co-ordinating more local plans.

Suggestions for the contents of such a plan vary, but most usually involve a target for the future in the form of a definitive plan—with proposals for the location of population, employment, major recreational and cultural facilities, the communications network and so on—and a programme of planned development towards that future. In their report on *Regional Planning Policy*, the Labour Party Study Group suggested the following as the approximate contents of a regional plan:[1]

a study of the region's resources—land and natural resources, population and manpower, capital and entrepreneurship—together with its regional and inter-regional industrial linkages, input–output relationships, travel-to-work patterns and so forth

b analysis of problems and needs, such as shortages of jobs and particular sorts of jobs, of manpower and particular skills, of transport facilities, housing, education and other social service provision, water and power resources, and so on

c working in existing plans and programmes for the future, e.g. for roads, hospitals, new towns, universities, together with the plans of the nationalised industries

d gathering information on the future plans of the private sector both directly and from known future investment plans, from share of the market targets, from analysis of regional, national

250

and international growth rates and trends, from input–output linkages and so on

e examination of changes that are likely to affect the present structure, e.g. demographic trends, changes in education, technology, social habits, investment

f working out the likely rates of expansion in sectors at given growth rates on the basis of examined linkages, and the consequences of this for job creation, public expenditure etc.

g analysis of the necessary action to be taken on incentives to industry (including guidelines on the types of industry and employment most needed), retraining, infrastructure development and the like

h land use pattern—agricultural land, water, areas of natural beauty and tourist attraction, communications, areas suitable for population and industrial growth.

The remainder of this chapter now examines the evolution of intra-regional planning in the United Kingdom, the regional planning process, emerging strategies and selected case studies. However, the vital question of administration and alternative forms of administrative machinery is left to the next chapter.

2 The evolution of intra-regional planning in the United Kingdom

The evolution of UK intra-regional planning followed a course somewhat similar to that for inter-regional planning. Although the original impetus dates back to the late nineteenth century, it was not until the inter-war years that planners became concerned about the conurbations and inter-urban development. This was followed by significant progress in the immediate post-war years, but then a lull in the 1950's. However since the early 1960's there have been considerable advances and the development of several alternative approaches to regional and sub-regional planning. [Appendix C lists the major UK Regional and Sub-Regional Studies by Economic Planning Region.]

THE EARLY DEVELOPMENT OF INTRA-REGIONAL PLANNING

The history of intra-regional planning can probably be traced back to Ebeneezer Howard. In his *Garden Cities of Tomorrow* he proposed the establishment of a cluster of new towns linked to a central city to deal with the rapidly expanding nineteenth-century city. These multi-centred regional clusters were to be separated from the existing cities, such as London or Glasgow, by means of green belts and were to contain both homes and jobs. But, apart from the early garden cities such as Letchworth and Welwyn, there was little immediate development of Howard's ideas. The most significant development in the inter-war years was the establishment of Joint Advisory Committees of Local Authority Planning Departments to attempt to co-ordinate the growth and interaction of towns. Unfortunately such bodies achieved little primarily due to the parochial infighting between the various County Boroughs and County Councils.

Towards the end of the Second World War there were more encouraging signs. The Barlow Report[2] realised the advantages of regional planning and the Scott Committee,[3] concerned with the problem of industrial development in rural areas and its effect on agriculture and rural amenities, recommended that planning should be carried out regionally as well as nationally so that local authority land-use plans conformed to national priorities. Out of this background emerged a series of advisory regional plans, the most notable being those for Greater London and the Clyde Valley. The *Greater London Plan 1944* was prepared by Professor Patrick Abercrombie for the Standing Conference on London Regional Planning, constituted in 1937; and the *Clyde Valley Plan 1946*, was prepared by Abercrombie and Matthew for the Clyde Valley Regional Planning Advisory Committee, composed of constituent local authorities and established in 1943.

These advisory urban regional plans were documents of considerable vision motivated by the social aims of accelerated redevelopment and dispersal and by the aesthetic concept of new regional forms against a background of green belt and countryside. But they were primarily physical planning documents with little economic content. In addition, their immediate implementation was limited by the lack of resources and inflationary pressure in the post-war years. Nevertheless they did have considerable influence on government decisions and local authority plans. From this period stems much of the important post-war physical planning legislation—the New Towns Act (1946), the Town and

252

Country Planning Act (1947) and the Town Development Act (1952)—all of which provided important tools for the implementation of urban regional planning. In the late 1940's, a number of new towns were designated including the eight London new towns and East Kilbride and Glenrothes in Scotland. Many of these were located in accordance with the principles laid down in the advisory plans. A start was also made in the preparation of development plans to cover the whole country. These also were influenced by the advisory plans.

With the advent of a Conservative Government in the 1950's, this early enthusiasm soon waned. Planning fell into disrepute and the political disinterest was reflected in several ways. There was a lack of a national lead on matters of overall policy, the regional offices of the Ministry of Town and Country Planning were abandoned, there was a failure to extend, revise and implement the advisory regional plans, and only one new town, Cumbernauld, was designated during the decade. The antiquated local government units continued to undermine the effectiveness of any form of regional planning, and the 'overspill controversies', such as that between Manchester County Borough and Lancashire County Council over the use of Westhoughton as an overspill location, were a typical result.

Only in Scotland was there any commendable progress. The *Clyde Valley Plan* was published in 1946 and was later adopted as the framework for resolving the general problems of the Clyde Valley and the congestion problems of Glasgow in particular. The designation of the new town of Cumbernauld in 1955 provided early evidence of the acceptance of the plan and, in spite of taking many hard knocks, it has continued to underpin the planning policies of the area. Scotland has also continued to figure prominently in both the practice and theory of UK regional planning, and this no doubt stems to a large extent from the degree of Scottish administrative independence in many matters, including planning.

A REVIVAL OF INTRA-REGIONAL PLANNING

A revival of interest in intra-regional planning was stimulated by a re-emphasis of the regional imbalance in the country at the beginning of the 1960's. The symptoms of economic distress became more marked in the problem regions and the Government was forced to take action. As outlined in Chapter 9, one response was the production, in 1963, of two White Papers on regional development programmes for Central Scotland and North East England designating eight growth areas for Central Scotland and a growth zone for the North East. These areas were to benefit from considerable investment in promotional infrastructure. This action implied a large degree of government commitment and represented an important fusion between the economic and physical aspects of inter- and intra-regional planning.

The government also took a renewed interest in the major conurbations where the problems of congestion were becoming worse and worse. A major stimulus came from the need to accommodate a far greater population growth than had originally been anticipated. A new generation of new towns, including Dawley, Redditch, Skelmersdale and Runcorn were designated to take the overspill of Birmingham and South Lancashire, and a new series of major regional studies were commissioned—the first since the *Clyde Valley Plan*. The *South East Study (1961–1981)* was produced in 1964. The proposals in this document introduced a new scale of planning, but they were essentially physical, seeking to accommodate the population growth of the area, and there was little economic content. The study was regarded primarily as a basis for discussion and implied no government commitment.

An interesting contrast at this time was the situation in Northern Ireland. In 1963, the government commissioned Professor Thomas Wilson to prepare a comprehensive plan for future economic development in Northern Ireland. The Wilson Report of 1965 provides a detailed programme of action covering the location of industry in centres of growth, amenity and tourism, transport services, training, inducements to industry, agriculture and the general investment programme. This Report was accepted by the Government, and together with Sir Robert Matthew's physically oriented *Belfast Regional Plan* (1963), has since formed the basis for the development of the province.

Following these initial developments, the 1960's and early 1970's have witnessed the production of a whole range of intra-regional studies, reports, plans and strategies which can be broadly divided into regional and sub-regional categories. The distinction between the two categories is bound to be somewhat arbitrary with wide areas of overlap, but for the purposes of discussion the regional studies are taken to relate to the large Economic Planning Regions and are primarily sponsored by departments of central government; whereas the sub-regional studies relate to smaller areas and have been more in the sphere of local planning authorities.

The regional level

The creation of a new Ministry, the Department of Economic Affairs (DEA), in 1964, and the establishment during 1965 and 1966 of a series of Regional Economic Planning Councils and Boards for eight English planning regions and Scotland, Wales and Northern Ireland marked the advent of a new phase of regional studies. The Councils of nominated members were given the tasks of studying the needs and potentialities of their regions, giving regional advice to the government, and preparing broad strategies for future development. The Boards of civil servants were to assist the Councils in their tasks and to co-ordinate the work of central government departments at the regional level.

The first studies, for the North West and the West Midlands, were produced by central government under the DEA. Later studies were produced by the respective regional councils and by 1968 were available for each region. The studies vary greatly in quality but overall have not matched up to many people's expectations. They have been criticised on several counts—for being descriptive studies rather than positive strategies, for their inability to link the physical and economic aspects of regional planning, and for their inward-looking nature and lack of integration.

It is certainly true that many of the studies have been more concerned with regional stocktaking seeking to clarify the regional planning problems rather than to put forward policies and propose solutions. Thus the aim of the *East Midlands Study* was:

'to present to the public an account of the region as it is, and as it is changing; it draws attention to problems and opportunities, with an indication of what is involved in them. It is hoped that the study will form an adequate basis for the

255

public discussion out of which the main lines of the region's planning will emerge, until adequate opportunity for that discussion has been provided it would be presumptuous to go further.'[4]

Similarly, *A Review of Yorkshire and Humberside*

'does not attempt to produce a regional plan, either economic or physical. It is the report of the Regional Economic Planning Council's first survey of the area, based mainly on information collected and analysed by the various departments of central government, constituting the Economic Planning Board. For the most part it presents a statement of the main demographic, economic and social circumstances of the region as a whole and of its sub-divisions.'[5]

This approach however can be partially justified by the fact that in many regions, particularly in the newly constituted Yorkshire and Humberside Region, there was at the time little in the way of official regional statistical data on which plans could be based.

This first round of studies was followed in the late 1960's by an attempt by the Economic Planning Councils to produce preliminary regional strategies. Outline strategies with an economic emphasis were produced for the North, North West and Yorkshire and Humberside, and a more physically oriented strategy was produced for the South East. But such strategies did not constitute firm plans, accepted by the Government. They were more initial sketches of the future principles of strategic planning to be discussed and amended with central government, local authorities and any other public agencies involved in large-scale regional investment. In contrast, the White Paper for Scotland *The Scottish Economy 1965–70. A Plan for Expansion* published in January 1966 by the Scottish Office carried more political commitment. The White Paper included an interesting survey of the existing situation and future potential of Scotland, and although it did not have the scope of a comprehensive regional plan, did deal in detail with proposals for immediate investment over a five-year period. It also provided a framework for more detailed sub-regional plans such as those for Central Scotland, Grangemouth–Falkirk, and South West Scotland produced by the Scottish Development Department.

Over the last few years, the work of the Regional Economic Councils and Boards in regional planning has been paralleled by that of the local authorities. Indeed, the formation of the Councils and Boards probably stimulated some coming together of local authorities within the same economic planning region, in the form of Standing Conferences, to push along the preparation of regional strategies. In the South East, this pressure resulted in the commissioning by the Standing Conference on London and the South East, the South East Economic Planning Council and the Government, of a new *Strategic Plan* for the region. The terms of reference of the strategy were:

> 'to report on patterns of development for the South East . . . with the objective of providing a regional framework for the local planning authorities to carry out their planning responsibilities . . . and for government decisions on investment and economic and social policies relating to the region's future development.'[6]

The comprehensive report, prepared by a team under the Chief Planner of the Ministry of Housing and Local Government, was published in 1970. In October 1971, it was accepted in principle by the Government as the framework for regional planning in the South East.

In the West Midlands, the Planning Authorities' Conference took the initiative into their own hands and in 1971 published *A Developing Strategy for the West Midlands* as a basis for consultation with individual local authorities, the Economic Planning Council and other interested bodies prior to the submission of proposals to the Government.

Such developments have prompted Government support for the joint preparation of regional plans.

> 'It is the Government's intention that future regional strategies should be prepared on a tripartite basis in collaboration between the regional economic planning councils, the local planning authorities, and central government. Ultimately, it is hoped to cover all the English regions in this way, but detailed arrangements and timing will vary from region to region.'[7]

Planning teams have since produced strategies for several other

regions, and some of the most important developments are outlined in the final section of this chapter.

The sub-regional level

The late 1960's have also witnessed the development of a whole
range of supra-urban studies. The origins and objectives of these
studies are diverse, but two major groups can be identified
which are now conventionally regarded as constituting the new
breed of sub-regional studies. The first group are studies carried
out for local planning authorities to co-ordinate the future natural
growth or interaction of large towns and cities. Included in this
group are the sub-regional plans for Teesside, Leicester and
Leicestershire, Nottinghamshire and Derbyshire, North Gloucestershire and Coventry–Warwickshire–Solihull. The Teesside
study published in 1969 dates from the transportation planning
era of the early 1960's and can be regarded as a bridge between
the transportation and sub-regional plans. The other studies
originate from an awakening of the sub-regional idea by Richard
Crossman, who as Minister of Housing and Local Government
in 1965

>·'believed that in advance of, and without prejudice to any
> subsequent reform of local government functions and boun-
> daries, co-operative planning ventures could begin between the
> towns and their surrounding authorities. His initial aim was to
> persuade the authorities in a small number of selected areas to
> come together and set up ad-hoc teams to prepare long term
> "broad-brush" plans for land uses and transportation. These
> were to be called 'sub-regional studies.'"[8]

Leicester City Council and Leicestershire County Council set up
one of the earliest of these studies in 1966, and the report was published in 1969. This was followed in quick succession by three
other studies, including the *Coventry–Solihull–Warwickshire* study
which was produced in 1971. All the studies have been produced by independent study teams set up for the purpose, with
the exception of the *North Gloucestershire Sub-Regional Study*
which was produced primarily by the local authority planning
departments. The studies have introduced many technical innovations in the planning process, with each study building on the

258

work of its predecessors, and will no doubt have a major impact on planning in the 1970s. Indeed, under local government re-organisation (discussed in Chapter 11), the new county structure plans will no doubt take on many of the attributes of the recent sub-regional studies. But sub-regional planning will still have a useful rôle to play. Many issues will continue to overlap local authority boundaries and the 1971 Town and Country Planning Act makes provision for joint studies. Here, sub-regional planning can perhaps be viewed as strategic planning at the scale of the whole or parts of at least two authorities, providing a link between the regional framework and the structure plans.*

The second group of studies are concerned with an examination of the feasibility of the large-scale planned expansion of selected areas of the country. They were commissioned by the central government and have been undertaken either by consultants or directly by government departments. Important studies in this category include those for South Hampshire, Humberside, Severnside and Tayside. The objective of the *South Hampshire Study* was to investigate the feasibility of large scale expansion of the area and its suitability for receiving some of the anticipated population increase of the South East in the form of overspill in the order of 250 000. The study, undertaken by Colin Buchanan and Partners, was completed in 1966 and makes an important contribution to the study of urban form. The three estuarial studies for Humberside, Tayside and Severnside arose out of the *Interim Report of the Long Term Population Distribution Group*, which raised the need to investigate possible reception areas for part of the then anticipated population increase of 20 million by the end of the century, and for industrial/maritime purposes. The objective of the studies was to investigate the physical possibilities and economic prospects for accommodating population increases in the order of 175 000–300 000 for Tayside, 300 000–750 000 for Humberside and 650 000–1 000 000 for Severnside by the end of the century. The *Humberside Study*, published in 1969 and the *Severnside Study*, published in 1971, were undertaken by a special Central Unit for Environmental Planning established under the

* The *Reading–Wokingham–Aldershot–Basingstoke Sub-Regional Study* (1975), a study for a major growth area designated in the Strategic Plan for the South East, provides an illustration of this rôle.

DEA, with some local authority assistance. The Scottish Study, published in 1970, was undertaken by a joint team from the Scottish Development Department and the University of Dundee. The collective consideration of both economic and physical planning aspects is a major strength of this group of studies.

3 The regional planning process

Planning is a continuous process concerned with guiding the development of a particular system—urban, regional, etc. Over the last decade or so, a systematic approach to such a process has developed. This approach has been well documented elsewhere (McLoughlin, Jackson, Boyce, Day and McDonald)[9] and this brief section seeks only to outline the main stages in such a process, as used in recent British and American studies.

A SYSTEMATIC APPROACH

Over the last few years, and particularly in the recent spate of British regional and sub-regional studies, the planning process of 'survey-analysis-plan' first formalised by Geddes has taken on a new terminology. The planning process is now seen as a sequence of operations involving the survey and analysis of the study area examining its needs and potential for development, the formulation of goals and/or objectives and the generation and testing of alternative strategies. However, although there may be some correlation between the main stages of the processes of recent studies, in detail they vary considerably, each geared and tailor-made to the requirements of its study area. Figures 10.1 and 10.2 provide simplified flow diagrams of the main stages in the processes used in the preparation of the *Coventry–Solihull–Warwickshire Sub-Regional Study* (CSW), and the *Strategic Plan for the South East*—two recent British sub-regional and regional studies.

The broad aims of a regional/sub-regional study are usually implicit in the initial terms of reference. From this starting point, generalised goals relating to factors such as social and economic balance and prosperity, choice and flexibility can be developed. But an assessment of how far alternative strategies might actually achieve these goals requires the definition of more specific objectives. Such objectives usually evolve from the survey and analysis stage which throws up identifiable problems. This may involve multi-stage development and refinement and the breakdown into sub-groups such as primary, secondary and tertiary objectives, grouped and provisional objectives, or essential and discriminatory objectives. Examples of objectives (discriminatory) used in the CSW Sub-Regional Study include:

Objective Number

2   To locate new development so that the loss of good quality farmland is kept to a minimum.

7   To locate new development so that physical disturbance to existing development is kept to a minimum.

16   To locate new population and employment where there is the greatest possible choice of transport route and mode available.

20   To retain as far as possible the option of switching from any preferred strategy to one of any other strategies examined once implementation has begun.

This stage of formulating goals and objectives is of vital importance in the planning process and has recently been assuming a much more significant rôle. Unfortunately the generality of the goals and objectives produced leaves much to be desired, as does the lack of public participation in their formulation. Apart from a limited number of public sample surveys the formulation has tended to be determined almost exclusively by the professional planning team.

Basic to all the studies are the stages of survey, analysis and forecasting, identifying the existing characteristics of the study area and exploring and projecting future characteristics. This can be seen as a two-sided, supply and demand exercise with the survey and analysis of regional characteristics providing a picture of existing regional needs and potential, but also clarifying the constraints on any future development; and the projection of future characteristics suggesting the scale of the demands to be made on the area resulting from future growth and change. At this stage, the adequacy or otherwise of the regional data base is

261

At these stages special reports were presented to the Planning Authorities viz:-

1. A sub-regional primer   3. Data report   5. Report on intended evaluation procedure   7. Detailing report
2. Study programme   4. Brief for the plan   6. Alternatives report   8. Draft final report

Fig. 10.1 Simplified flow diagram of main stages in study process: Coventry–Solihull–Warwickshire sub-regional study

SOURCE *Coventry–Solihull–Warwickshire: A Strategy for the Sub-region*, Coventry City Council, Solihull County Borough Council and Warwickshire County Council (1971).

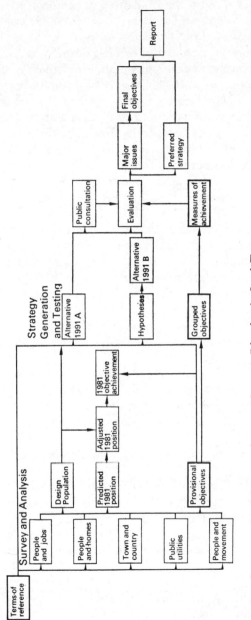

Fig. 10.2 Summarised diagram of process: Strategic Plan for the South East

SOURCE C. L. W. Minay, Department of Town Planning, Oxford Polytechnic (based on text of study report, *Strategic Plan for the South East*, HMSO (1970)).

of vital importance. A survey and analysis of regional activities such as population and employment, regional land use and communications makes heavy demands, as does the forecasting involved. Projections of population trends, changes in industry and employment, housing and shopping and many other associated activities are made on the basis of a variety of assumptions about natural population change and migration, trends in the major industrial sectors, rates of household formation and so on. The methods used vary in their complexity from simple trend projections to the use of complex mathematical models. But the length of the projection period (often greater than 25 years), the lengthy chains of reasoning and uncertainty about the future leave much room for inaccuracy and make forecasting extremely hazardous.

Given the projection of future characteristics and the formulation of specific objectives, the next stage involves the generation of alternative strategies. The contemporary approach to plan generation has been to produce a wide range of competing alternatives in an attempt to achieve the best solution. Although all studies consider factors such as the location of employment, housing demand and work–home relationships, there is no standard approach to plan generation and a variety of different methods can be identified:*

1. the use of simple, hypothetical concepts of urban form—linear cities, grid cities, growth corridors are examples
2. urban extensions determined primarily by land form and physical factors and problems using a simple 'sieve map' technique
3. trend growth—continuing the established pattern of development
4. sensitive analysis of the internal economic and social system which would be extended by the growth being planned—especially the distribution of basic employment
5. the construction of strategies derived directly or indirectly from the planning objectives emerging from survey and analysis.

* This classification is based partly on 'A background paper on the Coventry–Solihull–Warwickshire Sub-Regional Study.' *CES Next Stages in Sub-Regional Planning Conference,* pages 10–11, January 1972.

The generation of a range of alternative strategies necessitates the need for choice and most studies now identify a distinct evaluation stage in their planning process. It is the stage at which an identification is made of the comparative advantages and disadvantages of the alternatives. It logically follows the stage of analysis and alternatives generation and precedes decision making, although in practice there may be some blurring between them. For example, evaluation may provide new insights which may lead to recycling and the generation of a set of superior alternatives.

A wide variety of evaluation techniques are now available and have been used in regional and sub-regional planning (see: Lichfield[10]). They can be broadly subdivided into partial and comprehensive techniques. Of course, to some extent all evaluation techniques are partial in that they fail to include all the repercussions of a particular action. However, certain techniques make little attempt to be comprehensive. Narrow financial appraisal, cost effectiveness and cost-minimisation are the major categories of partial evaluation. The cost minimisation approach of threshhold analysis is of particular interest and has been used in several studies.[11] However, most studies prefer a more comprehensive form of evaluation such as Cost-Benefit Analysis (CBA). CBA involves taking a wide view and a long view of the repercussions of a particular action—the adoption of a strategic plan for an area. The method involves the identification, enumeration and evaluation of all relevant costs and benefits and their discounting to a standard base. This involves problems, not least the enumeration problems of defining the 'cut-off' point and dealing with intangibles, the problems of evaluating intangibles and considering equity factors, and the choice of discounting technique and interest rate.[12]

In this evaluation stage, the use of developments of CBA such as the Planning Balance Sheet (PBS) and the Goals Achievement Matrix (GAM) overcome some of the problems and may present more useful tools. The GAM Method involves the evaluation of alternative strategies against the stated goals and objectives and in some studies has been developed into a complex evaluation procedure. The existence of many diverse goals and objectives usually necessitates a system of weights as an input into the technique. This provides another opportunity for public participation which has largely been neglected to date. Similarly, there has been little attempt to incorporate the impact of alternative strategies on community groups.

The evaluation stage inevitably leads to a preferred strategy. But evaluation is not decision making, it is only an aid to the decision makers. If the plan is accepted by the responsible authorities it then remains to be implemented, for 'a form of planning which does not comprehend within itself the resources and means of implementation is not planning in any effective sense.'[13] This stage of the regional process constitutes a major stumbling block in the UK at the present time and the administrative questions involved are explored more fully in the next chapter. But this is not the end of the process. Planning, as envisaged in contemporary studies, has no end-product. It is part of a continuing process which must be kept under review and amended where necessary in the light of the monitoring of the key indicators of the region's condition.

ALTERNATIVE PERSPECTIVES
However, implicit in the preceding discussion, and now generally accepted, is the fact that a systematic 'look before you leap approach' ·has many problems. There is firstly the problem of *uncertainty*. Limited information and crude forecasting models mean that the planner has only a very partial picture of the environment of planning proposals. In the UK there have been rapid and unforeseen changes of fundamental regional significance in the last few years. A second problem relates to *community values*. How can they be determined especially with regard to nebulous strategic planning concepts? Even if group values could be determined at a particular point in time, they are likely to change over the plan period (note the rapidly changing climate of opinion on nuclear power in the UK in the 1970's); and how can/should the preferences of one group be traded off with those of another? Thirdly, there is the problem of *implementation and co-ordination*. Will the policies once formulated be carried out efficiently? This is a particular problem at the regional level, where in many countries (and certainly in the UK) regional development decision making powers are dispersed about a pluralist environment in which the regional planning agency

266

itself often has a weak advisory position.

In the face of such problems, a number of alternative approaches to the planning process have been suggested. Lindblom[14] for example advocates a *'disjointed incrementalist'* or *'muddling through'* approach, in which there is a continuous reaction to problems as they emerge. The approach is one of continuous short run marginal adjustments to policies rather than the evaluation of more radical alternatives. Such an approach avoids the problem of generating ideal goals and reflects the fragmentation of agencies in real life, but is ill equipped to deal with complex problems and may be a recipe for inertia planning constantly chasing after yesterday's problems.

A compromise approach is perhaps offered by Etzioni's[15] *'mixed scanning'* formulation, which seeks to combine a longer run broad framework to guide fundamental decisions with more specific shorter run studies to guide incremental decisions. The two tiers of this approach are inter-related through a series of rules (e.g. after a number of incremental decisions have been made the decision maker should undertake a more comprehensive review of the broad framework). Etzioni believes that the 'mixed scanning' approach may overcome the information requirement problem of the rational systematic approach and the conservative bias of the incrementalist approach. There is some evidence of an evolution in UK regional strategies from a comprehensive systematic approach towards such a 'mixed scanning' approach, as will be discussed later in the chapter.

In any one situation, the planning process adopted may be a combination of several ideas. In the UK context, such a combination might optimally include the logic of the systematic approach, plus the sensitivity of mixed scanning, set in an inter-organisational context. But in other countries it may be different, for the choice of a regional planning process for a particular regional planning exercise is very much influenced by the planning environment of that exercise. Thus, an environment where economic problems are seen as paramount, where there is scope for an innovative approach and where the planning agency has a high degree of control over plan implementation may result in a rather different approach from one in an environment with physical problems and where planning is largely allocative and advisory.

267

4 Growth centre policies

A recurrent feature of contemporary regional and sub-regional plans and strategies in this country and abroad is the concentration of growth and development in a limited number of centres. The advantages of such a policy relate back to the theoretical discussion of growth poles in Chapter 8. There it was suggested that such concentration brought industrial advantages (the various economies internal and external to the firm); urban advantages (economies of scale in the provision of social and economic infrastructure, reflected in factors such as good services and communications); and a nucleus from which growth could spread into the rest of the region. In addition, development in a limited number of growth centres may also bring 'rural' advantages, with concentration facilitating the retention of recreational and agricultural open space.

Growth centres have been liberally sprinkled over many of the contemporary British regional and sub-regional plans and strategies and it is interesting to briefly examine their use and misuse within the framework of the policy typology outlined in Chapter 8, prior to a more comprehensive discussion of strategies for the South East and North West. Growth centres have been advocated as remedies for the whole range of regional problems, although their suggested rôle is primarily twofold—firstly as centres of relief for congested urban areas and secondly as vehicles to secure regional development.

In the so-called *sparsely developed/underdeveloped* regions of Britain, growth centres have been proposed as a means of breaking out of the vicious circle of decline. In the North of Scotland, the Highlands and Islands Development Board has identified three areas as being capable of substantial growth based on industrial development—Fort William with a present population of approximately 16 000; Caithness (30 000); and the Moray Firth sub-region (75 000). Another planning scheme[16] suggested that the latter could be raised to 300 000 with high standards of amenity preserved. Yet there would seem to be little or no adequate foundation for such an increase for, although each of the three areas has been the scene of interesting new industrial developments over the last few years, there is little evidence as

268

yet of comprehensive development. However, North Sea oil may provide the necessary catalyst for major industrial development, but at what price?[17] The areas identified in the Highlands represent growth centres of development with the main function being one of at first stabilisation and then generation of growth; they also represent a 'passive' or 'reinforcing' strategy, accepting the rationality of the existing system of centres and concentrating on the most promising within them. In contrast, a plan for the Central Borders[18] proposed an 'active' or 'initiating' growth centre policy with the concentration of expansion in the area of the small community of St. Boswells, near to Galashiels. The application of threshold analysis suggested that this area would be one of the least expensive to develop, reaping economies of scale in the provision of public utilities. In the event, the plan was politically unacceptable, was rejected and growth was spread around the existing settlements. A similar proposal for a major new centre in Mid-Wales,[19] a linear settlement of 70 000 at the head of the Severn Valley based on the small centre of Caersws, met a similar fate, although a more limited scale of development has since been approved at nearby Newtown.

In the *depressed industrial regions*, growth centre policies have been clearly proposed for Northern Ireland, Central Scotland and the North East. In Northern Ireland, the problem is one of imbalance between east and west with overcrowding and congestion in the Belfast conurbation in the east and the lack of opportunities, decline in agriculture and population loss from the western counties. Yet even Belfast is not too prosperous, therefore the policy required was to establish strong relief centres to Belfast within the Belfast region, as well as the inauguration of development centres in the more remote western areas. It was recognised that 'in a region which had less than 1·5 million people, the number of centres must be limited'.[20] As such future growth is to be concentrated in three Major Centres of Accelerated Growth. The most important, Craigavon, lies 20–25 miles south-west of Belfast, centred on the towns of Lurgan and Portadown. The aim is a population increase from approximately 60 000 to 100 000 by 1981—and there have already been major infrastructural investments and industrial development. In the other growth centres, Antrim–Ballymena and Londonderry, proposed expansion is on a rather smaller scale but still quite substantial. All the centres represent primary developments in the Northern Ireland context. All also have development functions aimed at regenerating the south and west of the province, although Craigavon and Antrim–Ballymena can also be seen as centres of relief for Belfast. At a lower level in the settlement hierarchy, a number of smaller key centres have also been identified for the concentration of infra-structural investment.

In Central Scotland, the rôle of growth centres is again to act as relief centres to the older industrial congested centres like Glasgow and to serve as vehicles for regional development. Since 1947, a number of new towns have been developed for overspill purposes, but it was not until 1963 that eight growth centres were designated at Irvine, Vale of Leven, East Kilbride, North Lanark-shire, Cumbernauld, Grangemouth/Falkirk, Greater Livingston and Central Fife. The total population increase of the growth areas is expected to be in the order of 500 000. The growth areas are intended to 'form focal points of growth benefiting much wider districts'[21] through their initial relief of unemployment, followed by the spreading out of development into the surround-ing areas. Such benefits, it was realised, could be enhanced by a policy which would encourage 'industrial complexes . . . to build up around them'. It is with regard to the latter that the growth centre policy in Scotland differs from almost all other UK contexts, for since 1963 a deliberate policy of attracting science-based industry to the growth centres has been encouraged. The foundation of this policy was the existence at East Kilbride of the National Engineering Laboratory, the presence of the universities of Glasgow and Edinburgh, and the urbanisation economies of the growth centres themselves. There is, in fact, now commencing the birth of an industrial complex around the larger electronic firms, and

'Scotland now boasts an unrivalled concentration of electronic plants . . . its electronics and associated industry has mush-roomed from one firm to a host of more than 80 companies with a labour force now getting on for 40 000.'[22]

In the North-East, two growth centre policies have been produced. The 1963 proposals[23] reinforced the existing settlement hierarchy proposing main centres of expansion at the conurbations of Tyneside and Teesside and the Darlington/Aycliffe area. In contrast, the 1968 Outline Strategy by the Northern Economic Planning Council[24] proposed a hierarchy of major growth, growth and secondary growth centres and appeared to be an attempt to restructure the city system in the area. Growth centres have also been proposed in the two 'intermediate' depressed industrial regions of the North West and Yorkshire and Humberside. In the North West, the proposals for the Central Lancashire New Town (Preston–Leyland–Chorley) constitute a primary development in the regional settlement hierarchy, and are particularly interesting in that the area is seen not only as a centre for concentrated infrastructural investment, but also, as in Central Scotland, as a suitable location for an industrial complex development. In Yorkshire and Humberside a series of 'primary' growth centres have been proposed[25] for Dinnington/Maltby, Adwick/Bentley and 'Five Towns' (Castleford–Pontefract–Featherstone–Knottingley–Normanton). All the locations have good access to existing and proposed motorway interchanges and are aimed primarily at relieving the problems of the coalfield area.*

In the *pressured regions* there has been the gradual evolution of a strategy of 'concentrated decentralisation' to deal with the problems of population growth and overcrowding in particular urban areas. At first, growth was accommodated on the periphery of existing urban areas increasing the concentration at the centre and this will no doubt still be the inevitable approach for many smaller centres. But more recently there has been a deliberate attempt to create a better balance between the central urban areas and the, surrounding hinterlands, leading to less confused regional structures and combining growth with less rather than more congestion. This was first reflected in the dispersal of growth into small/medium sized towns not too distant from the major urban centre, such as the early overspill new towns for London. Unfortunately, such centres, with populations of less than 100 000 may not be large enough for the growth involved. In addition,

* Of course, such plans are relative to the envisaged levels of population growth which were dramatically revised downwards in the mid-1970's.

at distances of less than 30 miles from the central city, they may also lack functional independence. This has led to another alternative, the accommodation of growth in major new growth centres generally at much greater distances from the centre and with much larger populations. In the late 1960's, plans for expansion at Telford in the West Midlands and Northampton in the South East suggested ultimate populations in excess of 200 000, and the latest plans for growth centres in the South-East have much higher estimates still. Such centres can be expected to have a greater degree of functional independence than the smaller new towns.

This brief survey gives some indication of the many and varied uses of growth centre policies in contemporary UK regional plans. The centres have been used for purposes of relief and as vehicles for regional development and often both at the same time. Their population size varies greatly from a few thousand in remote rural areas to figures in excess of 0·25 to 0·5 million in the most populous regions. Their importance in the regional settlement hierarchy also various although most tend to be major centres at a primary or secondary level. Many centres seek to build on existing central places, a passive approach reinforcing the existing settlement structure, and tend to rely primarily on infrastructural investment to provide the necessary growth catalyst.

The survey also provides examples of the misuse of growth centres. A typical failing is the designation of too many centres which limits the concentration of investment in any one. This reflects the basic dilemma of a growth centre policy—the need to reconcile economic efficiency with social and political pressures. Areas not designated as growth centres tend to regard themselves as 'non-growth centres' and rebel accordingly. Another problem is the concentration on 'growth centre' policies and the failure to develop industrial 'growth poles'. A growth pole policy is much more likely to establish a state of self-sustaining growth in an area because of its stress on interlinkages between activities, and growth centres lacking a pole focus lose many of the benefits of concentration.

5 Regional planning in the metropolitan South East

The South East occupies a unique position both in the United Kingdom and in a wider international context. This uniqueness stems from the general strength and vitality of the economic base of the region, from the particular importance of London as the capital and seat of government and its rôle as a world centre of business and financial activity. Many of the political, financial and business decisions taken in the South East have important repercussions far beyond the region. Within the UK, one result of this high degree of interdependence is to make the actual definition of the South East a difficult task. It also reinforces the need to plan on an inter-regional as well as on an intra-regional basis.

Unfortunately however, the South East is also unique in the country in the scale of its problems, the various diseconomies of growth. These problems have existed in various guises for a long time and unrelated policies seeking to deal with them date back hundreds of years. But, as the previous chronology showed, it is only since the turn of the century that there have been any serious attempts to deal with them at the regional scale. At first these attempts were rather unco-ordinated, taking place as they were in a period of largely unconscious planning. Howard and his disciples pioneered the road to decentralisation policies by the early establishment of the satellite new towns in the 1920's, and Raymond Unwin and the London Society were largely instrumental in fostering the Green Belt Act of 1938 to restrain the outward growth of London. But it was not until the advent of Abercrombie's *Greater London Plan 1944* that a more comprehensive view was taken of the planning of the region. Although even here it is interesting to note that at the same time the then London County Council was asked to prepare a plan for London itself, which was published in 1943 as the *County of London Plan*. This duality seems to suggest that the interrelationship between London and its region was still not fully realised. Nevertheless these documents formed the framework for strategic planning in the metropolitan region for the next 20 years until they were replaced by a spate of more sophisticated studies and strategies—

the *South East Study* in 1964, *A Strategy for the South East* in 1967, and the *Strategic Plan for the South East* in 1970.[26]

DEFINING THE SOUTH EAST

A review of regional planning from pre-Abercrombie times shows that the region has been continuously growing in a vain attempt to catch up with its problems. In 1937, the Standing Conference on London Regional Planning took the London Traffic Area as its field of study, an area roughly coinciding with the old LCC boundary. Abercrombie defined his region as roughly 30 miles in radius from Central London although he was wise enough to qualify this by stating that the region consisted of:

'the one and indivisible Metropolis, whose boundaries are invisible to the naked eye, unrealised by the normal citizen— save when indicated by rate demands—and unmeaning to the planner.'[27]

The *South East Study* extended the region well beyond Abercrombie's original conception, taking in a massive area east of a line drawn from South Dorset to the Wash. This included the whole of the East Anglian and South Coasts, an area 100 miles north of Central London and beyond Oxford in the north west. The 1967 *South East Strategy* took a rather more conservative view contracting the boundaries in the north east and south west, and the most recent *Strategic Plan* takes a similar area defined on a grid basis.

THE REGIONAL PROBLEMS--TO GROW OR NOT TO GROW?

The growth of population and jobs is the major influence on regional planning in the pressured region of the South East. This growth has continued apace despite all attempts to restrain it and has imposed a severe strain on the resources of the region. Housing, communications and amenities such as attractive countryside are particularly vulnerable, and in the long run a wide range of social costs result.

The *Greater London Plan* was prepared in a climate of antipathy

274

towards any further growth of the London region. Growth in itself, rather than its form was considered undesirable. This clearly influenced Abercrombie's proposals which were based on a number of assumptions which were clearly stated in the plan. The first assumption was that, in conformity with the recommendations of the Barlow Report, no new industry would be admitted to London and the Home Counties, except in special cases. The second assumption was that there would be a decentralisation of persons and industry from the congested centre to achieve better environmental standards both inside and outside London. The third assumption was that the total population of the area would not increase, but on the contrary be somewhat reduced. All these assumptions, especially that of a static or declining population, were soon proved to be unrealistic. Growth continued and by not planning for it a situation arose where the pressure for land resulted in many *ad hoc* planning decisions and development completely unrelated to the objectives of the plan.

In contrast, the more recent regional plans adopted a more realistic approach. They all started from the premise that growth in the South East, at least that part attributable to natural increase, was inevitable and must be planned for. The *South East Study* estimated a population increase of approximately 3·5 million on the base population of 17 million between 1961 and 1981 and the *Strategic Plan* recognised a probable growth of approximately 5 million between 1966 and the end of the century.

However, the economic and demographic downturn in the mid-1970's undermined such projections. A Monitoring Report of 1973 suggested that there could be a shortfall in the projection of 1·25 million.[28] By 1976, the shortfall was projected at over 2·5 million, with the population increase by 1991 only expected to be slightly above the 1976 levels of 17 million. The falling impact on regional housing demand of this downturn is however considerably offset by falling household size and increasing household creation.

TOWARDS A REGIONAL PLANNING STRATEGY FOR
THE SOUTH EAST

In spite of the fundamental difference in attitude to the idea of growth in the South East, the concepts of the regional plans and strategies reveal a remarkable similarity over time. Two concepts are particularly dominant. These are the division of the region into a series of concentric zones with varying problems and the need for the concentrated decentralisation of population and employment from the inner zones to the outer zones to achieve a 'drawing-off' of influence from Central London.

Abercrombie divided the superficially apparent amorphous sprawl of the London region into the Inner Urban Ring, the Suburban Ring, the Green Belt Ring and the Outer Country Ring, all of which had quite different characteristics and problems. The Inner Urban Ring was characterised by serious environmental problems, with unhealthy, overcrowded development and a high level of sub-standard housing. The Suburban Ring was characterised by rapid, but anonymous and jumbled, growth which was beginning to leap the Green Belt creating a similarly undesirable pattern of development in the Outer Country Ring, destroying its rural and agricultural quality. The remedy for these problems, as Abercrombie saw it, was to decentralise industry and the overcrowded population from the problem areas such as the Inner Urban Ring to carefully chosen locations in the Outer Country Ring. This would both improve the environment of the inner areas and co-ordinate development around London into a limited number of towns providing good housing and job opportunities. He therefore proposed a policy of developing a series of satellite new towns and the enlarging of existing suitable towns in the Outer Country Ring to accommodate a possible overspill population of approximately one million. Just over a third of this number would be accommodated in eight new towns, which were to be finite self-contained communities of 40–60 000 population at about 30 miles from London. A further 250 000 would be accommodated in the expansion of existing towns in the Outer Country Ring, 125 000 would be in quasi-satellites and 250 000 would be dispersed in areas beyond the metropolitan influence. All this was against a background of an assumed static or even declining population.

The new town programme was implemented and has been a considerable success. But the rapid population growth after the Second World War demanded a reappraisal of policy. The *South*

276

East Study was set up to examine the growth and movement of population in the region, to lay down a broad strategy to deal with it, and to suggest ways and means of implementation. The Study again identified four concentric rings forming the region. These were labelled the London Conurbation, the Inner and Outer Country Rings which constituted the Outer Metropolitan

Fig. *10.3(a)* *Regional planning in the South East:* South East Study (1961–81) *Sub divisions of South East England*

Region, and the Remainder of the South East. Once again the suggested policy was one of decentralisation from the congested centre and the accommodation of the regional population growth in the outer rings, but the scale of the proposals was much larger. The London conurbation was to be stabilised at a population of eight million, with the one million moving out offset by natural increase, and the whole of the population growth of 3·5 millions

Fig 10.3(b)   Regional planning in the South East: South East Study (1961-81) *Areas suggested for expansion*

between 1961 and 1981 was to be housed in the outer areas, (Figure 10.3). It was suggested that a large proportion of this likely growth should be diverted into planned 'counter-magnets' between 50 and 100 miles from Central London. New cities were

278

proposed for the Southampton–Portsmouth, Bletchley and Newbury areas, and six other places were named, including Swindon, Ipswich and Northampton, where there might be substantial expansion, each with an import population of 50–100 000. Another twelve places were identified as possible locations for smaller expansion, each with an import population of at least 30 000. These schemes, plus the new and expanded towns programme, which was to take another 250 000, would account for 1–1·25 million, and it was anticipated that the remaining increase of approximately two millions would be accommodated under the normal development plans of local authorities outside the London conurbation. The *South East Study* enlarged the scale of regional planning in the South East, the rings had become wider and the 'counter magnets' were to be much larger and more distant from Central London, but in principle the underlying policy of decentralisation remained unchanged.

A *Strategy for the South East,* produced by the Regional Economic Planning Council, varied the pattern only slightly (Figure 10·4). Three basic zones were defined—Greater London, the Outer Metropolitan Area and the Outer South East. Within this framework it was again proposed that there should be no significant increase in the population of Greater London beyond eight million. All growth was to be accommodated in other parts of the region or nearby, taking account of existing plans for further development and existing and planned investment in the region, particularly in transport facilities. A number of 'major growth points' were recommended to form large 'counter magnets' such as Southampton–Portsmouth, Northampton–Milton Keynes and Ipswich–Colchester at the outer ends of 'growth sectors' radiating from the metropolis. In all nine such sectors or corridors were proposed following major transportation radials such as express inter-city rail links, motorways and trunk roads programmed for major investment (although in effect, they could be combined into four major groups radiating from the central hub to the north and north west, the east and north east, the south east and the west and south west). However, the strategy was not well received and in 1968 a new planning study was set in motion.

Legend:

Central London and sectors for future growth

Study areas

Green sectors

Main country zones

Approved metropolitan green belt

Strategic motorways and trunk routes

Strategic railways

■ Proposed major growth points

• Towns over 15,000 population (1966)

40 Miles

0

40 Kilometres

0

Fig. 10.4 Regional planning in the South East: A Strategy for the South East

The South East Joint Planning Team undertaking the preparation of the most recent *Strategic Plan* was required by its terms of reference to take as a starting point the strategy proposals of the South East Economic Planning Council. As such, in many ways, the resultant plan follows a similar pattern to its predecessor, with the same definition of concentric zones and the recommendation of growth points to accommodate the population and employment increase. Ten diverse patterns of population and employment distribution were designed and examined by the team and two of the alternatives for 1991 were considered in detail. 1991A suggests counter magnets 40–80 miles away from London, and 1991B suggests development closer to London. The result is 1991C, a compromise between the two hypothetical patterns identifying major and medium growth points (Figure 10.5). Three of the major growth points, South Hampshire, Reading–Aldershot–Basingstoke, and South Essex are each identified as locations for populations in excess of one million by the year 2001. The populations of the medium growth points vary between 0·25 and 0·5 million. As noted earlier, this strategy was accepted in principle by the government as the basis for regional planning in the South East.

At this most recent stage, it is interesting to note that the duality in planning for London and its region still continues. For on the central issue of whether the spontaneous outflow of households and jobs, especially manufacturing industries, from Inner London to the new and expanding towns beyond the green belt should be encouraged or restrained, the *Strategic Plan* and the *Greater London Development Plan* published in 1969 are diametrically opposed. The GLC speaks of 'retarding' the outflow of employment, whereas the Joint Planning Team believes that such dispersal is an essential component of its strategy.

When one compares the various plans and strategies it becomes evident that the main elements have changed very little over the last 30 years. Throughout the period, the aim has been to contain London within the area already developed, arresting the growth of employment in the conurbation and encouraging the necessary redevelopment, with the diversion of growth beyond the Green Belt to a series of more or less self-contained towns in the outer region. But although the principles have remained the same, there has been a considerable expansion in scale, with an extension of the South East and its constituent zones and a replacement of the early proposals for new towns of 40–60 000 population at about 30 miles from Central London, by cities with proposed populations of 0·25–1 million, usually based on existing major towns at distances from 50–100 miles from London. In addition, the scope of the subject matter of the various plans has also widened considerably, with a fuller coverage of both physical and economic aspects in the *Strategic Plan* in marked contrast to the physical orientation of the Abercrombie Plan, and even the *South East Study.*

A CHANGE IN DIRECTION?
Planning for any region, and especially one with the dynamism of the South East, must be capable of accommodating major new developments. The 1970 Strategic Plan aimed to provide for a considerable degree of flexibility which earlier experience had shown to be essential, while at the same time giving a firm guidance to the development of the region. But following a half decade of events of major importance affecting the development of the South East—massive forecast population growth/small population growth/no growth; Maplin Airport—no Maplin Airport; Channel Tunnel—no Channel Tunnel; the Greater London Development Plan Inquiry; local government reform; British membership of the EEC—to note but a few, the Government decided in November 1974 that it was time for an updating and development of the SPSE.

The *Strategy for the South East: 1976 Review* gives particular emphasis to the future of London in addition to the case for and nature of development in the Rest of the South East (ROSE). Over the period to 1990, it is anticipated that there will probably be minimal population increase in the region but significant intra-regional redistribution—out of London into ROSE. This continued outflow of population will be compounded by the problem of changes in household structure with the demand for many more smaller houses. For London, the report concludes that the main reasons why people are leaving seem to be environmental in the broadest sense. In contrast, the situation in ROSE is still rosy, although the potential of some of the 1970 growth

Road framework
Medium growth
Major growth
Agricultural area
Environmental area

Milton Keynes
-Northampton
-Wellingborough

Aylesbury

Bishops
Stortford
-Harlow

Chelmsford

South Essex

London

Maidstone-Medway

Ashford

Crawley

Eastbourne
-Hastings

Reading-
Basingstoke
-Aldershot

South Hants.

Bournemouth
-Poole

Fig. 10.5 Regional planning in the South East: Strategic Plan for the South East—preferred strategy areas, such as South Essex, now seems less. The report therefore does not recommend a completely new strategy, but opts more for significant changes of emphasis and adjustments to the 1970 SPSE framework. For London, the report advocates a slowing down of employment and population decline, with for example more emphasis on labour retraining, relaxing industrial controls and improving the environment. For ROSE, the broad essentials of the strategy remain much as in the 1970 SPSE, but with probable differences in the levels and pace of development. Some tightening up on development in restraint areas is suggested, but the growth areas remain.

There has therefore been some change of emphasis in favour of London, although many commentators thought the change was not enough. The Review is perhaps best seen as only one stage in a continuing process of regional planning in the South East, and the importance of continuity and monitoring is stressed in the report.

6 Regional planning in the industrial North West

WHAT IS THE NORTH WEST?[28]

In marked contrast to the South East, the North West embracing the geographical counties of Lancashire and Cheshire, and the High Peak of Derbyshire, covers less than 5% of the country and is the smallest UK region. On the other hand, with 6·7 million people it contains 14% of the total population of the country. Understandably it therefore has some of the highest population densities in the country as evidenced by the 9200 people per square mile on parts of Merseyside. Marked by hills and mountains to the north and east, by fine agricultural land to the south and by the Irish Sea to the west, it also has a much more defined physical identity than the sprawling South East and is much more of a 'natural' region. Within this framework there is a great sub-regional variety, including two major conurbations, a large number of major towns and beautiful and remote rural areas, and areas of growth and decline. The North West is in many ways a microcosm of the country. Yet it can also be seen as a functional unit, as a single city with many centres, large and small. Aspects

284

such as these, plus the attempts of this first major industrial region in the world to undertake major economic readjustments, make the tentative attempts at regional planning in the North West of particular interest.

STRATEGIC ISSUES—THE NORTH WEST'S LEGACY

Most of the problems of the North West stem from its industrial heritage. It was the cradle of the Industrial Revolution and in the nineteenth century the region's 'cotton–coal' economy boomed, population grew at a tremendous pace, towns doubled and re-doubled their size, and Manchester was the centre of gravity of industrial Britain. But such growth was achieved with nineteenth century machinery and sources of power and little thought for the environmental consequences, and even by 1900 the region had begun to regret and to pay for its reliance on a narrow industrial base and it has been paying for it ever since. As evidenced in Chapter 5, this decline in the traditional industries in the face of the changing internal and external factors of resources and markets, plus the region's rather disappointing record in the new growth sectors, have created major structural problems. A decline in the numbers employed in the Lancashire textile industry from over 600 000 at the turn of the century to a present figure of less than 100 000 has reduced the rôle of this major industry to one of secondary importance. Such economic malaise breeds all the usual symptoms, including high unemployment, falling activity rates and net outmigration. The incidence of economic problems of course varies and they have been particularly persistent in the North East Lancashire and Merseyside sub-regions.

Intrinsically linked with these economic problems are fundamental environmental problems. The region is seen by many as 'drab, dirty, dismal and dark'. As the oldest of the world's industrial regions it has an unwelcome legacy of dirty air and filthy rivers, of scarred and derelict land, and congested towns crammed with old and worn houses and factories. Housing problems are particularly acute. 20% of the 2·5 million poorest dwellings in the country are in the North West, the worst problems being in the two conurbations where urban renewal will continue to generate large overspill problems. But not all of these poor dwellings are necessarily ripe for demolition. Many of the houses are solid and capable of improvement although there may now be too much reliance by twentieth century planners on the improvement of nineteenth century houses to provide a twenty-first century environment. Houses thought at present 'too good to knock down' may be millstones around the necks of future generations. The problem is a vicious circle—the economic structure creates environmental problems, which in turn are not conducive to economic regeneration, and similarly environmental improvement. Nor is the situation helped by the apparent acceptance by the North West residents of low environmental standards and the 'image' of the North West by the British public at large.

The drabness of the local environment plus the lack of employment opportunities are the major causes of the long-standing problem of outmigration in the region. This factor plus the relatively low rate of natural increase makes the rate of population growth in the North West slower than that of any other English region. However, this does not mean that the area is not without population problems. In the period 1961–71, the total increase was approximately 200 000 persons and it has been estimated that the increase over the 1971–91 period may be in the order of 450 000. This of course means building more houses and finding more room in an already congested region. There are also specific sub-regional population problems, for although the region as a whole may be growing in population, areas in the major conurbations and North East Lancashire have suffered from an absolute decline. Thus, in addition to the fundamental industrial and environmental problems, the region also has to cope with population growth and redistribution.

Yet although the problems are many and widespread and cannot be ignored, they must not be overemphasised. The economic problems are balanced by rapid developments in major growth sectors such as chemicals, oil, glass and vehicles—perhaps heralding the birth of a new industrial revolution. The problem of large-scale environmental obsolescence, which in itself presents important opportunities for a fresh start, is partly offset by factors such as the excellent road system, new docks at Seaforth and a prosperous airport at Manchester. Over the years, such problems and opportunities have attracted a great deal of professional attention at the local level by local planning departments and consultants, and more recently at the regional level.

A MOVEMENT TOWARDS REGIONAL PLANNING

Prior to 1965, the North West had no overall regional planning body. Planning was in the hands of 24 independent planning authorities established under the 1947 Planning Act, each preoccupied with its own internal problems. The only authorities with any possibility of taking a wider view were the counties of Lancashire and Cheshire, but even here the problem was complicated—planning 'for a blanket with holes in'. As a result, the early approach to strategic issues was dealt with on an uncoordinated and piecemeal basis. Approaches to the overspill problems of Liverpool and Manchester included peripheral expansion on the fringes of the Liverpool city boundary, the promotion of a large number of small overspill expansion schemes by Manchester County Borough, and the initiation of new towns at Skelmersdale and Runcorn.

Since 1965, the North West Economic Planning Council and Board have been established and there have been a series of modern studies looking at the region as a whole. The *North West Study* was produced by a multi-department government team in 1965, and *An Economic Planning Strategy for the NW Region* (*Strategy I*) and *Strategy II: The North West of the 1970's* were produced in 1966 and 1968 by the Council.[29] Unfortunately, not one of these documents could be said to constitute a regional plan, and they all rightly disclaimed any pretensions of being such.

The *North West Study* was basically a factual survey of the region prepared by a group of civil servants as the basis for evolving a regional planning strategy. It included discussions of the population, employment, housing, transport and the general physical environment situation, highlighting major problems. Housing obsolescence was seen as the most important single problem. The study was particularly concerned with the physical accommodation of the population increase in the region, which, even with the continued net outmigration was estimated to be in

287

the order of 800 000–930 000 between 1964 and 1981. But it was markedly lacking in considered proposals merely stating that the existing new towns at Skelmersdale and Runcorn plus the major proposals for the development at Warrington and Preston–Leyland–Chorley (Central Lancashire New Town) would probably be adequate to meet the needs of at least the near future. The development of major new complexes in North Lancashire and South Cheshire were suggested as possible long-term locations. The study was also weak on economic content with little discussion of the fundamental industrial problems of the region as a whole and of the depressed sub-regions in particular.

Strategy I was similarly concerned with the accommodation of population in the area, and, rejecting the assumption of continued net outmigration as the probable course of future events, suggested that there could be a population increase of one million by 1981. This would certainly require the development of the two long-term growth areas in North Lancashire and South Cheshire. However it was left to *Strategy II* to introduce some economic realism into these suggestions. It realised that the region's future depended on its ability to provide good locations for the growth industries. One of its main conclusions was that 'the influence on the location of industry in the Region should be where it can operate most efficiently within a broad planning framework'. *Strategy II* also considered the problems and proposals of the nine regional sub-divisions in much more detail than its predecessors. Yet it was still 'only a stage in our thinking' and was quite some way from a regional strategy.

It is debatable whether the Planning Council and Board would have had the resources to produce the required strategy, and even more debatable whether such an advisory document would have been heeded by the local authorities. As it is, recent events are more encouraging. Following a series of studies of the region's main economic and social problems, such as land use and transportation problems in Merseyside and Greater Manchester, the costs and benefits of barrages across Morecambe Bay and the Dee Estuary, and the impact of Central Lancashire New Town (CLNT), a more detailed *Strategic Plan for the North West* (SPNW) was produced on a tripartite basis through the Planning Council, local authorities and government departments in 1974. It was

288

Fig. 10.6   The North West: regional planning proposals and commitments—late 1960's/early 1970's

urgently needed, for, with the designation of Warrington and CLNT as major urban developments and the spread of the motorway net, major strategic decisions were tending to go by default.

The Strategic Plan was preceded by a preliminary *Issues Report* which outlined the main problems at the regional level, the adopted regional planning process, provisional objectives and alternative hypothetical strategies. The *Strategic Plan* itself adopted an innovative approach and focused on the resource issue, especially financial resources, and on policies for deploying resources in particular sectors. In an interesting analysis of regional indicators (housing, health, education, pollution, etc.) the quality of life in the region was shown to be well below average and not 'in balance with the remainder of the country', and the report concluded that a decade of special effort was needed. The improvement of the urban environment was identified as the predominant regional issue, and the Mersey Belt, North East Lancashire and the Cheshire 'Salt Towns' were identified as major problem areas.

The spatial prescription in the Strategic Plan marks an interesting shift in the policy for the region. A spatial strategy for the North West is immediately constrained by a wide range of predominantly physical factors. Within such constraints, three alternatives appear to be viable—a 'trend' alternative with peripheral expansion on the perimeter of the Manchester and Liverpool green belts and limited overspill to new and expanded towns; more distant dispersal to the now fashionable 'growth points' or 'counter magnets' along the north–south M6 motorway axis; or a concentration in the belt between the two conurbations.

The various *ad hoc* policies for the region at first favoured a policy of limited dispersal with the development of small town expansion schemes followed by the designation of moderately sized new towns such as Skelmersdale. More recently, the designation of CLNT with an anticipated population of around 500 000 at a distance of 20–30 miles from the conurbations marked a confirmation of some changes to the second alternative. This was reinforced by the suggestions in the earlier regional studies of locations in North Lancashire and South Cheshire ('Weaver

290

National Parks and Areas of Oustanding Natural Beauty

Green Belts of regional significance

Areas of search for regional parks

Strategic areas of land release for urban development

Corridors of development

Conurbation cores

Areas of search for local green belts, positive open land policies and local growth

Liverpool

Manchester

Fig. 10.7   Regional planning in the North West: Strategic Plan for the North West (1974)—basic elements of the proposed physical pattern

City') as possible long term growth points taking advantage of the excellent mobility factor in the region. Throughout, the third alternative, the policy of concentration in the Mersey Belt, was continually rejected.

This evolving approach raised several questions with regard to economic realism. It is debatable whether a region such as the North West, with major structural and locational problems, can afford to ignore the inter-conurbation zone, which is undoubtedly the area of maximum economic potential, possessing many of the localisation and urbanisation economies referred to in earlier sections. It is also debatable whether new growth industries can be attracted to the more distant locations in the absence of particular inter-regional incentives. At present, a large amount of the new investment in the region is being channelled into Merseyside which has benefited from preferential Development Area treatment over a period of many years. The extension of 'intermediate area' status to the whole of the North West may help the new development at CLNT—the apex of the North West's 'Randstad' triangle. But the viability of a North Lancashire growth point is doubtful.

In the 1974 Strategic Plan, six spatial alternatives—ranging from a dispersed 'Lancaster' strategy to a concentrated 'Mersey Belt' strategy—were initially tested. In marked contrast to past proposals for the region, the strategy team effectively argued for a policy of concentration in the Mersey Belt. This was favoured because it was seen as offering more choice and access to urban facilities, better employment prospects, optimal utilisation of new town investment and the area was seen as urgently needing the resources in any event. The Central Lancashire New Town was relegated to a more long term rôle (Fig. 10.7).

7 UK regional strategies: progress and problems

The 1970's witnessed several important regional planning exercises in England and Scotland. In England, major strategic planning reports have been produced for the North West (1974), East Anglia (1975) and North (1977), and in the South East, a Review of the 1970 SPSE was completed in 1976. In Scotland, following

292

local government reorganisation, Regional Reports have been produced for the new regional authorities. Several promising new trends have emerged from these exercises although certain major problems still remain. Progress and problems are new assessed, focusing particularly on the evidence of the strategies for the English Regions.

PROGRESS

The process of regional strategic planning is still developing, but the evidence of UK planning practice in the 1970's suggests the emergence of some welcome trends. Of particular importance is the development of a more co-ordinated agency approach to strategy formulation. The tripartite approach, with regional strategies jointly sponsored by the DOE, the relevant Regional Economic Planning Council and local authorities, has been adopted in varying degrees in five of the eight English planning regions. The only exceptions are Yorkshire and Humberside and the South West, where the respective Economic Planning Councils continue to exercise the regional planning rôle; and the East Midlands, where the wide coverage of sub-regional studies has curtailed regional planning activities.

The nature and expectations of the products from a strategic planning exercise are also changing. The emphasis has shifted from the regional plan as a long run spatial blue-print for the year 2001, to the regional plan as a wide-ranging short run, regularly updated, corporate framework for decision making by the many public and private agencies in the region. Thus the Northern Region Strategic Plan (1977) is seen as 'a broad look at public policy which is not usually possible outside the Cabinet room or the political parties' policy committees'.[30] The Strategy for the South East: 1976 Review is seen as a contingent strategy for a five year period, although within more long run development parameters. Overall, strategic planning appears to be moving towards a mixed scanning approach.

Procedural proposals—the development of co-ordinative processes to bring agencies together and organisational innovations involving the creation of new structures—are developing as important complements to the usual substantive policy proposals. Further, there is an increasing recognition that in addition to the

293

'visible' products of the planning process already noted, there may be equally valuable 'invisible' products. Thus a strategic planning exercise might lead to changes in the communication networks and attitudes of agencies and individuals engaged in public and private decision processes in a region.

The emphasis on implementation has also increased, with planning teams increasingly stressing that their recommendations must be practicable—not for them the dusty shelves crowded with earlier regional plans! There is an increasing concern with resource, especially financial resource, questions and with the relationships between the regional strategy and the wide variety of executive agencies with the power to act. The resource question is especially developed in the Strategic Plans for the North West and Northern Regions. The Northern Region Strategy includes a recommended public expenditure programme for the region, disaggregated by sector, plus proposals for the financing of the programme. The North West Strategy concludes, from an analysis of public expenditure patterns, that the region has not had a 'fair deal', and suggests several financial reforms including a revision of the local authority rate support grant formula, and the setting up of a regional body to advise on resource allocation, with a limited regional fund for balancing spending priorities. The importance of a continuous regional planning process is also stressed in all the recent strategies.

Finally, there have been some significant changes in the substantive policy content of recent regional strategies reflecting the changing societal environment in Britain in the mid-1970's. There has been a shift from an environment of expansion and growth, reflected in long run horizons with plans for new cities, to an environment of low growth reflected in a more cautious approach, with an increasing premium on using existing resources more efficiently and effectively rather than relying on new resource inputs. This decline in growth, plus an increasing concern for 'inner city' problems, has also led to some shift in the spatial policies of recent regional strategies, as illustrated in the discussions of regional planning in the North West and to a lesser extent in the South East, earlier in this chapter.

Despite interesting progress and developments in the directions outlined, regional strategic planning still has many problems and of particular concern is the question of implementation. After a strategy team have reported, their report is appraised by central government. This may take up to 18 months to complete and includes an assessment of reactions from central government departments, local authorities and others. The final output is a government response, which, taken together with the strategy team's final report, constitutes the approved strategy for the region. With the exception of their blandness it is difficult to generalise on the nature of government responses. For example, with regard to substantive proposals, the government endorsed the Mersey Belt spatial emphasis in the Strategic Plan for the North West, but in East Anglia, the government felt that the strategy team's recommendation of a more even spread of growth throughout the region was neither essential nor very practicable.[31] Government responses to procedural proposals, especially with regard to organisational innovations, have tended to be very cautious.

The approved strategies are seen as influencing regional development in several ways. They provide a context for the guidance of planning authorities preparing structure plans, and in this respect help to discharge the commitments implicit in the 1971 Town and Country Planning Act (Section 7) to provide authorities with a regional planning framework. The government also sees the approved strategies as guiding and assisting other public and private bodies with investment programmes or other responsibilities for environmental, economic and social policies affecting the region concerned.

The rôle of structure plans is particularly important, and several government circulars have reinforced as a primary function of structure plans the interpretation of national and regional policies in terms of physical and environmental planning for their respective areas. In practice, this 'validation' of regional strategies through structure planning is less clear. Regional strategies are not statutorily binding on structure planning authorities, and this, plus the absence of up-to-date regional strategies in some regions and flexible strategies in others, provides some structure planning authorities with considerable scope for varied interpretations.

All of the recent regional strategy reports have emphasised the need for a continuous process, and there have been many suggestions for permanent regional planning units. The Strategic Plan for the North West saw such a unit as having the following purposes:[32]

(i)   'to continue the process of plan and policy formulation and revision;

(ii) to formulate policy advice on specific issues that arise in the region; and

(iii) to react to emerging policies and proposals of regional significance'.

But to date regional planning teams have been swiftly disbanded on the completion of their reports. Only in the West Midlands and in the South East has there been any evidence of a permanent regional planning unit with a continuous planning rôle.

Finally, there is the unanswered question of how do the various regional strategies fit together nationally?

FUTURE DIRECTIONS

Many of the evolving trends in regional planning are likely to gather momentum in the next few years. For example, the financial resource input is likely to increase in regional strategies, and it is hoped that regional financial data, especially on public expenditure, will continue to improve. But other resource issues—land, infrastructure, etc.—are also likely to become more important.

Hopefully, regional strategic planning might also develop into a continuous process. Rolling regional programmes are necessary for resource allocation, and also to provide a framework for evolving structure plans. In this context, an interesting model is the Scottish Regional Report. The Reports were called for by the Scottish Secretary of State, following 1975 local government reorganisation in Scotland, as a means for the new local authorities to take stock of their responsibilities and to establish priorities for the allocation of resources over the wide range of their activities. The Regional Reports have been produced quickly and corporately; they are wide ranging in content and have been useful for introducing new ideas and effecting quick decisions on strategic issues (e.g. the abandonment of Stonehouse new town in Scotland as advocated by the Strathclyde Regional Report).[33] But continuous though regional planning should be, it should not rule out the necessity from time to time for additional special reviews of a regional strategy on a more ambitious and perhaps radical scale.

Finally, there would seem to be a strong case for more meaningful guidance from regional strategies, which have tended to become increasingly bland in recent years. The Government's Response (1978) to the House of Commons Expenditure Committee Report on *Planning Procedures* (1977) admits as much, suggesting that there should be changes in the preparation and format of regional strategies to enable them to provide 'a crisper exposition of regional guidelines'.

8 Summary

British intra-regional planning has quite a long history dating back to the beginnings of the century. Yet it has only really come to the fore in the last decade with the production of a variety of regional and sub-regional reports, plans and strategies. The studies originate from varied sources reflecting the various pressures from above and below for regional planning. The regional level studies have largely been produced by central government and the regional arms of central government, and more recently by standing conferences and on a tripartite basis by local authorities, central government and the regional councils and boards. In contrast, sub-regional studies relating to smaller areas have been more in the sphere of local planning authorities. The studies also vary in their content with the early 'stocktaking' documents contrasting with the later strategic plans. An interesting trend in the more recent and positive documents is the increasing sophistication in the process of producing regional and sub-regional plans, with the studies introducing many technical innovations. There has also been a considerable use, misuse and questioning of growth centre policies. Such developments are reflected in the regional planning response to the regional problems of the metropolitan South East and the industrial North West. Yet however complex the process, and however satisfying the preferred plan, there cannot be effective regional planning without implementation.

References

1 Labour Party, *Regional Planning Policy,* pages 96–7 (1970).
2 *Report of the Royal Commission on the Distribution of Industrial Population,* Cmnd. 6153, HMSO (1940).
3 *Report on the Committee on Land Utilisation in Rural Areas,* Cmnd. 6378, HMSO (1942).
4 East Midlands Economic Planning Council, *The East Midlands Study,* HMSO (1966).
5 Yorkshire and Humberside Economic Planning Council, *A Review of Yorkshire and Humberside,* preface, HMSO (1966).
6 South-East Joint Planning Team, *Strategic Plan for the South-East,* HMSO (1970).
7 *Hansard,* 19 January 1972.
8 Leicester City Council and Leicestershire County Council, *Leicester and Leicestershire Sub-Regional Planning Study,* page 2, 1 (1969).
9 McLoughlin, J. B., *Urban and Regional Planning—A Systems Approach,* Faber and Faber (1969);
Jackson, J. N., *The Urban Future,* Allen and Unwin (1972).
Boyce, D. E., Day N. D., and McDonald, C., *Metropolitan Plan Making,* Regional Science Institute, Philadelphia (1970).
10 Lichfield, N., Evaluation methodology of urban and regional plans: A review, *Regional Studies,* **4,** 2 (1970).
11 See: Scottish Development Department, *The Central Borders: A Plan for Expansion,* **1,** HMSO (1968).
Scottish Development Department, *Grangemouth/Falkirk Survey and Plan,* **2,** HMSO (1968).
12 See: Pearce, D. W., *Cost-Benefiit Analysis,* Macmillan Studies in Economics (1971).
13 Smith, P. M., What Kind of Regional Planning?, *Urban Studies,* **3,** 3 (1966).
14 Lindblom, C. E., The Science of Muddling Through, article reproduced in Faludi, A. (ed.), *A Reader in Planning Theory,* Pergamon (1973).
15 Etzioni, A., *The Active Society,* Collier Macmillan (1968).
16 The Jack Holmes Planning Group, for the Highlands and Islands Development Board, *Moray Firth: A Plan for Growth* (1968).

298

17 See *Guardian*, 13 December 1972.

18 Scottish Development Department, *The Central Borders: A Plan for Expansion, op cit.*

19 Welsh Office, *A New Town in Mid-Wales* (Economic Associates), HMSO (1966).

20 Government of Northern Ireland, *Development Programme (1970–75)* 1970.

21 *Central Scotland: A Programme for Development and Growth*, Cmnd. 2188, HMSO, Edinburgh (1963).

22 Hamilton, D., The Scottish Miracle, *New Scientist*, 42 (1969).

23 *The North-East: A Programme for Development and Growth*, Cmnd. 2206, HMSO, London (1963).

24 Northern Economic Planning Council, *Outline Strategy for the North* (1968).

25 Yorkshire and Humberside Economic Planning Council, *Yorkshire and Humberside: Regional Strategy*, HMSO (1970).

26 See Appendix C for references.

27 Abercrombie, P., *op cit.*

28 For a comprehensive picture of the North West, see: Smith, D. M., *Industrial Britain: The North West*, David and Charles (1969).

29 See Appendix C for references.

30 NRST, *Strategic Plan for the Northern Region*, HMSO (1977).

31 DOE, *Government Response to Strategic Plan for North West* (1975); *Government Response to Strategic Choice for East Anglia* (1976).

32 SPNW Joint Planning Team, *Strategic Plan for the North West*, HMSO (1974).

33 Strathclyde Regional Council, *Strathclyde Regional Report* (1976),

34 House of Commons, 8th Report of the Expenditure Committee, Planning Procedures, HMSO (1977).

The gap between plan formulation and implementation, which is
a fact of life in most types of planning, is a particular problem in
regional planning, especially in the UK context. The gap sometimes exists because the plans and policies formulated are inappropriate for the region's problems. But perhaps of more
importance, the gap often exists because the powers to manage
the process of regional development lie in the hands of many
agencies. These agencies—private/public, local/regional/national
—often have different perspectives on regional development and
planning and their actions may not easily be co-ordinated. Thus,
central government departments may see regional planning primarily as the inter-regional correction of economic imbalances,
with little consideration of the location of investment within
regions. Local government on the other hand may tend to inter-
pret regional planning in terms of comprehensive strategies for
social, economic and physical development within regions. In this
sort of context, regional planning if it is to be effective, must seek
to guide and persuade agencies, advocating the region's case to
national agencies and seeking to influence agency decisions
within regions.

An important prerequisite in bridging the regional plan formulation–implementation gap is a recognition of the institutional
environment of regional planning and development. This can be
quite complex, with a wide range of agencies involved, but certain
key agencies can normally be identified. These are now outlined
in the UK context. This essential, but basically descriptive

approach, is a necessary step to the examination of alternative regional structures. A discussion of the 'devolution debate' concludes the chapter.

1   A framework

For the purposes of analysis, the complexities of the regional institutional environment are here simplified in several ways. The focus is on the British government and administrative systems, which—in contrast to countries with strong federal, state or provincial systems—are clearly polarised at the national (central) and local levels. More narrowly still, there is a concentration on England, but with a brief outline of Scottish and Welsh variations. The focus is also on the public rather than the private sector. Private sector agencies, such as large firms, are of course very important generators of regional change, but their complexity limits analysis and any direction of private actions towards regional social goals will often depend on the actions of public agencies (for example, the impact of IDC policy on businessmen's decisions). Even within the public sector, there is a selective focus on only some of the key agencies.

In Figure 11.1, the institutional environment is structured broadly by level and area of concern. Within this framework, a number of agency groups are identified. The private sector group is subdivided into commercial (private industry) and non-commercial (community groups). These tend to be motivated more by private goals than the societal goals of the public sector. Four public sector groups are identified. Of prime importance are the two sectors of central government departments and local authorities. But in addition, there are a whole range of other agencies, controlled by boards or councils appointed by government but otherwise exercising a high degree of autonomy. They include agencies of central government, with some, such as the Development Commission and the nationalised industries, operating nationally, and others, such as the Health and Water Authorities, operating regionally. There are also agencies of local government, such as Standing Conferences and Industrial Development Associations, operating on a regional or sub-regional scale. To complete the picture mention must also be made of supra-national

301

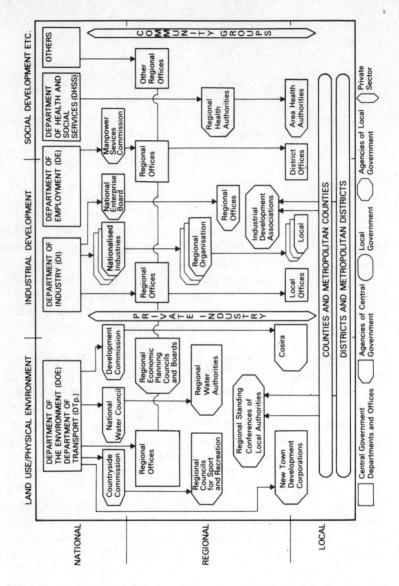

Fig. 11.1   Simplified institutional environment for regional development and planning in England (1978)

institutions, and especially the EEC, which is becoming of increasing importance in the regional field in Western Europe. (The regional rôle of the EEC will be discussed further in Chapter 12.)

The aims, organisation and functions of some of the key agencies in the various public sector groups are now outlined. Although the balance of the discussion reflects the contemporary situation, the institutional environment is not static, and the discussion is set in an historical perspective and seeks to draw out important changes over time.

2 Central government

CENTRAL GOVERNMENT DEPARTMENTS

Most departments of central government are involved in some way in regional development and planning, but the two most directly involved are the Department of Industry (DI) and the Department of the Environment (DOE). The DI exercises the collective responsibility over industrial development—the key to regional prosperity. The DOE has the overall aim of improving the physical environment and has many of the powers necessary for the implementation of regional policies.

Central government involvement in regional industrial development dates back to the pre-war depression years. This involvement was for many years handled by the Board of Trade. But in 1970, following a brief period in the Ministry of Technology, industrial development responsibilities were incorporated within a new Department of Trade and Industry. This was later split in 1974 into the separate Department of Industry and Department of Trade. Within the DI, the Industrial Development Executive co-ordinates the industrial part of regional policy. The evolution of central government involvement in environmental planning is rather more complex, developing from the Ministry of Health, via the 1943 Ministry of Town and Country Planning to the 1951 Ministry of Housing and Local Government (MOHLG). The MOHLG handled environmental issues into the 1960's, but in 1970, paralleling the industrial development machinery, and developing the Labour government's innovation of a co-ordinating Secretary of State for Local Government and Regional Planning, the new Conservative Government formally created the

DOE (including housing, transport, planning and local government). Transport was split off into a separate department in 1976 (DTp).

Both the DI and DOE devolve functions to regional offices. In general, policy formulation is dealt with at departmental headquarters while the administration and implementation of policy and the attendant casework (e.g. decisions on whether a particular firm should receive financial assistance under a scheme of selective assistance to industry) is handled and decided at the department's regional office.

This major DI/DOE division in central administration has mirrored and perpetuated the dichotomy in the UK regional planning. It was hoped that the creation of the Department of Economic Affairs in 1965, with the MOHLG working within its general directives, might bridge the gap between the environmental and industrial development aspects of regional planning. But its powers of execution were limited, and with its demise in 1969, the dichotomy has continued.

Of the other government 'home' departments, the rôle of the Department of Employment (DE) should also be noted. Operating through the Manpower Services Commission, the department's involvement in industrial training and aids to labour mobility constitute an important aspect of regional development policy. The DE also operates through a series of regional offices.

AGENCIES OF CENTRAL GOVERNMENT (NATIONAL)
Associated with the central government departments, especially the DI and DOE, are a growing number of agencies which, although operating nationally, have a considerable influence on the management of regional development. Examples of such agencies include the Development Commission, the National Enterprise Board and the various nationalised industries.

The Development Commission is a peculiarly British institution. It was established as long ago as 1909 to foster rural development. Armed with the finances of the Development Fund, its remit was wide, including aid to research, education and experiments in agriculture, forestry and rural industries; land reclamation; rural roads; harbours and inland waterways, and improvements of fisheries. Although its remit is now somewhat narrower, the Development Commission is still concerned with many aspects of rural development—industry, housing, transport and amenities.[1] For example, it has, since the mid 1960's become directly involved in the development of factories for new industry in small towns in rural areas. The Development Commission's factory programme in Mid-Wales is particularly notable.[2] Over time, the Commission has spawned many other agencies. Some are now independent, such as the Forestry Commission. Others, such as the Rural Community Councils and the Council for Small Industries in Rural Areas (COSIRA) still operate under the aegis of the Commission. COSIRA can provide financial aid, business and technical information and advice on a whole range of general problems (e.g. planning permission) to firms in manufacturing or service industries or trades employing not more than 20 skilled people, and located in a rural area or county town of not more than 10–15 000 people. Ministerial responsibility for the Development Commission was transferred to the DOE, from its original home, the Treasury, in 1971.

Another catalyst agency, but one of much more recent origin, is the National Enterprise Board (NEB). As outlined in the 1975 Industry Act, the NEB operates under the control of the Secretary of State for Industry, who appoints the Chairman and members of the Board. Its rôle is dramatic—the regeneration of British industry. More specifically, its functions are to establish new industrial enterprises or assist existing enterprises, promote reorganisation within industry, extend public ownership into profitable areas of manufacturing industry, promote industrial democracy in its subsidiaries and administer shareholdings and other property held in public ownership. The actions of the Board could be of considerable importance in regional development and it is seen as 'an instrument through which the Government can operate directly to create employment in areas of high unemployment'.[3]

By the very nature of their size, employment and output, nationalised industries are also of importance in regional development. Their proposals for expansion, or more usually decline, can have dramatic effects on the fortunes of an area. Although there have been efforts to make the industries more commercial in their outlook, there is probably some truth in the view that their responsibility to government and their greater sensitivity to public/political pressures tends to make them more 'regional conscious' in their planning and development of operations than private industry. Indeed, the British Steel Corporation (BSC) was required by Parliament in its acceptance of the BSC Organisation Report, to ensure that its efforts towards achieving the maximum long term return on its capital investment be consistent with ensuring the efficient and socially responsible utilisation of human resources. This social responsibility was seen as embracing four functions necessitating liaison with regional and local authorities:[4]

(i)   assessing, prior to any decision being taken with the Corporation, the social consequences of rationalisation;
(ii) developing policies and procedures to mitigate any harmful effects of rationalisation on employees and communities;
(iii) evaluating the external effects of major investment projects under consideration and those aspects of the local/regional socio-economic environment that might condition the viability of development in a particular area;
(iv) promoting good relations with communities where it operates.

But how has this apparent social responsibility operated in practice? It is probable that over the last 10–15 years (from the mid-1960's onwards) both the coal and steel industries have attempted to phase their decline and rationalisation plans to reduce the impact on local communities. Further, the steel industry also seeks to aid regional planners in attracting and smoothing the establishment of new firms in a locality, by for example developing its own sites as industrial estates, and, since 1975, BSC (Industry) Ltd has had the specific task of carrying out the Corporation's commitment to assisting national and local government agencies in creating new employment for redundant steelworkers in the Corporation's closure areas. But major constraints on initiatives by the nationalised industries tend to be the charters under which they operate, largely limiting their operations to their own narrow field of activity. Attempts have been made to widen NCB powers, to allow the industry to diversify into the petrochemical business, and there may be some useful progress made in this direction in the near future.

AGENCIES OF CENTRAL GOVERNMENT (REGIONAL)

The activities of regional agencies of central government, unlike those of national agencies, are limited to particular regions of the country. Such agencies are becoming of increasing importance in the UK institutional environment and include the Regional Water Authorities and the Regional Health Authorities, both set up in 1974, and the Regional Councils for Sport and Recreation set up in 1976.[5]

The ten Regional Water Authorities (RWAs) for England and Wales are of particular interest as examples of executive regional organisations.[6] They replace a large array of smaller water undertakings, and the aim of the reorganisation is to integrate the management of water in all its aspects. The National Water Council operates as a liaison unit but the regional authorities have a considerable degree of autonomy and executive power. The authorities are controlled by appointed councils; capital expenditure is financed through the DOE and the Treasury, and current expenditure is financed by service charges, largely through the rates. The water authorities must have twenty-year long term programmes, seven-year medium term, and five-year rolling programmes of investment. Such programmes are of vital importance in regional development because decisions on water and sewerage provision have a vital impact on housing and industrial development. Co-ordination between water and planning authorities is therefore of considerable importance, but, in the absence of approved local authority plans, and often in the face of conflicting advice, co-ordinated planning can be difficult. Even inter-water authority co-ordination can be problematic, as evidenced by the problems encountered by the Welsh National Water Development Agency and the Severn–Trent Authority with regard to the proposed Craig Goch reservoir development in the heart of Mid-Wales.

Of course, another set of regionally specific agencies are the Regional Economic Planning Councils set up in 1965. In contrast to the water authorities, they are primarily advisory in nature, having little executive power. Nevertheless they have played a vital rôle in the evolution of UK regional planning machinery and are discussed more fully later.

307

Finally, under the broad umbrella of 'central government', reference must also be made to certain important Scottish and Welsh variations within the institutional framework, which are of considerable importance for regional development and planning in those countries.

Scotland (since 1885) and Wales (since 1964) have enjoyed a much greater degree of administrative devolution than the English regions. A substantial proportion of central government responsibilities in Scotland, and a smaller but growing proportion of central government responsibilities in Wales, are handled respectively by the Scottish and Welsh Offices, with Secretaries of State of Cabinet rank. These Offices have the double advantage of being both regional and central government departments. In the Scottish Office, the Scottish Development Department (SDD) and the Scottish Economic Planning Department (SEPD) have played particularly significant rôles in regional development and planning. The Scottish and Welsh Secretaries also have 'oversight' powers over the activities of other central government departments operating in their countries, although the effectiveness of oversight varies greatly from Minister to Minister, being very much a matter of personalities.[7]

Other additional Scottish and Welsh agencies include the Highlands and Islands Development Board, the Development Board for Rural Wales and the Scottish and Welsh Development Agencies. These agencies are of particular interest as examples of executive regional development agencies and are considered in more detail later in the chapter.

3 Local government

LOCAL GOVERNMENT REORGANISATION

The recognition of the need to plan on a supra-urban scale has been paralleled over the last few years by a series of proposals for local government reform. The hotch-potch of 79 county boroughs, 45 counties, 227 non-county boroughs, 449 urban districts and 410 rural districts in England, and similar systems in Northern Ireland, Scotland and Wales, raised a host of problems. Many of the authorities were too small to carry out efficiently the services required of them, and the overall pattern of authorities no longer corresponded to the contemporary pattern of work and life. Increasing personal mobility has led to an increasing inter-dependence between town and country. More and more people now live in the countryside but go into the towns for work, shopping, education and entertainment. Similarly, people in towns go out into the countryside for recreation, and towns and cities with overspill problems look to the surrounding areas to provide a solution.

That such problems existed had been realised for some time, but it was not until the mid 1960's that the government decided to investigate the possible form of a completely new administrative structure. Prior to this, there had been Local Government Commissions charged with the duty of reviewing the structure of local government and of making changes considered desirable in the interests of effective and convenient government, but they were only tampering on the fringes of the problem. In 1966, the Royal Commission on Local Government in England was set up under the chairmanship of Lord Redcliffe-Maud:

'to consider the structure of Local Government in England, outside Greater London, in relation to its existing function; and to make recommendations for authorities and boundaries, and for functions and their division, having regard to the size and character of areas in which these can be most effectively exercised and the need to sustain a viable system of local democracy; and to report'.[8]

A similar commission under the chairmanship of Lord Wheatley was established to consider the situation in Scotland.

The Maud Report (1969)

The Redcliffe-Maud Commission produced its report in 1969. During its deliberations it received evidence on a variety of alternative solutions. One solution, strongly supported by the government departments, was to establish a primarily single-tier system of between 25 and 45 city regions which would perform all or nearly all the services of local government. A second solution, advocated by the County Councils Association, predictably proposed 40 or 50 modified counties, with a lower tier of enlarged urban or rural district councils. This two-tier system was very similar to the then-current division between the counties and county districts. In contrast, a third solution supported by the Association of Municipal Corporations, proposed a two-tier system with a greater number of city regions, between 60 and 140, and a limited number of regional or provincial bodies.

To choose between the alternatives the Commission formulated and applied certain general principles. Amongst others, these principles stressed that areas must be based upon the interdependence of town and country, all services concerned with the physical environment (planning, transportation and major development) must be in the hands of one authority, and all personal services must also be in the hands of one authority. In the interests of efficiency, the minimum population of the areas should be around 250 000; but in the interests of democracy it should not be much more than 1 000 000. The new local government pattern should also stem as far as possible from the existing one.

From the application of these principles a three-tier solution emerged, but with the emphasis strongly on the intermediate 'unitary' tier (Figure 11.2). This involved the creation of 61 new local government areas—somewhat similar to the third alternative above—each covering town and country. Fifty-eight of these were unitary areas with one authority responsible for all services; and three (Greater Merseyside, Greater Manchester and the Birmingham conurbation) were metropolitan areas, with services divided between three metropolitan authorities and 20 metropolitan district councils. The metropolitan authority was to be responsible for planning, transportation and also the major development functions. Above the intermediate tier were a limited number of provincial councils, and below them a series of local councils.

The Maud proposals brought about the unification of town and country and had much to commend them, allowing the planning and transportation problems of the urban regions to be tackled as a whole. They also did much for the big cities, extending their boundaries far beyond the built-up areas and the constricting green belts. But they were not acceptable to everyone, least of all to one of the Commissioners, Derek Senior.

Senior's alternative proposals

Senior first set out his ideas for local government reform in 1965.[9] He believed that the right approach to reform was to analyse functional and democratic needs in relation to the patterns of settlement, activity and community structure in which a motor age society organises itself. It is argued that people look for services to the nearest large urban centre, and thus the best unit for providing services, planning them and rallying local involvement is a city region. Senior saw this city region as 'a marriage between the built up core and its socially and economically dependent areas'.

Four types of city region were distinguished by Senior in 1965, dividing the whole of Britain into 42 areas:

(i)   The mature city regions were well defined areas already looking towards a major city of regional importance, with total populations of at least two million people. These were London, Birmingham, Liverpool, Manchester, Leeds, Newcastle and Glasgow.

(ii) The emergent city regions had hinterlands of over one million people, but their centres were not as well defined and developed as in the previous category. This type included Cardiff, Bristol, Southampton, Nottingham, Sheffield, Preston and Edinburgh.

(iii) The embryonic city regions were based on cities not yet of regional importance but of considerable local influence, with hinterlands of 300 000 to 800 000 people, such as Exeter, Brighton, Coventry, Middlesbrough and Aberdeen.

(iv) The potential city regions referred primarily to large rural areas with at present only limited links with central towns and cities, such as Plymouth, Peterborough, York and Carlisle. In some of these potential areas the population was as low as 250 000.

It was accepted that the latter two groups did not form regions readily, but it was thought that they could if given the opportunity.

311

North East province
1 Northumberland
2 Tyneside
3 Durham
4 Sunderland and East Durham
5 Teesside

Yorkshire province
6 York
7 Bradford
8 Leeds
9 Halifax
10 Huddersfield
11 Mid-Yorkshire
12 Sheffield and South Yorkshire
13 Doncaster
14 North Humberside
15 South Humberside

North West province
16 Cumberland and North Westmorland
17 Furness and North Lancashire
18 The Fylde
19 Preston-Leyland-Chorley
20 Blackburn
21 Burnley
22 Merseyside metropolitan area
23 SELNEC metropolitan area

West Midlands province
24 Stoke and North Staffordshire
25 West Midlands metropolitan area
26 Shropshire
27 Herefordshire and South Worcestershire
28 Coventry and Warwickshire

East midlands province
29 Derby and Derbyshire
30 Nottingham and Nottinghamshire
31 Leicester and Leicestershire
32 Lincoln and Lincolnshire

South West province
33 Cornwall
34 Plymouth
35 Exeter and Devon
36 Somerset
37 Bristol and Bath
38 North Gloucestershire
39 Wiltshire
40 Bournemouth and Dorset

East Anglia province
41 Peterborough-North Fens
42 Cambridge-South Fens
43 Norwich and Norfolk
44 Ipswich, Suffolk and North-East Essex

South East province
45 Oxford and Oxfordshire
46 Northampton and Northamptonshire
47 Bedford and North Buckinghamshire
48 Mid-Buckinghamshire
49 Luton and West Hertfordshire
50 East Hertfordshire
51 Essex
52 Reading and Berkshire
53 West Surrey
54 East Surrey
55 West Kent
56 Canterbury and East Kent
57 Southampton and South Hampshire
58 Portsmouth, South East Hampshire and Isle of Wight
59 West Sussex
60 Brighton and Mid-Sussex
61 East Sussex

100 0   60
Miles

——— Province
——— Unitary area

▨ Metropolitan area
▨ Greater London
23 Reference number

Fig. 11.2   Proposals of the Redcliffe-Maud Commission (1969)

When the Maud Commission came out in favour of the unitary authority in preference to the city region solution, Senior restated his views in a voluminous Memorandum of Dissent[10] accompanying the majority report. He believed that the Maud proposals suffered from a theoretical approach to the problem of local government reorganisation, with boundaries determined more by the population requirements for administrative efficiency and democratic control rather than by the facts of social geography. His proposals for a system of 35 English city regions (Figure 11.3) deviated little from his earlier views, with the exception of the creation of several new areas on the periphery of Greater London. The city regions would have directly elected regional authorities responsible for functions such as planning, transportation, development and capital investment programmes. Beneath them there would be 148 directly elected district authorities responsible for the more personal services.

The city region solution has undoubted attractions. It would end the division between town and country, create authorities large enough to handle the functions of local government, and receive the support of government departments. But it also has fundamental problems, the most obvious being that not all of the country fits neatly into a city region pattern. In many of the rural areas of the South West, the Wash Fens of East Anglia, the remoter Pennines and the Lake District, there is not the same emphasis on city life and there may be no one acceptable centre. In areas such as these Senior's proposals appear contrived, ironically lacking the basic clarity of the majority proposals they sought to replace.

The New Framework (1974)

Overall, the Maud proposals were widely welcomed. They redrew local government boundaries in a way that was particularly attractive to many town planners, and the Labour Government accepted them as a basis for reform. But that was not enough. Governments come and go and policies can change overnight. So it was that one of the first acts of the newly elected Conservative Government was to announce a standstill on the Maud

North East province
1 Newcastle upon Tyne
2 Teesside
3 York
4 Leeds
5 Kingston upon Hull
6 Sheffield
North West province
7 Carlisle
8 Preston
9 Liverpool
10 Manchester
Midlands province
11 Stoke-on-Trent
12 Nottingham
13 Lincoln
14 Birmingham
15 Leicester
16 Coventry

South-West province
17 Plymouth
18 Exeter
19 Bristol
20 Gloucester
South-East province
21 Peterborough
22 Norwich
23 Northampton
24 Cambridge
25 Ipswich
26 Oxford
27 St. Albans
28 Chelmsford
29 Reading
30 Guildford
31 Maidstone
32 Bournemouth
33 Southampton
34 Brighton
35 Ashford

—— Province
—— Region
▢ Greater London
25 Reference number

10 0   60 Miles

Fig. 11.3   Senior's alternative proposals (1969)

proposals. This was followed during 1971–72 by the publication of a new White Paper on Local Government Reform,[11] its subsequent discussion and amendment, and the passing of the Local Government Act (1972)[12] for the administration of local government in England from 1 April 1974.

The new proposals revealed a dramatic change around in policy, partly reflecting the pressure which had been exerted in the interim by the rural districts and counties. The Maud proposals for urban-based unitary authorities were swept aside in favour of a two-tier system of counties and county districts (1974) made up of 39 English counties with 296 new districts, and six Metropolitan counties with 36 metropolitan districts (Figure 11.4). The counties vary in size from the Isle of Wight with just over 100 000 population to Greater Manchester with a population in excess of 2 500 000. Similarly, the largest new district, Bristol in the new Avon county, has a population of over 400 000, yet several other districts have populations of less than 40 000. Wales was similarly reorganised into 8 counties and 37 districts.

The county councils handle major functions such as education, transport co-ordination and police, with the district councils taking more local functions such as house building and environmental health. In the field of planning there is a functional split. The preparation of structure plans and certain development control (strategic and reserved decisions) go to the counties, with the preparation of local plans and most development control in the hands of the district councils.

The new structure has received much criticism. The new county units closely follow existing county boundaries and in some areas separate towns from the rural areas with which they are closely associated. Although this allows for operational continuity and the preservation of local loyalties, it to some extent appears that social history has been allowed to obscure the importance of social geography. The division of the plan-making function may also bring problems, with the districts and counties having to agree on a 'development plan scheme' ('who does what and when?'). The planning system is designed to work from the structure plan downwards, with the formal adoption of local plans by the local planning authorities contingent on the prior approval of structure plans. In practice, the production of structure plans

1 Northumberland	18 Warwickshire	31 Norfolk
2 Tyne and Wear	19 Derbyshire	32 Suffolk
3 Durham	20 Nottinghamshire	33 Oxfordshire
4 Cleveland	21 Leicestershire	34 Northamptonshire
5 North Yorkshire	22 Lincolnshire	35 Bedfordshire
6 West Yorkshire	23 Cornwall	36 Buckinghamshire
7 South Yorkshire	24 Devon	37 Herefordshire
8 Humberside	25 Somerset	38 Essex
9 Cumbria	26 Avon	39 Berkshire
10 Lancashire	27 Gloucestershire	40 Surrey
11 Merseyside	28 Wiltshire	41 Kent
12 Greater Manchester	29 Dorset	42 Hampshire
13 Cheshire	30 Cambridgeshire	43 West Sussex
14 Staffordshire		44 East Sussex
15 West Midlands		45 Isle of Wight
16 Salop		46 Clwyd
17 Hereford and Worcester		47 Gwynedd
		48 Powys
		49 Dyfed
		50 West Glamorgan
		51 Mid Glamorgan
		52 South Glamorgan
		53 Gwent

County
Metropolitan
Greater London
8 Reference number

Miles 10 0 50 100
Kilometres 10 50 100 150

Fig. 11.4 Boundaries in the Local Government Act (1972)—introduced in April 1974 has tended to be a long drawn out process in most counties and the developing blockages in the system have generated considerable friction.[13]

Through their various activities, local authorities play a vital rôle in the development of a region. This is particularly significant in the planning field, where, although there is no statutory obligation to follow regional policies and plans, structure planning authorities are advised by central government to consider the regional framework and frame their own policies in a regional context.[14] Local authorities are also becoming more involved in industrial development and attempts to 'fill some of the gaps' left by central government regional incentives have gained accelerating momentum in the changed economic climate of the 1970's. Many local authorities are now beginning to initiate shareholding schemes to generate industrial development; finance is coming from hitherto untapped sources (e.g. the County Council Pension Fund in South Yorkshire) and several authorities are seeking to gain even wider powers in the industrial development field.[15]

In both these fields of planning and industrial development, local authorities have for some years found advantage in joint action. Several inter-authority agencies have been established and these are now outlined.

INTER-LOCAL AUTHORITY AGENCIES

Joint agencies develop from a group of local authority agencies combining together into some form of association. This type of agency is less well developed in Britain than in certain other West European countries, but two examples—industrial development associations and standing conferences of planning authorities—merit further discussion in the context of British regional development and planning.

Industrial development associations are groupings of local authorities, with local industry and trade unions. Notable examples in England include the North West Industrial Development Association (NWIDA), the North of England Development Council (NEDC) and the Yorkshire and Humberside Development Association (YHDA). Their particular concern is with the attraction of industry into their areas, although with the change in economic climate in the 1970's attention is also being focused

317

on indigenous industrial development. With only limited resources, the aid provided by the associations is more in the form of promotion, co-ordination and information rather than financial support. Nevertheless they have achieved some success in their aims.

Industrial development associations, reflecting the distribution of the traditional distressed industrial areas, have been concentrated in the North and West of the country. In contrast, the standing conferences of local planning authorities have developed furthest, in response to the need for co-ordination on physical planning problems, in the South East and West Midlands; although they are also found in varying degrees of activity in other regions. The conferences developed rapidly in the late 1960's, partly in response to the setting up of the Regional Economic Planning Council and Boards which were seen as a potential threat to the local authority planning rôle. Some of the conferences have become actively involved in regional planning exercises and some of them, such as the Standing Conference on London and South East Regional Planning (SCLSERP) and the West Midlands Planning Authorities Conference (WMPAC), produce regular and valuable studies and advice on regional issues. However, they do function in a consultative and advisory capacity and have no power to bind their members.

SCOTLAND

As a result of legislation that took effect in May 1975, the structure of local government in Scotland has also been reorganised. The reorganised system, as in England and Wales, succeeded an administrative framework that was complex and outdated. The old Scottish system was composed of five types of local authority —cities (4), large burghs (21), small burghs (176), counties (33), and districts (196). Such was the range of size within particular types that anomalies frequently occurred (e.g. a large burgh with a much greater population than a small county council may have had a more restricted range of functions).

Reform was first mooted in an exploratory White Paper of 1963. In 1966, a Royal Commission on Local Government in Scotland was set up under Lord Wheatley. Reporting in 1969, the Wheatley Commission recommended a two-tier structure of 7

Fig. 11.5 Local government reorganisation in Scotland: two-tier region and district system introduced in May 1975

regions and 37 district authorities.[16] After wide consultations, a further White Paper was produced in 1971 as the basis for the Local Government (Scotland) Bill (1972). The Local Government (Scotland) Act (1973) retained the broad framework laid down by Wheatley, but the number of regions was increased to 9 and the districts to 53. In addition, reflecting the problems of geography and demography, the Orkney Islands, the Shetland Islands and the Western Isles were each given single tier authorities with responsibility for most local government functions.

The wide ranging functions of the regional authorities, which include strategic planning, industrial development, transportation, education, water supply and sewerage, make them very powerful and comprehensive authorities. District functions include housing, environmental health, local plans and development control. But in three of the more sparsely populated and upland regions—Borders, Dumfries and Galloway, and Highland—all planning functions are allocated to the regional council. These regions are termed 'general planning authorities'; the remaining six regions being termed 'regional planning authorities' (Fig. 11.5).

The new regional authorities are interesting with regard to their planning activities, where there is a far greater degree of flexibility than in the English system. Of particular interest are the regional reports noted in the previous chapter, which have already proved very useful documents. It is to be hoped that this innovation can be continued and developed, either as a framework or possibly as a substitute for structure plans.[17]

Scottish local government reorganisation has introduced to Scotland the principles of the large city region and the unitary ethic. Not surprisingly, it is regarded by many, including Senior,[18] as a considerable improvement on its English equivalent.

4 Implications of a complex constitutional environment

Regions are complex in terms of their economic, social and spatial characteristics. The regional institutional environment is similarly organisationally complex. The preceding, albeit simplified, picture of the structure and changes in the UK regional institutional environment reveals a multiplicity of agencies affecting development and planning at the regional level. These agencies operate at various levels—central, local and intermediate—and have varying areas of concern. Some, such as a county council, may have a multi-sector rôle; others—for example Area Health Authorities, the National Coal Board—may be limited primarily to a single sector. Similarly, and perhaps of most importance, the agencies also have varying degrees of power. Some have statutory decision making powers, others are advisory—but may still play à most useful 'connective' rôle in the management of regional development.[19]

This complex institutional environment has important implications for the implementation of regional policies and plans. The generation of a co-ordinated approach to the implementation of a comprehensive regional programme is fraught with difficulties; indeed, the generation of such an approach to a more limited issue can be difficult. For example, there would seem to be a need for agency co-ordination in the area of UK regional industrial development, where our motley range of agencies must indeed be very confusing to the industrialist. Here perhaps we have something to learn from our European colleagues in the art of simplicity. There are also co-ordination problems within particular agency groups, reflected, for example, in the difficulty of persuading central government departments to substitute their normal 'vertical thinking' for a 'horizontal approach' in regional situations. There are even problems of co-ordination within particular agencies. The DOE/DTp, for example, operates its multifarious functions through eleven different regional structures, with widely differing boundaries (e.g. the Road Construction Unit Organisation divides England into six regions; the Traffic Area Organisations into eight and a half—half of one of its nine English regions including the northern half of Wales!). Although the main DOE/DTp regional structure, the DOE Regional Office, does operate through a unified structure based on the eight English economic planning regions, the overall variety of boundaries within this one particular agency hardly raises hope for cross-agency boundary correlation.

However, one must be wary of equating organisational complexity with waste and inefficiency.[20] Similarly, an over-emphasis on formal co-ordination can be counterproductive. The connective rôle of advisory agencies through informal networks and the

321

rôle of personalities can often be influential in guiding development and must not be overlooked. Nevertheless, if the regional planner is to influence regional development, he must be aware of the characteristics of the institutional environment, and seek to encourage agencies to adopt and use the guidelines of regional policies and plans. We now turn to an examination of regional planning institutional models, looking first at the existing UK regional planning machinery before considering some alternative approaches.

5 Regional economic planning councils and boards

The UK Regional Planning Councils and Boards were established during 1965–66. At the time this attempt to introduce an intermediate tier of planning seemed to mark an important turning point in regional planning heralding the start of a brighter future. The bodies are still in existence today and it is interesting to examine their operation in the interim period to assess whether in retrospect the early euphoria was either justified or perhaps a little premature. (For recent developments, see Appendix D.)

THEIR ROLE

After the 1964 General Election, the Department of Economic Affairs was established with the general aim ot putting 'muscles' into planning, and more specific responsibilities including the production of a national plan and the introduction of effective regional economic planning. The government defined regional economic planning as having:

'two main purposes: first to provide for a full and balanced development of the country's economic and social resources; and secondly to ensure that the regional implications of growth are clearly understood and taken into account in the planning of land use, of development—in particular of industrial development—and of services'.[21]

The regional planning rôle led to the establishment of Regional Councils and Boards for the eight English planning regions, and Scotland, Wales and Northern Ireland. The purpose of the

322

Councils was defined by the First Secretary in 1964 as follows:

'The economic planning councils will be concerned with broad strategy on regional development and the best use of the region's resources. Their principal functions will be to assist in the formulation of regional plans and to advise on their implementation. They will have no executive powers.'[22]

In addition the Councils were subsequently required 'to advise on the regional implications of national economic policies'. Their membership consists of about 25 unpaid members, with a paid Chairman. The members are all chosen by the responsible Minister and are not electorally responsible. They are chosen to represent a wide range of experience in the region, and include people with experience in local government, industry and social service, together with members drawn from universities in the region. The Chairmen include prominent citizens from various walks of life—industrialists, trade unionists, academics and local politicians. The Councils meet at roughly monthly intervals and most have found it necessary to appoint sub-committees to tackle particular aspects of regional planning in their areas.

The Regional Board's were seen as providing the technical backup to the Council's work and the:

'machinery for co-ordinating the work of Government Departments concerned with regional planning and development . . . their creation will not affect the existing powers and responsibilities of local authorities or existing Ministerial responsibilities'.[23]

They consist of civil servants from the regional offices of departments concerned with aspects of regional planning and development. In England, the Chairman is the DOE Regional Director.

In practice, the Councils have sometimes been consulted by central government on national policy affecting the affairs of their regions—such as the regional implications of railway closures and the effects of the reorganisation of the coal industry. But their advice has often had little impact and at times, where decisions have been dictated by national considerations, they have been bypassed completely. Within the regions the Councils have mounted limited 'ginger campaigns' such as 'Operation Spring-clean' in the North West, but above all their main work has been in the preparation of regional plan documents. In the period since 1965, a range of documents has been prepared for most of the regions (Appendix C). Yet, as noted in Chapter 10, many of these documents have come under much criticism, particularly for their descriptive, stocktaking approach outlining the region's structure and amenities, forecasting population and employment changes and spelling out problems rather than identifying solutions. In their reports, the Councils have also tended to adopt an introverted approach ignoring other regions and the aims of inter-regional planning in selfish bids on the nation's resources.

AN ASSESSMENT

In their short life the Regional Councils and Boards have run into many problems and there have been some notable resignations of members. One initial difficulty has been the weakness of the national planning body—the DEA until 1969—and the lack of a national planning framework; but there have also been fundamental problems specific to the Councils and Boards.

Basic problems of the Councils stem from their lack of executive powers and elective responsibility. Only if their advice commands general support in the region and is based on rigorous analysis can they exert any substantial influence on the major policy decisions. Yet their structure is not conducive to such an approach. They were set up on an amateur basis in the hope that they would function in the form of corporate consultants with their collective wisdom having more standing than the recommendations of individual advisers. But the Council members are busy men in other walks of life and, with limited support facilities, it was certainly unfair to expect much progress at an early stage.

The Regional Boards have given rise to less criticism although here also there are some fundamental problems. One problem is how to get members of government departments to switch from a vertical Ministry view to a horizontal regional view when 'their objective is not to win praise for putting the region's case possibly against the views of their masters in Whitehall but to please these masters so that they can return from exile in the provinces'.[24] The

324

Boards have also suffered from staff shortages, limited regional statistical data and knowledge of up-to-date regional planning techniques; although it should be added that substantial progress has been made in these areas over the last few years.

Partly as a result of these problems, the relationship between the Councils and Boards and central government on the one hand, and local government on the other have always been problematic. If a Regional Council objects to a particular aspect of national policy it can raise the matter with the responsible Ministry in Whitehall, but it carries very little weight to press its case for it represents no one and has little public support to fall back upon. Indeed the only communication with the regional public tends to be via the statements of the Chairman, and through the publication of regional studies. Similarly, the recommendations of the Council are not binding on the constituent local authorities of the region. The local planning authorities may exercise their statutory power to suit their own ends merely paying lip-service to the ideas of regional consultation. Alternatively they may organise their own regional consultation through the establishment of Standing Conferences of Local Planning Authorities.

Associated with this lack of power of the existing machinery is the lack of a political focus. This contrasts with Scotland, Wales and Northern Ireland, where there is a Secretary of State specifically concerned with the problems of the region. The introduction of some form of political focus might help to lift the Councils and Boards out of their present limbo.

Many of these difficulties facing the Councils and Boards are reflected in the regional studies produced, which probably provide evidence more of regional thinking than of regional planning. But it would be wrong to think that this new machinery has not achieved anything. It has at least established bodies for clarifying and analysing the problems of a region and for assessing the implications of various policies. Nothing like this existed before and it surely represents an advance, even if it is on the typically amateur basis beloved of the British. It also marks the formal acceptance by government of the concept of government action on a regional basis in Britain. The fact that there are certain fundamental problems and that questions are being asked about the effectiveness of the existing machinery, however, suggests that it would be premature to regard the present form of regional machinery as the final solution.

6 Regional reform: alternative approaches

If the existing regional machinery is not to become yet another 'false dawn' in the long history of British regionalism, there must be some changes. In the true spirit of the regionalist movement, there has been no shortage of suggestions of alternative regional planning institutional models. These range from the retention, with some modifications, of the existing machinery—that is, the *administrative decentralisation model* of the Regional Councils and Boards, or the *inter-agency model* represented by the tripartite approach; to the wider use of ad-hoc *regional development agencies*, or the adoption of a fully fledged system of *regional government*, with multi-purpose elected regional authorities. The relative merits of the suggested alternatives can be usefully examined with regard to their possible functions, boundaries and powers. Although this examination uses a UK context, the arguments are of wider relevance. Many of the alternatives refer to this large scale of regional organisation as 'provincial'. The relative merits of terms will not be discussed here and throughout this section *province* and *provincial* will be used interchangeably for *region* and *regional*.

FUNCTIONS

The various alternatives suggest a wide range of functions for the new regional tier, including some derived from existing regional bodies—such as regional economic planning councils and standing conferences; others taken from central government or its agencies; and some which local authorities have been increasingly unable to cope with (the extent of the latter are obviously influenced by the state of local government and local government reform). As such, any form of regional reform has an impact on adjacent levels of government and administration.

Key questions on the possible functions of regional planning machinery include the range of functions (limited to strategic planning?) and their status (statutory?). Associated here is the

326

further question of to what extent a planning function should be paralleled and possibly substituted by a development function? A regional development activity, with the public sector taking a positive and direct initiative (e.g. airport, new town, estuarial barrage, exhibition centre) may be of particular relevance in times of limited economic growth when there may be little private development of any significance to guide.

The Redcliffe-Maud Commission on Local Government in England included proposals for provincial councils,[25] and believed that their main function should be in the making and continual updating of the provincial framework of land use and economic strategy within which planning authorities must operate. Key elements in this framework would include the changing distribution of population, inter- and intra-regional migration, the location of major new growth points, the broad division of the province into urbanised, agricultural and recreational areas, major industrial developments, the provincial pattern of road and rail communications, the siting of airports, the future of seaports and the siting of cultural and recreational facilities. The provincial councils would have limited development functions, with such power remaining in the hands of the local authorities and central government. But reserve powers would be available to allow the council to act if such action was necessary to ensure the success of the provincial plan, and for the development of projects of benefit to the region as a whole (the development of a barrage could be one example of the latter). The provincial councils would also assess provincial priorities in certain specialist areas such as further education, child care, cultural and recreational services and tourism. In addition, they would ensure that central government was fully aware of provincial needs and aspirations, and would consider the impact on the province of national decisions and policies.

The Maud proposals represented a limited advance in the functional responsibilities of the intermediate tier. Yet to some even this was excessive. Senior, for example, in his Memorandum of Dissent on the Maud proposals,[26] while accepting the need for a strategic provincial plan to comprehend and resolve the interlocking spatial, social and economic problems that arise at the provincial scale, believed that its contents would be necessarily flexible and it would not carry any formal statutory approval. In contrast, others have advocated a much wider range of functions including road and housing development, and the control of public utilities such as electricity and gas.[27]

The existing Economic Planning Regions correspond closely to the earlier Standard Regions and, in shape and number, appear to have been delineated by the consideration of primarily administrative factors. The regional capitals each required about 80 000 square feet of office space which was available in centres which had been regional headquarters in the past. They also required specialist staff, and with a greater number of regions, the limited number of staff available would have been thinly spread. In addition, there was a reluctance to cross the boundaries of local planning authorities which might result in some local planning authorities being divided between two Economic Planning Regions.

Administrative viability is undoubtedly a major factor in the delineation of regions, and the administration of the variety of functions outlined in the previous section has been a major consideration in suggestions of alternative regional boundaries. But Chapter 2 illustrates that regions also have formal and functional characteristics which must also be considered. Regional boundaries should be chosen so as to interfere as little as possible with the economic unity of an area. They should also pay due regard to physical boundaries, and should preferably reflect the range of social, economic, political and informational relationships between the hierarchy of centres within the region, paying due regard to any sense of regional identity.

Discounting the extremes such as the division of England into only two provinces—prosperous Metropolitan England and distressed Industrial England—most of the alternative proposals include between 10 and 15 major regions for England. The Maud Commission, for example, believed that the existing Economic Planning Regions provided an appropriate model for the provinces, arguing that not only do they provide areas of suitable size for the administration of provincial functions but also reflect some sense of provincial identity, building on areas already fami-

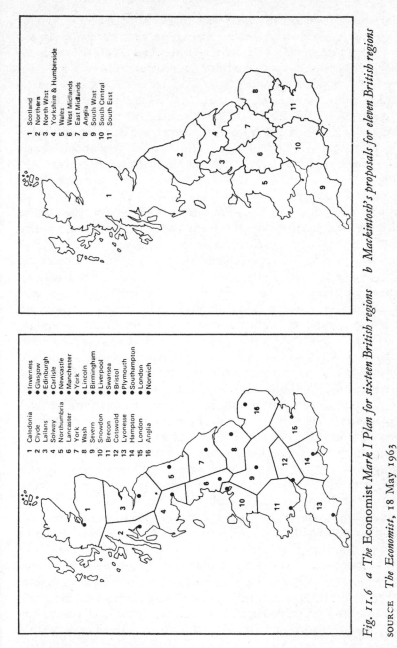

Fig. 11.6 a The Economist Mark I Plan for sixteen British regions   b Mackintosh's proposals for eleven British regions

SOURCE   *The Economist*, 18 May 1963

J. P. Mackintosh, *The Devolution of Power*, page 192. Penguin (1968).

liar to people. Hence only minor boundary changes were proposed (Fig. 11.2). There have been other more radical proposals, as illustrated in Fig. 11.6. The variations between them are explained mainly by alternative proposals for the difficult areas in the South West, the South East and the 'area in between', and there has tended to be agreement on many of the remaining regional boundaries. Finally, however, and of considerable interest, are the five major English provinces proposed by Senior in his 1969 Memorandum of Dissent (Fig. 11.3), which are much more comparable with Scotland and Wales than other proposals.

POWER

Associated with suggestions for various regional functions are a variety of suggestions for the form and power of the regional machinery. One approach is to develop the *administrative decentralisation model*, as represented by the Regional Economic Planning Councils and Boards. The Councils are a non-executive/non-elected 'advisory' form of body. Such a body has the advantage of having no electoral inhibitions in preparing and presenting strategies for the region, being able to take a regional view and to consider what is best for the region rather than what is politically acceptable. But the experience of the Regional Economic Planning Councils suggests that much of their impotence stems from this advisory rôle. Without executive power and/or elective responsibility, they exert only limited influence on local and central government. Senior[28] seeks to counter this argument by attributing their ineffectiveness more to the failure of central government to complement the regional machinery with machinery for the exercise of its own executive powers, and hypothesises on the possibility of a Minister of Regional Development with Ministers of State and support staff in each of his 5 provinces.

Such a development would certainly give the Councils a stronger political focus, similar to the French Regional Prefects (see Chapter 12). The Councils and Boards occupy a useful position between agencies at the regional level, but the work of the Boards could be improved by the inclusion of members from other government departments concerned with regional development but not yet represented (e.g. the Departments of Education and Science, and Health and Social Security). Further, both the

Boards and Councils would benefit from a stronger national framework. National guidelines have been missing since the demise of the DEA in 1969. In this context, Hall suggests that the Councils and Boards should be given the function they were originally supposed to have—that of providing the regional input to a national plan.[29]

A second approach is to develop the *inter-agency approach* to regional planning and development, reflected in Britain in the inter-local authority agencies and the tripartite approach to the production of regional strategies. Such advisory arrangements do tend to be problematical and it is easy to be sceptical. The matter was put rather succinctly by Aneurin Bevan when he said that a joint board 'has no biological content, it has no mother and it has no progeny, it is a piece of paperwork'.[30] Yet such bodies can improve inter-agency understanding, which may in some situations lead to co-ordinated action in the regional field. As in all the institutional models, an advisory inter-agency approach would benefit from improved knowledge and training in the processes of agency interaction. But improving the catalyst rôle of existing agencies may not be enough; Friedman, for example, argues that effective implementation requires the power.

One approach to increasing the power of the regional machinery is through the creation of *regional development bodies* with executive powers. Over the years there have been several proposals for regional development commissions, regional planning commissions and regional development corporations. One of the most notable was presented in the report of the Steering Group to the *Traffic in Towns* study.[31] The group, under the chairmanship of Sir Geoffrey Crowther, recommended the setting up of a number of Regional Development Agencies for each of the recognisable 'urban regions' in Britain. Such bodies, similar to huge new town development corporations, would 'oversee the whole programme of modernisation in their regions', and 'should be given far-reaching legal powers'. In addition to co-ordinating and encouraging the work of local and national authorities at the regional level, they would have powers to act in their own right, reviewing plans, controlling grants and acting 'like a gigantic property development company'.

The Highlands and Islands Development Board provides an

early example of this type of executive body in the UK. The board is a statutory body responsible to the Secretary of State for Scotland. It was set up in 1965 with the task of assisting the people of the seven counties of North West Scotland to improve their economic and social conditions, and to enable them to play a more effective part in the economic and social development of the nation. For these purposes it has been given finance and a wide range of powers. Although the financial resources are not excessive, it does have the power to borrow money, to acquire land and business by compulsory purchase, to enter into partnership with commercial and industrial concerns and to broaden the capital structure of a company. In recent years there have been further examples of the regional development agency. The Development Board for Rural Wales was established in 1977 to carry out a similar pump priming rôle for development in rural Wales. In 1976 the Scottish and Welsh Development Agencies were set up with remits for the whole of Scotland and Wales respectively. Their aims are to help to regenerate the economies and environments of Scotland and Wales. The agencies have substantial budgets, and powers to make industrial investments and take share-holdings, to carry out factory building and to finance schemes for environmental improvement.

The work of these agencies is more a regional development activity than a regional planning activity, but it does have the advantage of introducing the positive and innovative element needed, implementing by direction as well as by persuasion.[32] The HIDB has had notable economic successes, but as with all the suggested forms of regional development bodies, there is no electoral responsibility. Members of development bodies are nominated by central government—by the relevant Secretaries of State in the case of Scotland and Wales—and although their freedom of action may benefit from the resultant lack of democratic control it may also suffer by not having the strength of democratic authority.

The alternative is to have a democratically elected *regional/ provincial government*, and this idea has been popular throughout the history of UK regionalism. A provincial government approach involves provincial executive or executive and legislative powers, but still within a national government framework.

332

Proponents of the idea claim that it would reintroduce the democratic principle into many spheres which were too complex for local authority control and have now been either centralised under central government control or taken over by regional *ad hoc* bodies. It has also been suggested that it would attract greater public interest and participation than local government has ever done. But the approach is not without its problems. How will the councils be financed; can an electoral system be devised to avoid the domination of the councils by the more powerful local authorities; and is there indeed popular interest at the regional scale?

The Stormont Parliament of Northern Ireland (1921–72) represented a working example of regional government in the UK. Under this system many innovations were introduced into the province especially in the field of regional industrial development. There have also been many suggestions for regional government elsewhere in the UK, varying widely in terms of the degree of devolved power.

The Redcliffe-Maud Commission[33] opted for a limited form of provincial council to replace the existing regional economic planning councils. It proposed that council members should be indirectly elected from the constituent authority councils in the province (unitary and metropolitan authority councils). To prevent the swamping of the councils by members from the larger authorities, it was proposed that each authority should have two council members for the first 250 000 of its total population and one further member for each additional 250 000 or part of 250 000. On this basis, omitting the South East province, the number of provincial council members would range from 14 in East Anglia to 41 in the North West. In the South East, the same principles would apply except that there would be a limit of 20 on the Greater London members. The councils would also co-opt between 20% and 25% of their total membership from outside local government thereby complementing the democratic element with particular experience and expertise of relevance to the region. In pursuing their functions, the councils would not be heavy spenders and would cover their mainly administrative costs by precepting on the main authorities.

In contrast, Mackintosh[34] suggested a more radical change with

English regional councils and Scottish and Welsh assemblies directly elected for a fixed period of three years. The councils and assemblies would have between 100 and 150 members with an executive consisting of a prime minister and cabinet. The members would continue with their normal occupations, but the executive would have to be full time and be paid a full salary. To carry out the wide range of functions proposed by Mackintosh, the councils would each receive a share of national taxation calculated on a *per capita* basis but with deficiency allowances for special problems.

The alternative institutional models present considerable variations, especially with regard to functions and powers. They all have their strengths and weaknesses and the more powerful bodies, development agencies and provincial government, may not necessarily produce more effective regional planning machinery than the advisory bodies with their co-ordinating and catalyst rôles. Further, what is suitable for one country or region may not be suitable for another. There may be a need for a combination of models and perhaps different models for different regions. Regional reform has wide-ranging impacts, and in the last resort, the type of regional reform depends on the political will available. Hence we now turn to the UK 'devolution debate'.

7 The devolution debate

BACKGROUND: COMMISSION ON THE CONSTITUTION
The possibility of regional devolution has generated a great deal of debate in Britain in recent years. It has also generated a large number of official and semi-official documents which are outlined in Table 11.1. This section should be read in association with the details in that table.

In 1969 a Royal Commission on the Constitution was established, chaired by Lord Crowther and later by Lord Kilbrandon,

'to examine the present functions of the central legislature and government in relation to the several countries, nations and regions of the United Kingdom.

'To consider, having regard to developments in local government organisation and in the administrative and other relationships between the various parts of the United Kingdom and to the interests of the prosperity and good government of our people under the Crown, whether any changes are desirable in those functions or otherwise in present constitutional and economic relationships.'[35]

The Commission reported in 1973 with a Majority Report produced under the chairmanship of Lord Kilbrandon and a dissenting Minority Report produced by Lord Crowther Hunt and Professor Peacock. The main points of issue concerned the devolution of legislative power and the variations in devolved power for different parts of the UK. The Majority Report advocated directly elected assemblies for Scotland and Wales with legislative responsibility for matters such as local government, town and country planning, new towns, housing and roads. An independent exchequer board would mediate between central government and the new assemblies in the allocation of funds. For the English Regions (Fig. 11.7a), more limited non-executive co-ordinating and advisory councils, partly indirectly elected by local authorities and partly composed of central government nominees, were proposed. These would express regional needs to relevant agencies, advising on government spending in the region and playing a co-ordinating rôle over local government activities.

In contrast, the Minority Report, less motivated by satisfying the nationalist discontent in Scotland and Wales, and more concerned with a fundamental solution, believed that it was unfair to discriminate between Scotland and Wales and the English Regions. It also believed that, within the EEC framework, the proposed Scottish and Welsh Assemblies would not have the scope for the suggested legislative freedom. Hence, Peacock and Crowther Hunt suggested a uniform system of executive devolution for Scotland, Wales and 5 large English regions (Fig. 11.7b). The assemblies proposed for each of these regions would have substantial powers—responsibilities for executing central government policies for the regions and filling out the details, control over all central government regional outposts and regional non-industrial *ad hoc* bodies, and supervisory powers over regional *ad hoc* industrial bodies—but not legislative powers.

Faced with an immense task, the approach of the Commission was often circumscribed, and there was plenty of criticism of the

335

Table 11.1. *The 'devolution debate': a chronology of events (1969–77)*

1969 *Commission on the Constitution* set up under the chairmanship of Lord Crowther, and then Lord Kilbrandon.
Aim: 'to examine the present functions of the central legislature and government in relation to the several countries, nations and regions of the United Kingdom. To consider . . . whether any changes are desirable in those functions or otherwise in present constitutional and ecnomic relationships.'

1969 *Report of the Royal Commission on Local Government in England* (1966–69). Chairman: Lord Redcliffe-Maud. Cmnd. 4040. HMSO.
In addition to its proposals for unitary local authorities, the Report also advocated the need for 8 English provincial authorities.

1970 *White Paper, 'Reform of Local Government in England'*. Labour Government accepted Redcliffe-Maud's message that there are highly practical functions of government which must be considered in a regional/provincial context, but felt that it would be premature to reach conclusions on the subject before Kilbrandon reported.

1973 *Report of the Royal Commission on the Constitution* (1969–1973). Chairman: Lord Kilbrandon. Vol. 1 (Cmnd. 5460) and Vol. 2 (Cmnd. 5460–1), plus 10 Research Volumes. HMSO.
The Majority Report (Vol. 1) suggested directly elected assemblies for Scotland and Wales, with legislative devolution in many matters; and non-executive co-ordinating and advisory councils for the eight English regions.
The Memorandum of Dissent of Crowther Hunt and Peacock (Vol. 2) advocated a uniform devolution to Scotland, Wales and five English regions. Each region would have substantial but not legislative powers.

1973/ *Devolution debate accelerated* by economic crisis (and impact on depressed
1974 regions), development of North Sea oil, membership of EEC, and growth of nationalist political weight after the 1974 (Oct) General Election.

1974 *Green Paper, 'Devolution within the United Kingdom, some Alternatives for*
June *Discussion'*. HMSO.
Summarised the seven main schemes for devolution which emerged from the Royal Commission on the Constitution, and posed the administrative and other questions involved in each (i.e. legislative devolution, elected assemblies, executive devolution, Welsh advisory council, Scottish council, regional co-ordinating and advisory councils for the English Regions, co-ordinating committees).

1974 *White Paper, 'Democracy and Devolution: Proposals for Scotland and Wales'*.
Sept Cmnd. 5732. HMSO.
After consultations in the summer of 1974, the government decided to focus on proposals for Scottish and Welsh devolution, arguing that it would be premature to reach conclusions about change in England until further consultations had been carried out. The Sept. White Paper focused on possibilities (re powers, functions, finance, etc.) for Scottish and Welsh devolution.

1975 *Labour Party, 'Devolution and Regional Government in England: A*
Sept *Discussion Document'.* London.
      This document sought to clarify some of the issues involved in
      English regional government. It discussed the cases for and against
      regional government, and the possible powers, functions and boun-
      daries of regions.

1975 *White Paper, 'Our Changing Democracy: Devolution to Scotland and Wales'.*
Nov   Cmnd. 6348. HMSO
      Major policy document on devolution, which outlined the form,
      functions and finance of proposed Scottish and Welsh Assemblies,
      i.e. Scotland to have an executive and legislative assembly; Wales to
      have policy making and executive powers, but no legislative powers.
      Finance of the Assemblies to be by block grant allocation from central
      government.

1976 *Establishment of the Scottish and Welsh Development Agencies* (SDA,
Jan   WDA), to help regenerate the economy and improve the environment
      in Scotland and Wales. Their establishment probably increased the
      devolution 'backlash' from the English Regions.

1976 *Publication of the 'Scotland and Wales Bill'.* HMSO.
Nov   The Bill outlined the detailed legislation for constitutional change. Its
      main contents differed little from those outlined in the Nov. 1975
      White Paper, i.e. legislative devolution to a Scottish Assembly,
      executive devolution to a Welsh Assembly. Both Assemblies to be
      directly elected.

1976 *White Paper, 'Devolution: The English Dimension'. A Consultative*
Dec   *Document.* HMSO.
      This document argued that there would be minimal impact on the
      English Regions of Scottish and Welsh devolution. A number of
      'radical' (e.g. elected regional assemblies on the proposed Welsh
      model) and 'limited' (e.g. more effective REPC's) alternatives for the
      English Regions were outlined for discussion.

1977 *Government defeat on guillotine motion* to restrict discussion on Scotland
Feb   and Wales Bill and speed its passage through Parliament. Government
      rethink of entire devolution strategy.

1977 *Labour Party, 'Regional Authorities and Local Government Reform'. A*
July *Consultation Document.* London.
      This document proposed abolishing the present network of districts,
      counties and metropolitan counties in England, replacing them with a
      two-tier system of about 12 powerful elected regional councils and
      200 multi-purpose district councils.

1977 *Publication of separate 'Scotland Bill' and 'Wales Bill'.* HMSO.
Nov   Similar in content to previous joint bill with legislative devolution for
      Scotland and executive devolution for Wales. Some reduction in
      Westminster veto power. Guillotine motion passed.

(For subsequent developments, see Appendix D.)

recommendations—especially the Majority Report's unequal treatment of the various UK regions.[36] Nevertheless, the Commission does represent an important stage in the UK regionalist movement, and one which produced a wealth of important research into regional issues.

THE GOVERNMENT RESPONSE

The government response to Kilbrandon and the events of the mid-1970's was to separate the discussion on devolution to Scotland and Wales from that on devolution to the English regions, which was seen as less urgent and less clear cut.

For Scotland and Wales, a series of consultative documents were produced (Table 11.1), leading to a major policy statement in the 1975 (November) White Paper, 'Democracy and Devolution: Proposals for Scotland and Wales'. The objective was to give more democratic control and to help foster the distinctive national traditions of Scotland and Wales, but within the continuing framework of the UK. For Scotland, an executive and legislative assembly of 142 members was proposed, with responsibilities for local government (including powers to effect another reform), health, social work, education, science and the arts, housing, physical planning and the environment, roads and transport, natural resources, tourism, legal system and aspects of industrial development (e.g. responsibility for the economic and social activities of the HIDB, but not the industrial finance functions of the SDA). The proposed Welsh Assembly was to have policy making and executive powers, but unlike its Scottish counterpart, would not have the power to pass legislation. The main arguments for this discriminatory treatment were that Scotland already had more power than Wales and that public opinion, reflected for example in the nationalist vote in Wales, was not in favour of a legislative assembly. Subjects for transfer to the Welsh Assembly were as for Scotland, excluding the legal system. The White Paper proposed that the assemblies be financed by block grants from central government, allowing them to determine priorities within that sum. A proposal for limited tax raising powers, with an optional surcharge on local authority rates, was later removed in a government supplementary state-

338

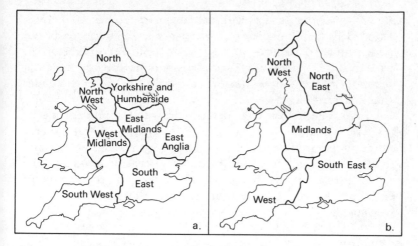

Fig. 11.6   The Kilbrandon Report: boundary proposals—a Majority
Report   b Minority Report

SOURCE   Royal Commission on the Constitution 1969–73, Vols. I and II (Cmnd. 5460, 5460–1), HMSO (1973).

ment. The subsequent 'Scotland and Wales' Bill differed little in content from the 1975 White Paper.

The English regions were accorded a much lower priority, although a Labour Party document of 1975 produced some useful background material. However the development of the Scottish and Welsh devolution movement, plus the establishment of the Scottish and Welsh Development Agencies, initiated a ground-swell of concern, particularly in the North of England. The government's response was a White Paper on 'Devolution: the English Dimension' (1976). Unfortunately this did not take the discussion very far, and the document was unconvincing on the impact of Scottish and Welsh devolution on the English regions. A series of regional institutional models, divided into 'radical' and more 'limited' were outlined for discussion:

'Radical'—elected regional assemblies on the proposed Welsh model with the ability to exercise functions in specified fields at present carried out by central government; or, elected regional bodies drawing powers more from local government and nominated bodies such as the health and water authorities.

339

'*Limited*'—more effective regional advisory bodies, i.e. a re-vamped EPC machinery with its rôle enlarged to encompass a wider range of central and local government interests; or, modification of local government functions and the development of *ad hoc* combinations of local authorities to tackle wider than local problems.

Factors suggested for consideration in weighing up the merits of reform included the advantages of lightening central government administrative loads, democratising nominated bodies and providing intermediate government for intermediate issues; disadvantages relate primarily to the undermining of central government control, financial implications and the impact on local government.

KEY ISSUES

The devolution debate raised many issues, but of particular concern were the control of the industrial development function, the extent of financial autonomy of the proposed assemblies, and possible impacts on other areas and institutions. The various devolution proposals left the control of regional industrial development (e.g. Industry Act finance) largely in the hands of central government, thereby reducing the impact of inter-regional competition in the industrial development field and maintaining central control over this vital sector of public expenditure. Needless to say, the nationalist movements in Scotland and Wales pressed for more independence in this field. Similarly, there was pressure from within Scotland and Wales for more financial autonomy, with regional taxation as a substitute, at least partially, for centrally allocated block grants. The proposed veto of the Westminster Parliament on Assembly legislation also generated considerable opposition.

Concern over the impact of possible devolution developed intra- and inter-regionally. In Scotland for example, the peripheral areas were concerned that the composition of the Assembly would be heavily weighted in favour of West Central Scotland. The Shetlands were particularly vociferous in their concern over the possible impact of devolution on the financial position they had established with the oil companies operating off their coast. Similarly, in the English regions, and especially in Wales, there

340

Table 11.2. *Regionally relevant public expenditure by PESC Programme,* by region. Per capita indices (GB=100), 1969/70–1973/74*

PESC Programme†	N	Y+H	NW	WM	EM	SW	EA	SE	Sc	Wa
Agriculture, fisheries and forestry	116·0	90·7	36·0	65·3	94·7	152·0	257·3	49·3	242·7	209·3
Trade, industry and employment	221·2	59·7	105·1	55·1	108·1	114·8	61·0	68·6	168·2	160·6
Nationalised industries capital expenditure	104·9	91·0	95·6	69·0	99·6	104·9	92·2	103·7	128·2	101·6
Roads and transport	128·0	86·7	105·2	90·5	68·7	118·0	88·2	96·7	110·0	118·0
Housing	111·3	65·6	88·1	73·1	72·2	59·1	82·5	127·2	139·7	79·7
Other environmental services	91·8	89·3	97·9	88·4	93·3	109·1	107·9	110·1	84·5	101·1
Law, order and protective services	98·4	76·4	96·9	84·3	89·0	92·9	79·5	120·5	96·9	88·2
Education and libraries, science and arts	93·8	94·2	95·1	91·8	93·2	89·6	100·5	106·8	111·0	102·7
Health and personal social services	89·0	78·0	95·9	85·1	101·6	88·4	91·4	114·1	111·8	99·2
Social security	118·8	102·7	108·0	90·0	92·4	101·2	91·1	93·6	104·4	116·4
Total	112·4	87·0	98·0	83·4	92·4	97·1	94·7	102·8	117·0	110·5

* Classification of expenditures used by the official Public Expenditure Survey Committee (PESC). 'Regionally relevant' expenditures are those which are made 'in and for' the region, the purposes of which are for the specific benefit of that region.

† N–North; Y+H–Yorkshire and Humberside; NW–North West; WM–West Midlands; EM–East Midlands; SW– South West; EA–East Anglia; SE–South East; Sc–Scotland; Wa–Wales.

SOURCE Northern Region Strategy Team, *Technical Report No. 12: Public Expenditure in the Northern Region and other British Regions, 1969/70–1973/74*, NRST, Newcastle (1976).

was concern from the new county councils which would be very much at risk, especially in the planning and development field, with the emergence of a regional tier of government.

Inter-regionally, the English regions were concerned that Scotland and Wales, with their proposed Assemblies and new Development Agencies, would carry more political and economic 'clout' in the regional development field. This they saw as increasing an already imbalanced inter-regional distribution of public funds, under which Scotland and Wales had for several years been receiving a higher proportion of public expenditure than other UK regions. Research for the Commission on the Constitution revealed evidence to this effect, later reinforced by the detailed analysis of regional public expenditure carried out by the Northern Region Strategy Team. Table 11.2 outlines some of the inter-regional variations in regionally relevant public expenditure (i.e. public expenditure in and for the region); although it should be noted that a consideration of the distribution of nationally relevant public expenditure (much of which takes place in the South East), the relationship of expenditure to need, inter-regional expenditure leakages and inter-regional cost variations can somewhat change the analysis.

The English regions were also concerned that Scottish MPs would still sit in Parliament at Westminster and legislate on English matters, that Scotland and Wales would still have Cabinet-ranked Secretaries of State, and that, on equity grounds, why should they be treated any differently from Scotland and Wales?

8 Summary: future regional structures?

Stronger intermediate regional tiers of planning and government now seem likely in Britain, but their form and timing are still uncertain.

For Scotland and Wales, the initial outcome of the devolution debate, reflecting some of the issues discussed in the previous section, was a defeat on the guillotine motion to speed the Scotland and Wales Bill through Parliament. Scottish and Welsh MPs voted in favour of the Bill, but an English 'backlash' developed, with 20% of the Labour MPs who voted against or abstained coming from the North East of England. But when devolution was re-introduced in separate bills for Scotland and Wales later in 1977, progress was a little smoother. This may have been due, among other things, to some modifications in the proposed legislation and to the provision, at about the same time, of extra regional industrial development assistance to the English regions via the regionalisation of the NEB. The debate continues but some form of devolution for Scotland and Wales seems likely. (For recent developments, see Appendix D.)

For the English regions, a Labour Party Consultative Document of 1977 proposed radical reform with the establishment of around 9 to 12 powerful elected Regional Councils and the abolition of counties. The proposals met with considerable opposition, especially from local government. However, the incremental organic approach to regional reform discussed in the report, with perhaps firstly a regional takeover of central government outposts through a strengthening of the regional economic planning machinery, followed by a takeover of *ad hoc* regional agencies and then major local government restructuring, may be the most likely outcome for the English regions.

But whatever the outcome, there will still be a need for a recognition of the inter-corporate dimension and the development of inter-agency co-ordination if the regional planner is to guide more effectively the process of regional development.

References

1 Chapman, Donald, The Development Commission: its new role in the rural areas, RSA Conference on 'Planning for Areas of Population Decline', *Regional Studies Association* (1975).
2 Development Commission, *Mid-Wales: An Assessment of the Impact of the Development Commission Factory Programme*, HMSO (1972).
3 *Industry Act*, HMSO (1975).
4 Fisk, T. A., and Jones, T. K., Regional Planning from the Viewpoint of a Major Employer, RSA Conference on 'Regional Development—Self Sufficiency or Inter-Dependence', *Regional Studies Association* (1971).

343

5 *A Background to Water Reorganisation in England and Wales*, HMSO (1973); *The Reorganisation of the National Health Service*, Cmnd. 5055, HMSO (1972); *Sport and Recreation*, Cmnd. 6200, HMSO (1975).

6 See: Proceedings of Conference on 'Water and the Regions', *Regional Studies Association* (1977), for fuller discussion.

7 Rowlands, E., The Politics of Regional Administration: the Establishment of the Welsh Office, RSA Conference on 'Regional Development' (1971), *op. cit.*

8 *Report of the Royal Commission on Local Government in England 1966–69 (Chairman: Lord Redcliffe-Maud)*, I, Cmnd. 4040, HMSO (1969).

9 Senior, D., The City Region as an Administrative Unit, *Political Quarterly*, **36**, January–March (1965).

10 *Report of the Royal Commission on Local Government in England 1966–69*, II, Memorandum of Dissent by Mr. D. Senior, Cmnd. 4040-1, HMSO (1969).

11 *Local Government in England—Government Proposals for Reorganisation*, Cmnd 4584, HMSO (1971).

12 *Local Government Act (1972)*, HMSO (1972).

13 See: *Aspects of Structure Planning in Britain, CES.RP.* **20**, Centre for Environmental Studies, London (1975).

14 DOE, *Circular 98/74*, HMSO (1974).

15 See: Proceedings of Conference on 'The Economic Crisis and Local Manufacturing Employment', *Regional Studies Association* (1976).

16 *Report of the Royal Commission on Local Government in Scotland 1966–69 (Chairman: Lord Wheatley)*, Cmnd. 4150 (1969).

17 Robinson, P., Regional reports: a step in the right direction?, *The Planner*, **63**, 3 (1977).

18 Senior, D., Scotland: Strathclyde shows the way, *Town and Country Planning*, **41** (1973).

19 Friend, J. K., Power, J. M., and Yewlett, C. J. L., *Public Planning: the inter-corporate dimension*, Tavistock (1974).

20 Rondinelli, D., *Urban and Regional Development and Planning— Policy and Administration*, Cornell U.P. (1975).

21 Statement in the House of Commons by the First Secretary of State for Economic Affairs, The Rt. Hon. George Brown MP, 10 December 1964.

22 *Op. cit.*

23 *Op. cit.*

24 Mackintosh, J. P., *The Devolution of Power*, Penguin (1967).

25 *Royal Commission*, **I**, *op. cit.*, Chapter X.
26 *Royal Commission*, **II**, *op. cit.*, Chapter V.
27 Mackintosh, *op. cit.*; Liberal Party, *Power to the Provinces* (1967).
28 *Royal Commission*, **II**, *op. cit.*, Chapter V.
29 Hall, P., The Regional Economic Planning Councils and Boards
    —Past, Present and Future, Conference on 'The Regions,
    Strategies and Agencies', *Regional Studies Association* (1977).
30 From Robson, W. A., *The Development of Local Government*, 3rd
    ed., Allen and Unwin (1954).
31 Ministry of Transport, *Traffic in Towns*, HMSO (1963).
32 See: Annual Reports of HIDB and SDA.
33 *Royal Commission*, **I**, *op. cit.*
34 Mackintosh, *op. cit.*
35 *Report of the Royal Commission on the Constitution 1969–73*
    (Chairman: Lord Kilbrandon), **I**, Cmnd. 5460, HMSO (1973).
36 RSA Study Group on Kilbrandon, *Perspective on Devolution*,
    Regional Studies Association (1975).

Note: A publication by the International Union of Local Authorities,
Regional Planning and Regional Government in Europe, E. Kalk (ed.), provides an interesting discussion of the relationship between regional
planning and regional government in the wider European context.

Much can be learnt from regional planning experience elsewhere and interesting examples can be drawn from all over the world. Each example would merit a text in its own right rather than the few pages that are available here. Hence, if the study is not to be too superficial, it is only possible to take a very limited number—and even then this may be only scratching the surface of each one. Of particular relevance to regional planning in Britain is the experience of other neighbouring countries in Western Europe. Thus this chapter examines the practice of regional planning in France, the Netherlands and Eire, set in the wider context of the EEC. The chosen countries vary greatly. Both France (*c*. 200 000 square miles, 50 million people) and the smaller but more densely populated Netherlands (*c*. 14 000 square miles, 13 million people) can be regarded as relatively prosperous countries. In contrast, the more sparsely populated Eire (*c*. 26 000 square miles, 3 million people) is, in a Western European context, a comparatively rural, developing country, occupying a peripheral location. But all face major regional problems which have given rise to interesting and often contrasting experience in inter- and intra-regional planning.

1 Regional planning in France

Regional planning is a recent phenomenon in France. Prior to the Second World War there were neither regions nor plans, but since that period there have been many interesting developments. Some of these developments are similar to those that have been taking place in the UK and some have directly influenced British think-

346

ing. Others, such as the development of French regional planning within the framework of an established system of national planning, are fundamentally different. (Useful references on French regional planning include those by Allen and Maclennan,[1] Boudeville,[2], Hansen[3] and Hall[4] (on the problem of the Paris Region).)

REGIONAL PROBLEMS IN FRANCE

Paris et le Désert Français

As in the UK, regional planning in France is a response to two types of problems—the problems of socio-economic disparities between the regions of the country and the physical environmental problems of growing urban areas which can only be tackled effectively on a supra-urban scale.

The regional disparities in economic and social development are particularly acute in France and nowhere are they more marked than in the contrast between the Paris region and the rest of the nation. Paris dominates France and the life of the country is centralised around it. This centralisation has a long history stemming back to the days of Louis XIV and Napoleon. Today, Paris is not only the political and intellectual capital of the country but also the industrial and business capital, with one quarter of all industrial workers and over a half of the country's business turnover. This dominance is reinforced by the lack of other large metropolises, with the only other major urban agglomerations at Lyons and Marseilles. This is in marked contrast to the situation in other Western European countries such as the UK and West Germany where there are several major conurbations counterbalancing the attraction of the centre.

The disparity between the Paris region and the rest of the country is however not the only one. Another major cleavage can be identified between the east and west of the country. An imaginary line drawn from Le Havre in the north-west to Marseilles in the south-east roughly divides France into a 'prosperous' eastern industrial zone enlivened by the influence of Paris and a 'poor' western agricultural zone. The latter has over 50% of the area of the country but less than 40% of the population and less than 30% of its labour employed in industry. It furnishes many clear examples of the underdeveloped problem region although there are exceptions to the general rule with pockets of growth and prosperity in centres such as Toulouse, Lacq and Rennes. In contrast the eastern zone, even excluding the Paris region, has about 43% of the area of the country, 44% of the population and almost 50% of its labour employed in industry and is relatively much more prosperous. Nevertheless here also there are exceptions to the rule, with areas of the Nord Coalfield and Alsace-Lorraine providing examples of depressed industrial regions.

The east–west disparity is a function of both structural and locational factors. In contrast to the industrially based economy of the eastern zone, industrial activity in the west is restricted to a small number of individual centres and there is a high degree of dependence on agriculture—a sector where increased mechanisation and land reform are leading to a progressive decline in employment opportunities. In addition, the physical structure of the area and its peripheral nature (especially within the context of the EEC) constitute additional locational problems, as do the conservative culture and political traditions prevalent in such areas.

This threefold division of France into the Paris region, the eastern zone and the western zone has been evident for many years. Yet there was, perhaps not surprisingly, some reluctance to interfere especially in the growth of Paris for fear of jeopardising French economic development which in such a highly centralised country was closely linked to the fortunes of the Paris region. However, the widening of the disparities plus the recognition of the need for the second aspect of regional planning to deal with the environmental problems of growing urban areas, especially Paris, on a large scale, finally began to have some effect. It was the publication of a book entitled *Paris et le Désert Français* by J. F. Gravier[5] in 1947 which probably lit the fuse. This book, which in its impact on public opinion was the French equivalent of the UK Barlow Report, focussed attention on the regional problems and particularly the effects of excessive centralisation and the growth of Paris.

Out of an appraisal of these problems emerged the objectives of French regional planning which can be briefly summarised as

348

the reduction of regional disparities, with the control of the growth and excessive centralisation around Paris, the development of the under-developed west and south, and the regeneration of problem industrial areas. The achievement of such objectives however requires an efficient regional planning machinery.

THE ADMINISTRATIVE FRAMEWORK

The French administrative framework of the early post-war period was not at all well fitted to the task of regional planning. With 90 *départements* and 38 000 *communes* it was a relic from the Napoleonic era. But over the next 20 years, with the development of regional planning, this framework was to undergo major changes resulting in the development of a regional planning machinery of great administrative complexity. This development stemmed from two sources—the spontaneous efforts of private regional committees concerned with the future of their areas and the need for a regional tier in the French national planning machinery.

In 1955 local regional pressure was finally recognised by the government and local representatives were encouraged to set up 'regional expansion committees' in 21 embryonic regions. In 1959, after studying the boundary problem for four years, the government formally set up 21 planning regions (*régions de programme*). The regions contained between two and eight *départements* and populations of roughly two million inhabitants. The regional boundaries (see Figure 12.1) were very much a compromise delimited to correlate as closely as possible with the existing administrative boundaries of government agencies and taking little account of functional associations. Even so, central government was loath to adopt them until a decree of 1960 enforced 30 government agencies to do so. For each region a social and economic plan was to be drawn up by an interdepartmental conference of civil servants chaired by the co-ordinating prefect and in consultation with the regional expansion committees.

The regional administrative machinery continued along this path until 1964 when there were far-reaching reforms creating a

349

completely new system. In each of the 20 regions outside Paris the administration is headed by a Regional Prefect responsible for co-ordinating development programmes within his region. The prefect, assisted by a technical team, the *Mission Économique Régionale* is responsible for the preparation of five-year regional programmes for economic development. He is supported by a *Conférence Administative Régionale* (CAR) similar to the UK

Fig. 12.1   France: planning regions

Regional Economic Planning Boards, and a new consultative body the *Commission de Développement Économique Régionale* (CODER), similar to the UK Regional Economic Planning Councils. In addition, in six regions, there are also new sub-regional planning bodies known as *Organismes d'Études d'Aménagement d'Aires Métropolitaines* (OREAM), created in 1966 to prepare plans for metropolises including two cities—Lille–Dunkerque, Nantes–St. Nazaire, Nancy–Metz, Lyons–St. Etienne and Marseilles–Aix. In the Paris region, a separate body—the *District de la Région de Paris*—was set up in 1961 to deal with planning problems. This body is distinct from the others in that it is headed by a full-time director. *Délégue-Général*, and has a budget of its own raised through Parliament by the levying of taxes on the Paris region. The District has a consultative regional assembly and being a financial power also has a board consisting of elected local council members and government appointees. The annual budget is not great but is useful for initiating schemes of regional importance.

To meet those developments at the regional level, the government introduced new co-ordinating bodies for regional planning at the national level.[6] Underneath the main body for national economic planning, the *Commissariat Général du Plan* (CGP), two further institutions were formed—the *Délégation à l'Aménagement du Territoire* (DATAR) and the *Commission Nationale d'Aménagement du Territoire* (CNAT). DATAR is a small body charged with co-ordinating regional plans in the short run and pushing them along. It can draw upon the resources of a regional development fund, amounting to 1·5% of the public investment budget to facilitate its tasks. CNAT is a much larger body concerned with the preparation of long-term perspectives (up to 20 years ahead) for urban and regional development. It produces long-term guidelines on matters such as population and employment trends and the distribution of jobs and people. In 1967 CNAT and CGP merged to form a single medium/long run planning institution, successfully integrating spatial and economic planning at the national scale.

INTER-REGIONAL PLANNING IN FRANCE

In contrast to the UK, inter-regional planning in France has the advantage of a well tried, accepted and effective framework of national planning. Such a framework, perhaps at first sight somewhat alien to the French *laissez-faire* attitude, developed shortly after the end of the Second World War in response to the need

351

for some central direction to rebuild the country. French national planning is of the indicative form with the government setting down guidelines for economic growth and seeking to effect their achievement by the use of the range of economic tools at its disposal. The plan is produced by a sophisticated planning machinery centred on the CGP, and since 1947 six major plans have been produced and implemented with ever increasing levels of success, and the seventh is now in operation.

At first, inter-regional planning was regarded as more of a social and political necessity than an essential input into the strategy for national economic growth. During the 1950's attempts were made to divert growth from the Paris region to a number of critical zones defined primarily by the criteria of unemployment, using a system of financial incentives and controls. This industrial location policy had some success although most of the decentralisation tended to be to a zone within 70 to 200 km of Paris. Towards the end of the decade however, ever widening regional disparities prompted a fresh look at the regional level. The administrative reforms already outlined were effected and during the 1960's inter-regional planning was pursued more vigorously within the framework of the Fourth and Fifth National Plans.

Industrial location policy was continued, but in 1964 sweeping changes were made in an attempt to make it more effective. The system of critical zones was replaced by the division of the country into five zones, each with a different kind of financial aid (Figure 12.2). The first zone covers the under-industrialised western and south western periphery—over one third of the area of the country. Within this area investment grants for new establishments are available (1969) ranging from 25% in certain specific localities such as Cherbourg, Bordeaux and Toulouse to 12% for the majority of the area. Grants for the extension of existing factories range from 15% to 6%. Fiscal exonerations— involving the exemption or reduction in taxes on land purchase, local taxation, and capital gains taxes—plus training and resettlement aid, are also available. The second zone, a 'conversion zone', is a more fragmented area of eastern France, where the traditional mining and textile areas are in a state of decline. Here an equally wide range of incentives are also available, but whereas in zone 1

0   200   Miles

0   320   Kilometres

Zones 1 and 2 (investment grants and fiscal exonerations)

Zone 3 (guaranteed fiscal exonerations)

Zone 4 (selective fiscal exonerations)

Zone 5 (no assistance)

Fig. 12.2   France: zones of financial aid for industrial development they are available over an indefinitely long period, in zone 2 the availability is determined by the persistence of the structural problems and the number of jobs created. Zones 3 and 4 are more extensive and constitute the 'grey areas'. In the third zone expanding firms automatically qualify for tax exemptions. In the fourth zone, the procedure is more selective. Finally in the fifth zone, the region around Paris, no government assistance is available and industrial development is actively discouraged by the use of a system of development controls. Overall, this system has much in common with the UK approach, although the fact that the French system of incentives and controls applies more rigorously to the 'services' sector constitutes one fundamental difference.

This system of incentives and controls has been complemented by a policy of increasing public investment in infrastructure in the problem regions. In the Fourth Plan, the distinction was made between a policy of *accompagnement*, aimed at reinforcing desirable aspects of growth in developing problem regions by the use of social infrastructural investment, and *entrainement*, aimed at inducing growth, using government investment as a propulsive tool. The Plan also emphasised the need to promote self-sustaining growth rather than to just simply alleviate pockets of unemployment and introduced the strategy of growth centres into French regional planning.

The growth centre approach has since been developed as an integral element in French plans for decentralisation and regional development, and in 1966 a policy of building up counter magnets in the form of *métropoles d'équilibrium* throughout France to counterbalance the influence of the Paris region and provide foci for regional development was officially endorsed. The country is divided into nine functional regions based on Paris and eight other centres (Figure 12.3). The latter were chosen on the basis of a range of criteria but with the size of the cities and their central-place status being the major considerations. Excluding Paris, the chosen centres ranged in population size from less than 400 000 in Toulouse to almost 1·5 million in Lyons–St. Etienne. The policy is now to concentrate public investment in these centres creating the urbanisation economies which are at present mainly limited to Paris. It is hoped that these will be attractive to new firms, which, when they come, will create their own localisation economies of linked industries.

The success of this growth centre policy obviously depends on the ability of the new centres to reduce the influence of Paris. Some of the centres in the west are quite small and the Paris zone of influence is extensive. It is unfortunate that a new centre could

Fig. 12.3   France: regional metropolises and their functional regions

SOURCE   J. R. Boudeville, *Problems of Regional Economic Planning*, Edinburgh University Press (1966).

not have been designated in the south-central area of France to offset this central domination, but the most likely centres such as Clermont-Ferrand and Limoges simply do not possess the necessary initial facilities. The success of the policy also depends on the ability of the centres to transmit growth into their regions, although it is anticipated that the introduction of a series of intermediate regional centres, *centres-relais*, might fulfil this rôle (Figure 12.3). Overall, the policy represents a fascinating attempt to introduce a more discriminating spatial dimension into interregional planning.

FRENCH INTRA-REGIONAL PLANNING

Intra-regional planning in France tends to be synonymous with the attempts to deal with the metropolitan scale problems of the Paris Region, although developments in other regions such as the development of *métropoles d'equilibrium* mentioned above are not without significance and also merit some consideration. As mentioned earlier, Paris dominates France. It is one of the major cities of the world. The Paris region, roughly the area within 50 miles of Notre Dame, now has a population approaching ten million—almost 20% of the total French population—and since the turn of the century its population has been growing at almost twice the national average. Perhaps even more important, the region also has a concentration of economic activity, political power and cultural facilities out of all proportion even to this large proportion. It is from this excessive degree of concentration that the physical planning problems of Paris stem. The city region is congested. Its radial growth along the main lines of communication has placed excessive strain on the centre and the interstices between the radials. The net results are the typical diseconomies of growth—long journeys to work with the associated problems of time wastage and fatigue, very high inner densities and conflicting land uses with industry hemmed in on unsuitable sites.

These were some of the problems highlighted by Gravier in 1947 but it was not until 1960 that a comprehensive and coordinated plan for the region was approved by the government. This plan, *Plan d'Aménagement et d'Organisation Générale de la Région Parisienne* (PADOG),[7] was short-term in perspective dealing with the period from 1960 to 1970. It firstly assumed that the population growth of the area could be limited by cutting the future annual migration into Paris from 100 000 to 50 000. A limit was then proposed on the physical growth of the Paris agglomeration, accommodating population growth through the redevelopment of the structure of the existing city, creating suburban nodes, and the expansion of major towns like Orleans and Rouen some 60 miles or so from Paris. This approach was widely criticised partly on the failure to fully consider Paris in the context of its region, and particularly on the grounds that a total stop on the further growth of the agglomeration was unrealistic. As it was, the innate attraction of Paris led to a much faster rate of population growth than had been assumed and the plan was rapidly overtaken by events.

In 1965, a new plan was produced under the new regional planning body, the District de la Région de Paris. This plan, the *Schéma Directeur d'Aménagement et d'Urbanisme de la Région de Paris*[8] (Figure 12.4) mapped out the general guidelines for the development of the region up to the year 2000. It differed markedly from its PADOG predecessor in that it estimated a much faster rate of population growth with an approximate total figure of 14 million by 2000, including an extra two million jobs. It further accepted that there was a need to plan to accommodate this growth rather than restrict it and this would inevitably involve expansion—but planned expansion—of the agglomeration of Paris.

The aim of the new plan was to rectify the region's present monocentric form creating a new intermediate level of centre. Using the Paris region as a functional planning unit, the plan sought to accommodate the anticipated growth by the renovation of urban centres within the existing agglomeration and the development of new urban centres along preferential axes tangential to the main agglomeration. The former involves the continuation of some of the PADOG proposals, such as the comprehensive renewal scheme at La Défense. The latter, involving the organisation of growth into major centres along broad NW–SE twin corridors at a distance of between 15 and 30 miles from the city, represents a fundamental shift of approach. It is a determined approach to break away from the radial–concentric structure. As such, it involves a rejection of a green belt/new town

357

Fig. 12.4 *The Schéma plan (1965) for the Paris region*

Scale:
0 ___ 10 Miles
0 ___ 10 Kilometres

Legend:
- Central area
- City of Paris
- Surburban area
- Nodes (1960 plan, retained)
- Growth axis
- New urban zones
- Rivers
- Motorways

Meaux
Marne
Bry-sur-Marne Nasy-le-Grand
Bobigny
Paris
Créteil
St. Denis
Beauchamp
Oise
La Défense
Rungis
Seine
Versailles
Cergy Pontoise
Trappes Sud-Est
Trappes Nord-Ouest
Mantes
Mantes-Sud
Evry
Tigery-Lieusaint
Melun

approach which was regarded as unnecessarily constricting on the agglomeration and as possibly intervening with town development programmes outside the region. It also means a rejection of a 'second Paris' solution, or the development of several major axes—which was regarded as an expensive and inefficient solution. The proposed growth along the axes will be in the form of major sub-regional service and employment centres with populations of 300 000 to 500 000. Three such centres—Cergy-Pontoise, Beauchamp and Bry-sur-Marne—were proposed for the 45-mile northern axis; and five for the 55-mile southern axis. The specific locations were chosen where the main routes from Paris intersect the tangential axes. It is argued that this solution is efficient in terms of transportation investment and, by preserving an open wedge along the Seine Valley, will also guarantee easy access to open space for the bulk of the population. Of course, not everyone is convinced and such a radical solution has raised much opposition. The plan has been strongly criticised especially on the question of the excessive costs involved and on the likely impact on development in the more distant problem regions. Although the plan has since been reviewed, it nevertheless represents a courageous attempt to deal with these major regional problems.

Elsewhere in France there was little progress in planning at the intra-regional level until comparatively recently. In most regions in the 1950's the extent of regional planning was limited to the work of the regional expansion committees which were mainly concerned with the diagnosis of regional problems—although there were some interesting exceptions. During the same period, a limited number of quasi-public development corporations were set up to implement redevelopment programmes. One such organisation was the *Compagnie Nationale d'Aménagement de la Région du Bas-Rhône et du Languedoc* (CNARBL), which after much study initiated the Lower Rhône–Languedoc programme to tap water from the Rhône to irrigate a vast area of southern France freeing it from an economy narrowly based on vine culture. The programme soon developed a much wider range of projects concerned with many aspects of the life of the region.

More recently, the new sub-regional agencies (OREAM), established to produce plans for the development of the major *métropoles d'équilibrium* have begun to produce results. To date they have produced a series of *livres blancs* (white books) on demographic and economic prospects as a basis for planning, and some have produced *schémas d'aménagement* which constitute more concrete plans for the development of their areas. The OREAM Marseilles for example, following interesting exercises in public consultation, has now produced plans[9] to accommodate a population increase of up to 140% in its 2600 square mile area by the year 2000. However the agencies are purely study teams with no executive powers and the powers of implementation rest with the central government and local authorities.

THE FUTURE

France has now developed a sophisticated if perhaps somewhat complex planning system for dealing with its regional problems. But this system is not without problems. In spite of its elaborate structure, it is still highly centralised with the regional bodies, CODER and CAR, having only limited powers and the main power and control remaining in the hands of central government. This issue provoked a referendum in 1969, when proposals for greater regional autonomy, involving the creation of more representative and powerful regional assemblies, were put forward. In the event, the referendum was clouded by other issues and the proposals were rejected. But this is only a temporary halt and greater regional autonomy to counter the excessive centralisation on Paris seems to be only a matter of time.* A positive step in this direction could be to reduce the number of regions. Boudeville believes that the population of the French *régions de programme* should be in the order of four to five million. Yet only Paris, Rhône–Alpes and Nord fit into this scale, and ten regions have populations of less than 1·5 million. It could be

---

* Indeed, modest steps have recently (1972) been taken towards regional reform with some widening of the functions and composition of the regional bodies. But this is more concerned with streamlining the existing regional structure rather than changing it and each region will continue to be administered by a Government-appointed prefect.

argued that this present balkanisation is one of the major factors favouring the continuing domination of Paris.

2 Dutch regional planning

The Netherlands is a thriving and prosperous nation occupying an important strategic position in Western Europe. It is also a small country. In spatial terms it is considerably smaller than either the United Kingdom or France—indeed it is no larger than the largest regions in these countries. Yet despite its overall prosperity and small size, it still presents a striking diversity of problems. Within the country there are varying shades of prosperity and even prosperity itself brings problems.

In this small country a factor of vital importance is the growth and distribution of population. Round about the year 1800 a growth of one million in population took 50 years, now it only takes six years and by the year 2000, it may only be four years. It has been estimated (1966) that the 1971 population of 13 100 000 may increase to 20 000 000 by the end of the century.[10] The impact of population growth is further complicated by its high concentration in a small economically prosperous area in the west of the country which for many years has acted as a magnet for migrants from the more rural peripheral provinces to the north, east and south. In 1971, the three provinces of North Holland, South Holland and Utrecht, the Dutch 'Randstad', accounted for 46% of the total population on only 21% of the total land area. There are many reasons for this higher level of economic activity in the western provinces but of particular importance is their juxtaposition to the major trading axes of the North Sea and the Rhine, and their continued historical ascendancy in the administrative and cultural spheres.

For many years, Dutch planners have realised the need for an enlargement of the scale of planning to meet the problems now and in the future of this most densely populated country, and their advances in developing administrative structures, inter-regional planning frameworks, and both allocative and innovative forms of intra-regional planning offer important lessons of more general relevance. (Useful references on aspects of Dutch

361

regional planning include those by Burke,[11] Hall,[12] Heywood[13] plus official Dutch government publications.)

THE STRUCTURE OF PLANNING

To reconcile the competing claims on its scarce resources, the Dutch nation has evolved a hierarchical planning structure which is carried out at three levels—national, provincial and municipal—with each level being generally regulated by the policies laid down by those above it.

At the national level, responsibility for spatial planning policy falls to the Minister of Housing and Spatial Planning. He is advised and assisted by the National Physical Planning Agency which carries out much of the day-to-day work of policy preparation; a National Physical Planning Committee which is an inter-departmental consultative body; and an Advisory Physical Planning Council which functions as a channel of communication between the government and the community. Economic planning however comes under a separate ministry, the Ministry of Economic Affairs, and thus considerable onus lies upon inter-ministerial co-ordination.

At the intermediate level there are eleven provinces (Figure 12.5). These provinces, developed from the seventeenth-century United Provinces, are autonomous administrative units which have, over the course of time, gradually gained influence and are now of considerable importance for effective regional planning. In outline, the organisational structure of provincial planning closely resembles the national level. The provinces are authorised to adopt regional plans which can cover all or parts of their areas. This plan preparation is carried out by Provincial Physical Planning Agencies in consultation with Provincial Physical Planning Committees. The municipal authorities must also be consulted and the plan must be approved by the elected regional decision-making body, the Provincial Council.

The municipality constitutes the third level of planning. There are in total some 861 municipal councils in the Netherlands. They are obliged to draw up an allocation plan for the whole of the municipal territory that is not built up and may also do the same for built-up areas. They may also draw up a structure plan for their area, indicating future development. Neither plan should transgress the regional plan. However, should the municipality feel strongly opposed to the restraints set by the province, then it may appeal directly to the Crown, which can overrule the regional plan. In this respect, a recent development of some importance has been the grouping of several municipalities into

Provinces

1 Friesland
2 Groningen
3 Drenthe
4 North Holland
5 Overijssel
6 South Holland
7 Utrecht
8 Gelderland
9 Zeeland
10 North Brabant
11 Limburg

A Waddenzee Project
B IJsselmeer Polder Scheme
C Delta Plan Area

Fig. 12.5   The Netherlands: provinces

Agglomeration Boards which tend to be more effective planning units.

It is possible to identify two elements in Dutch inter-regional planning. Historically, the first element is an industrial location policy, carried out by the Ministry of Economic Affairs and initiated to meet the same problems encountered in other Western European countries (namely, the fact that certain regions of the country lag behind in economic development). In the Netherlands, it is the northern rural provinces (Groningen, Drenthe, Friesland and part of North Holland) and the more industrialised province of Limburg in the south which suffer from economic malaise. In the latter there was a risk of structural unemployment following the closure of the coal mines; whereas in the north, the general problem is one of static or even shrinking employment opportunities owing to the mechanisation of agriculture, as a consequence of which farm labourers are obliged to look for jobs elsewhere. The policy response has been one of 'stimulation and reconversion' with the concentration of government support, through the provision of infrastructural facilities and industrial incentives, in specific primary and secondary nuclei in the problem regions. This policy has met with considerable success especially in the southern part of the country.

The second and more recent element of inter-regional planning involves the preparation of National Physical Plans by the National Physical Planning Agency in an attempt to structure the competing demands on the scarce physical resources of the country, especially in the West. In the Second Report on Physical Planning in the Netherlands (1966), the government proposed a possible physical structure for the year 2000 aimed at improving the irregular distribution of the population over the various parts of the country. The broad urbanisation pattern proposed was one of 'concentrated deconcentration' with some stabilisation of urbanisation in the West conserving the 'green heart' of the Randstad and with dispersal directed especially to the North, certain parts of the province of Overijssel, the Southern IJsselmeer Polders and the province of Zeeland.

364

The more detailed structural scheme distinguished a four-tier hierarchy of physical planning units (Figure 12.6). Yet, despite the innate attraction and theoretical sophistication of the approach, the Second Report constitutes more an indicative proposal rather than an effective national framework for spatial planning. Nevertheless, even broad guidelines as to how current trends could be accommodated in the light of existing policies are of considerable relevance, especially to regional planners.

However, by the early 1970's, the underlying assumptions of the 'concentrated deconcentration' strategy were being superseded. In particular, demographic projections suggested a population of not more than 16 millions by the year 2000 rather than the 20 millions forecast in 1966. Further, the aims of the Second Report were not being realised, and there were fears that the dispersal policy would lead to the elimination of any good sized areas of open land in the country, and that harm would be done to the economic, social and cultural functions of the Randstad. A Third Report was initiated, and the 'Urbanisation' part of that report, published in 1976, abandoned the stringent dispersal policy in favour of a policy directed much more towards concentrating further urbanisation, both inside and outside the Randstad, into a limited number of designated growth nuclei and growth towns (Fig. 12.7).

INTRA-REGIONAL PLANNING

It is also possible to identify two forms of Dutch intra-regional planning—provincial planning and regional development planning. *Provincial planning* is primarily allocative regional planning concerned with maintaining the smooth functioning of the existing system over time in accordance with evolving policies. This involves several rôles. Provincial planning must firstly bridge the gap between national and municipal planning, allowing the consideration of regional priorities in the formulation of national investment decisions and vice versa. In the Netherlands this is done through a series of regular consultations between the various planning levels and is also aided by provincial regulation of two major items of expenditure—roads and town centre redevelopment.

A second rôle involves the co-ordination of municipal planning—reconciling local conflicts and avoiding the duplication of expensive infrastructural investment. On paper this is achieved through the preparation and implementation by the Provincial Council of the regional and sub-regional plans—documents which hopefully take a wider view of issues than the individual municipalities. Unfortunately this can sometimes result in major provincial–municipal disagreements as exemplified by the conflicts between the major cities of Amsterdam and Rotterdam and their provinces over restrictions on their growth potentials along the North Sea Canal and in the Rhine Delta respectively. In such situations, the strength of democratic authority may not be sufficient for the provincial bodies and in reality the municipality

Fig. 12.6 The Netherlands (Randstad)—hierarchy of settlements, from the Second Report on Physical Planning in the Netherlands (*1966*)

often wins the day. It has been argued that this may reflect the physical orientation of the regional plans and their failure to appreciate economic forces, and the greater financial and political resources of the larger municipal authorities.[14]

Finally, provincial planning can also bee seen as an input into national planning. This is certainly the case in the Netherlands where the existence of a series of regional plans greatly facilitated the preparation of the Second National Physical Plan.

The second form of intra-regional planning, *Regional Development Planning*, predates the provincial form and is somewhat of a Dutch speciality for which the nation is rightly famous. Regional

Fig. 12.7 The Netherlands urbanisation strategy, from the Third Report on Physical Planning in the Netherlands (*1976*)

development planning is innovative involving the moulding of change on a large scale. It is concerned with integrated development schemes, schemes of great impact which require planning at the regional scale to ensure the greatest possible benefit for all activities in the region. In the Netherlands, the IJsselmeer Polders scheme to reclaim the Zuyder Zee, the Delta Plan to close the Rhine–Maas Delta, and the Waddenzee project to reclaim large areas of land between the West Frisian Islands and the north coast, all fit into this category.

The varying objectives of such schemes have been discussed by Van den Berg.[15] Originally, the main objective was one of economic growth (the Zuyder Zee reclamation scheme was proposed as early as 1848 to foster commerce, shipping and agriculture). But it was the threat to the Dutch people of the ravages of both sea and river inundations which in the end proved to be the most forceful objective and the most powerful political argument. Over time however multiple objectives have developed including water supply, the improvement of communications and land reclamation and its subsequent use for agriculture, industry and housing.

Of the three schemes, reclamation of the IJsselmeer Polders has progressed furthest. Of the area of 870 000 acres closed to the North Sea, 300 000 have already been reclaimed and three polders have been settled. A further 250 000 will be reclaimed by 1980 with the rest remaining as a fresh-water reservoir. In contrast to the older polders which are being developed primarily for agriculture, rather more space in the newer reclaimed areas will be set aside for recreation, industrial sites and new residential areas. Thus the 1965 structure plan for the South IJsselmeer Polders[16] was made to fit in with the aim of national planning— releasing pressure from the crowded and growing cities of Amsterdam and Utrecht. Within this broad structure a detailed hierarchy of centres is planned.

These major multi-purpose projects are carried out by semi-autonomous regional development agencies under the auspices of the Department of Water Management. Although such an approach might be viewed as undemocratic it does have the advantages of achieving impressive results in a relatively short period of time unhindered by inter-departmental and provincial-municipal conflicts. Further, as the projects proceed, reclaimed land is returned to the control of adjacent provinces.

The Dutch approach to regional planning has much to commend it. The possession of an intermediate level of provincial planning with statutory powers and an elected provincial council would seem to be a major administrative asset; the national physical plan provides useful guidelines for regional planning and the regional development agencies fulfil a valuable innovative rôle. But there are also problems. At all levels there appears to be a failure to integrate economic and physical planning. This lack of effective horizontal co-ordination is particularly clear at the national level and it has been suggested 'that on the national planning level all financial, economic and technical means should be concentrated in one ministry'.[17] Provincial planning could also be more effective; at present it is politically and financially rather weak and is in consequence squeezed from above and below.

3 Regional planning in Eire

PROBLEM BACKGROUND
Most of Eire's planning problems stem from the two interrelated factors of slow industrial growth and population decline. Lack of coal and mineral resources meant that Ireland was largely by-passed by the industrial revolution in Western Europe, and its fortunes were tied to a not very efficient agriculture (in 1922, at the time of Irish independence, 50% of the labour force were engaged in agriculture which accounted for 75% of total merchandise exports). This has resulted in a dispersed settlement pattern, a relatively unskilled labour force and a weak tradition of industry-based urban development. Apart from Dublin and Cork, only 13 towns in Ireland have populations of more than 10 000 persons and in 1966, 50·8% of the population were still living in rural areas or centres of less than 1500 population. The most significant demographic feature has been emigration which exceeded natural increase almost continuously between 1841 and 1961, leading to a continuous fall in population. This, in itself, resulted in a declining home market too limited to easily support a wide range of modern industry. Thus, economic and demo-

369

graphic factors have worked together in a self-reinforcing vicious circle.

There are also wide disparities in economic and social levels between regions in Eire. A line running from Dundalk in the north east to just west of Cork in the south west, roughly divides the less developed regions to the north and west from the more developed south and east. The weakest regions, in terms of social and economic development, are Donegal, North West, West and Midlands, all of which have ranked consistently badly on socio-economic indicators (Fig. 12.8). For example, Donegal had a population loss of 4·6% (1961–66), an unemploy-

Fig. 12.8   Eire—planning regions and Buchanan's recommended growth centres

ment rate of 9·7% (1966), average *per capita* personal income of £215 (1965) and only 16·6% of its labour force employed in industry. In contrast, in the most prosperous Eastern Region (including Dublin), the respective figures were population growth of 9·1%, unemployment rate of 3·5%, average personal income of £359 and 36% industrial employment. Within the less developed regions, the Gaeltacht (Irish speaking) areas have constituted a particular problem with in nearly all cases greater proportionate population losses than other rural areas in the counties of which they form part.

From the foundation of the state, Irish governments have actively sought to deal with these problems, developing a range of policies administered by a variety of agencies. (Useful background references on regional planning in Eire include those by Buchanan, Viney and Roberts.)[18]

THE INSTITUTIONAL FRAMEWORK

As in the United Kingdom, government and administration in Eire is concentrated at the national and local levels. Most government departments are involved in some way in regional development but, in addition, since the 1950's a number of semi-autonomous government agencies have been established with particular regional rôles.

The Ministry of Local Government exercises the central control over environmental planning. Within this Ministry, an inter-departmental Regional Development Committee was set up in 1965 to advise on regional problems and to co-ordinate regional policies at a national level. The planning regions illustrated in Fig. 12.8 were also introduced at this time. Since 1969, the Regional Development Committee has had the additional responsibility for co-ordinating and monitoring the work of the Regional Development Organisations (RDOs). The nine RDOs, one for each planning region, were created in 1969 as a result of a recommendation in the Buchanan Study.[19] Their rôle is to promote the co-ordination of planning and development within their regions. They are also required to produce reports outlining the region's problems and the potential for and constraints on development. Representatives from the local planning authorities, central government and other development agencies, including tourist and industrial development interests, sit on these organisations, each of which has a majority of locally elected representatives. The RDOs are non-statutory bodies, they have no executive powers and are unable to raise finance. To date, this weak power base has tended to limit their co-ordinating rôle and the organisations have not yet developed a corporate image. Nevertheless they do have the potential to perform a valuable connective rôle. Note should also be taken of An Foras Forbartha (AFF), the central government agency for physical planning and construction research, which has played a valuable catalyst rôle in the evolution of regional planning through its funding and publishing of relevant research.

Industrial development policies come under the central control of the Ministry of Industry and Commerce. Responsible to the Ministry is the Industrial Development Authority (IDA), which is the single most important development agency in Eire and the key agency in Irish regional development and planning. The IDA was created in 1949 with the responsibility for promoting the industrial development of all the regions. Under the 1969 Industrial Development Act its statutory functions were consolidated to include the furtherance of industrial development, the provision of financial incentives, the provision of industrial estates and factories, the provision of housing for employees in industry and the fostering of regional industrial development. In 1971, as part of its work of promoting regional industrial development, the IDA opened an office in each planning region, with the exception of the Mid-West where the Shannon Free Airport Development Company acts as the agent of the Authority. The offices provide information and advisory services, covering for example grants and other incentives, and handle after-care services for industry. They also assist in the preparation of the regional industrial plans.[20]

The Ministry for the Gaeltachts also has a regional perspective. Established in 1956, its rôle is to promote the cultural, social and economic welfare of the Gaeltachts, and to encourage the preservation and extension of the use of Irish as a vernacular language. Gaeltarra Eireann, a statutory body, has the responsibility and financial powers for industrial development in the Gaeltachts.

At the local level, the 27 county councils and 4 county boroughs

(Dublin, Cork, Limerick and Waterford) are the major government units with planning powers. At a lower level, there are a further 135 assorted borough, urban district and 'town' authorities. In only a limited number of the larger authorities has planning made much progress. Many of the authorities have very limited resources, and in 13 western counties they have been augmented by County Development Teams (CDTs). These teams, responsible to the Central Development Committee of the Finance Ministry, seek to foster the development of the counties in every sphere of economic activity and to co-ordinate the work of public services. They are small 'action' groups of top officials, chaired by the County Manager, with a sound record of success in implementing development policies.

INTER-REGIONAL PLANNING IN EIRE
The overriding aim of Irish government policy has been the generation of industrial development to absorb the population increase and offset the debilitating flow of emigrants. But in the pursuit of this aim, successive Irish governments have had to confront the problem facing many developing countries; namely, the nature of the trade off between concentrated development in the areas of greatest potential in order to foster self-sustaining national economic growth, and the dispersal of development to counter inter-regional imbalance. This problem is intensified by the weak urban structure of the country with many areas lacking the sizeable urban centres which might be the natural locations for new industrial projects. If the industrial base was to be concentrated on the eastern coast of the country, the economic growth of the nation as a whole and greater international competitiveness might be achieved. But such concentration might also intensify existing regional imbalances and accelerate emigration from the weaker regions.

Until the 1950's a policy of dispersed development, influenced more by welfare than economic considerations, was favoured. However, this policy often resulted in sub-optimal locations and higher operating costs, as exemplified by the programme of peat-fired electricity generating stations in the Midlands and West. Lack of success prompted the establishment of the IDA (1949) and, under the 1952 Underdeveloped Areas Act, an increase in

373

financial incentives for firms located in development areas. But little was achieved until, in 1956, financial incentives were widened to the whole country. A further impetus was provided in 1958, when it was recognised, in the First Programme for Economic Expansion,[21] that industrial growth based upon a home market, protected behind high tariff walls, was not adequate and that future industrial development needed the establishment and attraction of new industries catering mainly for export markets. Tax exemption was introduced as an incentive for firms if their products were for export only. The net result of these new measures was a rapid growth in industrial development, but also a reintensification of development in the economically attractive eastern locations, especially around Dublin.

A new balanced approach was needed, and was provided by the Committee on Development Centres and Industrial Estates, set up by the Minister for Industry and Commerce in 1963, which concluded that development centres were attractive to industry and desirable from a social viewpoint. The government endorsed a development centre policy but decided to await the completion of studies of the Limerick and Dublin regions before identifying regional centres. When the studies were completed in 1966,[22] it became clear that a comprehensive national strategy for regional development was required, embracing all the regions. Buchanan and Partners were engaged through the United Nations Organisation to prepare physical development policies for seven of the nine planning regions and their study similarly recommended a preferred strategy based upon a limited number of growth centres (Fig. 12.8). It was proposed that Cork and Limerick/ Shannon should act as national counter magnets to the capital, and only natural growth shoud be allowed in Dublin. The development of the counter magnets was to be achieved by a concentrated drive for expansion involving much internal migration of population. The development of the second level or regional growth centres would be based on industrial growth or service sector expansion or both. Local growth centres at a third level were also suggested and the need was seen for even smaller centres to act as local growth points. Overall, the Buchanan study argued that growth centre policy offered 'the best, perhaps the only, chance of achieving the rate of industrial development

374

needed for getting a full employment society'.[23]

The Buchanan study generated considerable critical reaction, especially in rural areas, and the government, mindful of possible political implications, neither accepted nor rejected the proposals. Several studies argued that the alternative dispersed pattern of industrial location had been successful,[24] and in its Regional Industrial Plans of 1972,[25] the influential IDA opted for more dispersal than suggested by Buchanan. While both the IDA and Buchanan proposals were designed to bring about improvements in the country's urban and industrial structures, the IDA proposed that approximately 50% of new jobs in the period 1961–86 should be located in the nine growth centres recommended in the Buchanan study, rather than the 75% advocated by Buchanan. IDA proposals also included a policy for the smaller population centres, and a development strategy for those parts of the country (North West, Midlands) for which the Buchanan study did not provide a solution. The IDA proposals were published in conjunction with the government's 'Review of Regional Policy', which expressed similar views noting that 'an overall regional strategy should not merely seek the attainment of required national growth rates but should also provide for the maximum spread of development, through all regions, giving an increased and wider range of economic and social opportunities and so minimising population dislocation through internal migration'.[26] This policy statement together with the Buchanan and IDA proposals, formed the basis for regional development policies in Eire in the 1970's.

In its 1972 Regional Industrial Plans, the IDA set out a target of 55 000 new manufacturing jobs for the period 1973–77. With anticipated manufacturing job losses of 17 000 in the same period, this gave a net increase of 38 000 jobs, which represented a substantial increase on earlier net changes in manufacturing employment of 19 000 jobs (1961–66) and 24 000 jobs (1966–71). The highest percentage regional growth targets were proposed for the problem regions (e.g. 48% net increase in manufacturing employment in the West region). To achieve its targets, the IDA pursues an active policy of both developing home industry and marketing Ireland as a location for overseas industry. A range of industrial incentives are available, including training grants, non-repayable cash grants, relief from tax on export profits, ready-made facilities, loan guarantees, equity participation and housing for key workers. The IDA has the discretionary power to offer the cash grants, towards the costs of fixed assets, at any level up to a maximum of 60% in designated areas and 45% elsewhere, and this power can be used to encourage industrialists to choose locations in accordance with the proposals made in the various Regional Plans (see following section).

Between 1973 and 1975, gross job creation was already in excess of 50 000, but unfortunately the job loss prediction over this same period proved a gross underestimation, and over 57 000 manufacturing jobs were lost. Over 50% of these losses occurred in the East region, principally in the traditional industries in Dublin City. Nevertheless there have been some notable net gains in the four most problematic regions, with the West region for example increasing manufacturing employment by over 25% between 1973 and 1975.[27] Such gains are helping to deal with the regional imbalances within the country. Continuing policies are seeking to reinforce these gains, although more attention is also being given to the major urban areas, especially Dublin, so badly hit by the shake out of jobs from the traditional industries in the mid-1970's.

INTRA-REGIONAL PLANNING

Intra-regional planning in Eire has several strands. Firstly, following on from the previous discussion, the IDA produces a series of Regional Industrial Plans which are designed to influence the pace, structure and location of industrial development within particular regions over a five-year period. Features of the plans are an analysis of the region's problems and potential, the development of an industrial strategy, the establishment of manufacturing industry job creation targets for particular 'town groupings' within the region, and the identification of approaches to plan implementation. With the IDA operating not only as a planning agency, but also a development agency in its own right, the Regional Industrial Plans are rightly termed 'action' plans. Secondly, there are the reports of the Regional Development Organisations. These documents are seen as providing a framework for the co-ordinated planning and development of a region,

376

covering for example programmes for infrastructure provision. To date, the regional reports have tended to be largely stock-taking documents, somewhat limited by their advisory nature. Finally, there are the various consultant plans, such as those produced for the Dublin and Limerick regions and the Cork sub-region. These *ad hoc* regional plans have performed a useful interim rôle in the evolution of regional planning in Eire.

A particular interesting example, illustrating some of the innovative aspects of the Irish approach to regional development and planning, is the Shannon Airport Scheme which, over a period of 20 years, has acted as a vital catalyst in the rapid industrial development of the previously depressed Mid-West region.

Shannon International Airport is located in County Clare on the sheltered deep water estuary of the Shannon River, 12 miles downstream from the regional 'capital' of Limerick. The airport rose to prominence in the post-war period as the eastern refuelling halt for most transatlantic services. But with the introduction of

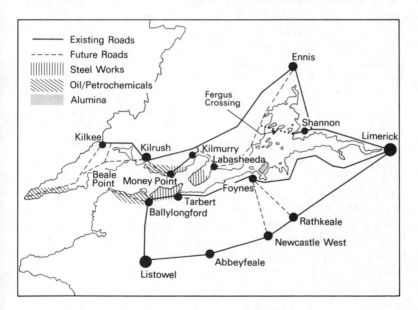

Fig. 12.9   Shannon Estuary—development recommendations

SOURCE   SFADCO, *Shannon Estuary: Outline Development Framework* (1974).

'long haul' jet aircraft in the late 1950's, the airport was over-flown and its future was in jeopardy. Closure would have meant a considerable loss in foreign revenue and the loss of the single largest employer in the Mid-West region. The government response was a vigorous attempt to generate traffic for the airport and the Shannon Free Airport Development Company (SFADCO), a semi-autonomous government agency, was given the responsibility for promoting the growth.

SFADCO has pursued the task through the improvement of the runway, warehousing and freight handling services at the airport; the establishment of an industrial estate within a Customs Free Zone adjacent to the airport; and the development of tourist facilities and tourism based on Shannon. A package of financial incentives, including a complete exemption from Irish taxes on export profits on goods manufactured in the Free Zone and some exemption of customs duties on goods imported for processing in the Free Zone have, since 1960, attracted over 70 prosperous international manufacturing and service industries to the indus-trial estate, employing 4000 people and contributing 11% of the country's exports. The airport and industrial estate together employ over 7000 people, roughly equal to the population of the adjacent Shannon New Town which was established, also under SFADCO, to complement the industrial development.

The impact of the Shannon development has not been limited solely to the Shannon locality. In 1966, the consultants' study of the Limerick region advocated a Limerick–Shannon–Ennis 'Central Growth Area' with a number of subsidiary growth centres. Since 1968, SFADCO has been the regional agent of the IDA for the whole of the Mid-West region. Development has spread outwards, primarily to the Limerick–Shannon–Ennis triangle, but also to other smaller towns, and the industrial environment in the region has improved considerably over the years to meet the needs of modern industry. For the future, attention is being focused on the development of the Shannon Estuary. Recent reports suggest that the combination of the deep water estuary and possible offshore oil may augur well for the development of maritime industry, including aluminium smelting and petrochemicals.[28]

Since the early 1960's Eire has been experiencing a period of major social and economic change. The country has been industrialising quite rapidly, the net migration loss has been reduced and sometimes reversed, and the population is increasing. Regional planning is now accepted as an important aspect of this development. Although there still exists a major centre–periphery dualism within the country, there have been some notable improvements in the performance of peripheral areas. One important step has been the introduction of a knowledge of a modern work environment which was often quite alien to the rural way of life. This can of course have detrimental side effects on local cultural patterns,·and in the Gaeltacht Areas the aim is to combine industrial development with cultural preservation. However, the rôle of manufacturing industry development, especially via foreign investment, can be overemphasised. Greater use could be made of a decentralisation of the rapidly growing office employment out of its Dublin concentration; and the central rôle of agriculture in Eire must not be minimised. An efficient agriculture, in combination with modern industrial development, could provide a strong base for Eire, especially in an EEC context.

The institutional framework for regional planning in Eire presents an interesting contrast. On the one hand, there is a strong group of state sponsored agencies, headed by the IDA, and presenting a forceful and innovative approach to planning and development which provides a model for other countries. On the other hand there is a seemingly inefficient government system, with problems of overlap between central government departments and many weak local authorities. The 1969 Devlin Report on the Organisation of Public Services in Eire[29] suggested that the system could be improved by reducing the centralised nature of state administration through the devolution of more executive power to the local authorities, which themselves should be reorganised so as to reduce the number of small local authorities. There might also be merit in strengthening the Regional Development Organisations and increasing the public accountability of the various development agencies.

4 Regional planning in a European community

In addition to dealing with their problem regions within a national framework, some countries are now having to allow for the effects of integration into major international blocs such as the EEC. It is possible that such integration may aggravate existing regional problems or even create new ones. With the recent expansion of the EEC from the original six—France, Germany, Holland, Belgium, Luxembourg and Italy—to nine, with the addition of the UK, Eire and Denmark, this factor is particularly relevant to a discussion of UK regional problems.

INTEGRATION AND REGIONAL PROBLEMS

In assessing the effects of economic integration it is important to differentiate between the immediate impact effects and the long-run dynamic effects. The impact effects result from given supply and demand conditions and often reveal themselves most clearly via price changes (the expected rise in UK food prices on joining the Common Market provides an example of this effect). The dynamic effects result from changes in the underlying conditions of supply and demand arising from opportunities for rationalisation, economies of scale, specialisation and centralisation in a supra-national market—250 million people in the enlarged EEC.

Three long-run effects may have a particular significance for regional problems. In the first place, the elimination of internal tariffs and the adoption of common policies for transport will lead to the creation of a large and competitive market. This will stimulate greater efficiency favouring the most efficient enterprises which can best take advantage of the economies of scale. This will inevitably lead to increased *specialisation*, bringing greater prosperity to some regions, but also aggravating the problem of the depressed industrial and agricultural areas. (In Belgium, the winds of EEC competition have had a traumatic impact on the admittedly inefficient coal industry of the Borinage.) An open market will also tend to lead to an *equalisation of factor prices* with capital and labour flowing from locations where earnings are low to those where earnings are high until some equilibrium position is reached. The level of factor earnings will be determined by the most productive enterprises in the prosperous

380

regions. The weaker enterprises in the problem areas which had only survived by paying lower rates will have to either improve their efficiency or, more likely, decline. This introduces a third major effect, the tendency for increasing *centralisation* of economic activity in the prosperous centre of the wider community to the detriment of the partners on the fringe. The centre reaps the advantage of scale economies and the net effect may be the replacement of national centre–periphery disparities with a wider community centre–periphery. In Western Europe, the impact of this effect could be to concentrate economic activity in the Rhine–Rhône axis or the so-called 'Golden Triangle'.

THE EEC AND UK REGIONAL PROBLEMS

As a country on the periphery of Europe, the effects of EEC membership, especially those of increased centralisation and specialisation, on regional problems, are of considerable importance in the UK. It would seem likely that, in the absence of controls, economic activity will tend to gravitate towards the centre of the market it is mainly aiming to supply. For although, as noted in Chapter 6, the micro-location of industry is becoming more flexible, the macro-location is tending to a greater concentration on a limited number of areas. What will be the impact on the UK of this centralisation in the Golden Triangle of Western Europe—will it become the Northern Ireland of the EEC? The areal extent of this Golden Triangle tends to vary according to the nationality of the delineator. Accepting the implicit British bias it can perhaps be roughly identified as the area bounded by Birmingham, Amsterdam, the Ruhr, Milan and Paris, although it isn't a static phenomenon.

Clark, Wilson and Bradley[30] ingeniously attempted to identify which regions in Western Europe were the most attractive to industry and the likely effects of both economic integration in the EEC and transport developments on the most favoured regions, using a quantitative approach based on the concept of economic potential. The latter is derived from Stewart's[31] form of demographic potential and has also been used by Clark[32] in an estimate of the economic potentials in Britain. The countries of Western Europe were subdivided into major regions, and the

Areas with potentials over 2800
Areas with potentials 2600-2800

(a)

(b)

(c)

Fig. 12.9   Economic Potential in a European Community

a Pre-Treaty of Rome

b Post-Treaty of Rome

c Enlarged Community

SOURCE: Clark, C., Wilson, F., and Bradley, J., Industrial location and economic potential in Western Europe, *Regional Studies*, **3**, 2, pages 197–212 (1969).

economic potential of a focal point in each region was defined by summing regional incomes around it—each regional income having been first divided by the 'distant costs' of reaching it. The distance costs included tariffs, and land and sea transport costs. The areas with the highest economic potential were assumed to be those most attractive to industrial location. The validity of the approach rests of course on the assumptions that firms are attracted by the large markets and scale economies of the areas of dense population, and that the capacity of a region to act as a market and supplier of inputs is directly related to regional income and inversely to the distance costs from other markets.

Using this method, contours of equi-potential were constructed for Western Europe for several different situations. Prior to the Treaty of Rome, clearly identifiable centres of equally high potential could be identified in South East England, the Paris region and the Rhine–Ruhr area. These areas were in marked contrast to the Benelux countries where major troughs of depression were apparent. Other attractive regions in the UK included the Midlands, the South East and North West regions; although potential fell quickly in the peripheral regions to the north and west.

But with the advent of Customs Union and the elimination of trade barriers between the original 'Six', the model revealed a marked shift in potential with the formation of a single central region of high potential concentrated in the Rhine Valley, Eastern Belgium and South East Netherlands, from which potentials diminished with distance on all sides. The net result was to relegate the whole of the UK to a European periphery of low potential. The enlargement of the EEC to include the UK, Eire, Norway* and Denmark, is shown to bring about some improvement in the relative UK position, as is the impact of increased containerisation and the building of a channel tunnel. Yet even with these improvements, the concentric pattern persists with Britain lying outside the areas of greatest potential.

Obviously the results are very sensitive to the approach used and can be questioned by attacking the structure, inputs and assumptions involved in the model. Nevertheless it provides an interesting attempt at analysis of an important issue, and at the

* Norway was included in the model.

384

least suggests that unless there is some form of positive intervention there may be considerable aggravation of existing UK regional problems and perhaps the creation of new ones.

The impact of increasing specialisation in the UK resultant from economic integration is equally difficult to assess, although it is probable that the existing efficient growth industries of the UK economy would be the ones most likely to benefit.[33] In the secondary sector, industries such as petro-chemicals, electronics and heavy electrical engineering might hope to benefit. Mechanical engineering, vehicles and aerospace might also be 'moderate gainers'. It is probable however that the tertiary sector and quaternary sector (high expertise services) might stand to gain most. In the tertiary sector, several British retailing firms are already expanding into continental markets to the benefit of the UK. In the quaternary sector, the South East is established as a world centre for finance, banking, insurance, marketing, research and development, and has several factors in its favour. It has the advantages of the established contacts of 'the City', the fact that the internationally accepted quaternary language is English, a strong tradition of scientific research and that elusive asset, the 'quality of the English way of life'. Offset against such advantages are the low degree of 'Europeanness' of the UK capital, the barrier of the English Channel (necessitating some reliance on public transport), the low salary for brainpower in the UK, and the rapidly inflating prices for office accommodation, all of which may over time constitute major constraints.

Whatever the particular effects of increased specialisation and centralisation, the likely general effect on the UK will be to relatively favour the already prosperous regions and especially the South East at the expense of the already ailing problem regions. The peripheral areas, Northern Scotland, Wales and Northern Ireland may face particularly difficult problems. But given better air and sea links, the North East and Central Scotland are both well placed for export to the Continent, and may enjoy better long-term prospects in the market than some people seem to fear.

REGIONAL POLICY IN THE EEC[34]

The dynamic effects of economic integration on all countries in

385

the Community are in themselves a major reason for policy at an EEC level. The aims of economic and perhaps ultimately political unity will not be furthered if some regions suffer badly from such union. As in the UK national context, widening regional disparities may encourage separatist tendencies and there are therefore important political motives for intervention. The Treaty of Rome setting out why the original Six countries wanted to create the EEC, includes the following reason, 'to ensure their harmonious development by reducing the differences between the existing regions'. This view was reiterated by the communiqué on the 1972 Common Market Summit, 'The Heads of State or of Government agreed that a high priority should be given to the aim of correcting in the Community, the structural and regional imbalances which might affect the realisation of Economic and Monetary Union.' There is also a need to intervene to co-ordinate the variety of national regional policies to prevent the development of situations where governments are actively outbidding each other to attract foreign investment.

For reasons such as these, the EEC is today more than ever aware of the need to work towards a co-ordinated regional policy. But this is not synonymous with the replacement of national regional policies. M. Borschette, a Community Commissioner recently said:

'the Commission and the Community recognise it is unlikely that a single regional policy could ever apply in all its details in all regions of the Community. We know that each region is a special case, often requiring special treatment. We also know that it is primarily for national governments to produce the ideas for dealing with these special problems. It is not our task to seek to intervene with the efforts of national governments directed towards this end. But we think that a common Regional Policy is necessary to supplement national efforts.'

The rôle of Community regional policy can therefore be seen as one of co-ordinating and 'topping up' the efforts of individual countries as and when necessary.

Three major elements in Community policy to date can be identified. Firstly the Commission has sought to create an awareness of regional problems organising studies and sponsoring conferences on the theory, techniques and practice of regional planning. A particular interesting development in this field was the commissioning by the EEC of the study into the feasibility of promoting an industrial development pole at Bari-Taranto in the heel of Southern Italy.

In the second place, the Commission has sought to co-ordinate the regional measures of the various member countries in an attempt to prevent excessive and wasteful competition between countries seeking to attract foreign, especially American, investments. In this area there has been notably less success. However, in 1971, a new set of guidelines were proposed which would limit industrial investment aid to a maximum of 20% of the total cost for any project in the so-called 'central area' of the Community. The central area includes the more developed areas. There would be no such limitation in the peripheral areas. Yet even if such proposals to control direct aid were successful the situation would still be open to abuse through the use of indirect aids such as the generous provision of social and economic infrastructure. The problem of co-ordinating regional measures presents a thorny problem.

The third and rather more successful element of EEC regional policy is the provision of capital to regions, 'topping up' the various national regional measures. Several community institutions, financed by subscriptions from the member states, have been established with this purpose in mind. By 1971, the European Investment Bank had loaned over £600 million for regional development, primarily to Southern Italy; the European Social Fund had aided the training and resettlement of over a million workers, again mainly from Italy; the European Coal and Steel Community had allocated loans of over £400 million to coal and steel modernisation projects largely in Germany and Belgium; and the European Agricultural Fund had provided major grants towards the rationalisation of farming, with approximately 80% of the total going to France. However the 1972 Community Summit gave a fresh impetus to a common Community regional policy initiating several new developments [35] and at the beginning of 1975, two new measures were adopted as the basis of a new European regional policy. [36]

The *European Regional Development* Fund is a source of grants and interest rebates on loans to industrial schemes, service activities and infrastructure projects in those areas which are covered by national regional policies. The Fund had a difficult birth, with considerable controversy over its size and distribution. After much political infighting, a modest fund of 1300 million units* of account (*c.* £540 million) was agreed for the first three years 1975–77, and the lion's share of the fund was to be distributed to projects in only two of the member states—Italy (40%) and the UK (28%).[37] Fig. 12.10 shows the allocation of grants from the fund for 1975 and the preference for aid to the more peripheral problem regions. In practice, however, the final form and destination of fund aid within any one country may not be easily identified. Aid tends to percolate down to individual projects in member states via central government ministries and linked with national regional policy measures. This raises the contentious issue of how additional are the EEC resources?[38] The principle of additionality, whereby fund aid must be additional to the normal regional policy expenditure of member states, and not a substitute, is a basic principle of the fund, but its observance is difficult to test. In some countries the principle appears to be observed (e.g. Danish acceleration of specific projects in Greenland); but in other countries, the fund aid appears to be used more as a general budget transfer.

A *Regional Policy Committee* and a Fund Committee, both set up in 1975, advise on various applications for aid from the EEC Regional Development Fund. The Regional Policy Committee also has wider responsibilities for examining more general questions of Community regional policy and in particular, ways of co-ordinating national and Community regional policies. To facilitate comparison, the Committee is encouraging a progression towards a standard method of preparing regional development programmes.

COMMUNITY POLICY: FUTURE DIRECTIONS
Community regional policy has made significant advances in the

* Each unit is the equivalent of a pre-Smithsonian US dollar—approx. 42p. A new 'floating' European Unit of Account (EUA) tied to a basket of Community currencies is to be introduced in 1978. (One 1978 EUA=approx. 65p.)

Fig. *12.10* *Distribution of EEC Regional Development Funds Grants* *(1975)*

SOURCE Adapted from *First Annual Report on ERDF*, EEC (1976).

1970's, but what of the future? The co-ordinating rôle over national regional policies is still weak, but the advent of the system of Regional Development Programmes may improve the situation. By the end of 1977, member states had to submit such programmes for each of their problem regions. The programmes, covering periods of three to five years, include diagnoses of economic and social problems in the regions; precise and, as far as possible, quantified regional objectives; regional development measures envisaged; size and sources of financial resources; and an implementation schedule. Aid from the Regional Development Fund will only be given to projects falling within the framework of a regional development programme. Each country is also required to produce an annual statistical summary indicating by region the results achieved during the previous year, identifying those to which the fund has contributed.

Table 12.1.   *EEC grants and loans to the UK (Jan. 1973–Nov. 1977)*

	£m
Regional Development Fund (grants)	132·2
European Social Fund (grants)	172·4
European Agricultural Guidance/Guarantee Fund (grants) including hill-farming grants	66·0
European Coal and Steel Community (grants)	35·8
(loans)	746·0
European Investment Bank (loans)	768·0
Miscellaneous grants	7·9
Total grants	414·3
Total loans	1514·0

SOURCE   EEC (London Office).

Regional development programmes may help to overcome the 'additionality' problem of the Regional Development Fund; but increasing the size of the fund brings more problems. The fund is increasing—2880 million units of account (*c.* £1200 million) have been allocated for the 1978–80 period—but allowing for inflation this increase is only modest. The fund is small in comparison with national regional policy aids; the sum received by Britain in the 1975–77 period was less than one tenth of national aid. But proposals for increasing its size meet resistance from those countries, such as West Germany, which are net subscribers. Perhaps

390

herein lies the most difficult task for future Community regional policy—that of convincing nations, such as France and Germany, that it is in their interests that their neighbours, such as Britain, Italy and Eire, should have a larger share of Community finances.

It should be remembered, however, that the fund is only one tool of EEC regional policy, and others, such as the European Investment Bank, are at least as important for Community regional·development. For the future, it is possible that the EEC may attempt to co-ordinate the various financial instruments at its disposal to focus on a limited number of regional projects of major Community interest.

Finally, there would also seem to be merits in a supra-national approach to the growing power of multi-national companies in regional industrial development, with for example an EEC Regional Development Corporation seeking to guide multi-nationals in the interests of Community regional development. But of course national political pressures present even more formidable problems here! (A brief summary of the major EEC regional policy measures can be found in Appendix B.)

5 Summary

In France, the Netherlands and Eire the incidence of socio-economic disparities between different areas of the country and the need to co-ordinate physical, economic and social development at a supra-urban scale have necessitated an intermediate level of planning. For this purpose the highly centralised France has been divided into 21 planning regions, in the Netherlands the eleven provinces provide the regional framework and Eire has 9 planning regions. As in the United Kingdom, the duality of problems has led to a duality in regional planning. Within the regions there has been an emphasis on spatial plans to 'deconcentrate' the capital cities—Paris and the polycentric Randstad. There have also been interesting developments in innovative planning using semi-independent regional development bodies. Between regions, all the countries have developed industrial location policies. They have also sought to introduce a more discriminatory spatial dimension—as represented in the French policy of *métropoles d'équilibrium*, the Dutch national physical plans and the Irish

391

growth centres. But as in the United Kingdom the regional level of planning is still lacking in power and autonomy, with France still heavily centralised around Paris, the Dutch provinces unable to combat national and municipal pressures and the Irish Regional Development Organisations still very much in their infancy. In a wider context, it is possible that within the expanded European Economic Community certain regional problems may be aggravated by the market trends of increasing centralisation, specialisation and equalisation of factor prices. Peripheral areas of the Community, including large areas of Britain, may be particularly vulnerable, and this may necessitate a reappraisal and more vigorous pursuance of regional planning in the member countries and a more extensive European regional policy.

References

1 Allen, K., and MacLennan, M. C., *Regional Problems and Policies in Italy and France,* Allen and Unwin (1970).
2 Boudeville, J. R., *Problems of Regional Economic Planning,* Edinburgh UP (1966).
3 Hansen, N. M., *French Regional Planning,* Indiana UP (1968).
4 Hall, P., *The World Cities,* Weidenfeld and Nicolson (1966). See also: Gravier, J., *La question régionale,* Flammarion, Paris (1970).
5 Gravier, J. F., *Paris et le Désert Français,* Paris (1958).
6 Hackett, J. and A. M., *Economic Planning in France,* Allen and Unwin (1963).
7 France, Ministère de la Construction, *Plan d'Aménageemnt et d'Organisation Générale de la Région Parisienne* (1960).
8 France, Premier Ministre. *Délégation Générale du District de la Région de Paris, Schéma Directeur d'Aménagement et d'Urbanisme de la Région de Paris* (1955).
9 OREAM: Marseilles, *Schéma d'Aménagement de l'Aire Métropolitaine Marseillaise* (1970).
10 *Second Report on Physical Planning in the Netherlands,* Government Printing Office of the Netherlands, The Hague (1966).
11 Burke, L., *The Greenheart Metropolis,* Macmillan (1966).
12 Hall, P., *The World Cities, op cit.*
13 Heywood, P., Regional planning in the Netherlands and England and Wales, *Journal of the Town Planning Institute,* December 1970.
14 Dunham, D. M., The Processes of Spatial Planning in the Netherlands, in Dunham, D. M., and Hilhorst J. G. M. (eds.),

Issues in Regional Planning, Mouton (1971).
15 Van den Berg, G. J., Changing Regional Planning Goals in a Changing Country, *Town and Country Planning Summer School*, Keele (1966).
16 Rijkswaterstraat Communications, **6**, *Structure Plan for the Southern IJsselmeer Polders* (1965).
17 Steigenga, W., 'Recent Planning Problems in the Netherlands', *Regional Studies*, page 106, **2** (1968).
18 Buchanan, C., and Partners, *Regional Studies in Ireland*, An Foras Forbartha, Dublin (1969); Viney, M. (ed.), *Seven Seminars: An Appraisal of Regional Planning in Ireland*, An Foras Forbartha and Ministry of Development (Northern Ireland) (1970); Roberts, P. W., *Regional Planning in the Republic of Ireland*, Liverpool Polytechnic (1975).
19 Buchanan, C., *op. cit.*
20 Industrial Development Authority, *Regional Industrial Plans 1973–77*, Part 1 and Part 2 (plans for each region), IDA Ireland (1972).
21 Irish Government, *Economic Development*, Stationery Office, Dublin (1958).
22 Lichfield, N., and Associates, *Report and Advisory Outline Plan for the Limerick Region*, Stationery Office, Dublin (1966); Wright, M., *Advisory Regional Plan and Final Report for the Dublin Region*, Stationery Office, Dublin (1967).
23 Buchanan, C., *op. cit.*
24 O hUiginn, P., *Regional Development and Industrial Location in Ireland*, An Foras Forbartha (1972).
25 IDA, *Regional Industrial Plans 1973–77*, Parts 1 and 2, *op. cit.*
26 Irish Government, Statement in *Regional Policy Review*, Dublin (1972).
27 *IDA News*, April 1976, **2**, 8, IDA (1976).
28 SFADCO, *The Shannon Estuary: An Outline Development Framework*, Shannon (1974); Mid-West Regional Development Organisation, *The Impact of Offshore Oil on the Shannon Estuary* (1976).
29 Report of the Public Services Organisation Review Group (1966–69), Stationery Office, Dublin (1969).
30 Clark, C., Wilson, F. and J., and Bradley, J., Industrial location and economic potential in Western Europe, *Regional Studies*, **3**, 2, pages 197–212 (1962).
31 Stewart, J. Q., Empirical mathematical rules concerning the distribution and equilibrium of population. *Geog. Review*, **37** (1947).

32 Clark, C., Industrial location and economic potential, *Lloyds Bank Review*, **82**, pages 1–17 (1966).
33 For an interesting discussion and further references,
    See: Wise, M. J., Britain on the Brink of Europe, in Chisholm, M., (ed.), *Resources for Britain's Future*, David and Charles (1972).
34 See: Europe Community Information Service, Community Topics, 33: *Regional Policy in an Integrated Europe* (1969);
    Lind, H., *Regional Policy in Britain and the Six*, and Flockton, C., *Community Regional Policy*, Chatham House/PEP European Series, 15 (1970).
    McCrone, G., *Regional Policy in Britain*, Chapter XI, Allen and Unwin (1969).
35 *Report on the Regional Problems in the Enlarged Community*, Commission of the European Communities, May 1973.
36 *A New Regional Policy for Europe*, Commission of the European Communities (1975).
    The Community and Its Regions, Commission of the European Communities (1977).
37 *First Annual Report on the European Regional Development Fund*, Commission of the European Communities (1976).
38 Glasson, J., Regional Aid from the EEC, *Town and Country Planning*, March (1977).

Conclusion: retrospect and prospect

There is a growing awareness of the need for regional planning in many countries of the world. In some this awareness has provoked positive action. This has certainly been the case in the United Kingdom which today has a more extensive system of regional planning than most. But this development of British regional planning has not been smooth, and at first was somewhat intermittent. In the early years of this century, the functional problems of urban regions arising from rapid population growth, increasing urbanisation and increasing standards of living and personal mobility highlighted the need for intra-regional planning; similarly, the 'economic malaise' of the depressed industrial and rural regions aroused concern over regional variations and the need for the inter-regional allocation of resources to remedy the imbalance. But at this stage, the motivation for regional planning was founded more on emotion than considered argument and the achievements were minimal. The Barlow Report (1940) gave a welcome stimulus, which was reflected in major regional planning developments in the immediate post-war period (1945–51). Unfortunately this initiative was soon dissipated in the 1950's, and it was not until the last decade that regional planning reappeared in earnest. Now, supported by economic as well as social and political arguments, it is tempting to conclude that regional planning has finally arrived on the British scene. Inter-regional planning has an extensive armoury of incentives and controls designed to effect industrial relocation to assisted areas and these appear to be having some effect. In addition specific regional and sub-regional plans are being produced for many areas of the country. But while it is true that progress has been made and that the need for regional planning is now widely accepted—even in government circles—it still only represents a start and there are many fundamental issues yet to be resolved. Of particular concern is the gap between the goals of regional policies and plans and regional development in practice—the plan formulation–implementation gap. Such a gap raises several issues which need to be further explored if regional planning is to play more useful rôle in guiding the process of regional development.

The first issue relates to *goals*. There are innumerable potential conflicts between, for example, national and regional goals, the goals of one region and those of another, short run and long run, social and economic goals, which may greatly hinder a co-ordinated approach to the development of a region. In addition goals are often not made explicit, which greatly complicates co-ordination and the measurement of policy effectiveness. There is a particular lack of goals and general guidelines on the most desirable future inter- and intra-regional distributions of population and employment. As compared with France, the UK national planning framework is weak. In particular, there is a marked absence of policies on spatial priorities at the national level. Intra-regional strategies lack a published national framework linking each of the strategies together, and inter-regional policies, although becoming increasingly selective, lack an urban focus. In the early 1960's, there were several suggestions for a national framework for future population distribution, and the Central Unit for Environmental Planning was established in the mid 1960's to consider such problems. But the net result was the production of the *Long Term Population Distribution Study*[1] which merely suggested the need to investigate the feasibility of Severnside, Humberside and Tayside as future reception centres for national population growth. More recently the rôle of a national settlement strategy as a framework for regional development has been explored by an EFTA study group[2] who suggest that a national settlement strategy would be a broad strategy for the development of the national system of settlements rather than a rigidly defined spatial plan.

The plan formulation–implementation gap sometimes exists because the plans and policies formulated are inappropriate to the region's problems, and the rôle of *alternative policies* constitutes a second major issue. Contemporary UK regional policies and strategies have tended to suffer from a certain rigidity of approach. In inter-regional planning this rigidity has been reflected in the approach to the delineation of assisted areas, which until quite recently followed a 'blanket' approach based on rather narrow criteria. The emphasis on attracting private manufacturing industry, with only a minor rôle for the public sector and service industry, provides another example. Even the industrial location policies themselves could be more flexible relating more closely to the needs of particular industries and regions (perhaps the advent of new Regional Development Agencies may provide the necessary stimulus here). In intra-regional planning there has been a similar rigidity with a tendency for a rather narrow approach, often with a strong physical emphasis. There is a need for an integrated approach considering the interrelationships of a wide range of factors—physical, economic, social and the like—at the regional level, with a multi-alternative dynamic view of future situations. Some recent UK regional strategies are now adopting such an integrated approach.

The distributional impact of regional policies also merits further attention. Regional policies which may be efficient in economic terms and which may be to the advantage of the region as a whole, may discriminate against particular groups and areas within the region. There is a need to balance efficiency with equity, making equity more than a word and giving it some form of operational basis, so that the trade off between the two becomes clearer.

Overall there is some confusion over the roles and effectiveness of alternative policy measures, which may to a large extent reflect the state of regional substantive theory, and its relationship with regional planning practice. Much regional theory, although promising, is still in its infancy. Further, even though the principles outlined in earlier chapters provide a valuable insight into regional growth and change and the spatial structure of regions, there is still a wide gap between theoretical possibilities and the *ad hoc* rule-of-thumb practice. There are of course examples where the gap is narrowing, but there are also some examples of the misuse of concepts (the growth pole theory is a point in question). One explanation of this gap in many countries could be the poor state of the regional information system, for a good regional data base is essential for effective planning.

A third issue concerns the *institutional framework* for regional planning. The management of the process of regional development lies in the hands of many unco-ordinated agencies. If the regional planner is to guide this process, he must be aware of the characteristics of these agencies and seek to encourage them to adopt and use regional policy guidelines. But effective guidance may involve some reform of the regional planning machinery. Regional reform raises many questions of boundaries, functions and powers. What is the most suitable framework for co-ordinating local plans? How much of the administration of inter-regional planning can be devolved to the regional level? With regard to the latter it would seem that whatever the degree of regional autonomy, the inter-regional allocation of resources would still require some degree of co-ordinated central control. Regional reform is occurring in many countries. In the UK, the 1970's have witnessed the arrival of many new regional agencies, and the process is likely to gather momentum with the possibility of devolved regional government. But even this is only a stage in a continuing process, and any system must be adaptable to future changes.

The exploration of such issues is of course complicated by the rapidly changing environment in many countries. In Britain during the 1970's, events such as the economic recession, the discovery and exploitation of North Sea oil and the collapse of the birth rate led to much questioning of regional policies. Which are the problem regions, what should be the balance of resource allocation between inner city problems and outer growth area locations? Further, the emerging presence of the EEC has introduced a supra-national element into the regional debate.

The issues raised here create the need for new perspectives by regional planners and by educational programmes for regional planners. In addition to offering convincing diagnoses of and prescriptions for regional problems, the planner must also have

398

an understanding of the agencies involved in bringing about change. Yet, however skilful the approach of the regional planner and however efficient the regional machinery, regional problems will persist for many years to come. But the failure to tackle them now, and with vigour, will result in even greater social, economic and political problems in the future.

References

1 Department of the Environment, *Long term population distribution in Great Britain—a study*, HMSO (1971).
2 EFTA Economic Development Committee, *National settlement strategies: a framework for regional development*, EFTA Secretariat, Geneva (1974).

APPENDIX A
UK regional statistics:
major published sources

This summary of the major published sources of regional statistics makes no attempt to be comprehensive. It seeks merely to outline some of the sources relevant to regional planning. The general sources, although composed mainly of secondary sources derived from the original statistics, provide a useful framework. The selection of supplementary sources provides a basis for more detailed investigation of particular aspects of the regional environment. The regions referred to in the sources are primarily the eleven standard regions of the UK. These coincide with the Economic Planning Regions.

General Sources

Regional Trends (Central Statistical Office)—annually since 1981, and previously as *Abstract of Regional Statistics* since 1965. It is a compilation of 178 tables (1991) of economic, social and environmental statistics for the UK standard regions. Major categories of statistics are (1991):

1 Regional profiles	8 Law enforcement
2 Sub-regional statistics	9 Education
3 District statistics	10 Employment
4 Population	11 Personal income and expenditure
5 Housing	12 Regional accounts
6 Transport and environment	13 Industry and agriculture
7 Health	14 European Community regional statistics

Scottish Abstract of Statistics (Scottish Office)—published annually

Digest of Welsh Statistics (Welsh Office)—published annually

Northern Ireland Annual Abstract of Statistics (Northern Ireland Office)—published annually

Various Regional and Sub-Regional Studies, Plans, Reports and Strategies, and Structure Plans/Scottish Regional Reports, which contain much useful information specific to the particular region, sub-region or county (See Appendix C).

Key Data (Central Statistical Office)—an annual publication which presents basic statistics on the main social and economic areas. Information is primarily for the UK, with limited regional data. *Key Data 1991* contained over 130 tables, maps and coloured charts; each is accompanied by a reference to sources.

Guide to Official Statistics (Central Statistical Office)—first published in 1976, and now in its fifth edition, provides a comprehensive guide to UK statistics.

Local Government Trends (Chartered Institute of Public Finance and Accountancy)—provides useful annual overview of data, with some sub-national disaggregation, on topics including local authority expenditure, political trends, demographic features, employment and earnings, education, environmental health, housing, leisure, social services, public protection, transportation and development.

Supplementary Sources

1 *Population*

Census of Population (Office of Population Censuses and Surveys (OPCS), General Register Offices for Scotland and Northern Ireland). The most important single source on population, this has been taken every 10 years from 1801, with the exception of 1941 (wartime conditions) and 1966 (10% sample census). The most recent Census of Population was in April 1991. Census data provides a great deal of information on basic demographic characteristics, housing, household composition and economic activity, for all levels from the national and regional to the smallest possible enumeration district—a group of 150 or so households. Summary results for counties and districts in England and Wales are published in a series of County Monitors, one for each county. In Scotland, similar Regional Bulletins covering regions, districts and island authorities are published. Each Monitor and Bulletin contains a brief commentary and comparisons with earlier censuses. County Reports and Scottish Regional Reports are the most important source of census data for counties/Scottish regions and districts. They are much more comprehensive than the Monitors and Bulletins. In England and Wales there are two parts for each county; the first has statistics on population, economic activity, households and housing, and the second contains statistics on socio-economic characteristics. In addition, there are a series of national topic reports, which normally include data on standard regions and sometimes on local authority areas. The 1991 Census will include topic reports on:

1	Historical Tables	11	National Migration—Part 1
2	Population: Sex, Age, and Marital Status	12	National Migration—Part 2
		13	Regional Migration—Part 1
3	Usual Residence	14	Regional Migration—Part 2
4	Persons Aged 60 and Over	15	Economic Activity
5	Housing (including cars)	16	Workplace and Transport to Work
6	Communal Establishments		
7	Household Composition	17	Household and Family Composition
8	Limiting Long-term Illness	18	Qualified Manpower
9	Welsh Language in Wales	19	Children and Young Adults
10	Ethnic Group and Country of Birth		

For the 1991 Census, the sub-national monitors and reports are all planned to be available by early 1993. All national topic reports are planned to be published by the end of 1993.

Key Population and Vital Statistics (OPCS)—produced annually, and providing a wealth of population data (including resident population by sex/age groups, natural change and net migration, and vital statistics) for local and health authority areas.

Population Trends (OPCS)—published quarterly, this journal of OPCS contains a regular series of quarterly and annual tables on population and vital statistics for regions and health authority areas in England and Wales, and articles on a variety of population and medical topics. Similar information for Scotland and Northern Ireland is available in publications of the appropriate Registrar General.

Population Projections—Sub-National (OPCS)—biennial, provides population projections for regions and local government areas of England (excluding non-metropolitan districts).

Social Trends (Central Statistical Office)—published annually since 1970, provides much useful information about British society. The material is arranged in 12 chapters, corresponding closely to the administrative functions of government. Regional coverage is limited.

2 Employment

Employment Gazette (Department of Employment)—published monthly. This is the major source on employment. At the regional level there is monthly information on employment, redundancies, vacancies, unemployment and Regional Development Grants, and annual information on number of employees (age/sex/SIC/MLH), activity rates, seasonal unemployment and new employment data breakdowns by travel-to-work areas, Assisted Areas and Parliamentary Constituencies are also available. There are also occasional labour force projections (male/female/total) by region.

New Earnings Survey (Department of Employment)—has been produced annually since 1971. It relates to earnings of employees by industry, occupation, region etc. at April each year. Part E of the six parts includes detailed analysis of earnings (weekly, hourly) by occupation and industry for regions.

Skills and Enterprise Network (Department of Employment)—introduced in 1991 and produced quarterly. It provides an important data source on skills, employment and training.

Labour Market Quarterly Report (Department of Employment)—provides a commentary, including tables and charts, on current labour market trends and the implications for training, employment, unemployment, and includes special features on particular labour market topics. It includes some regional data.

National Online Manpower Information System (NOMIS) (Department of Employment/University of Durham)—a pay-as-you-use nationally networked information system offering rapid access and integrated analysis for data on employment, unemployment, job vacancies, population and migration, at various geographical levels.

3 Industry: Agriculture/Production Industries/Distribution and Other Services

Agricultural Statistics: United Kingdom (Ministry of Agriculture, Fisheries and Food)—information is obtained (on holdings, crops, livestock, labour force, tenure, farm type) by counties once a year on a census basis with sample enquiries at other times within the year.

Report on the Census of Production (Central Statistical Office)—was originally produced every four years and included numbers of establishments, total sales and volumes of employment for 130 industries at the regional level. It is now produced annually, as part of a comprehensive system of industrial statistics, in over 100 separate Business Monitors (e.g. for aerospace equipment, brewing and malting). Each Monitor gives regional distributions of employment, net capital expenditure, net output and gross value added at factor cost. The Census and Monitors use the Standard Industrial Classification (revised 1980, and to be revised again in 1993).

Census of Distribution/Business Monitors for Distribution and Other Services (Central Statistical Office)—was originally published approximately every five years by the Board of Trade. It provided estimates of the number of retail establishments, sales and employment by kind of business, for areas with population over 20,000. It has now been replaced by a set of Business Monitors for Retailing, Retail Trade and specific trades (e.g. motor trades, catering and allied trades), which provide a similar range of information, with limited spatial disaggregation.

4 Income and Expenditure: Individual and Community

Inland Revenue Statistics (Inland Revenue Board)—produced annually, the reports contain statistics on all taxes administered by the Inland Revenue, i.e. income tax, corporation tax, petroleum revenue tax, inheritance tax, capital gains tax and stamp duties. They also contain data on numbers of taxpayers and on various transactions. Regional surveys of personal incomes are published annually; data on property transactions, agricultural land prices and industrial investment are also available for regions.

Family Expenditure Survey (Central Statistical Office)—published annually, this shows, in great detail, income and expenditure by type of household for the UK. At the regional level the Survey includes data on household characteristics (size, composition, tenure of dwellings), and on weekly income by household and average weekly household expenditure on over 100 goods and services.

Local Government Financial Statistics (Department of the Environment)—an annual publication presenting details of local authority expenditure and income during the past financial year. Main figures relate to local authorities in England, but summary figures are also shown separately by the various types of authority (counties and districts, metropolitan and non-metropolitan) in both England and Wales.

5 Housing, Construction and Land Use

Local Housing Statistics (Department of the Environment)—quarterly statistics including information on the progress of house-building (private/housing association/ local authority), on a wide range of grants for renovations, on sales of land and council houses, and on local authority action under the homelessness provisions of the Housing Act. All data can be aggregated from the local authority upwards.

Private House Building Statistics (National House Building Council)—provides comprehensive quarterly information, disaggregated by regions and counties, on housing starts, completions, average prices and types.

Household Projections, England: 1989–2001 (Department of the Environment)—summary results of 1989-based household estimates for England, the regions, counties, metropolitan districts and London boroughs. An occasional series.

Development Control Statistics (Department of the Environment)—published annually it provides details of planning statistics handled by Local Planning Authorities in England. It also contains information on planning appeals and data on land with outstanding planning permission for private housing development.

Planning and Development Statistics (Chartered Institute of Public Finance and Accountancy)—provides annual information disaggregated by local authority, on a wide range of topics of relevance to the planner, including population, hereditaments, development applications, expenditure on planning and economic development, and staff.

Commercial and Industrial Floorspace Statistics for England (Department of the Environment)—published quarterly. A comprehensive source of commercial and industrial floorspace statistics, compiled from rating valuations, and broken down to local authority level.

Enterprise Zone Information (Department of the Environment)—available annually since 1986, and including information on employment, establishments, development (floorspace and land), EZ measures, land values and rental and capital values of premises, and investment, for 25 Enterprise Zones.

Land Registers (Department of the Environment)—the DoE's Computerized Land Register contains information about 8,300 sites (86,500 acres) of unused or under-used land in the public sector. Public access to the Land Register is available through the Department and most regional offices.

6 Transport

Transport Statistics Great Britain (Department of Transport)—published annually, it includes a wealth of information on road, rail, water and air transport, and international comparisons. There are limited disaggregations to sub-national levels.

British Road Statistics (British Road Federation)—a useful source of annual data on road statistics (e.g. network, traffic, expenditure, travel by mode, accidents) with considerable regional and county disaggregation.

7 Environment

Digest of Environmental Protection and Water Standards (Department of the Environment)—a useful publication, produced annually since 1978, with considerable regional disaggregation, and including over 100 figures and tables in the following categories:

1 Air quality and global atmospheric change
2 Inland water quality and use
3 Coastal and marine waters
4 Radioactivity
5 Noise
6 Waste and recycling
7 Land and nature conservation
8 Supplementary tables

Environment Digest for Wales (Welsh Office)—annual

The Scottish Environmental Statistics (Scottish Office)—biennial

Hydrological Data UK: Yearbook (Institute of Hydrology)—published annually since 1981, it provides a wealth of data on rainfall, river flow, groundwater and river water quality, with very detailed disaggregation.

8 Education, Health and Law Enforcement

Statistics of Education (Department of Education and Science)—published annually, it includes a wide variety of information (e.g. on staff/student ratios, distribution of pupils in different types of schools, school leavers and examinations, further education) with regional and local education authority disaggregation.

Health and Personal Social Services Statistics for England and Wales (Department of Health and Social Services, Welsh Office)—annual, including data on vital statistics, NHS hospitals, general practitioners and many other topics, primarily for health authority regions.

Scottish Health Statistics (Scottish Office)—annual.

Criminal Statistics, England and Wales (Home Office)—annual, including notifiable offences, prosecutions and police manpower.

offences, prosecutions and police manpower.

9 European Community
Eurostat: Regional Statistics (Statistical Office of the European Communities)—first published in 1975, it contains a wide variety of statistics including demography, labour market, the economy, living conditions, environment, investment under various Community financial instruments, for a three-level hierarchical classification of regions for each member state. The nomenclature of territorial units for statistics (NUTS) is based primarily on the institutional divisions currently in force in the member states, rather than an analysis by function or homogeneity. The present NUTS nomenclature subdivides the territory of the European Community into 66 regions at Level 1, 174 at Level 2 and 829 at Level 3 (see Table A1).

Table A1: NUTS levels and national administrative divisions in the European Community

Member State	NUTS 1		NUTS 2		NUTS 3	
Belgium	Regions	3	Provinces	9	Arrondisements	43
Denmark[1]	—	1	—	1	Amter	15
Germany[2]	Länder	11	Regierungsbezirke[3]	31	Kreise	328
Greece	Groups of Development Regions	4	Development Regions	13	Nomoi	51
Spain	Agrupción de comunidades autonomas	7	Comunidades autonomas + Melilla y Ceuta	18	Provincias	52
France	Zeat + DOM	8 1	Régions	22 4	Départements	96 4
Ireland	—	1	—	1	Planning regions	9
Italy	Gruppi di reggioni	11	Regioni	20	Provincie	95
Luxembourg	—	1	—	1	—	1
Netherlands	Landsdelen	4	Provincies	12	COROP-Regio's	40
Portugal	Continente + Regioes autonomas	3	Comissãoes de coordenação regional + Regioes autonomas	7	Grupos de Concelhos	30
United Kingdom	Standard regions	11	Groups of counties[4]	35	Counties/Local authority regions	65
EUR 12		66		174		829

1 A breakdown of Denmark into three regions is given in most of the tables and maps
2 Regions of the former GDR not yet included (5 Länder, 15 Bezirke, 218 Kreise)
3 26 Regierungsbezirk + 5 Länder, not subdivided into Regierungsbezirke
4 Grouping for Community purposes.
Source: Commission of the European Communities (1991) The Regions in the 1990s, CEC.

APPENDIX B
Summary of British government regional policy measures (1978)

Key: SDA = Special Development Areas; DA = Development Areas;
IA = Intermediate Areas

Measures directed at the individual firm

Regional Development Grants (on SIC III to XIX)—available to firms already established in the assisted areas as well as to incoming firms, on New Machinery, Plant and Mining Works, and on Building Works (other than Mining Works). SDA (22%), DA (20%), IA (20%—on Building Works only).

Tax Allowances—initial (first-year) tax allowances on New Machinery and Plant of 100%, and on New Industrial Buildings of 54%, in all assisted areas. Subsequent annual tax allowances (calculated on balance of costs after deducting initial balance) of 4% on new industrial buildings.

Selective Assistance—for all assisted areas.

Loans: on preferential terms for general capital purposes for projects providing additional employment; on non-preferential terms for projects that maintain or safeguard employment.

Interest Relief Grants: available towards the interest costs of finance provided from private sources which provide additional employment. Removal Grants: available on up to 80% of certain expenses involved in moving any undertaking from any part of Britain to an assisted area (i.e. expenses of removal of plant and machinery, stock, travel and accommodation by management, and termination of employment payments).

Government Factories for rent or sale—for all assisted areas. Rents at favourable rates and (subject to a 'cost per job limit') there may be a rent-free period for the first two years of occupation. Some factories may be available for sale with the repayment of capital and interest spread over a period of up to 15 years at a fixed rate of interest.

Regional Employment Premium—for all assisted areas. The premium was available to any employer with a manufacturing establishment, at the rate of £1.50 per week for a man, and 75p per week for a woman or juvenile (phased out in 1977).

Service Industry Support—£1,500 per employee moving with work to assisted area. Grants for jobs created: £1,500 per job (SDA), £1,000 (DA). Approved rent grant up to 7 years (SDA), 5 years (DA) and 3 years (IA).

Locational Controls—Industrial Development Certificates (IDCs) required for developments of greater than 15,000 sq. ft. (12,500 in the South East Region), with the exception of those in SDAs and DAs.

Office Development Permits (ODPs) required for office developments of more than 3,000 sq. ft. in Greater London and 10,000 sq. ft. in the rest of the South East Region and urban parts of the East and West Midlands Regions.

Measures directed at labour mobility and re-employment—for all assisted areas
Training—where an employer provides training for workers to fill new jobs, the Department of Employment may pay the employer weekly grants over an approved period at the rate of £15 per man and £12 per woman.

Other schemes provide grants for training apprentices and technicians; the purchasing of machinery and equipment needed for additional off-the-job training, and assistance with training older workers. Government Training Centres are also sited in most assisted areas.

Transferred Workers—a Key Workers' Scheme provides grants (towards costs of settling in, lodgings, removals, etc.) for key workers transferring to install plant or machinery, train local employees or form a nucleus for a new labour force.

A Resettlement Transfer Scheme provides a housing grant of £600 for workers who live in assisted areas and move home to get a job, or who undertake training and then have to move to use their skills.

General measures—for SDAs and DAs only
Environmental Improvement—grants available to local authorities towards the costs of clearing derelict land: 85% of costs (SDA and DA), 75% (IA).

Preference Schemes—under the General Preference Scheme, a firm in an assisted area will receive preference over firms in other areas, where price, quality, delivery date and other considerations are equal.

Under the Contracts Preference Scheme, a firm which has been unsuccessful in its original tender may still be given an opportunity to tender for up to 25% of the contract price, provided that it can meet the accepted price.

APPENDIX C
Major UK regional and sub-regional planning studies

This Appendix lists the major post-war (predominantly post-1965) Regional and Sub-Regional Planning Studies. The studies are grouped according to major regional divisions. The list is a representative rather than comprehensive bibliography of such studies undertaken within this period. Although there has been a continuity of strategic planning activity via Structure Plans for England and Wales, and Regional Reports for the Scottish Regions, it will quickly become apparent that there was a major lull in the output of regional studies for the standard regions towards the end of the 1970s and throughout the 1980s. The following Preface seeks to put such trends in context, and provides some relevant references.

Preface
Strategic planning for regions in the UK reached its peak in the early to mid-1970s; thereafter the locus of planning shifted dramatically down the hierarchy towards local planning. The pioneering *Strategic Plan for the South East* (1970) ran to six large volumes, yet in little over a decade the Secretary of State for the Environment saw fit to summarize the strategic guidance for the South East region in only two pages. The Regional Economic Planning machinery was disbanded in 1979. During their 15-year life, the Regional Economic Planning Councils played an important if not always readily appreciated role, as regional spokesmen, highlighters of key regional economic issues and contributors to the preparation and revision of strategic plans. They provided a base for many important innovations in regional planning in England and were unfortunate to be swept away after the 1979 election in the reduction of the number of quangos, without a more rigorous assessment of their worth.

Before these changes and not directly related to the change in government, was the checking of the devolution momentum which had been building up in the 1970s. The separate Scotland and Wales Acts received parliamentary approval in 1978 but, in March 1979, failed to clear a referendum hurdle, whereby 40% of the electorate had to vote in favour of the devolution proposals. In Scotland, the vote was split, with 32.5% of the registered electorate voting 'yes', 30.4% voting 'no' and 37.1% not voting. The Wales Act was more clearly rejected by the Welsh electorate, with only 11.8% voting 'yes', 46.5% 'no' and 41.7% not voting. There has been much speculation as to why the Scottish and Welsh electorates did not support the proposals. It may be that they saw the benefits as more illusory than real or were perhaps fearful of the gradual break-up of the United Kingdom. Some regions within Scotland and Wales were also very wary of losing out in the new provincial assemblies: in the Shetlands, for example, only 13.6% voted 'yes'. The devolution campaign perhaps also suffered from too much emphasis on an extra level of government and, implicitly, more bureaucracy, and not enough on the reform and possible replacement of the county level of government. Finally, it could also be argued that, by nature, referenda are inappropriate instruments for the assessment of progressive legislation. Interestingly, the devolution pressures built up again before the 1992 General Election. Several political parties, including Labour, indicated that they would support some measure of independence, especially for Scotland. The Conservative victory in the election has now checked the momentum; their line on devolution is decidedly low key.

Another major loss for strategic planning in the 1980s was the abolition of the Greater London Council and six English Metropolitan Councils (1986). This removed the strategic level of planning from most of the major metropolitan city regions in Britain. This 'streamlining' left the statutory County Structure Plan as the only 'strategic' survivor, and more recently these, and the county councils themselves, have come under threat.[1] There were of course some exceptions to this strategic planning cull, particularly in Scotland where the 1970s reform of local government produced a set of powerful Regional Councils. The Celtic fringes also have their Regional Development Agencies, which do have the resources to provide more effective implementation, although there has been concern in Scotland about the recent merging of the SDA and the Training Agency under a single agency—Scottish Enterprise—with a radical new decentralised structure.[2]

Breheny succinctly summarized the demise of strategic planning in the 1980s:
To be an advocate of strategic planning in the United Kingdom just three or four years ago seemed to be a rather exotic role to adopt; one felt something of an outsider or dissident. Occasionally a few fellow travellers would meet and bemoan the mainstream obsession with the immediate and the local, with 'getting things done', to use a professional slogan of the time.[3]

However, towards the end of the 1980s and into the 1990s there does appear to be a change towards strategic planning; and it is now back on the agenda of various pressure groups, academics, professional planners and politicians (see Glasson,[4] Breheny[5]). There is a growing concern about random development, especially in the south of England, fuelled by an unlikely alliance of the concerned NIMBY ('not in my backyard') lobby and big business. The former wish to fight off unwelcome development; the latter seek more certainty in the planning system and more infrastructure planning. The Nuffield Report, *Town and Country Planning*, in 1986,[6] took a 'top-down' approach to strategic planning, calling for national planning guidelines articulated at the regional level with Regional Reports, and with a regional dimension to the Public Expenditure Survey Committee annual cycle. The Royal Town Planning Institute (RTPI) in its 1986 report,[7] *Strategic Planning for Regional Potential*, took a 'bottom-up' approach, proposing a set of regional local authorities to replace the counties. These would have elected members and wide-ranging responsibilities, including physical planning, economic development, water and transport. A modified set of regions would be needed, and there would be a role for Regional Development Agencies. Strategic planning for regions was also firmly on many political agendas in the run-up to the 1992 General Election.

Of more significance, however, than all of these were the views of the Conservative government. These were set out in a Department of the Environment Planning Policy Guidance Note *(PPG15), Regional Planning Guidance, Structure Plans and the Content of Development Plans.*[8] They are usefully summarized in the Department of Environment publication, *This Common Inheritance*,[9] as follows:

The Government's regional planning guidance sets broad strategic policies for land use and development where there are issues which, though not of national scope, apply across regions or parts of regions and need to be considered on a wider scale than a single county or district. Such policies are not the prescriptive economic planning of the type attempted in the past, but flexible guidance on ways of responding to economic forces to help local authorities plan for their areas.

The current model of strategic planning starts with conferences of local planning authorities getting together to produce proposals for guidance on issues affecting the region as a whole. Central and local government then confer before the government publishes draft advice for public comment. It considers all the views expressed before formally issuing guidance for the region: in England in the form of a regional planning guidance paper. This model is an extension, to the whole of England and Wales, of the approach followed by SERPLAN (South-East Regional Planning Standing Conference) during the 1980s. Although SERPLAN's role during the 1980s was primarily one of monitoring regional change, it has produced strategic planning advice for the region,[10] and the approach has spread to other regions (e.g. East Anglia, South-West). However, in all cases, the advice offered has been 'thin' and, where there has been a government response, the guidance is inadequate and offers little in the way of a 'cascade of guidance', for the lower tiers of planning, which the government had hoped for.

The current (1992) situation for strategic planning for the UK regions is far from satisfactory, but there does now seem to be some commitment to this level of planning. There has also been no shortage of recent ideas to 'toughen up' the system. Hall,[11] for example, suggested either an appointed or elected authority for the South East. The RTPI South-west branch has produced proposals[12] of a preferred regional planning process, involving the production of a Regional Plan within a statutory planning process. The Town and Country Planning Association (TCPA)[13] has launched a Campaign for Strategic Planning.

References

1 Department of the Environment, *The Future of Development Plans*: Cmnd. 569, London: HMSO (1989).
2 Danson, M., Lloyd, G. and Newlands, D. Scottish Enterprise: towards a model agency or a flawed initiative? *Regional Studies*, **23**(6), pages 557–64 (1989).
3 Breheny, M. The renaissance of strategic planning, *Environment and Planning B*, **18**(2) pages 233–50 (1991).
4 Glasson, J., Lloyd, G., McMillan, A., and Wood, C. *Models of Regional Planning*, Working Paper No 124, School of Planning, Oxford Polytechnic (1990).
5 Breheny, M. *op.cit.*
6 Nuffield Committee of Inquiry, *Town and Country Planning: Report of a Committee*, London, Nuffield Foundation (1986).
7 Royal Town Planning Institute (RTPI), *Strategic Planning for Regional Potential: A Discussion Document*, London, RTPI (1986).
8 Department of the Environment, *PPG15: Regional Planning Guidance, Structure Plans and the Content of Development Plans*, London, HMSO (1990).
9 Department of the Environment, *This Common Inheritance: Britain's*

Environmental Strategy: Cmnd. 1200, London, HMSO (1990).
10 SERPLAN, *Shaping the South-East Planning Strategy*, London, SERPLAN (1990).
11 Hall, P. *London 2001*, London, Unwin Hyman (1989).
12 Royal Town Planning Institute (RTPI), *The Regional Planning Process*, London, RTPI (1991)
13 TCPA, *The People and the Land: Strategic Planning for the Future—A Discussion Paper*, London, TCPA (1990).

Regional and Sub-Regional Planning Studies
(omitting Structure Plans produced for English and Welsh counties, and Regional Reports produced for each Scottish region)

Scotland
Report of the Committee of Inquiry into the Scottish Economy (Toothill Report), Scottish Council. Cmnd. 1835, HMSO 1962.
The Scottish Economy 1965–70. Cmnd. 2864, HMSO 1966.
Clyde Valley Regional Plan, a Report prepared for the Clyde Valley Regional Planning Committee by Abercrombie and Matthew, HMSO 1946.
Central Scotland: A Programme for Development and Growth, Cmnd. 2206, HMSO 1963.
The Lothians Regional Survey and Plan, 1: Economic and Social Aspects; 2: Physical Planning Aspects, Scottish Development Department, HMSO 1966.
The Central Borders: A Plan for Expansion 1: Plan and Physical Study; 2: Economic and Geographical Report, Scottish Development Department, HMSO 1968.
Grangemouth–Falkirk Regional Survey and Plan, 1: Economic and Social Issues; 2: Physical Planning Aspects, Scottish Development Department, HMSO 1968.
A Strategy for South-West Scotland, Scottish Development Department, HMSO 1970.
Tayside: Potential for Development, Scottish Development Department, HMSO 1970.
North East Scotland: A Survey of its Development Potential, Scottish Office Department, HMSO 1969.
Moray Firth: A plan for growth, The Jack-Holmes Planning Group for the Highlands and Islands Development Board, 1968.
Cairngorm Area, Report of the Technical Group, HMSO 1967.
West Central Scotland Plan, Colin Buchanan and Partners for the West Central Scotland Plan Steering Committee, Glasgow, 1974. Plus the *Regional Reports* (1976) produced for the various Scottish Regional and Islands Councils.

Northern Ireland
An Economic Survey of Northern Ireland, Iles and Cuthbert, HMSO 1957.
Report of the Joint Working Party on the Economy of Northern Ireland (Hall Report), Cmnd. 1835, HMSO 1962.
Economic Development in Northern Ireland (Wilson Report), Cmnd. 479, HMSO 1965.
The Belfast Regional Survey and Plan, Prof. Robert Matthew, HMSO 1963.
Area Development in Northern Ireland, Northern Ireland Economic Council HMSO, 1969.
Development Programme (1970–75), Government of Northern Ireland 1970.
Regional Physical Development Strategy: 1975–1995, Department of Housing, Local

Government and Planning, Northern Ireland 1975.
Economic Strategy in Northern Ireland, Report No 88, Northern Ireland Economic Council 1991

Wales
Wales: The Way Ahead, Secretary of State for Wales, Cmnd. 334, HMSO 1967.
Strategy for Rural Wales, Welsh Council 1971.
Strategy for North West Wales, Welsh Council 1971
Deeside Planning Study, Shankland Cox and Associates, HMSO 1970.
Mid-Wales: The Growth Town Programme, Welsh Council 1973.
The Valleys: A Programme for the People, Welsh Office 1988.
Strategic Planning Guidance in Wales, Consultation Report, Assembly of Welsh Counties 1992.

Northern Region
The North East: A Programme for Development and Growth, Cmnd. 3206, HMSO 1963.
Challenge of a Changing North, Northern Economic Planning Council, HMSO 1966.
Outline Strategy for the North, Northern Economic Planning Council 1969.
Cumberland and Westmorland: A Sub-Regional Study, Department of Economic Affairs, HMSO 1965.
Teesside Survey and Plan, 1: Policies and Proposals; 2: Analysis Parts 1 and 2, Wilson, H., and Wolmersley, L., Scott Wilson Kirkpatrick and Partners, HMSO 1969 (Vol 1), 1971 (Vol 2).
Carlisle and West Cumberland Sub-Region: A Social and Economic Study, R.S. Taylor for DDoE, Cumberland County Council and Carlisle Borough Council 1972.
First, Second and Third Interim Reports, Northern Region Strategy Team 1975 and 1976.
Strategic Plan for the Northern Region, Northern Region Strategy Team HMSO 1977. Volumes 1: *Main Report; 2: Economic Development Policies; 3: Social and Environmental Policies; 4: Settlement Pattern and Transport Priorities; 5: Public Expenditure Priorities.*
Northern Region Prospectus, annual 'state of the region' report, Northern Region Councils Association, since 1979.
Regional Planning Guidance for North East England; Advice to the Department of the Environment, North East County Councils Regional Guidance Steering Group 1992.

North West
The North West: A Regional Study, Department of Economic Affairs, HMSO 1965.
The Problems of Merseyside (An Appendix to 'The North West: A Regional Study' 1965.
Strategy II: The North West of the 1970s, North West Economic Planning Council 1968.
Strategic Plan for the North West: Issues Report, SPNW December 1971.
North East Lancashire Plan: A Report on Sub-Regional Development, Lancashire County Council, Blackburn and Burnley County Borough Councils 1972.
Strategic Plan for the North West, SPNW Joint Planning Team, HMSO 1974.

412

The North West, Profile of an English Region, North West County Planning Officers 1985.
North West 2010: The Pressing Case for Strategic Planning, RTPI North West Branch 1990.

Yorkshire and Humberside
A Review of Yorkshire and Humberside, Yorkshire and Humberside Economic Planning Council HMSO 1966.
Yorkshire and Humberside Regional Strategy, Yorkshire and Humberside Economic Planning Council HMSO 1970.
Area Studies: Halifax and the Calder Valley 1968; Huddersfield and the Colne Valley, 1969; Doncaster, 1969, Yorkshire and Humberside Economic Planning Council,HMSO.
Humberside: A Feasibility Study, Central Unit for Environmental Planning, HMSO 1969.
The Pennine Uplands, Yorkshire and Humberside Economic Planning Council, HMSO 1975.
Yorkshire and Humberside Regional Strategy Review: the Next Ten Years, Yorkshire and Humberside Economic Planning Council, HMSO 1976.
A New Deal for Yorkshire and Humberside, Yorkshire and Humberside County Councils Association 1983.
Turning the Corner: A Strategy for the Yorkshire and Humberside Region, Yorkshire and Humberside County Councils Association, undated 1986.

East Midlands
The East Midlands Study, East Midlands Economic Planning Council, HMSO 1966.
Opportunity in the East Midlands, East Midlands Economic Planning Council, HMSO 1969.
Leicester and Leicestershire Sub-Regional Planning Study, Leicester City Council and Leicestershire County Council 1969.
Nottingham and Derbyshire Sub-Regional Study, Nottinghamshire County Council, Derbyshire County Council, Nottingham City Council, Derby County Borough Council 1969.
East Midlands: Draft Regional Strategy, East Midlands Regional Planning Forum 1991

West Midlands
The West Midlands: A Regional Study, Department of Economic Affairs, HMSO 1965.
The West Midlands: Patterns of Growth, West Midlands Economic Planning Council, HMSO 1967.
A Developing Strategy for the West Midlands, West Midlands Planning Authorities Conference, Birmingham 1971.
The West Midlands: An Economic Appraisal, West Midlands Economic Planning Council, HMSO 1971.
Coventry–Solihull–Warwickshire: A Strategy for the Sub-Region, Coventry City Council, Solihull County Borough Council, Warwickshire County Council 1971.
A Developing Strategy for the West Midlands (Conference Report, Addendum and letter from Secretary of State, DoE, known collectively as the 'Orange Book'), West

Midlands Planning Authorities Conference 1974

A Developing Strategy for the West Midlands, First and Second Reports of the Joint Monitoring Steering Group, DDoE and WWMPAC 1975, 1976.

A Developing Strategy for the West Midlands, Updating and Rolling Forward to 1991, 1: Main Report; 2: The Regional Economy, DDoE and WWMPAC, 1979.

The West Midlands: Your Region, Your Future, West Midlands Regional Forum of Local Authorities 1991.

East Anglia

East Anglia: A Study, East Anglia Economic Planning Council, HMSO 1968.

Small Towns Study, East Anglia Consultative Committee and East Anglia Planning Council, Shire Hall, Cambridge 1972.

A Study of the Cambridge Sub-Region, East Anglia Consultative Committee, HMSO 1974.

Strategic Choice for East Anglia, East Anglia Joint Planning Team, HMSO 1974.

East Anglia: Regional Strategy, Standing Conference of East Anglian Local Authorities, Ipswich 1989.

East Anglia: Regional Commentary, annual 'state of the region' reports, Standing Conference of East Anglian Local Authorities, Ipswich.

Regional Planning Guidance for East Anglia, Department of the Environment, Eastern Region, Bedford 1991.

South East

Greater London Plan, 1944, a Report prepared on behalf of the Standing Conference on London Regional Planning by Professor Abercrombie, HMSO 1945.

The South East Study, 1961–1981, Ministry of Housing and Local Government, HMSO 1964.

A Strategy for the South East, South East Economic Planning Council, HMSO 1967.

Strategic Plan for the South East, South East Joint Planning Team, HMSO 1970.

Studies: 1: Population and Employment; 2: Social and Environmental Aspects; 3: Transportation; 4: Strategies and Evaluation; 5: Report of Economic Consultants Ltd.

Report of the Monitoring Group on Strategic Planning in the South-East, Department of the Environment, HMSO 1973.

South East: A Study of Sub-Divisions, South East Economic Planning Council 1969.

South East Kent Study, South East Economic Planning Council, HMSO 1969.

South Hampshire Study: Report on the Feasibility of Major Urban Growth, Colin Buchanan and Partners, HMSO 1966.

> *Supplementary 1: The area, its people and activities; Supplementary 2: Methods and policies.*

Reading–Wokingham–Aldershot–Basingstoke Study, Report of the Study Team, Berkshire, Hampshire and Surrey County Councils Joint Steering Committee 1975.

Development of the Strategic Plan for the South East: Interim Report, South East Joint Planning Team 1976.

Strategy for the South East: 1976 Review, South East Joint Planning Team, HMSO 1976.

Strategic Plan for the South East: Review Government Statement, Department of the Environment, HMSO 1978.

414

Regional Trends in the South East (annual Regional Monitors), South East Regional Planning Conference, London.
A New Strategy for the South East, South East Regional Planning Conference, London 1989.
Shaping the South East Planning Strategy, South East Regional Planning Conference, London 1990.
Regional Planning Guidance for the South East, Department of the Environment, London 1989.
From Bologna to Basildon: Regional Initiatives for the 1990s, South East Economic Development Strategy, Basildon 1989.
South–South Divide, South East Economic Development Strategy, Basildon 1987.

South West
A Region with a Future: A Draft Strategy for the South West, South West Economic Planning Council, HMSO 1967.
The Plymouth Area Study, South West Economic Planning Council, HMSO 1969.
Severnside: A Feasibility Study, Central Unit for Environmental Planning, HMSO 1971.
North Gloucestershire Sub-Regional Study, Gloucestershire County Council 1970.
A Strategic Settlement Pattern for the South West, South West Economic Planning Council, HMSO 1974.
Towards a Regional Strategy: A Report for Public Consultation, South West Regional Planning Conference, Taunton 1991.

APPENDIX D
Major UK regional policy changes:
1979, 1984, 1988 to 1992

1979

May 1979 saw the return of a Conservative Government in Britain with a large majority and a clear mandate to restrain public spending. Initial steps towards exercising such restraint quickly had a significant impact on regional policy. The major principle behind the changes announced in July 1979[1] and introduced over the period to August 1982 was greater selectivity in regional aid, concentrating on those parts of the country with the most intractable problems of unemployment. The changes were designed to produce major savings in regional aid—an estimated £233 million off the £609 million projected for 1982-3 in the 1978 Public Expenditure White Paper, as revalued at 1979 prices.

The savings were to be achieved largely by changes in Assisted Area (AA) boundaries and gradings, and by cutting the rate of grants. The AA coverage was reduced from over 40% of the working population to around 25%. Figure A.1 illustrates the situation for 1982, with a reversing of the southward advance of the map of regional aid. Some anomalies, such as the availability of aid to the prosperous North Sea oil development-related locations of the North of Scotland, are corrected. More significant however was the removal of AA status from a large expanse of 'grey areas', particularly in Lancashire and Yorkshire. Most of the worst economic black spots, such as Clydeside and Merseyside, remained as Special Development Areas (SDAA). The Regional Development Grant (RDG) remained at 22% for SDAAs, but was reduced from 20% to 15% in Development Areas (DAA) and ceased altogether in the Intermediate Areas (IAA). The sole financial incentive available to the IAAs was discretionary aid. Other areas of saving included a raising of the threshold of investment projects which qualified for grants.

The changes were met with cries of anguish from many quarters. Downgrading to non-assisted area status means not only a loss of British regional policy assistance but also reduced access to EC sources of finance. Areas such as North East Lancashire, which had benefited greatly from the IAA status, felt particularly aggrieved, especially when areas such as Southport and Lytham St Annes retained that status. Yet, although the map of regional aid changed dramatically, the changes still left the basic framework of regional policy, as established in the 1972 Industry Act, largely intact. Advance factory building continued as a useful and relatively inexpensive measure, although the aim was to generate more self-financing in the programme. Industrial development certificates were retained, being seen as useful in identifying at an early stage large projects which might be located in the AAs. However the exemption limit was raised to 50,000 square feet throughout the non-AAs, including the South East, and the IAAs, like the SDAAs and DAAs were exempted

---

1 *Trade and Industry*, Government's new regional policy, 20 July 1979.

from 1.8.82

from 1.8.80

Special Development
Areas

Development Areas

Intermediate Areas

Miles

0   50   100

Fig. A.1 Proposed Assisted Areas, 1980 and 1982

from the need for IDCs. Discretionary aid continued as a useful policy safety valve and provided some scope for 'topping up' aid packages when, for example, it was felt necessary to offer assistance to enable internationally mobile projects to locate in the UK. The changes introduced in mid-1979 were planned to last unchanged for at least five years, in marked contrast to the fragmented and variable Development District policy operated during the 1960–66 period.

1984

During the early 1980s, there was considerable discussion of British regional policy, which was generally seen to be in need of a thorough overall. Pre-1983 general election reports by the Labour Party, TUC and Alliance parties called for, inter alia, more emphasis on service industry, more devolution (e.g. to regional development agencies) and more emphasis on job creation. An important review document was the *Report of an Inquiry into Regional Problems in the United Kingdom,* produced by the Regional Studies Association in 1983. In addition to the points already noted, the report recommended that the criteria of 'need' used in assessing an area's eligibility for assistance should cover a wider range of indicators, including an area's potential; regional development grants should be subject to a cost-per-job limit; more selectivity should be introduced to increase the cost-effectiveness of assistance; a regional dimension should be introduced into national public expenditure planning and the institutional gap which exists at the regional level in England should be filled through the creation of regional planning authorities. The Government contribution to the review was a White Paper on *Regional Industrial Development* 1983, which affirmed a commitment to an effective regional industrial policy but also argued that proposed changes in the regional aid package provided opportunities for a further reduction in public expenditure.

In November 1984, the Government announced its new regional policy. From that date there was to be a two-tier map of assisted areas (see Figure A.2) instead of the traditional three tiers. Developments in the 'inner tier' Development Areas, qualified automatically for regional development grants of 15% (compared with pre-November 1984 rates of 22%), and were also eligible for selective assistance. Developments in the 'outer tier' of the map, Intermediate Areas, were eligible only for regional selective assistance, which included grants towards the capital expenditure costs of projects and towards in-plant training schemes. Capital grants were subject to a limit of £10,000 per job created, for firms employing over 200 people. As an alternative to capital grants, firms could qualify for £3,000 for each net new job created. The DTI decided between the two forms of grant on the basis of which was most favourable to the applicant. The range of qualifying activities for regional aid was extended to include certain service industries, including transport and communications; banking, finance, insurance, business services and leasing; and research and development in the industrial field.

In modifying the map of Assisted Areas to include regions such as the West Midlands, in the inclusion of service activities and in establishing a link between grant and jobs created, the revised policy met some of the issues raised in the preceding review. But the Government's limited index of 'need' left out many blackspots, and services related to recreation and tourism were a glaring omission from the list of qualifying service activities. More generally, the new policy reduced

Orkney Islands   Shetland Islands

Development Areas
Intermediate Areas

Glasgow ● Edinburgh

Newcastle upon Tyne

Leeds ●

Manchester ●

Nottingham ●   Norwich ●

Birmingham ●

Cardiff ● ● Bristol   ● London

● Southampton

● Plymouth

Isles of Scilly

Fig. A2   Assisted Areas as from 29 November 1984
Source: Department of Trade and Industry (DTI)

the level of regional aid, reduced access to EC aid, and no encouragement was given to regional and local development agencies. More fundamentally, the revised policy did little to address the regional implications of new technology. There is a marked concentration of research and development activity in the South East region of the country where the social and economic infrastructure facilitate innovations. It seems inevitable that, without a more effective regional policy, a disproportionate number of new job opportunities in Britain in the next decade will be in this region.

1988 to 1992

Further pruning of regional policy followed in 1988. Although the 1984 pattern of Assisted Areas was maintained, changes were made to policy measures. The most significant was the ending of the automatic Regional Development Grant system. Regional selective assistance was still available and a package of measures was added, with a focus on small firms and local enterprise. These included Investment Grants, for firms with fewer than 25 employees, up to 15% of fixed assets (max. £15,000), Innovation Grants to support product and process development, up to 50% of costs involved (max. £25,000), and funded business and consultancy advice. The net effect was a further reduction in real terms of Government expenditure on regional preferential assistance to industry (Table A.2).

Table A.2: Government expenditure on regional preferential assistance to industry (£ million)

	1981-2	1985-6	1989-90
Great Britain	865.5	578.0	540.8
North	176.6	94.6	117.3
Yorkshire & Humberside	61.6	35.4	32.5
East Midlands	8.6	8.3	9.5
East Anglia	0.0	0.0	0.0
South East	0.0	0.0	0.0
South West	14.8	12.0	10.8
West Midlands	0.0	6.4	20.0
North West	173.8	85.9	74.5
England	435.4	242.6	264.5
Wales	197.5	138.4	131.7
Scotland	232.5	197.0	144.6

Source: Regional Trends

In June 1992, the Government issued a consultation paper on a 'Review of the Assisted Areas of Great Britain'. This announced that the Government planned to introduce a revised map of Assisted Areas in early 1993. The new map would continue to have two tiers—Development and Intermediate Areas—based on existing Travel-To-Work Areas. Key criteria for designation as Assisted Areas would include statistical measures of unemployment: current rates, persistence of above national average rates, and proportion of long-term unemployed in the locality. Other criteria were likely to be the future demand for jobs in an area, other measures of economic performance, activity rates, inner-city and urban problems, peripherality, and, for some areas, the prospect of major closures or rundowns.

Current thinking appears to be to switch support from areas (particularly old steel communities) which Government ministers perceive as recovering from the recession, to newly emerging problem areas such as the Lincolnshire coast, Great Yarmouth, and Thanet and Folkestone, which may suffer from the opening of the Channel Tunnel in 1993. Other possible losers include large areas of the Highlands & Islands. Opposition politicians suspect a major shift towards Conservative Party constituencies in the redistribution. Whatever the outcome, it is possible that the coverage of the new Assisted Areas map may be less than the 35% of the working population of the country (Development Areas 15%, Intermediate Areas 20%) when it was last designated in 1984.

APPENDIX E
Summary of European Community regional policy measures

Preface

In contrast to UK regional policy activity, there has been a significant growth in the scope and size of European Community regional policy measures in the 1980s and 1990s. This growth is a response to several factors, including widening membership of the Community and further moves towards greater European integration. The 1980s enlargements to include Greece, Spain and Portugal have accentuated the centre–periphery issues in the Community, with a major increase in the population of the least-favoured regions (those with a per capita GDP of less than 50% of the Community average). Statistics can distort, but disparities in GDP per capita of over 4:1 between many regions in Germany and regions in Greece, Portugal and Spain do constitute major divergence and a major problem for the European Community objective of economic and social cohesion. The completion of the Single European Market in 1993, with the removal of all fiscal, material and technological barriers between member states within the Community market of 320 million people, is seen by most observers as a recipe for a further widening of centre–periphery disparities.

The European Community response has been to introduce major reforms to the Community's Structural Funds: the European Regional Development Fund (ERDF), the European Social Fund (ESF) and the Guidance Section of the European Agricultural Guidance and Guarantee Fund (EAGGF/EEOGA). Under the 1989 Reform, the resources committed to the Structural Funds will double, in real terms, from 7 billion ECU (1987) to 14 billion ECU (1993), at 1988 prices. Financial assistance now concentrates on achieving five complementary objectives which focus attention on the regions and social groups in need of assistance. These are outlined in Table A.3. In most cases the Structural Funds are restricted for use in designated areas (see Fig. A.3). All parts of the UK qualify for assistance under Objectives 3 and 4, but only Northern Ireland qualifies under Objective 1 (which accounts for 60% of Structural Funds in 1993). The UK is a major beneficiary under Objective 2. Community Support Frameworks (CSFs) have been introduced to provide programmes of funding for particular objectives for countries and their designated areas.

Other elements of the 1989 Reform include a further shift from a project-based to a programme-based approach; plus commitments to more efficiency in procedures, to additionality (whereby annual allocations of EC funds to member states result in at least an equivalent increase in the total volume of structural aid in the member state concerned), and to partnership between the Commission and designated competent authorities (at national, regional and local levels) in member states. Although good progress has been made on many elements of the reforms, additionality has been problematic especially in the UK, and there is considerable scepticism that the reforms will not be enough to counterbalance pressures towards centralization in the Community.

Eligible regions under Objectives 1, 2 and 5b

- Objective 1: Lagging regions
- Objective 2: Declining industrial areas
- Objective 5b: Rural areas
- Objective 2 and Objective 5b

Figure A.3: Areas eligible for EC Structural Fund under Objectives 1, 2, 5b. Source: Commission of the European Communities (1991),
The Regions in the 1990s, CEC.

Table A.3: Priority objectives in 1989 reform of European Community Structural Funds

Objective 1:
Promoting the development and adjustment of the regions whose development is lagging behind (i.e. where per capita GDP is less than, or close to, 75% of the Community average)
(list of regions revised every five years)

Main instruments which may be used:
ERDF, ESF, EAGGF, Guidance Section, and EIB princip ECSC (80% of ERDF resources are devoted to th regions)

Objective 2:
Converting the regions, frontier regions or parts of regions (including employment areas and urban communities) seriously affected by industrial decline (criteria: average unemployment rate above the Community average, industrial employment rate above the Community average, decline in industrial employment)
(list revised every three years)

ERDF, ESF, EIB, ECSC

Objective 3:
Combating long-term unemployment (above the age of 25, unemployed for more than 12 months)

ESF, EIB, ECSC

Objective 4:
Facilitating the occupational integration of young people (job-seekers below the age of 25)

ESF, EIB, ECSC

Objective 5:
With a view to the reform of the common agricultural policy:
5(a) adapting production, processing and marketing structures in agriculture and forestry;
5(b) promoting the development of rural areas.
      Criteria: agricultural employment accounting for a high proportion of total employment; low level of agricultural income; low level of socio-economic development in terms of per capita GDP

EAGGF, Guidance Section only

EAGGF, Guidance Section, ERDF, ESF, EIB

Source: Commission of the European Communities (1989), Guide to the Reform of the Community's Structural Funds, CEC

Outline of EC Structural Funds

European Regional Development Fund (ERDF)—established in 1975, its aim is to reduce the regional disparities in the Community and to stimulate economic development in the least prosperous regions. In general terms support is provided for industrial investment, infrastructure projects, local initiatives, studies and environmental protection measures. In the least favoured regions (Objective 1), such as Northern Ireland, a maximum of 75% of the total cost of projects and a minimum of 50% of the total public expenditure costs is allowed. In other parts of the UK, the corresponding rates are 50% and 25%. The Commission allocates 85% of the ERDF budget in advance between types of regions in each member state over a five-year period (currently 1989–93). The remaining 15% of ERDF resources is reserved for programmes of particular Community benefit. These include (1992):

ENVIREG:	waste management in coastal regions
INTERREG:	development in border areas
PRISMA:	improving responses to the Single Market with reference to quality standards and access to public procurement
RECHAR/	for regions heavily dependent upon the coal and steel
RESIDER	industries
REGEN:	energy networks in the least developed regions
	socio-economic integration of peripheral regions into the larger Community market
RENAVAL:	support for old shipbuilding areas
STRIDE:	support for regional research, development and innovation
TELEMATICS:	promotion of advanced telecom services
VALOREN:	exploitation of indigenous energy potential of most disadvantaged regions.

European Social Fund (ESF)—established in 1958, to expand employment opportunities and to improve job prospects, with a major focus on training. Financial assistance is targeted on measures to help the long-term unemployed (Objective 3) and young people (Objective 4). Special attention is given to those with special employment difficulties, notably women, migrant workers and the disabled. There is some regional preference, with additional ESF contributions to measures in areas designated under Objectives 1, 2 and 5b. Levels of ESF grant aid are as for ERDF (above).

European Agricultural Guidance and Guarantee Fund (EAGGF)—established in 1958, it is principally concerned with Objective 5. Grant aid is provided to modernize and diversify agricultural holdings, and to improve the processing and marketing of agricultural and fishery products.

European Investment Bank (EIB)—established in 1958, it provides long-term finance for investments which further the balanced development of the Community. There is some preference for the financing of projects (e.g. communications, energy, pollution control, SMEs including tourism) in the less favoured regions. Aid is in the form of loans of up to 50% of a project's cost (on average 25%–30%).

European Coal and Steel Community (ECSC)—established in 1951, it provides loans, grants and guarantees to improve economic and social conditions in the coal-

and steel-producing regions of the EC, which have suffered particular hardship as a result of industrial decline and contraction. Conversion loans are provided to finance projects which bring employment to areas suffering from coal- and steel-industry job losses; loans (normally at 1% interest) are provided for housing programmes; re-adaptation grants are made to supplement the income of redundant coal and steel workers, and there are other special programmes (e.g. RECHAR, RESIDER).

Index

Mezzogiorno region (Italy), 180, 242–3
migration, regional
  costs of, 206–7
  trends, UK, 198, 227, 229, 401
mixed scanning, 267
models, spatial interaction, 185
  Garin–Lowry, 87, 186–8
  holistic models, 186–8
  partial models, 100
monitoring, 266, 284, 296
Moseley, M. J., 179
motorways, regional impact, 184
movement of industry, 230–2
multi-nationals, 117–19, 135, 143
multiplier analysis, regional, 87–91
Myrdal, G., 116, 179

National Enterprise Board, 305, 343
National Plan (UK), 21–2, 203
national spatial planning (UK), 259,
  396–7
nationalised industries, 305–7
nationalism and regional planning,
  25–6, 49, 55, 204, 205–6, 335,
  338
Needleman, L., 205–7
Netherlands, 361–9
  national physical plans, 163,
  364–7
  provincial planning, 365–7
  regional development planning,
  367–8
  regional problems, 361–2
  structure of planning, 362–4
Nevin, E., 79, 205
new towns, 222, 252–4
Nichols, V., 179
North, D. C., 107
North Sea oil, 26, 237, 269
North-East Lancashire, 176–7, 285–6
Northern Ireland, 200, 204, 254,
  269–70, 405–9, 412
  indicator trends, 225–33
Northern Region (UK), 119–20, 412–13
  indicator trends, 225–33
  North-East England, 200, 210,
  216,

Northern Region Strategic Plan,
  237–8, 293–4, 341–2
North-West Industrial Development
  Association, 140
North-West Region (UK), 184, 217,
  255, 271, 413
  indicator trends, 225–33
  North West Study, 255, 287–8
  regional planning, 284–92
  Strategic Plan for the North West,
  288–92, 294–6
Norway, 31

Odber, A. J., 214
Office Development Permits (ODPs),
  218, 407
office location, government, 223, 243
Ohlin, B., 109
Oxford, 148

Pahl, R., 121
Paris region, 347–9, 356–9
Peacock, Prof., 335
Pedersen, P. O., 167
Perroux, F., 171–2
Petit, C., 33–4
planning allocative/innovative, 20
  imperative/indicative, 21
  key features, 19
  levels of planning, 21–4
  multi-/single objective, 20–1
  physical/economic, 19
  reasons for, 17–18
  types of, 19–21
  see also inter-regional planning,
  intra-regional planning, regional
  planning, regional planning process
Planning Balance Sheet, 265
polarisation effects, 175–9
political factors
  and regional growth, 121–2
  and regional policy, 204–6
population, UK regions, 55
  statistical sources, 64–6, 401–2
problem regions
  depressed industrial, 199–200
  dynamic classification, 201–2

431